Praise from Job Seekers for the
Knock 'em Dead Books

"I got the position! I was interviewed by three people and the third person asked me all the questions in *Knock 'em Dead*. I had all the right answers!"
— **D.J., Scottsdale, Arizona**

"I just finished writing the letter I have dreamed of writing for three years: my letter of resignation from the Company from Hell. Thanks to you and the book, *Knock 'em Dead*, I have been offered and have accepted an excellent position with a major international service corporation."
— **C.C., Atlanta, Georgia**

"My previous employer asked me to resign. Your book got me through my depression, and in only four weeks, got me four job offers. This is the first time in my career I have this many options to choose from."
— **D.H., North Canton, Ohio**

"After college graduation, I searched and searched for a job, and ended up taking a few low-paying ones I was overqualified for. Finally, I read your book and have been offered *every* job I have applied for since."
— **L.E. (no address given)**

"I followed the advice in *Knock 'em Dead* religiously and got more money, less hours, a better hospital plan, and negotiated to keep my three weeks vacation. I start my new job immediately!"
— **A.B., St. Louis, Missouri**

"I found your book to be absolutely invaluable during my recent job search. Since then I have had a chance to speak with my interviewer, who informed me that it was my strong interview that landed me my job offer. He went on to outline what had turned him off about other candidates, and it was some of the very same mistakes I used to make before reading your book!"
— **D.D., Houlton, Maine**

"Every time I've used your book, I've gotten an offer! This book is incredible. Thanks for publishing such a great tool."
— **W.Z., Columbia, Maryland**

"Just a quick note to let you know how much your book has helped me. I was chosen for my job out of over one hundred applicants! I later loaned the book to a friend and circled the things that had helped me. She interviewed on a Thursday, and she was offered the position that Thursday night! Thanks for writing such a helpful book."

— S.G., Sacramento, California

"Your book is simply fantastic. This one book improved my yearly income by several thousand dollars, and my future income by untold amounts. Your work has made my family and myself very happy."

— M.Z., St. Clair Shores, Michigan

"Thank you for all the wonderfully helpful information you provided in your book. I lost my job almost one year ago. I spent almost eight months looking for a comparable position. Then I had the good sense to buy your book. Two months later, I accepted a new position. You helped me turn one of the worst experiences of my life into a blessing in disguise."

— L.G., Watervliet, New York

"I was out of work for four months—within five weeks of reading your book, I had four job offers."

— S.K., Dallas, Texas

"Yesterday I received two job offers in the space of fifteen minutes. I am now using the 'Negotiating the Offer' chapter to evaluate these positions."

— W.B., Thornhill, Ontario

"I read every page in the book and, after a two-month search, got ten interviews with top-performing companies and six offers (five of which I declined)."

— M.V., Millington, Tennessee

"I was sending out hordes of resumes and hardly getting a nibble—and I have top-notch skills and experience in my field. I wasn't prepared for this tough job market. When I read your book, however, I immediately began applying some of your techniques. My few nibbles increased to so many job interviews I could hardly keep up with them!"

— C.S., Chicago, Illinois

RESUMES THAT KnOCK 'em DEaD

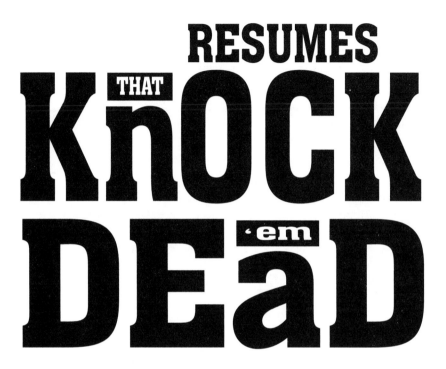

Martin Yate

Adams Media Corporation
Avon, Massachusetts

Acknowledgments

Knock 'em Dead is now in its 16th year of publication, and has become a staple for job hunters around the world. This is due to the ongoing support of my publisher Bob Adams, and the tireless encouragement of the Adams Media sales team. In addition, I am indebted to: Wayne Jackson, Ed Walters, Jennifer Lantagne, and Jill Alexander—their hard work has been critical to the success of the *Knock 'em Dead* books.

Published by Adams Media Corporation
57 Littlefield Street, Avon, MA 02322. U.S.A.
www.adamsmedia.com

ISBN: 1-58062-794-3

Printed in the United States of America.

J I H G F E D C B A

Library of Congress Cataloging-in-Publication Data
  Yate, Martin John.
  Resumes that Knock 'em Dead / Martin Yate. — Rev. and expanded ed.
    p.   cm.
  ISBN 1-58062-794-3
  1. Resumes (Employment) I. Title.
  HF5383.Y38   1997
  808'.06665—dc21   97-41514
                                                                        CIP

This publication is designed to provide accurate and authoritative information with regard to the subject matter covered. It is sold with the understanding that the publisher is not engaged in rendering legal, accounting, or other professional advice. If legal advice or other expert assistance is required, the services of a qualified professional person should be sought.
  —From a *Declaration of Principles* jointly adopted by a Committee of the American Bar Association and a Committee of Publishers and Associations

Rear Cover Photo: ARIEL JONES

This book is available at quantity discounts for bulk purchases.
For information, call 1-800-872-5627.

Contents

Introduction

Most of the books on writing resumes haven't changed to accommodate today's dynamic work environment. That is the reason for this book: To help "now" people get the very best jobs!

Look at the other resume books on the market; they are full of resume examples with dates going back to what seems, to most job seekers, like the Bronze Age. They use job titles that no longer exist and techniques that no longer work—techniques that in many instances can be downright damaging to your job hunt.

This book is unique in two very important ways.

First, you'll get to read real resumes from real people. Each of the resumes in this book is based on a "genuine article" that worked wonders for its writer. Included are resumes for today's and tomorrow's in-demand jobs, as defined by the Bureau of Labor Statistics and confirmed by the professionals on the front lines: Corporate recruiters and other employment industry professionals across the country. The odds are that you are already working in one of these jobs, or wishing you were.

Also included in the "real-life" section of this book is a selection of resumes from people with special challenges. These reflect the pressures and needs of a modern, profession-oriented society struggling into the information age. Like the resume that got a six-dollar-an-hour factory worker a $70,000-a-year job; or the one that helped a recovering alcoholic and drug-abuser get back on her feet again. There are winning resumes of people recovering from serious emotional challenges and mental problems, of people reentering society after jail, starting over after the divorce, and changing careers. And what's more, these examples have proved themselves effective in every corner of the nation; their writers landed both interviews and jobs.

Second, I explain the ins and outs of putting a resume together as painlessly as possible. I'll show you the three best ways to look at your background and present your resume. Then I'll show you all the available options for inclusion. Why certain things should be in your resume and how they should look, and why other things should never appear. Wherever industry experts disagree, I'll give you both sides of the argument, and my reasoned solution to the dispute.

That way you can make a prudent decision about your unique background, based on possession of all the facts and the best advice going. In addition, you will see the infinite variety of styles and approaches that can be used within my guidelines to help you create a truly individual resume.

These two unique concepts, the numerous resume examples, and the nuts-and-bolts sections about resume production and distribution give you everything needed to create a distinctive, professional resume: one that will knock 'em dead!

1 | The Marks of a Great Resume

Who needs a resume? Everyone. Certainly you do, unless you are so well known that your reputation is already common knowledge to all potential employers. If that were the case you probably wouldn't be reading this book in the first place.

Anyone, in any job, can be viewed more favorably than his or her competition—if he or she is better organized and prepared, which is what a good resume demonstrates. It's a staunch friend who only speaks well of you and can gain you entrance into undreamed-of opportunities.

Now, no resume ever gets carefully read unless a manager is trying to solve a problem. That problem may be finding a quicker way to manufacture silicon chips. It may be getting the telephone calls answered, now that the receptionist has left. As disparate as these examples might seem, both are still concerned with problem solving. And invariably, the problem that needs a solution is the same: productivity. The simple question is, "How on earth are we going to get things done quicker/cheaper/more efficiently without a _____?"

Resumes that get acted upon are those that demonstrate the writer's potential as a problem solver.

Your resume must speak loudly and clearly of your value as a potential employee. And the value must be spoken in a few brief seconds, because, in the business world, that's all the attention a resume will get. The resume takes you only the first few paces toward that new job. It gets your foot in the door, and because you can't be there to answer questions, it has to stand on its own.

A resume's emphasis is on what has happened in your business life, what actions you took to make those things happen, and what supportive personal characteristics you brought to the job. It is about how you contributed to solving a business' problems. It has nothing to do with generalizations or personal opinions.

The resume itself came about as a solution to a problem: How does a manager avoid interviewing every applicant who applies for a job? Can you imagine what would happen to a business if everyone who applied for a job was given even a cursory ten-minute interview? The company would simply grind to a halt, then topple into bankruptcy. The solution: Come up with a way to get a glimpse of applicants' potentials before having to meet them face-to-face. The resume appeared and evolved into an important screening and time-saving tool.

While that solved one problem for the employer, it created another for the job applicant: "Considering that my background isn't perfect, how do I write a resume that shows off my best potential?" The first attempt to answer that question is how the gentle art of resume writing came into being.

In the world of recreational reading, resumes are pretty far down on the list. They are usually deadly dull and offer little competition to murder mysteries, tales of international intrigue, and love stories.

Nevertheless, resumes are a required part of every manager's daily reading, and, exactly because they are usually deadly dull, are generally avoided. To combat this deep-seated avoidance, there is a general rule that will help your resume get read and acted upon in the quickest possible time: It needs to be short and long. Short on words, but long on facts and an energy that reflects the real you.

Good resume writing focuses attention on your strengths and shows you as a potential powerhouse of an employee. At the same time, it draws attention away from those areas that lack definition or vigor. You can do this even if you are changing your entire career direction, or starting your life over for other reasons, and I'll show you how.

There is a hidden benefit, too, in the resume-writing process: It focuses your attention and helps you prepare for job interviews. In a very real sense, putting a resume together is the foundation for succeeding at the job interview. Preparation for one is preparation for the other.

For example, the interviewer's command to "tell me about yourself" is one of those tough interview demands that almost all of us have difficulty answering satisfactorily. Were you totally satisfied with your response the last time it came up? I doubt it. You can only answer it well if you have taken the time to analyze and package all your strengths and weaknesses in an organized fashion. It is the only way you will ever learn to speak fluently about your background and skills in a fashion guaranteed to impress the interviewer. So, why not kill two birds with one stone—prepare for the interview by preparing a resume that will open all the right doors for you.

Interestingly enough, the majority of interviewers accept the contents of a resume as fact. Additionally, a good number of interviewers base all their questions on the resume content: This means that in a very real way you can plan and guide the course of the majority of your interviews by preparing an effective resume.

Those without resumes are forced to reveal their history on a job application form, which does not always allow the perfect representation of skills, and which gives the interviewer no flattering starting point from which to base the interview questions.

In addition to helping you get your foot in the door and easing the course of the interview, your resume will be your last and most powerful advocate. After all the interviewing of all the candidates is done, how do you think the interviewers review and evaluate all the contenders? They go over their notes, application forms, and the resumes supplied by the job candidates. You will want to make yours something powerful and positive.

Finally, the preparation of a good resume has the broad, intangible benefit of personal discovery. You may find, as you answer some of the questions in chapter 4, that your experience is deeper than you imagined, that your contributions to previous employers were more important than you thought. You may look on your career direction in a new light. And you may see your value as a solid employee increase. You will gain confidence that will be important not only for a good performance at the interview; but for your attitude toward the rest of your career.

No sane person will tell you that resume writing is fun, but I will show you the tricks of the trade, developed over the years by executive recruiters and professional resume writers, that make the process easier.

What makes this book truly different is that the resume examples in it are all real resumes from real people, resumes that recently landed them real jobs in "in-demand" professions. They were all sent to me by employment specialists from around the nation. For example, the health care examples were screened initially by professional health care recruiters, and those in the data processing by computer recruiters. These are the pros on the firing line, who know what works and what doesn't in today's business marketplace.

You will find everything you need to make resume writing fast, effective, and painless. Just follow my instructions, and in a few hours you'll have a knock-out resume and never have to read another word about the damn things as long as you live. With that in mind, do it once and do it right—you'll generate a top-flight resume without knocking yourself out!

So now, for your delight and edification, we'll review the marks of a great resume: What type of resume is right for you, what goes in (and why), and what always stays out (and why), and what might go in depending on your special circumstances. This is followed by countless resume examples and a "painting-by-numbers" guide that makes resume writing easy for anyone!

With the changing times and circumstances, there are few rigid rules for every situation. So in those instances where there are exceptions, I'll explain them and your choices. The judgment call will be yours. And when you are finished, you will have one of the very best resumes, one that will be sure to knock 'em dead.

2 | Three Ways to Sum Yourself Up

"Give me a moment of your busy day! Listen to me, I've got something to say!"

That's what your resume must scream—in a suitably professional manner, of course. Not in the manner of the would-be retail clothing executive who had his resume "hand-delivered"…attached to the hand and arm of a store window mannequin.

As it happened, that was only the first surprise in store for the personnel director who received the delivery: The envelope was hand-decorated in gothic script; the cover letter inside was equally decorative (and illegible); the resume writer had glued the four-page resume to fabric, and stitched the whole mess together like a child's book. The crowning glory, however, was yet to come: All the punctuation marks—commas, colons, periods, and the like—were small rhinestone settings. Yes, it got noticed, but its success had to depend entirely on the recipient's sense of humor—which in this case was most noticeable for its absence.

Here's the point: trying to do something out of the ordinary with any aspect of your resume is risky business indeed. For every interview door it opens, at least two more may be slammed shut.

The best bet is to present a logically displayed, eye-appealing resume that will get read. That means grabbing the reader right away—on that first page. And that's one big reason for short, power-packed resumes.

We all have different backgrounds. Some of us have worked for one company only, some of us have worked for eleven companies in as many years. Some of us have changed careers once or twice, some of us have maintained a predictable career path. For some, diversity broadens our potential, and for some concentration deepens it. We each require different vehicles to put our work history in the most exciting light. The goals, though, are constant:

- To show off achievements, attributes, and cumulation of expertise to the best advantage;
- to minimize any possible weaknesses.

Resume experts acknowledge just three essential styles for presenting your credentials to a potential employer: Chronological, Functional, and Combination (Chrono-Functional). Your particular circumstances will determine the right format for you. Just three styles, you say? You will see resume books with up to fifteen varieties of resume style. Such volumes are, alas, merely filling up space; in the final analysis, each additional style such books mention is a tiny variation on the above three.

The Chronological Resume

This is the most common and readily accepted form of presentation. It's what most of us think of when we think of resumes—a chronological listing of job titles and responsibilities. It starts with the current or most recent employment, then works backward to your first job (or ten years into the past—whichever comes first).

This format is good for demonstrating your growth in a single profession. It is suitable for anyone with practical work experience who hasn't suffered too many job changes or prolonged periods of unemployment. It is not suitable if you are just out of school or if you are changing careers. The format would then draw attention to your weaknesses (i.e., your lack of specific experience in a field) rather than your strengths.

The exact content of every resume naturally varies depending on individual circumstances. A chronological resume usually incorporates these six basic components:

- *Contact Information*
- *A Job Objective*
- *A Career Objective*
- *A Career Summary*
- *Education*
- *A Description of Work History*

This last item is the distinguishing characteristic of the chronological resume, because it ties your job responsibilities and achievements to specific employers, job titles, and dates.

There are also some optional categories determined by the space available to you and the unique aspect of your background. These will be discussed in chapter 3.

Chronological

Jane Swift, 9 Central Avenue, Quincy, MA 02169. (617) 555-1212. jswift@careerbrain.com

SUMMARY:	Ten years of increasing responsibilities in the employment services industry. Concentration in the high-technology markets.

EXPERIENCE: Howard Systems International, Inc.   1995-Present
Management Consulting Firm
Personnel Manager

Responsible for recruiting and managing consulting staff of five. Set up office and organized the recruitment, selection, and hiring of consultants. Recruited all levels of MIS staff from financial to manufacturing markets.

Additional responsibilities:

- Coordinated with outside advertising agencies.
- Developed P.R. with industry periodicals—placement with over 20 magazines and newsletters.
- Developed effective referral programs—referrals increased 32%.

EXPERIENCE: Technical Aid Corporation   1988-1995
National Consulting Firm. MICRO/TEMPS Division

Division Manager	1993-1995
Area Manager	1990-1993
Branch Manager	1988-1990

As Division Manager, opened additional West Coast offices. Staffed and trained all offices with appropriate personnel. Created and implemented all divisional operational policies responsible for P & L. Sales increased to $20 million dollars, from $0 in 1984.

- Achieved and maintained 30% annual growth over 7-year period.
- Maintained sales staff turnover at 14%.

As Area Manager, opened additional offices, hiring staff, setting up office policies, and training sales and recruiting personnel.

Additional responsibilities:

- Supervised offices in two states.
- Developed business relationships with accounts—75% of clients were regular customers.
- Client base increased 28% per year.
- Generated over $200,000 worth of free trade-journal publicity.

As Branch Manager, hired to establish the new MICRO/TEMPS operation. Recruited and managed consultants. Hired internal staff. Sold service to clients.

EDUCATION: Boston University
B.S. Public Relations, 1987.

The Functional Resume

This format focuses on the professional skills you have developed over the years, rather than on when, where, or how you acquired them. It de-emphasizes dates, sometimes to the point of exclusion. By the same token, job titles and employers play a minor part with this type of resume. The attention is always focused on the skill rather than the context or time of its acquisition.

This functional format is suited to a number of different personal circumstances, specifically those of:

- Mature professionals with a storehouse of expertise and jobs
- Entry-level types whose track records do not justify a chronological resume
- Career changers who want to focus on skills rather than credentials
- People whose careers have been stagnant or in ebb, who want to give focus to the skills that can get a career under way again, rather than on the history in which it was becalmed in the first place
- Military personnel embarking on a civilian career
- Those returning to the workplace after a long absence
- People closer to retirement than to the onset of their careers

The functional resume does present a major challenge for the writer. Because it focuses so strongly on skills and ability to contribute in a particular direction, you must have an employment objective clearly in mind. When this is achieved, such a resume can be very effective.

Though a functional resume is a bit more free-form than a chronological one, there are certain essentials that make it work. In addition to contact information and a job and/or career objective, these include the elements that follow.

- *A Functional Summary.* Different skills are needed for different jobs, so the functional summary is where you make the tough decisions to determine what goes in and what stays out.
- *Dates.* Strictly speaking, a functional resume needn't give dates. Until recently, you could sometimes get away without them. Today, a resume without dates waves a big red flag. So, what if your employment history doesn't have stability? The functional resume is perfect for you—because dates can be de-emphasized by their placement.
- *Education.* Including education and other optional categories is determined by the space available and the unique aspects of your background.

Functional

Jane Swift
9 Central Avenue
Quincy, MA 02169
(617) 555-1212
jswift@careerbrain.com

OBJECTIVE: A position in Employment Services where my management, sales, and recruiting talents can be effectively utilized to improve operations and contribute to company profits.

SUMMARY: Over ten years of Human Resources experience. Extensive responsibility for multiple branch offices and an internal staff of 40+ employees and 250 consultants.

SALES: Sold high-technology consulting services with consistently profitable margins throughout the United States. Grew sales from $0 to over $20 million a year.

Created training programs and trained salespeople in six metropolitan markets.

RECRUITING: Developed recruiting sourcing methods for multiple branch offices.

Recruited over 25,000 internal and external consultants in the high-technology professions.

MANAGEMENT: Managed up to 40 people in sales, customer service, recruiting, and administration. Turnover maintained below 14$^{\%}$ in a "turnover business."

FINANCIAL: Prepared quarterly and yearly forecasts. Presented, reviewed, and defended these forecasts to the Board of Directors. Responsible for P & L of $20 million sales operation.

PRODUCTION: Responsible for opening multiple offices and accountable for growth and profitability. 100$^{\%}$ success and maintained 30$^{\%}$ growth over seven-year period in 10 offices.

WORK EXPERIENCE:

1995 to Present   HOWARD SYSTEMS INTERNATIONAL, Boston, MA
National Consulting Firm
Personnel Manager

1988-1995   TECHNICAL AID CORPORATION, Needham, MA
National Consulting & Search Firm
Division Manager

EDUCATION: B.S., 1987, Boston University

REFERENCES: Available upon request.

The Combination Chrono-Functional Resume

For the upwardly mobile professional with a track record, this is becoming the resume of choice. It has all the flexibility and strength that come from combining both the chronological and functional formats. If you have a performance record, and are on a career track and want to pursue it, then this is the strongest resume tool available. This format, in addition to contact information and a job objective, incorporates a number of identifying factors, outlined below.

- *A Career Summary.* The combination resume, more often than not, has some kind of career summary. Here you spotlight a professional with a clear sense of self, a past of solid contributions, and a clear focus on future career growth. The career summary, as you might expect, will include a power-packed description of skills, achievements, and personal traits that fairly scream "Success!"
- *A Description of Functional Skills.* This is where the combination of styles comes into play. Following the summary, the combination resume starts out like a functional resume and highlights achievements in different categories relevant to the job/career goals, without any reference to employers.
- *A Chronological History.* Then it switches to the chronological approach and names companies, dates, titles, duties, and responsibilities. This section can also include further evidence of achievements or special contributions.
- *Education.* Then come the optional categories determined by the space available to you and the *unique* aspects of your background.

Combination

Jane Swift
9 Central Avenue
Quincy, MA 92169
(617) 555-1212
jswift@careerbrain.com

OBJECTIVE:

Employment Services Management

SUMMARY: Ten years of increasing responsibilities in the employment services marketplace. Concentration in the high-technology markets.

SALES: Sold high technology consulting services with consistently profitable margins throughout the United States. Grew sales from $0 to over $20 million a year.

PRODUCTION: Responsible for opening multiple offices and accountable for growth and profitability. 100% success and maintained 30% growth over seven-year period in 10 offices.

MANAGEMENT: Managed up to 40 people in sales, customer service, recruiting, and administration. Turnover maintained below 14% in a "turnover business." Hired branch managers and sales and recruiting staff throughout the United States.

FINANCIAL: Prepared quarterly and yearly forecasts. Presented, reviewed, and defended these forecasts to the Board of Directors. Responsible for P & L of $20 million sales operation.

MARKETING: Performed numerous market studies for multiple branch opening. Resolved feasibility of combining two different sales offices. Study resulted in savings of over $5,000 per month in operating expenses.

EXPERIENCE: Howard Systems International, Inc.   1995-Present
Management Consulting Firm
Personnel Manager

Responsible for recruiting and managing consulting staff of five. Set up office and organized the recruitment, selection, and hiring of consultants. Recruited all levels of MIS staff from financial to manufacturing markets.

Additional responsibilities:

- developed P.R. with industry periodicals—placement with over 20 magazines and newsletters.
- developed effective referral programs—referrals increased 320%.

Technical Aid Corporation   1988-1995
National Consulting Firm. MICRO/TEMPS Division

Division Manager   1993-1995
Area Manager   1990-1993
Branch Manager   1988-1990

As Division Manager, opened additional West Coast offices. Staffed and trained all offices
with appropriate personnel. Created and implemented all divisional operational policies.
Responsibilities for P & L. Sales increased to $20 million dollars, from $0 to 1984.

- Achieved and maintained 30% annual growth over seven-year period.
- Maintained sales staff turnover at 14%.

As Area Manager, opened additional offices, hiring staff, setting up office policies, and
training sales and recruiting personnel.

Additional responsibilities:

- Supervised offices in two states.
- Developed business relationships with accounts—75% of clients were regular customers.
- Client base increased 28% per year.
- Generated over $200,000 worth of free trade journal publicity.

As Branch Manager, hired to establish the new MICRO/TEMPS operation. Recruited and
managed consultants. Hired internal staff. Sold service to clients.

EDUCATION: B.S., 1987, Boston University

One of these styles is perfect for you. Pick one, and in the next chapter we'll begin to fill it
in with the resume basics.

3 | The Basic Ingredients

It used to be that there were just a few set rules for writing a great resume. Now, however, many of the jobs for which those rules were made no longer exist—so many of the traditional rules no longer apply.

New technologies are creating new professions overnight, and, with them, new career opportunities. The content of these new professions and careers is dramatically different from the employment world of a few years ago.

What used to be strictly off-limits in all resumes is now acceptable in many and required in some. (The need for technical jargon to explain skills, for example, comes to mind.) Elements that were once always included, such as the mug shot, are now frowned upon in almost every instance. And so, what are the rules?

Today, writing a resume can be likened to baking a cake. In most instances, the ingredients are essentially the same. What determines the flavor is the order and quantity in which those ingredients are blended. There are certain ingredients that go into almost every resume. There are others that rarely or never go in, and there are those special touches that are added (a pinch of this, a dash of that), depending on your personal tastes and requirements.

Sound complicated? It really isn't. If a certain ingredient must always go in, you will understand why. In circumstances where the business world holds conflicting views, these views will be explained so that a reasoned judgment can be made.

First, let's look at the ingredients that are part of every successful resume.

What Must Always Go In

Name

We start with the obvious, but there are other considerations about your name besides remembering to put it on your resume. Give your first and last name only. It isn't necessary to include your middle name(s). My name is

Martin John Yate—but my resume says simply Martin Yate, because that is the way I would introduce myself in person. Notice also that it isn't M. J. Yate, because that would force the reader to play Twenty Questions about the meaning of my initials. Even if you are known by your initials don't put them on your resume. If you use quotation marks or parentheses, those on the receiving end might think it a little strange. Better that it come out at the interview when the interviewer asks you what you like to be called: At the very least you'll have some small talk to break the tense interview atmosphere.

It is not required to place Mr., Ms., Miss, or Mrs. before your name. But what if your first name is Gayle, Carrol, Leslie, or any of the other names that can easily be used for members of either sex? In such instances it is acceptable to put Mr. Gayle Jones, or Ms. Leslie Jackson. The reasoning is based on the ever-present foot-in-mouth syndrome: In contacting you to follow up on your resume, your interviewer is likely to make the mistake of asking to speak to Ms. Gayle Jones, or Mr. Leslie Jackson. Though it is a little mistake that is easily corrected, the possible future employer is immediately put in the awkward position of starting the relationship with an apology.

Finally, for those who are the IInd, IIIrd, Junior, or Senior holders of their name: If you always add "Jr." or "III" when you sign your name or if that is the way you are addressed to avoid confusion, go ahead and use it. Otherwise, it is extraneous information on the resume, and therefore not needed.

Address

Always give your complete address. Do not abbreviate unless space restrictions make it absolutely mandatory—you want the post office to have every possible advantage when it comes to delivering those offer letters efficiently. If you do abbreviate—such as with St. or Apt.—be consistent. The state of your residence, however, is always abbreviated to two capitalized letters (for example, MN, WV, LA), according to post office standards. The accepted format for laying out your address looks like this:

Maxwell Krieger
9 Central Ave. Apartment 38
New York, NY 23456

Notice that the city, state and zip code all go on the same line, with a comma between city and state.

Telephone Number

Always include your telephone number: Few businesses will send you an invitation for an interview in the mail. Including your area code is important even if you have no intention of leaving the area. In this era of decentralization, your resume might end up being screened in another part of the country altogether!

The inclusion or exclusion of a work telephone number is a little bit more of a problem.

> *The case for inclusion:* Featuring your daytime contact number allows prospective employers to reach you at a time of their convenience.
>
> *The case for exclusion:* Being pulled out of the Monday meeting every five minutes to take calls from headhunters and *Fortune 500* executives can ruin your whole day. The funny thing about employers is that they always prefer to lose you at their convenience rather than yours. In addition, keeping the company number off the resume adds to its life expectancy. Who needs another detail that may be obsolete in short order?
>
> *The solution:* Unless your current employer knows of your job search, leave the business number off the resume, but put it in your cover letter. Good cover letters do this with a short sentence that conveys the information and demonstrates you as a responsible employee. For example, something like this can work very well:
>
> "I prefer not to use my employer's time taking personal calls at work, but with discretion you can reach me at 202/555-5555, extension 555, to initiate contact."

E-mail

Your e-mail address has become an integral part of your contact information. An e-mail address implies that you have already adapted to the new technology of the workplace. That's a must for any worthwhile job in the new century. If you have an e-mail address, use it. If you don't, get one—and get with it.

If you are planning on using your e-mail address from work, keep in mind that it increases the odds of your boss learning that you are looking at broader horizons. E-mails leave a trail that an employer can follow, and as many as 35 percent of managers are believed to track their employees' e-mail. So using your company e-mail address is almost as stupid as listing your immediate supervisor as the principal contact for your job hunt.

Using company e-mail outside regular working hours won't work either—the trail is still there for prying eyes to see. And think about what it tells potential employers about how you're likely to act once you're on their payroll!

Job Objective

This section sometimes appears on resumes as:

Position Desired	Objective
Job Objective	Employment Objective

All are acceptable. Regardless of the heading, the job objective has traditionally meant one or two sentences about the kind of job you want and what you can contribute to the company in return for such a job. You will recall from chapter 2 that the use of a job objective in your resume will depend in part on the style of resume you employ to present your qualifications. Remember that the functional resume in particular almost demands one.

That notwithstanding, feelings run strong about whether or not to include a job objective in the resume, so let's review the cases for and against, then reach a considered conclusion.

The case for inclusion: Without a job objective, a resume can have no focus, no sense of direction. And if you don't know where you are going, you can't write a resume, because the body copy has nothing to support. The resume revolves around your objective like the earth around the sun.

The case for exclusion: A job objective is too constricting and can exclude you from consideration from countless jobs you might have been interested in, and for which you are qualified. And after creating a resume with the intent of opening as many doors as possible, you wouldn't want to have half of them slammed shut. Besides, employers are not generally believed to be overly concerned about what you want from them until they have a damn good idea about what they can get out of you.

The solution: You do need an objective, but it needn't fit the traditional definition. The best resumes have objectives written in broad, nonspecific terms. They are often little more than a categorization, such as:

Job Objective: Marketing Management

Sometimes these objectives appear at the top of a resume, as a headline and attention grabber. If they go beyond that, they focus on skills, achievements, and relevant personal characteristics that support the argument.

Job Objective: To pursue an accounting career

STAFF ACCOUNTANT—REAL ESTATE

To obtain a responsible position in a company where my experience, accomplishments, and proficiency will allow me the opportunity for growth.

This last approach is best, because it considers the forces at work in business these days. Including job objectives has as much to do with filing and retrieval systems and computers as it does with people. On the one hand, the resume reader is looking for a problem solver, so, by seeing that you fit into a general area, will want to rush on to the rest of the resume (where there are more specifics). Then what happens? In the best-case scenario, you will get a frantic call asking you to state your terms and a start date right away. But what happens when there isn't a need for your particular talents that day? Your resume gets filed or logged onto the company's database. They will file your resume according to your instructions. And unless you give it the right help, it may not be filed under the right category; it may never see the light of day again. The broader your objective, the greater frequency with which it will be retrieved and reviewed in the future.

The same argument holds true for resumes sent to employment agencies and executive recruiters, who have been known to keep them on file for as long as ten years. Just recently, in fact, I heard one of those wonderful tales of an eight-year-old resume that landed a job for its writer because it had a general objective. Why is this relevant? Had the specific job objective of an entry-level professional been on that resume, the writer would never have been considered.

Such considerations are encouraging many job seekers to include brief and nonspecific job objectives in their resumes. You will learn how to come up with the right tone for your specific needs later in the book.

Employment Dates

Resume readers are often leery of resumes without employment dates. If you expect a response, you can increase your odds dramatically by including them—in one form or another.

With a steady work history and no employment gaps you can be very specific (space allowing) and write:

> January 11, 1997 to July 4,1998   or   1/11/97 to 7/4/98

> or, to be a little less specific:
> January 1997–February 1998

But if there are short employment gaps, you can improve the look of things:

> 1997–1998
> instead of
> December 12, 1997–January 23, 1998

There is no suggestion here that you should lie about your work history, but it is surprising just how many interviewers will be quite satisfied with such dates. There seems to be a myth that everything written on 20-lb. rag paper needs no further inquiry.

While this technique can effectively hide embarrassing employment gaps, and may get you in for an interview, you should of course be prepared with an adequate answer to questions about your work history. Even if such questions are posed, you will have the opportunity to explain yourself—*mano a mano,* as it were—and that is a distinct improvement over being peremptorily ruled out by some faceless non-entity before you get a chance to speak your piece. The end justifies the means, in this case.

Again, if you abbreviate months and years, do so consistently.

Keywords

Just as computers have helped streamline your job-hunting activities, they have done the same for the recruiting work of many human resources departments. One of the changes gaining ground in corporate America is the use of resume screening and tracking systems. Understanding how this technology affects the way your resume is received will dramatically affect your chances for success in your job hunt.

While electronic resume distribution makes your life easier, it's created an avalanche of electronic paper on the other side of the desk. If a company once had to deal with 100 resumes a day, it now probably sees 1,000 or more. With the high cost of human handling, the wholesale adoption of resume screening and tracking systems by businesses is a given. These systems are already in place in the most forward looking companies.

When computer screening replaces human judgment, the whole game changes. The computer program can't use human logic (although it is already getting pretty close); instead, the computer searches for keywords that describe the position and the professional skills needed to execute the duties effectively.

Your resume—and a thousand like it—can be scanned for the necessary keywords in seconds. The user receives a list of the resumes that contain the appropriate keywords. The greater the number of relevant keywords in your resume, the higher your ranking. The higher your ranking, the greater the likelihood that your resume will be rescued from the avalanche and passed along to a person for further screening.

In the resume examples you'll see a section that lumps a string of keywords together. A keyword section can be labeled with a variety of names: Special Knowledge, Keyword Preface, Keyword Section, or Areas of Expertise. Here's what the keyword section of a taxation specialist's resume looks like:

AREAS OF EXPERTISE

SBT, C-Corporation and S-Corporation State Income Tax Returns • Vehicle Use Tax Returns • State Income Tax Budgeting and Accrual • Multistate Property Tax Returns • Federal, State and Local Exemption Certificates • State and Local Sales, Use and Excise Tax Management • Tax Audit Management • Tax License and Bonding Maintenance • Certificates of Authority and Annual Report Filing Maintenance • State Sales and Use Tax Assessment • Federal Excise Tax Collection and Deposits • Determination of Nexus • Tax Amnesty Programs

---

This section will become mandatory in the very near future. You would be smart to be ahead of the curve on this one! This keyword section not only dramatically increases your chances of getting the computer's attention, but HR people appreciate them as a brief synopsis of the whole resume.

Job Titles

The purpose of a job title on your resume is not to reflect exactly what you were called by a particular employer, but rather to provide a generic identification that will be understood by as many employers as possible. So if your current title is "Junior Accountant, Level Three," realize that such internal titling may well bear no relation to the titling of any other company on earth. I remember looking over the personnel roster of a New York bank and learning, to my astonishment, that it had over one hundred systems analysts. (The typical number for an outfit this size is about twelve.) Then I noticed that they had no programmers. The reasoning that I eventually unearthed was remarkably simple. The human resources department, finding people to be title-conscious in this area, obligingly gave them the titles they wanted. (Another perceived benefit was that it confused the heck out of the raiding headhunters, who got disgusted with systems analysts who couldn't analyze their way out of a wet paper bag!)

This generic approach to job titles also holds true as your job takes you nearer the top of the corporate ladder. The senior executive knows that the higher up the ladder, the more rarefied the air and the fewer the opportunities. After all, a company only has one Controller or one VP of Operations. Again, to avoid painting yourself into a career corner, you can be "specifically vague" with job titles like:

Administrative Assistant   *Accountant*
instead of   instead of
Secretary   *Junior Accountant Level II*

It is imperative to examine your current role at work, rather than relying on your starting or current title. Job titles within companies change much more slowly than the jobs themselves, so a job change can be the opportunity for some to escape stereotyping and the career stagnation that accompanies it. Take the typist hired three years ago, who has now spent two years with a word processor. Such a person could be identified as a word processor instead of a typist.

This approach is important because of the way titles and responsibilities vary. Often, more senior titles and responsibilities are structured around a person's specific talents, especially so outside the *Fortune* 1000.

There are two situations that don't lend themselves to this technique.

- When you apply for a specific job where you know the title and the responsibilities, and where the position's title is similar but not the same as your own. (Then the exact title sought should be reflected in your resume—as long as you are not being misleading.)
- When you apply for a job in certain specific professions, such as health care. (A brain surgeon wouldn't want to be specifically vague by tagging herself as a Health Aide.)

Company Name

The names of employers should be included. There is no need to include street address or telephone number of past or present employers, although it can be useful to include the city and state. The company will find the complete address on your employment application.

When working for a multiple-division corporation you may want to list the divisional employer: "Bell Industries" might not be enough, so you would perhaps want to add "Computer Memory Division." By the way, it is quite all right to abbreviate words like Corporation (Corp.), Company (Co.), Limited (Ltd.), or Division (Div.). Again, be consistent.

Here is how you might combine a job title, company name, and address:

> DESIGN ENGINEER.
> Bell Industries, Inc., Computer Memory Div., Mountain View, CA.

The information you are supplying is relevant to the reader, but you don't wish it to detract from space usable to sell yourself. If, for instance, you live in a nationally known city, such as Dallas, you need not add "TX."

There is a possible exception to these guidelines. Employed professionals are justified in omitting current employers when their industry has been reduced to a small community of professionals who know, or know of, each other, and where a confidentiality breach is likely to have damaging repercussions. This usually happens to professionals on the higher rungs of the ladder. Of course, if you don't quite fit into this elite category but are still worried about identifying your firm, you are not obliged to list the name of your current employer.

One approach is simply to label a current company in a fashion that has become perfectly acceptable in today's business climate.

> A National Retail Chain
> An Established Electronics Manufacturer
> A Major Commercial Bank

You will notice that usually a company name is followed by a brief description of the business line:

> A National Retail Chain: Women and junior fashions and accessories.

> An Established Electronics Manufacturer producing monolithic memories.

This requirement is obviated when the writer can get the company's function into the heading.

> A Major Commercial Bank

The writer who can do this saves a line or two of precious space which can be filled with other valuable data.

Responsibilities

This is what is referred to as the meat, or body copy, of the resume, the area where not only are your responsibilities listed, but your special achievements and other contributions are also highlighted. This is one of the key areas that sets the truly great resume apart from the rest. This is a crucial part of the resume; it will be dealt with in detail in chapters 4 and 5.

Endorsements

Remember when you got that difficult job finished so quickly? And all the good things the boss said about your work? Well, in a resume you can very effectively quote him, even if the praise wasn't in writing (though of course it is best to quote directly). A line such as "Praised as 'most innovative and determined manager in the company'" can work wonders.

These third-party endorsements are not necessary, and they most certainly shouldn't be used to excess. But one or two can be a useful addition to your resume. Such quotes, used sparingly, can be very impressive; overkill can make you sound too self-important and reduce your chances of winning an interview.

Such endorsements become especially effective when the responsibilities have been qualified with facts, numbers, and percentages.

Accreditation and Licenses

Many fields of work require professional licensure or accreditation. If this is the case in your line of work, be sure to list everything necessary. If you are close to a particular accreditation or license (a C.P.A., for example), you would want to list it with information about the status:

Passed all parts of C.P.A. exam, September '00 (expected certification February '01).

Professional Affiliations

Your affiliation with associations and societies dedicated to your field shows your own dedication to your career. Membership is also important for networking, so if you are not currently a member of one of your industry's professional associations, give serious consideration to joining. Note the emphasis on "professional" in the heading. An employer is almost exclusively interested in your professional associations and societies. Omit references to any religious, political, or otherwise potentially controversial affiliations.

An exception to this rule is in those jobs where a wide circle of acquaintances is regarded as an asset. Some examples would include jobs in public relations, sales, marketing, real estate, and insurance. In that case, include your membership in the Kiwanis or the Royal Lodge of the Raccoons.

By the same token, a seat on the town board, charitable cause involvement, or fundraising work are all activities that show a willingness to involve oneself and can often demonstrate organizational abilities. Space permitting, these are all activities worthy of inclusion because they show you as a sober and responsible member of the community.

These activities become more important as one climbs the corporate ladder of the larger companies. Those firms that take their community responsibilities seriously look for staff who feel and act the same way—an aspect of corporate culture applying itself at the most immediate levels.

As for method of inclusion, brevity is the rule.

American Heart Association: Area Fundraising Chair

My personal observation is that these activities increase in importance with the maturity of the individual. Employers, quite selfishly perhaps, like to think of their younger staff burning the midnight oil solely for them.

Civil Service Grade

With a civil service job in your background, you will have been awarded a civil service grade. So, in looking for a job with the government, be sure to list it. In transferring from the government to the private sector, you are best advised to translate it into generic terms and ignore the grade altogether, unless you are applying for jobs with government contractors, subcontractors, or other specialized employers familiar with the intricacies of civil service ranking.

Publications and Patents

Such achievements, if they appear, are usually found at the end of the best resumes. Although they serve as positive means of evaluation for the reader, these achievements are of relatively minor importance in many professions.

Nevertheless, both publication and patents are manifestations of original thought and extended effort above and beyond the call of accepted professionalism. They tell the reader that you invest considerable personal time and effort in your career and are therefore a cut above the competition. Publication carries more weight in some industries and professions (where having literary visibility is synonymous with getting ahead); patents are a definite plus in the technology and manufacturing fields. You will notice in the resume examples how the writers list dates and names of publications, but do not usually include copyright information.

> "Radical Treatments for Chronic Pain." 2000. *Journal of American Medicine.*

> "Pain: Is It Imagined or Real?" 1998. *OMNI* Magazine.

Languages

Technology is rapidly changing our world into the proverbial global village. This means that today, as all companies are interested in client-based expansion, a linguistic edge in the job hunt could be just what you need. If you are fluent in a foreign language, you will want to mention it. Likewise if you understand a foreign language, but perhaps are not fluent, still mention it.

Fluent in French   Read German
Read and write Serbo-Croatian   Understand Spanish

Education

Educational history is normally listed whenever it helps your case, although the exact positioning of the information will vary according to the length of your professional experience and the relative strength of your academic achievements.

If you are recently out of school with little practical experience, your educational credentials, which probably constitute your primary asset, will appear near the beginning of the resume.

As you gain experience, your academic credentials become less important, and gradually slip toward the end of your resume. The exception to this is found primarily in certain professions where academic qualifications dominate a person's career—medicine, for instance.

You will notice that all examples for education are in reverse chronological order: The highest level of attainment (not necessarily a degree) always comes first, followed by the lesser levels. In this way, a doctorate will be followed by a master's degree, then a bachelor's. For degreed professionals, there is no need to go back further into educational history. (It is optional to list your prestigious prep school.) Those who attended school but did not graduate should nevertheless list the school in its proper chronological position, but should not draw attention to the fact that they did not receive a degree.

Those who did not achieve the higher levels of educational recognition will list their own highest level of attainment. A word on attainment is in order here. If you graduated from high school, attended college, but didn't graduate, you may be tempted to list your high school diploma first, followed by the name of the college you attended. That would give the wrong emphasis: it says you are a college drop-out and focuses on you as high school graduate. In this instance you would in fact list your college and omit reference to earlier educational history.

While abbreviations are frowned on in most circumstances, it is acceptable to abbreviate educational degrees (Ph.D., M.A., A.B., etc.), simply because virtually everyone understand them.

Those with scholarships and awards will list them, and recent graduates will usually also list majors and minors (space permitting). The case is a little more confused for the seasoned professional. Many human resources professionals say it makes life easier for them if majors and minors are listed, so they can further sift and grade the applicants. That's good for them, but it might not be good for you. All you want the resume to do is get you in the door, not slam it in your face. So, as omitting these minutiae will never stop you from getting an interview, I strongly urge you to err on the side of safety and leave 'em out.

If you are a recent entrant into the workplace, both your scholastic achievements and your contributions have increased importance. List your position on the school newspaper or the student council, memberships in clubs, and recognition for scholastic achievement; in short, anything that demonstrates your potential as a productive employee. As your career progresses, however, prospective employers care less about your school life and more about your work life.

Changing times have also changed thinking about listing fraternities and sororities on resumes. A case could be made, I think, for leaving them off as a matter of course: If such organizations are important to an interviewer he or she will ask. My ruling, however, is that if the resume is tailored to an individual or company where membership in such organizations will result in a case of "deep calling to deep," then by all means, list. If, on the other hand, the resume is for general distribution, forget it.

Professional Training

Under the educational heading on smart resumes, you will often see a section for continuing professional education, focusing on special courses and seminars attended. Specifically, if you are computer literate, list the programs you are familiar with.

Summer and Part-time Employment

This should only be included when the resume writer is either just entering the work force or re-entering it after a substantial absence. The entry-level person can feel comfortable listing dates and places and times. The returnee should include the skills gained from part-time employment in a fashion that minimizes the "part-time" aspect of the experience—probably by using a Functional resume format.

What Can Never Go In

Some information just doesn't belong in resumes. Make the mistake of including it, and at best your resume loses power. At worst, you fail to land the interview.

Titles: Resume, Fact Sheet, Curriculum Vitae, etc.

Never use any of these variations on a theme as a heading. Their appearance on a resume is redundant: If it isn't completely obvious from the very look of your piece of paper that it is a resume, go back to square one. By the way, there is no difference in meaning among the above terms. "Curriculum Vitae" (or CV, as it is sometimes known) was an early term much favored in English and American academia—basically to prove that the users knew a little Latin. Its use today is outmoded and affected. "Fact Sheet," on the other hand, was a term developed by the employment agencies to imply they were presenting unvarnished facts. The phrase has never caught on.

Availability

Saying anything about your availability for employment on a resume is another redundancy. If you are not available, then why the heck are you wasting everyone's time? The only justification of the item's inclusion is if you expect to be finishing a project and moving on at such and such a time, and not before. But your view should be that intelligent human beings always have their eyes and ears open for better career opportunities. If leaving before the end of a project could affect your integrity and/or references, O.K. There's a lot to be said for not burning your bridges, and as careers progress, it's surprising how many of the same people you bump into again and again.

Let the subject of availability come up at the face-to-face meeting. After meeting you, an employer will often be prepared to wait until you are available, and will probably appreciate your integrity.

Reason for Leaving

There is no real point to stating your reasons for leaving a job on a resume, yet time and again they are included—to the detriment of the writer. The topic is always covered during an interview anyway. Mentioning it in advance and on paper can only damage your chances for being called in for that meeting.

References

It is inappropriate and unprofessional to list the names of references on a resume. You will never see it on a top example. Why? Interviewers are not interested in checking them before they meet and develop a strong interest in you—it's too time-consuming. In addition, employers are forbidden by law to check references without your written consent (thanks to the 1972 Fair Credit and Reporting Act), and they have to meet you first in order to obtain it, right?

Most employers will assume that references are available anyway (and if they aren't available, boy, are you in trouble). For that reason, there's an argument to be made for leaving that famous line—References Available Upon Request—off the end of the resume. I disagree, however. It may not be absolutely necessary to say that references are there for the asking, but those four extra words certainly don't do any harm and may help you stand out from the crowd. Including the phrase sends a little message:

"Hey, look, I have no skeletons in my closet."

A brief but important aside. If you have ever worked under a different surname, you must take this fact into account when giving your references. A recently divorced woman wasted a strong interview performance not too long ago because she was using her maiden name on her resume and at the interview. She forgot to tell the employer that her references would, of course, remember her by a different last name. The results of this oversight were catastrophic. Three prior employers denied ever having heard of anyone by that name the woman's interviewer supplied. She lost the job.

Written Testimonials

Even worse than listing references on a resume is to attach a bunch of written testimonials. It is an absolute no-no. No one believes them anyway.

Of course, that doesn't mean that you shouldn't solicit such references for your files. They can always be produced when references are requested and can be used as a basis for those third-party endorsements we talked about. This will be especially helpful to you if you are just entering the work force, or re-entering after a long absence, because the content of the testimonials can be used to beef up your resume significantly.

Salary

Leave out all references to salary, past and present—it is far too risky. Too high or too low a salary can knock you out of the running even before you hear the starting gun. Even in responding to a help-wanted advertisement that specifically requests salary requirements, don't give them. A good resume will still get you the interview, and in the course of your discussions with the company, you'll certainly talk about salary anyway. If you somehow feel obliged to give salary requirements, simply write "competitive" or "negotiable" (and then only in your cover letter).

Abbreviations

With the exceptions of educational attainments, and those required by the postal service, avoid abbreviations if at all possible. Of course, space constraints might make it imperative that you write "No. Wilshire Blvd." instead of "North Wilshire Boulevard." If that is the case, be sure to be consistent. But bear in mind that you will always seem more thoughtful and professional if everything is spelled out.

Jargon

A similar warning applies to industry slang. Your future boss might understand it, but you can bet your boots that neither his or her boss nor the initial resume screener will. Your resume must speak clearly of your skills to many different people, and one skill that we all need today is a sensitivity to the needs of communication.

If you are in one of the high-technology industries, however, avoiding jargon and acronyms is not only impossible, it is often inadvisable. All the same, keep the nontechnical resume screener in mind before you wax lyrical about bits and bytes.

Charts and Graphs

Even if charts and graphs are part of your job, they make poor use of the space available on a resume—and they don't help the reader. In fact, you should never even bring them out at an interview unless requested. The same goes for other examples of your work. If you are a copywriter or graphic artist, for example, it is all right to say that samples are available, but only if you have plenty of resume space to spare.

Mention of Age, Race, Religion, Sex, National Origin

Government legislation was enacted some years ago forbidding employment discrimination in these areas. If the government had to take action, you know things were bad. Although today it's much better, I urge you to leave out any reference to any of these areas in your resume.

Photographs

In days of old when men were bold and all our cars had fins, it was the done thing to have a photograph in the top right-hand corner of the resume. Today, the fashion is against photographs; including them is a waste of space that says nothing about your ability to do a job.

(Obviously, careers in modeling, acting, and certain aspects of the electronic media require photos. In these instances your face is your fortune.)

Health/Physical Description

Who cares? You are trying to get a job, not a date. Unless your physical health (gym instructor, for example) and/or appearance (model, actor, media personality) are immediately relevant to the job, leave these issues alone.

Early Background

I regularly see resumes that tell about early childhood and upbringing. To date, the most generous excuse I can come up with for such anecdotes is that the resumes were prepared by the subjects' mothers.

Weaknesses

Any weakness, lack of qualifications, or information likely to be detrimental to your cause should always be canned. Never tell resume readers what you don't have or what you can't or haven't had the opportunity to do yet. Let them find that out for themselves.

Demands

You will never see demands on a good resume. Don't outline what you feel an employer is expected to give or to provide. The time for making demands is when the employer extends a job offer with a salary and job description attached. That is when the employer will be interested and prepared to listen to what you want. Until then, concentrate on bringing events to that happy circumstance by emphasizing what you can bring to the employer. In your resume you should, to paraphrase the great man, ask not what your employer can do for you, but rather what you can do for your employer.

Exaggerations

Avoid verifiable exaggerations of your skills, accomplishments, and educational qualifications. Research has now proven that three out of every ten resumes feature inflated educational qualifications. Consequently, verification, especially of educational claims, is on the increase. If, after you had been hired, you were discovered to have told a sly one on your resume, it could cost you your job and a lot more. The stigma of deceit will very likely follow you for the rest of your professional days. On the other hand, I don't notice 30 percent of the work force stumbling around with crippled careers. Matters are tightening up in this area, and ultimately it will be a personal judgment call.

Judgment Calls

Here are some areas that fall into neither the do nor the don't camp. Whether to include them will depend on your personal circumstances.

Summary

The Summary, when it is included in a resume, comes immediately after the Objective. The point is to encapsulate your experience and perhaps highlight one or two of your skills and/or contributions. You hope, in two or three short sentences, to grab the reader's attention with a power pack of the skills and attributes you have developed throughout your career. Good summaries are short; you don't want to show all your aces in the first few lines! (You can see examples of resumes with strong summaries in the resume section of this book.)

On the other hand, many experts feel that the content of the summary must be demonstrated by the body of the resume, and that therefore summaries are pointless duplications and a waste of space. The choice is yours. Used wisely and well, they can work.

Personal Flexibility, Relocation

If you are open to relocation for the right opportunity, make it clear. It will never in and of itself get you an interview, but it won't hurt. On the other hand, never state that you aren't open to relocation. After all, that factor usually comes into play only when you have a job offer to consider. Let nothing stand in the way of a nice collection of job offers!

Career Objectives

These are okay to include at the very start of your career, before your general direction has been confirmed by experience and track record. Inclusion is also acceptable if you have very clearly defined objectives and are prepared to sacrifice all other opportunities. If that is the case, state your goals clearly and succinctly, remembering not to confuse the nature of long-term career objectives with short-term job objectives.

Beware, though, of the drawbacks. First of all, resume readers aren't famous for paying much attention to objectives. Second, I have seen these used on many occasions to make a hiring decision between two candidates. The resumes are compared, A has no objective, B has an objective that doesn't match the initial expectations. Result? A gets the job. Another consideration is that your resume may be on file for years, during which time your objectives are bound to change.

Marital Status

If you think mention of your marital status will enhance your chances (if you are looking for a position as a long-distance trucker, marriage counselor, or traveling salesperson, for example), include it. In all other instances leave it out. Legally, your marital status is of no consequence.

Military

Include your good military record with highest rank, especially if you are applying for jobs in the defense sector; otherwise exclude it. It is no longer any detriment to your career not to have a military history.

Personal Interests

A recent Korn Ferry study showed that executives with team sports on their resumes were seen to be averaging $3,000 a year more than their more sedentary counterparts. Now, that makes giving a line to your hobbies worthwhile, if they fit into certain broad categories. These would include team sports, determination activities (running, climbing, bicycling), and "brain activities" (bridge, chess). The rule of thumb, as always, is only to include activities that can in some way contribute to your chances.

Personal Paragraphs

Here and there throughout the resume section of this book you will see resumes that include—often toward the end—a short personal paragraph that gives you a candid snapshot of the resume writer as a person. Done well, these can be exciting, effective endings to a resume, but they are not to everyone's taste. Typically, they refer to one or two personal traits, activities, and sometimes, beliefs. These are often tied in with skills required for the particular job sought.

The idea is to make the reader say, "Heh, there's a real person behind those Foster Grants, let's get him in here; sounds like our kind of guy." Of course, as no one can be all things to all people, you don't go overboard in this area.

4 | Resumes That Knock 'em Dead

This is the part of the book that requires you to do some thinking. I will ask questions to jog your memory about your practical experience. The outcome will be a smorgasbord of your most sellable professional attributes. Whether you are a fast-tracker, recent graduate, work force reentrant, career changer, or what-have-you, if you are considering new horizons, you must take stock before stepping out.

People change jobs for a multitude of reasons. Perhaps your career isn't progressing as you want it. Perhaps you have gone as far as you can with your present employer, and the only way to take another career step is to change companies. Maybe you have been in the same job for three or more years, without dramatic salary increases or promotions, and you know that you are going nowhere. You have been stereotyped, classified, and pigeonholed.

You need to know where you've been, where you are, and where you're headed. Without this stock taking, your chances of reaching your ultimate goals are reduced, because you won't know how best to use what you've got to get what you want.

Believe it or not, very few people have a clear fix on what they do for a living. Oh, I know; you ask a typist what he or she does, and you get, "Type, stupid." You ask an accountant, and you hear, "Fiddle with numbers, what do you think?" And that is the problem. Most people don't look at their work beyond these simplistic terms. They never examine the implications of their jobs in relation to the overall success of the company. Most people miss not only their importance to an employer as part of the business, but also, their importance to themselves. Preparing your resume will give you a fresh view of yourself as a professional and your role in your chosen profession.

Employers all want to know the same thing: How can you contribute to keeping their ship afloat and seaworthy? Companies hire only one type of person—a problem solver. Look at your work in terms of the problems you solve in the daily round, the problems that would occur if you weren't there.

Some people find the prospect of taking stock of their skills to be an ominous one. They feel it means judging themselves by others' standards, by the job title and salary assigned to by someone else. Then, knowing their own weaknesses too well, they look at other people in their position, of whom they see only the exterior, and are awed by those persons' seemingly superior competence, skills, and professionalism. "Seemingly" is the key word here. You are as good as the next person, and to prove it, all you have to do is look yourself squarely in the eye and learn that you have a great deal more to offer than you may ever have imagined.

The Secret of Resume Writing

As a resume writer, you have a lot in common with journalists and novelists. Beginners in each field usually bring some basic misconceptions about how writing is done: I always thought that Stephen King or James Clavell sat down, wrote "Page 1," then three weeks later wrote "The End," and placidly returned the quill to the inkwell. In fact, many professional writers—and resume writers—have more in common with sculptors. What they really do to start the creative process is to write masses of notes. This great mass is the raw material, like a block of stone, at which you chip away to reveal the masterwork that has been hiding there all along.

The key is that the more notes you have, the better. Just remember that whatever you write in the note-making part of your resume preparation will never suffer public scrutiny. It is for your private consumption; from these notes, the finished work of art will emerge for public view.

Questionnaire, Part One: Raw Materials

This questionnaire is set up to follow your entire career.

1. *Current or Last Employer:* This includes part-time or voluntary employment if you are a recent graduate or about to reenter the work-force after

an absence. Try looking at your school as an employer and see what new information you reveal about yourself.

> Starting Date:
> Starting Salary:
> Leaving Date:
> Leaving Salary:

2. *Company Description:* Write one sentence that describes the product(s) your company made or the service(s) it performed.
3. *Title:* Write your starting job title (the one given to you when you first signed on with the company). Then write a one- or two-sentence description of your responsibilities in that position.
4. *Duties:* What were your three major duties in this position?
5. *Methods, Skills, Results:* Now, for each of the above three duties, answer the following questions:

> What special skills or knowledge did you need to perform this task satisfactorily?
>
> What has been your biggest achievement in this area? (Try to think about money saved or made, or time saved for the employer. Don't worry if your contributions haven't been acknowledged in writing, as long as you know them to be true without exaggeration.)
>
> What verbal or written comments were made about your contributions in this area, by peers or managers?
>
> What different levels of people did you have to interact with to achieve your job tasks? How did you get the best out of superiors? Co-workers? Subordinates?
>
> What aspects of your personality were brought into play when executing this duty? (For example, perhaps it required attention to detail, or determination, or good verbal and writing skills.

To help you address that last issue (it's a vitally important one), you should look over the following list of a number of personality traits that are in constant demand from all employers.

Analytical Skills: Weighing the pros and cons. Not jumping at the first solution to a problem that presents itself.

Chemistry: Your willingness to get along with others.

Communication Skills: More than ever, the ability to talk with and write effectively to people at all levels in a company is a key to success.

Confidence: Poise, friendliness, honesty, and openness with all employees—high and low.

Dedication: Doing whatever it takes to get the job done.

Drive and Determination: A desire to get things done. Goal-oriented. Someone who does not back off when a problem or situation gets tough.

Economy: Most problems have an expensive solution and an inexpensive one that the company would prefer to implement.

Efficiency: Always keeping an eye open for inefficient uses of time, effort, resources, and money.

Energy: Extra effort in all aspects of the job, the little things as well as the important matters.

Honesty/Integrity: Responsibility for all your actions—both good and bad. Always making decisions in the best interests of the company, rather than on whim or personal preference.

Listening Skills: Listening, rather than just waiting to speak.

Motivation: Enthusiasm, finding reasons to accept challenges rather than avoid them. A company realizes that a motivated person accepts added challenges and does that little bit extra on every job.

Pride: Pride in a job well done. Paying attention to detail.

Reliability: Follow-through, a willingness to keep management informed, and a predisposition toward relying on oneself—not others—to see your job done.

Sensitivity to Procedures: Following the chain of command, recognizing that procedures exist to keep a company functioning and profitable. Those who rush to implement their own "improved procedures" wholesale, or organize others to do so, can cause untold chaos in an organization.

6. *Supporting Points:* If you asked for a promotion or a raise while in this position, what arguments did you use to back up your request?

7. *Most Recent Position:* Write down your current (or last) job title. Then write a one- or two-sentence description of your responsibilities in that position, and repeat steps 3 through 6. In this step it is assumed that you have a title and responsibilities that are different from those you had when you first joined the company. If this is not the case, simply ignore this step. On the other hand, many people have held three or four titles with a specific employer, and gained breadth of experience with each one. In this instance, for each different intermediary title, repeat steps 1 through 6. The description of responsibilities should be reserved for your departing (or current) title.

8. *Reflecting on Success:* Make some general observations about work with this employer. Looking back over your time with this employer, what was the biggest work-related problem that you had to face? What solution did you find? What was the result of the solution when implemented? What was the value to the employer in terms of money earned or saved and improved efficiency? What was the area of your greatest personal improvement in this job? What was the greatest contribution you made as a team player? Who are the references you would hope to use from this employer, and what would they say about you?

9. *Getting All the Facts:* Repeat the last eight steps for your previous employer, and then for the employer before that, and so forth. Most finished resumes focus on the last three jobs, or last ten years before that, and so forth. In this developmental portion of the process, however, you must go back in time and cover your entire career. Remember that you are doing more than preparing a resume here: You are preparing for the heat of battle. In the interview preparation, throughout any telephone screening interviews, and especially before that crucial face-to-face meeting, you can use this Questionnaire to prepare yourself for anything the interviewer might ask. One of the biggest complaints interviewers have about job candidates, and one of the major reasons for rejection, is unpreparedness: "You know, good as some of this fellow's skills are, something just wasn't right. He seemed—slow somehow. You know, he couldn't even remember when he joined his current employer!" You won't have that problem.

Questionnaire, Part Two: Details, Details, Details

The hard work is done and it's all downhill from here. Just fill in the facts and figures relating to the following questions. Obviously, not everything will apply to you. The key is just to put it all down; you can polish it later.

Military History

Include branch of service, rank, and any special skills that could further your civilian career.

Educational History

Start with highest level of attainment and work backward. Give dates, schools, majors, minors, grade-point averages, scholarships, and/or special awards.

List other school activities, such as sports, societies, social activities. Especially important are leadership roles: Any example of how you "made a difference" with your presence could be of value to your future. Obviously, this is important for recent graduates with little work experience.

Languages

Specify fluency and ability to read and write foreign languages.

Personal Interests

List interests and activities that could be supportive to your candidacy. For example, an internal auditor who plays chess or bridge would list these on a resume, because they support the analytical bent so necessary to work.

Technological Literacy

In this new era of work, every potential employer is concerned about your ability to work with new technologies. If you are computer and Internet literate, let's hear the details. If not, it's time to catch up with today's technology—before you get left behind with the industrial era dinosaurs. You should be able to identify the equipment and applications you need to function effectively in your field.

Patents

Include patents that are both pending and awarded.

Publications

If you have published articles, list the name of the publication, title of article, and the publication date. If you have had books published, list the title and publisher.

Professional Associations

Include membership and the details of any offices you held.

Volunteer Work

Also include any volunteer work you performed. It isn't only paid work experience that makes you valuable.

Miscellaneous Areas of Achievement

All professions and careers are different. Use this section to itemize any additional aspects of your history where you somehow "made a difference" with your presence.

Questionnaire, Part Three: Where Are You Going?

Knowing where you want to go will determine both the wording and the layout of your resume. Remember that there is a difference between valid objectives and pipedreams. Dreams aren't bad things to have, but they mustn't be confused with making a living.

Your first step is to write down a job title that embraces your objectives. Having taken this simple step, you need to note underneath it all the skills and qualifications needed to do that job successfully. List them like this:

Job Title
1. First skill
2. Second skill
3. Third skill

Take a trip to the library and ask to see a copy of the *Dictionary of Occupational Titles*. It gives you endless job titles, as you might expect, and brief job descriptions. Make notes by all means, but don't copy it out word for word. The book is full of dead prose that's copper-bottom guaranteed to send the average resume reader to sleep in three seconds flat.

When you have decided on an objective, and defined what it takes to do that job, go back through the first part of the questionnaire and flag all the entries you can use to build a viable resume. Just underline or highlight the appropriate passages for further attention when the time comes for putting pen to paper.

The chances are that you will find adequate skills in your background to qualify you for the job objective. And remember: Few people have all the qualifications for the jobs they get!

If you still aren't sure, develop a "Matching Sheet" for yourself. List the practical requirements of your job objective on one side of a piece of paper and match them on the other side with your qualifications. A senior computer programmer, looking for a step up to a systems analysis position with a new job in financial applications, might develop a Matching Sheet that looks like this:

Job Needs	*My Experience*
Mainframe IBM experience	6 yrs. experience
IBM COBOL	COBOL, PL/1, Assembler
Financial experience	6 yrs. in banking
Sys. dev. methodology	Major sys. dev., 3 yrs.
Communication	Ongoing customer service work OS/MVS, TSO/SPF, CICS, SNAOS/MVS, TSO/SPF, ROSCOE, IMS, DB/DC, SAS

But what about the junior accountant who had VP of finance as a goal? Naturally, at this stage, many of the needed skills—and much of the experience—aren't in place. If you fall into this category, don't worry. You just happened upon a career objective rather than a job objective. To solve the dilemma, list all the title changes between your present position and your dream job. This will show you how many career steps stand between you and your ultimate goal.

At best, job and career objectives are simply a tool to give you focus for writing the resume, and to give the reader something to take sightings on. The way the world is changing, by the time you can reasonably expect to reach your ultimate career goal, that particular position may not even exist.

Be content with a generalized objective for the next job. And don't be afraid of that objective—who knows what the next few years will hold for you?

Sample Questionnaire

This sample questionnaire was filled out by a fellow professional using the questionnaire guidelines.

1. Current or Last Employer:
   This includes part-time or voluntary employment if you are a recent graduate or about to reenter the work force after an absence. That does not mean you should ignore this section: Try looking at your school as an employer and see what new information you reveal about yourself.

   BRANCH MANAGER
Starting Date	*11/92*
Starting Salary	*$13,000*
Leaving Date	*8/95*
Leaving Salary	*$26,000*

   AREA MANAGER
Starting Date	*8/95*
Starting Salary	*$31,200*
Leaving Date	*8/98*
Leaving Salary	*$41,600*

   DIVISION MANAGER
Starting Date	*8/98*
Starting Salary	*$62,400*
Leaving Date	*3/00*
Leaving Salary	*$62,400*

2. Write one sentence that describes the products your company made or the services it performed.

   BRANCH MANAGER through DIVISION MANAGER: MICRO/TEMPS sold software consulting services to the computer-user industry.

3. List your starting job title (the one given to you when you first signed on with the company). Then write a one- or two-sentence description of your responsibilities in that position.

    BRANCH MANAGER
    Started a new division of the Technical Aid Corporation called MICRO/TEMPS. Was responsible for developing a client and applicant database, while showing a profit for the division.

    AREA MANAGER
    Opened an additional office in the Washington area. Was accountable for the profitability of both the Boston and Washington offices.

    DIVISION MANAGER
    Responsible for market studies for future branches to be opened. Directly involved in choosing new locations, opening office, training staff, and having the office profitable in less than one year's time.

4. What were your three major duties in this position?

    BRANCH MANAGER
    A) Selling software services to clients.
    B) Interviewing applicants and selling them on consulting.
    C) Setting up interviews for applicants and clients to meet.

    AREA MANAGER
    A) Training sales and recruiting staff.
    B) Developing and implementing goals from forecasts.
    C) Interfacing with other divisions in order to develop a working relationship between different divisions.

    DIVISION MANAGER
    A) Hired and trained Branch Managers for all new offices.
    B) Developed P & L forecasts for the B.O.D.
    C) Developed and implemented division policies.

5. Now, for each of the above three duties, answer the following questions.

What special skills or knowledge did you need to perform this task satisfactorily?

BRANCH MANAGER
A) Knowledge of the computer industry.
B) Key contacts in the Massachusetts computer industry.

AREA MANAGER
A) Knowledge and experience developing a branch.
B) Experience training sales and recruiting staff.

DIVISION MANAGER
A) Knowledge and understanding of developing a profitable division.
B) Knowledge and experience hiring and training branch managers.

What has been your biggest achievement in this area? (Think about money saved or made, or time saved for the employer. Don't worry if your contributions haven't been acknowledged in writing, so long as you know them to be true.)

BRANCH MANAGER
Successfully developed a new division of the Technical Aid Corporation. Now generating $18,000,000 in revenues.

AREA MANAGER
Successfully opened new branches for the division and hired and trained the staff.

DIVISION MANAGER
Built division to $20 million in annual sales.

What verbal or written comments were made about your contributions in this area, by peers or managers?

BRANCH MANAGER
Hard-working, stay-at-it attitude.

AREA MANAGER
Hires good people and knows how to get the best out of them.

DIVISION MANAGER
Her division always makes the largest gross profit out of any of the divisions.

What different levels of people did you have to interact with to get this particular duty done? How did you get the best out of each of them?

BRANCH MANAGER
A) Superiors—Listened to their ideas and then tried to show them I could implement them.
B) Co-workers—Shared experiences and company goals—set up some competition.
C) Subordinates—Acknowledged their responsibilities as very important for the team.

AREA MANAGER
A) Superiors—Explained situations clearly and made them understand our options.
B) Co-workers—Challenged to reach goals.
C) Subordinates—Complimented when and where it was necessary.

DIVISION MANAGER
A) Superiors—Asked for their experience and advice in difficult situations.
B) Co-workers—Set up and accepted contest between managers.
C) Subordinates—Made them feel they were extremely important as a member of the team.

What aspects of your personality were brought into play when executing this duty?

PERSONALITY: BRANCH MANAGER TO DIVISION MANAGER

strong willpower	*high achiever*	*high goal setter*
stick-to-it attitude	*aggressive*	

6. If you asked for a promotion or a raise while in this position, what arguments did you use to back up your request?

BRANCH MANAGER—Increase in sales.
AREA MANAGER—Increase in responsibility.
DIVISION MANAGER—Increase in gross profit and responsibilities.

7. Write down your current (or last) job title. Then write a one- or two-sentence description of your responsibilities in that position, and repeat steps 3 through 6.

Current title—*Personnel Manager*

Step 3: Description of responsibilities. *Hiring all internal staff of technical managers and sales people, additionally responsible for hiring all external consultants.*

Step 4: Three major duties:
A) *Hiring of all internal and external consultants*
B) *Setting up wage and salary guidelines*
C) *Establishing the Boston office so it could become profitable quickly*

Step 5: Skills or knowledge needed:
A) *Ability to source qualified candidates*
B) *Experience in start-up situation*
C) *Knowledge of the Boston marketplace*

Biggest achievement: *Helped in making the branch profitable in nine months.*

Verbal or written comments: *A no-nonsense kind of person, aggressive and hard-working; good at getting the best out of people.*

Superiors: *Was up-front with any problems and clearly and concisely laid out all the alternatives.*

Co-workers: *Set up good networking of communications to have information flow quickly and easily.*

Subordinates: *Made them aware that we all had a lot to do, but that we were all important.*

Step 6: Raise or promotion.
Increase in sales figures and was responsible for hiring more consultants than we had originally discussed.

8. Make some general observations about work with this employer.
Looking back over your time with this employer, what was the biggest
work-related problem that you had to face?
*They wanted to grow rapidly, but didn't want to invest the money it took to
recruit and attract good consultant talent.*

What solution did you find?

*Got consultants through Boston Computer Society and other related
organizations, and set up a very aggressive referral program.*

What was the result of the solution when implemented?

*We started to attract quality consultants, and our name was beginning to
circulate.*

What was the value to the employer in terms of money earned or saved and
improved efficiency?

*Company did not spend a lot of money on recruiting efforts and was able to
attract quality people.*

What was the area of your greatest personal improvement in this job?

Made many key contacts in some excellent organizations.

What was the greatest contribution you made as a team player?

Brought internal staff members closer together as a working team.

Who are the references you would hope to use from this employer, and
what do you think they would say about you?

*Ken Shelly—He was one of our first external consultants hired. He would
probably say that I identified some key consultants for this project at
Sheraton, and that he could always rely on me to help him no matter what.*

*Dave Johnson—He was our technical manager. He would say that I did my
job extremely well considering the little resources I had, and that I
identified many quality applicants.*

5 | Writing the Basic Resume

Advertisements and resumes have a great deal in common.

You will notice the vast majority of advertisements in any media can be heard, watched, or read in under thirty seconds. That is not accidental. The timing is based on studies relating to the limit of the average consumer's attention span.

And that is why you sometimes notice that both resumes and advertisements depart from the rules that govern all other forms of writing. First and last they are an urgent business communication, and businesses like to get to the point.

Before getting started, good advertising copywriters imagine themselves in the position of their target audience. They imagine their objective—selling something. Then they consider what features their product possesses and what benefits it can provide to the purchaser.

You will find a similar procedure beneficial in your own writing. Fortunately, your approach is simplified somewhat, because you can make certain generalizations. You can assume, for instance, that the potential employer has a position to fill and a problem to solve, and that he or she will hire someone who is able to do the job, who is willing to do it, and who is manageable.

For the next fifteen minutes, imagine yourself in one of your target companies. You are in the personnel department on resume detail. Fortunately it is a slow morning, and there are only thirty that need to be read. Go straight to the example section now and read thirty resumes without a break, then return to this page.

Now you have some idea of what it feels like. Except that you had it easy— the resumes you read were good, interesting ones; resumes that got real people real jobs. Even so, you probably felt a little punch drunk at the end of the exercise. But I know that you learned a very valuable lesson: Brevity is to be desired above all other things.

Preparation

Collect an old resume, some generic job descriptions, and of course, the completed Questionnaire. Then get comfortably set up at your computer (or with a pad of paper) and you're ready to go!

Now, just write. Don't even try for style or literacy—you can tend to that later. Think of yourself as speaking on paper. You'll find your personal speech rhythms will make for a lively resume, once they have been edited.

Choose a Layout

You have seen the basic examples of chronological, functional, and combination resumes in chapter 2, and certainly you have browsed through the dozens of actual resumes. Find one that strikes your fancy and fits your needs, and use it as your model. It need not reflect your field of professional expertise. Obviously, you will have to tinker with any model, adding or deleting jobs and making other subtle adjustments as necessary.

This first step is just like painting by numbers. Go through the model and fill in the obvious slots—name, address, telephone number(s), e-mail address, employer names, employment dates, educational background and dates, activities and the like. Shazam! Now the first half of your resume is complete.

Filling in the Picture: Chronological Resumes

Objectives

You can have a simple nonspecific objective, one that gives the reader a general focus, such as, "Objective: Data Processing Management." It gets the message across succinctly; and if there is no immediate need for someone of your background, it encourages the employer to put your resume in the file where you feel it belongs. That's important, because even if you are not suitable for today's needs, there's a good chance that the resume will be pulled out when such a need does arise.

If you choose to use an expanded, detailed objective, refer to chapter 3. You will of course:

- Keep it short, just one or two sentences.
- Not get too specific—no one is that interested.
- Focus the objective on what you can do for the company and avoid mention of what you want in return.
- State exactly the job title you seek, if the resume is in response to a specific advertisement.
- Keep your objectives general to give yourself the widest number of employment options, if the resume will be sent out "blind" to a number of companies.

Of course, with your resume produced on a computer, your objective can go through subtle variations for each specific job.

If you want to use both a nonspecific and a detailed objective, headline the resume with the nonspecific title, and then follow with the more detailed one.

Company Role

Now, for each employer, edit your response from step 2 of the Questionnaire, which outlines that company's services or products. Make it one short sentence: Do not exceed one line or ten words.

Job Titles

Remember what we said in chapter 3. There is nothing intrinsically wrong with listing your title as "Fourth-Level Administration Clerk, Third Class," as long as you are prepared to wait until doomsday for it to be considered by someone who understands what it means and is able to relate it to current needs. With this in mind:

- Be general in your job title. All companies have their particular ways of dispensing job titles, and they all vary. Your title with employer A will mean something entirely different to employer B, and might not make any sense at all to employer C.

- Whenever possible, stay away from designations such as trainee, junior, intermediate, senior—as in Junior Engineer—and just designate yourself as Engineer, Designer, Editor, or what have you.

Responsibilities

In a chronological resume, the job title is often followed by a short sentence that helps the reader visualize you doing the job. Get the information from the completed questionnaire and do a rough edit to get it down to one short sentence. Don't worry about perfection now; the polishing is done later.

The responsibilities and contributions you list here are those functions that best display your achievements and problem-solving abilities. They do not necessarily correspond with how you spent the majority of your working day, nor are they related to how you might prefer to spend your working day. It can perhaps best be illustrated by showing you part of a resume that came to my desk recently. It is the work of a professional who listed her title and duties for one job like this:

> Sales Manager: Responsible for writing branch policy, coordination of advertising and advertising agencies. Developed knowledge of IBM PC. Managed staff of six.

Is it any wonder she wasn't getting responses to her resume-mailing campaign? She has mistakenly listed everything in the reverse chronological order, not in relation to the items' relative importance to a future employer. Let's look at what subsequent restructuring achieved:

> Sales Manager: Hired to turned around stagnant sales force. Successfully recruited, trained, managed and motivated a consulting staff of six. Result: 22 percent sales gain over first year.

In the rewrite of this particular part of the resume, notice how she thought like a copywriter and quickly identified the problem she was hired to solve.

> Hired to turn around stagnant sales force. (Demonstrates her skills and responsibilities.)

Successfully recruited, trained, managed and motivated a consulting staff of six. Result: 22 percent sales gain over first year. (Shows what she subsequently did about them, and just how well she did it.)

By doing this, her responsibilities and achievements become more important in the light of the problems they solved.

Some More about Contributions

Business has very limited interests. In fact, those interests can be reduced to a single phrase: Making a profit. Making a profit is done in just three ways: By saving money in some fashion for the company; by saving time through some innovation at the company, which in turn saves the company money and gives it the opportunity to make more money in the time saved; or by simply making money for the company.

That does not mean that you should address only those points in your resume and ignore valuable contributions which cannot be quantified. But it does mean that you should try to quantify as much as you can.

Achievements

Your achievements will be listed in step 5 of the first part of the Questionnaire. The achievements you take from step 5 will not necessarily be the greatest accomplishments that can help you reach your stated (or unstated) employment objective. Concentrate solely on those topics that relate to your objectives, even if it means leaving out some significant achievement; you can always rectify the situation at the interview.

Pick two to four accomplishments for each job title and edit them down to bite-size chunks that read like a telegram. Write as if you had to pay for each entry by the word—this approach can help you pack a lot of information into a short space. The resulting abbreviated style will help convey a sense of immediacy to the reader.

Responsible for new and used car sales. Earned "Salesman of the Year" awards, 2000 and 2001. Record holder for:

- Most Cars Sold in One Year
- Created an annual giving program to raise operating funds. *Raised $2,000,000.*

- Targeted, cultivated, and solicited sources including individuals, corporations, foundations, and state and federal agencies. *Raised $1,650,000.*
- Raised funds for development of the Performing Arts School facility, capital expense, and music and dance programs. *Raised $6,356,000.*

Now, while you may tell the reader about these achievements, never explain how they were accomplished. After all, the idea of the resume is to pique interest and to raise as many questions as you answer. Questions mean interest, and getting that interest satisfied requires talking to you!

You probably have lots of great accomplishments to share with the reader that will tempt you to add a second page, or even a third. Your resume, however, is designed to form the basis for tantalizing further discussions, so just be content with showing the reader a little glimpse of the gold vein. You have to save some of your heavy firepower for the interview, so that the meeting will not be an anticlimax for the interviewer. And that, in turn, will lend you some leverage and control in the discussions.

Prioritize the listing of your accomplishments as they relate to your job objective, and be sure to quantify your contributions (that is, put them into tangible, profit-oriented terms) wherever possible and appropriate.

Now is the time to weave in one or two of those laudatory quotes (also from step 5). Don't include every one, but do incorporate enough to show that others think well of you.

- Sales volume increased from $90 million to $175 million. Acknowledged as "the greatest single gain of the year."
- Earnings increased from $9 million to $18 million. Review stated, "always a view for the company bottom line."

Functional or Combination Resumes

In a functional or combination resume, you will have identified the skills and attributes necessary to fulfill the functions of the job objective, and will highlight the appropriate attributes you have to offer. In this format, you will have headings that apply to the skill areas your chosen career path demands, such as: Management, Training, Sales, etc. Each will be followed by a short paragraph packed with selling points. These can be real paragraphs, or the introductory sentence followed by the bullets usually recommended for the chronological formats. Here are examples of each style.

COLLECTIONS:

Developed excellent rapport with customers while significantly shortening pay-out terms through application of problem-solving techniques. Turned impending loss into profit. Personally salvaged and increased sales with two multi-million dollar accounts by providing remedial action for their sales/financial problems.

COLLECTIONS:

Developed excellent rapport with customers while significantly shortening pay-out terms:
- Evaluated sales performance; offered suggestions for financing/merchandising.
- Performed on-the-spot negotiations; turned impending loss into profit.
- Salvaged two multi-million-dollar problem accounts by providing remedial action for their sales/financial problems. Subsequently increased sales.

Keep each paragraph to an absolute maximum of four lines. This ensures that the finished product has plenty of white space so that it is easy on the reader's eye.

Editing and Polishing

Sentences gain power with verbs that demonstrate an action. For example, one client—a mature lady with ten years at the same law firm in a clerical position—had written in her original resume:

I learned to use a computer database.

After discussion of the circumstances that surrounded learning how to use the computer database, certain exciting facts emerged. By using action verbs and an awareness of employer interests, this sentence was charged up, given more punch:

> I analyzed and determined need for automation of an established law office. Responsible for hardware and software selection, installation and loading. Within one year, I had achieved a fully automated office.

Notice how the verbs show that things happen when you are around the office. These action verbs and phrases add an air of direction, efficiency, and accomplishment to every resume. They succinctly tell the reader why you did and how well you did it.

Now look at the above example when a third party endorsement is added to it:

> I analyzed and determined need for automation of an established law office. Responsible for hardware and software selection, installation and loading. Within one year, I had achieved a fully automated office. Partner stated, "You brought us out of the dark ages into the technological age, and in the process neither you nor the firm missed a beat!"

Keywords

With the advent of electronic resume screening tools, it's become more and more important to use specific keywords in your resume. Internal job descriptions are usually built of nouns and verbs that describe the skill sets required for the job. Your resume should be built the same way, with nouns that identify the skill sets and verbs/action phrases that describe your professional behavior and achievements with these skill sets.

This is an important distinction in the initial screening process. Screening software focuses on the skill sets, which invariably are nouns. If you are a computer programmer the screening device might search for words like "HTML"; if you are an accountant it might search for words like "financial analysis." Only when the computer has identified those resumes that include matching skills do human eyes enter into the picture; and only then can the verbs/action phrases that describe your competencies and achievements have the desired impact. With an electronic resume, the nouns/skill sets are the skeleton, while the verbs/action phrases are designed to put flesh on the bones—for human eyes hungry for talent.

For our purposes the keyword nouns are the words commonly used to describe the essential skill sets and knowledge necessary to carry out a job successfully. They are likely to include:

- Skill sets/abilities/competencies
- Application of these skills sets
- Relevant education and training

You may also want to study the keywords that appear frequently in help wanted ads and electronic job postings. If you do, you'll notice that different words (synonyms) are used to describe the same job or skill set. If you identify yourself as a secretary, a computer searching for an administrative assistant might pass you over. So if you are a secretary, you might also want to include the phrase "administrative assistant" in your resume. Likewise, an attorney might want to include "lawyer"; someone in HR management might want to include "personnel administration." You get the idea.

You'll want to weave these synonyms for job titles and skill sets into the main body of your resume as much as possible. However, that won't always be possible. The logical flow of your resume—or insufficient space—might prevent you from using the keywords in place. That's where a separate keyword section comes in handy. It is the perfect spot to list the technical acronyms and professional jargon that you can't fit into the body copy.

Here's an example of a keyword box from a sales management professional:

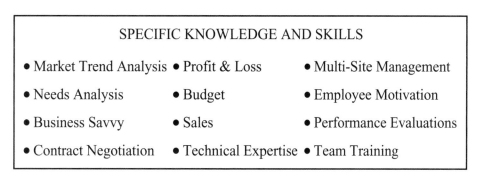

SPECIFIC KNOWLEDGE AND SKILLS

- Market Trend Analysis
- Needs Analysis
- Business Savvy
- Contract Negotiation
- Profit & Loss
- Budget
- Sales
- Technical Expertise
- Multi-Site Management
- Employee Motivation
- Performance Evaluations
- Team Training

This innovation in resume writing allows you to add a host of additional information to your resume in a space-efficient way—usually in 20 or 30 words.

Using a keyword section will increase the odds of an electronic screening agent making multiple matches between your resume and an open job requisition. Human eyes will view the list of keywords as an expansion of the body copy—and a ready source for topics for discussion.

This compels me to offer you a warning: Don't use keywords to extend the "reach" of your resume. You must have real experience in each of the areas you include. Including keywords for areas where you have no professional expertise may get you a telephone conversation with an employer, but it will also quickly reveal you as an impostor. End of story.

Where does the keyword section go? As far as the computer is concerned it doesn't matter. The computer doesn't care about the niceties of layout and flow. However, human eyes will also see this section, so there is a certain logic in putting it front and center, after any summary or objective or immediately after the contact information. The keyword section acts as a preface to the body copy, in effect saying, "Hey, here are all the headlines. The stories behind them are immediately below." To put it another way, the keyword section acts as a table of contents for your resume, with the body—with its action words and phrases—explaining and expanding on the list of topics.

Your keyword section can be as long as you require, though they typically don't run longer than 40 items and usually are a little shorter. There's no need to use definite or indefinite articles or conjunctions. Just list the word, starting with a capital and ending with a period: "Forecasting," or a phrase, such as "Financial modeling."

You can also think of your keyword section as an electronic business card that allows you to network with computers!

Action Verbs

Here are over 175 action verbs that will see which ones you can use to give punch to your resume writing.

accepted
accomplished
achieved
acted
adapted
addressed
administered
advanced
advised
allocated
analyzed
appraised
approved
arranged
assembled
assigned
assisted
attained
audited
authored
automated
balanced
budgeted
built
calculated
catalogued
chaired
clarified
classified
coached
collected
compiled
completed
composed
computed
conceptualized
conducted

consolidated
contained
contracted
contributed
controlled
coordinated
corresponded
counseled
created
critiqued
cut
decreased
defined
delegated
demonstrated
designed
developed
devised
diagnosed
directed
dispatched
distinguished
diversified
drafted
edited
educated
eliminated
emended
enabled
encouraged
engineered
enlisted
established
evaluated
examined
executed
expanded

expedited
explained
extracted
fabricated
facilitated
familiarized
fashioned
focused
forecast
formulated
founded
generated
guided
headed up
identified
illustrated
implemented
improved
increased
indoctrinated
influenced
informed
initiated
innovated
inspected
installed
instigated
instituted
instructed
integrated
interpreted
interviewed
introduced
invented
launched
lectured
led

maintained
managed
marketed
mediated
moderated
monitored
motivated
negotiated
operated
organized
originated
overhauled
oversaw
performed
persuaded
planned
prepared
presented
prioritized
processed
produced
programmed
projected
promoted
proposed
provided
publicized
published
purchased
recommended
reconciled
recorded
recruited
reduced
referred
regulated
rehabilitated

remodeled
repaired
represented
researched
resolved
restored
restructured
retrieved
revamped
revitalized
saved
scheduled
schooled
screened
set
shaped
solidified
solved
specified
stimulated
streamlined
strengthened
summarized
supervised
surveyed
systemized
tabulated
taught
trained
translated
traveled
trimmed
upgraded
validated
worked
wrote

Use these words to edit and polish your work, to communicate, persuade, and motivate the reader to take action.

This stage is most challenging, because many people in different companies will see and evaluate your resume. Keep industry "jargon" to a minimum. You need to share your technical or specialist wisdom with the nonspecialists, too.

Varying Sentence Structure

Most good writers are at their best when they write short punchy sentences. Keep your sentences under about twenty words; a good average is around fifteen. If your sentence is longer than the twenty mark, either shorten it by restructuring, or make two sentences out of the one.

At the same time, you don't want the writing to sound choppy, so vary the length of sentences when you can. You can also start with a short phrase and follow with a colon:

- Followed by bullets of information
- Each one supporting the original phrase

All these different techniques are designed to enliven the reading process. Here's an example of how the above suggestions might be put into practice.

Analyzed and determined need for automation of an established law office:

- Responsible for hardware and software selection;
- Coordinated installation of computer database and six work stations;
- Operated and maintained equipment, and trained other users;
- Achieved full automation in one year.

Partner stated, "You brought us out of the dark ages, and neither you nor the firm missed a beat!"

Just as you use short sentences, use common words. They communicate quickly and are easy to understand. Stick to short and simple words wherever possible without sounding infantile. Of course, you need action words and phrases. But the real point is to stay away from obscure words.

*Short words for short sentences help
make short, gripping paragraphs:
Good for short attention spans!*

Within your short paragraphs and short sentences, beware of name and acronym dropping, such as "Worked for Dr. A. Witherspoon in Sys. Gen. SNA 2.31." Such coinage is too restricted to have validity outside the small circle of specialists to whom they speak. Your resume deserves the widest possible readership. Apart from the section on the resume that includes your educational qualifications, stay away from jargon unless you work in a highly technical field.

Voice and Tense

The voice for your resume depends on a few important factors: getting a lot said in a small space, being factual, and packaging yourself in the best way.

The voice you use should be consistent throughout the resume. There is considerable disagreement among the experts about the best voice.

Sentences can be truncated (up to a point) by omitting pronouns—*I, you, he, she, it, they*—and articles—*a* or *the*. In fact, many authorities recommend the dropping of pronouns as a technique that both saves space and allows you to brag about yourself without seeming boastful. It gives the impression that another party is writing about you. Many people feel that to use the personal pronoun ("I automated the office") is naive and unprofessional. These experts suggest you use either the third person ("He automated the office") or leave the pronoun out altogether ("Automated office").

At the same time, there are others who recommend that you write in the first person because it makes you sound more human. Use whatever style works best for you. If you do use the personal pronoun, try not to use it in every sentence—it gets a little monotonous and takes up valuable space on the page.

A nice variation I have seen is a third-person voice used through the resume and then a final few words in the first person appended to the end of the resume, to give an insight into your values. Here is an example:

> *Regular third person:*
> James Sharpe is a professional who knows Technical Services from the ground up. He understands its importance in keeping a growing company productive, and takes pride in creating order in the chaos of technology.

Abbreviated third person:

Responsible for machine and system design, production scheduling, procurement and quality control. Redesigned conveyors and simplified maintenance while improving quality. Instituted a system of material control to account for all materials used.

First person:

I am accustomed to accepting responsibility and delegating authority, and am capable of working with, and through people at all levels. Am able to plan, organize, develop, implement, and supervise complex programs and special projects. All of this requires a good sense of humor and a personal dedication to producing timely, cost-effective results.

Many people mistake the need for professionalism with stiff-necked formality. The most effective tone is one that mixes the conversational and the formal, just the way we do in our jobs. The only overriding rule is to make it readable, so that another person can see the human being shining through.

Length

The accepted rules for length are one page for every ten years of your experience. If you have more than twenty years under your belt, however, you won't want to appear to be too steeped in the annals of ancient history, and so will not want to exceed the two-page mark.

Occasionally a three- or four-page resume can be effective, but only when:

- You have been contacted by an employer about a specific position and have been asked to prepare a resume for that opportunity.
- An executive recruiter who is representing you determines that the exigencies of a particular situation warrant an extensive dossier. Usually, such a resume will be prepared exclusively by the recruiter.

You'll find that thinking too much about length considerations while you write will hamper you. Think instead of the story you have to tell, then layer fact upon fact until it is told. When that is done, you can go back and ruthlessly cut it to the bone. Ask yourself the following questions.

- Can I cut out any paragraphs?
- Can I cut out any sentences?
- Can I cut out any superfluous words?
- Where have I repeated myself?

If in doubt, cut it out—leave nothing but facts and action words!

The Proofreading Checklist for Your Final Draft

There are really two proofing steps in the creation of a polished resume. The first you do at this point, to make sure that all the things that should be in are there—and that all the things that shouldn't, aren't. The final proofing is addressed later in the book. In the heat of the creative moment, it's easy to miss critical components or mistakenly include facts that give the wrong emphasis. Check your resume against these points:

Contact Information
- Is the pertinent personal data—name, address, personal telephone number, and e-mail address—correct? (You will want to make sure that this personal data is on every page.)
- Is your business number omitted unless it is absolutely necessary and safe to include it?

Objectives
- Does your objective briefly state your employment goals without getting too specific and ruling you out of consideration for many jobs?
- If you gave a detailed objective (up to—but no more than—two sentences), does it focus on what you can bring to the employer, rather than what you want from the employer?
- Is your stated objective supported by the facts and accomplishments stated in the rest of your resume?

Summary
- If you choose to include a summary, is it no more than two or three sentences long?

- Does it include at least one substantial accomplishment that supports your employment goals?
- Does it include reference to some of your personality or behavioral traits that are critical to success in your field?

Keywords

- If you include a keyword section, this is probably the place to put it.
- Do you have experience in each of the areas you've listed?
- Can you illustrate your experience in conversation?
- Does it include commonly used synonyms for your skill sets that you have not already used in the body of the resume?
- Is the spelling and capitalization correct? (It's easy to make mistakes here, especially with acronyms.)
- Are there any other justifiable keywords you should add?

Body of Resume

- Is your most relevant and qualifying work experience prioritized throughout the resume to lend strength to your application?
- Have you avoided wasting space with inessential employer names and addresses?
- Have you been suitably discreet with the name of your current employer?
- Have you omitted any reference to reasons for leaving a particular job?
- Have you removed all references to past, current, or desired salaries?
- Have you removed references to your date of availability?

Education

- Is education placed in the appropriate position? (It should be at the beginning of the resume if you have little or no work experience; at the end if you are established in your field and your practical experience now outweighs your degree.)
- Is your highest educational attainment shown first?
- Have you included professional courses that support your candidacy?

Chronology

- If you've done a chronological resume, is your work history stated in reverse chronological order, with the most recent employment coming at the head of the resume?

- Within this reverse chronology, does each company history start with details of your most senior position?
- Have you avoided listing irrelevant responsibilities or job titles?
- Does your resume emphasize the contributions, achievements, and problems you have successfully solved during your career? Is this content made prominent by underlining, bolding, italicizing, etc.?
- Does the body copy include at least one, and possibly two or three, laudatory third-party endorsements of your work?
- Have you avoided poor focus by eliminating all extraneous information? (This category includes anything that doesn't relate to your job objective, such as captaining the tiddlywinks team in kindergarten.)
- Have you included any volunteer or community service activities that can lend strength to your candidacy?
- Is the whole thing long enough to whet the reader's appetite for more details, yet short enough not to satisfy that hunger?
- Have you left out lists of reference and only included mention of the availability of references (if, of course, there is nothing more valuable to fill up the space)?
- Have you avoided treating your reader like a fool by highlighting the obvious (i.e., heading your resume, "RESUME")?

Writing Style

- Have you substituted short words for long words? And one word where previously there were two?
- Is your average sentence ten to twenty words? Have you made sure that any sentence of more than twenty words is shortened or broken into two?
- Have you kept every paragraph under five lines, with many paragraphs considerably shorter?
- Do your sentences begin, wherever possible, with powerful action verbs and phrases?
- If you are in a technical field, have you weeded out as much of the jargon as possible?

Crossing the T's, Dotting the I's

Before your resume is finished, you have to make sure that your writing is as clear as possible. Three things guaranteed to annoy resume readers are incorrect spelling, poor grammar, and improper syntax. Go back and check all these areas. If you feel uneasy about your syntax, get a third party involved.

An acquaintance of mine recently came up with an eminently practical solution to the "style" problem. She went around to the local library, waited for a quiet moment, and got into conversation with the librarian, who subsequently agreed to give her resume the old once-over for spelling, grammar, and syntax. You say you're on bad terms with the library because of overdue books? Surely you know someone whose opinion you trust in these matters. You must do everything you can to make the resume a "perfect" document before it is sent out.

It simply isn't possible for even the most accomplished professional writer to go directly from final draft to print, so don't try it. Your pride of authorship will blind you to the blemishes, and that's a self-indulgence you can't afford.

You need some distance from your creative efforts to gain detachment and objectivity. There is no hard and fast rule about how long it takes to come up with the finished product. Nevertheless, if you think you have finished, leave it alone as long as you can—at least overnight. Then you can come back to it fresh and read almost as if it were meeting your eyes for the first time.

More Than One Resume?

Do you need more than one type of resume? It depends. Some people have a background that qualifies them for more than one job. If this applies to you, the process is as simple as changing your objective for various employers and rewriting along the lines directed in this chapter.

There is a case for having resumes in more than one format. I was once engaged in an outplacement experiment for a group of professionals. With a little work, we developed chronological, functional, and combination resumes for everyone. The individuals sent out the resume of their choice. Then, in those instances where there was no response, a different version of the resume was sent. The result from just a different format: 8 percent more interviews.

6 | The Final Product

When it comes to clothes, style has a certain feel that everyone recognizes but few can define. Fortunately, with resumes, there are definite rules to follow.

I Need TWO Resumes?

One of these rules is that in today's job market you can't get by with just one perfect resume any more. Because an astounding 78 percent of resumes are read by machines. Your resume may be an aesthetic marvel, but if it goes into the computer as gobbledy-gook, it won't do you much good. This chapter will cover "the traditional" resume—the resume designed for human eyes. The other kind, the "computer-friendly" resume, is designed to get through a computer scanner with data intact. It is so vital in today's job market that I have devoted a separate chapter to it (see chapter 7). The two kinds of resumes do have certain basics in common.

The Circular File

The average resume arrives on a desk with dozens of others. Your resume will get only thirty to forty seconds of initial attention. And that's if it's laid out well and looks clear. What are the biggest complaints about those resumes that reach the trash can in record time?

> *Impossible to read.* They have too much information crammed into the space.

> *No coherence.* Their layout is unorganized, illogical, and uneven. They look shoddy and slapdash.

> *Typos.* They are riddled with misspellings.

Here are some tips garnered from the best resumes in America that will help yours rise above the rest.

Get Your Computer Ready!

If you plan to be employable in the year 2003, you'd better wake up and smell the coffee—computer literacy is a must. Typing your resume or using a typing service is the equivalent of carving your resumes in tablets of stone. It looks old-fashioned, and it must be redone every time you need to send one to someone else or customize it for another purpose. If you cannot now prepare your resume in a computer, engage the services of a good wordprocessing outfit while you get up to speed.

Fonts

Business is rapidly coming to accept the likes of Bookman, New York, and Palatino as the norm. When choosing your font, stay away from heavy and bold for your body copy (although you may choose to take a more dramatic approach with key words or headlines). Bold type takes up too much space, and if it needs to be copied on the receiving end, it can blur. Avoid "script" faces similar to handwriting; while they look attractive to the occasional reader, they are harder on the eyes of the person who reads any amount of business correspondence. Capitalized copy is tough on the eyes too; we tend to think it makes a powerful statement when all it does for the reader is cause eye strain.

How to Brighten the Page

Once you decide on a font, stick with it, because more than one on a page looks confusing. You can do plenty to liven up the visual impact of the page within the variations of the font you have chosen.

Most fonts come in a selection of regular, bold, and italic. Good traditional-style resumes try to take advantage of this—they can vary the impact of key words with italics, underline important phrases, or use boldface or capital letters in titles for additional emphasis. (Computer-friendly resumes, by contrast, keep type variations to a minimum.) You will notice from the examples in this book that the best resumes pick two or three typographical variations and stick with them.

Proofing

When you have the printed resume in hand, you *must* proofread it.

- Is everything set up the way you want it?
- Are there any typographical errors?
- Is all the punctuation correct?
- Has everything been underlined, capitalized, bolded, italicized, and indented, exactly as you specified?

Once you read the resume, get someone else to review it. A third party will always provide more objectivity, and can catch errors you might miss.

Appearance Checklist

- Have you remembered that the first glance and the first feel of your resume can make a powerful impression?
- Have you used only one side of the page?
- If you have employed more than one page for your resume, did you check to make sure that your name, address, and telephone number are on every page?
- If more than one page, did you paginate your resume ("1 of 2" at the bottom of the first page, and so on)?

Choosing Your Paper

While you should not skimp on paper cost, neither should you be talked into buying the most expensive available. Indeed, in some fields (health care and education come to mind), too ostentatious a paper can cause a negative impression. The idea is to create a feeling of understated quality. The right paper will take the ink better, giving you clean, sharp print resolution.

Paper can come in different weights and textures. Good resume-quality paper has a weight designation of between 16 and 25 lbs. Lighter, and you run the risk of appearing nonchalant and unconcerned. Heavier, and the paper is unwieldy, like light cardboard.

As for color, white is the prime choice. Cream is also acceptable, and I'm assured that some of the pale pastel shades can be both attractive and effective. Personally, I think that most professionals just don't show up in the best light when dressed in pink—call me old-fashioned if you will. White and cream are straightforward, no-nonsense colors.

Cover letter stationery should always match the color and weight of your resume. To send a white cover letter—even if it is written on your personal stationery—with a cream resume is gauche, and detracts from the powerful statement you are trying to make.

A good idea, in fact, is to print some cover-letter stationery when you produce your finished resume. The letterhead should be in the same font and on the same kind of paper, and should copy the contact data from your resume.

Copies

Every resume should be printed on standard, 8½" x 11" (letter-size) paper. If the original is set up like this, you will be able to take it to a good-quality copy shop for photocopying. Technology has improved so much in this area that as long as the latest equipment is used, you should have no problems. (Bear in mind, though, that the computer-friendly resume is always an original—to ensure a clean scan.)

If you choose to have your resume printed—rather than photocopied— for whatever reason, you must go to a multilith or photo-offset printer. Both produce really smart, professional copies. Shop around for prices, as printers vary quite dramatically in their price structures. While you are shopping, ask to see samples of their resume work—they are bound to have some. If not, keep shopping.

The Final Checklist

- Have you used a good-quality paper, with a weight of between 16 and 25 lbs.?
- Does the paper size measure 8½" x 11"?
- Have you used white, off-white, or cream-colored paper?
- If your resume is more than one page, have you stapled the pages together (one staple in the top left-hand corner)?
- Is your cover letter written on stationery that matches your resume?

7 | How the Internet Can Help in Your Job Hunt

The Internet can be of great assistance in your job hunt.

This chapter focuses on giving you the facts and most effective techniques for online job-hunting. Knowing these facts, you can decide on the merits of Internet searches for yourself. I think that you will clearly see value in including online job-hunting techniques in your arsenal of search strategies. It will not, however, effectively replace your other job-hunting activities. A job search becomes more effective when you widen its geographic scope, and the Internet easily allows you to access numerous job openings in major metropolitan areas. The usefulness of an Internet search diminishes when you are only looking for jobs in your immediate area. Nevertheless, online searches can still provide valuable information about local opportunities as well.

The vast majority of companies are now using their Web sites as recruiting portals. From the corporate perspective, Internet recruitment serves a dual purpose: Their personnel openings are posted on the Web to attract candidates, and the technologically challenged are screened out by virtue of default.

The Internet allows you to:

- Create customized electronic documents and communicate with potential employers and recruiters within seconds.
- Find job openings through job banks and employers' job sites.
- Be accessible to employers.
- Research companies, potential employers, and your industry.
- Make better career and life decisions through the use of career tools and online services.

Anyone can use the Web to find opportunities for climbing the corporate ladder. The Internet offers you access to millions of job openings, and tens of thousands of companies and recruiters. You'll be able to communicate your qualifications to the world in minutes, resulting in more responses; you can post your resume on the Internet so that companies and recruiters can find you; and you'll have access to more information about prospective employers, making you a better-informed candidate.

What You Need to Start an Online Job Search

You need computer access from outside the workplace. Using your office computer for writing your resume, sending out e-mails, or surfing the net for job listings is the Internet equivalent of stealing company stationery and postage stamps. Studies show that 50 percent of all companies either read their employees' e-mail and/or track their Internet usage. Some companies have even implemented programs offering a "finders' fee" if a staff member's resume appears online. Originating primarily in the high tech industries, this practice seems to be on the rise in industries across the board. Don't ignore this warning because you feel your boss is computer illiterate or too stupid to catch you. Almost all companies are using the Internet for recruitment purposes; someone in Human Resources could accidentally stumble across your online resume. Moreover, tracking software allows your employer to spy on company computer usage and it is legal for them do so. Bottom line: do not use an employer's computer or e-mail address for job-searching activities.

Online Privacy and Organization

Personal privacy and confidentiality become real issues when you use the Internet for job-hunting and resume distribution. It's a good news/bad news situation—with the ease of electronic document distribution comes the fear of prying eyes. So take precautions to protect your privacy.

If you have Internet access at home, it is probably through a local ISP (Internet Service Provider) such as MSN, AOL, or Earthlink. These accounts typically come with one e-mail address, and most people set it up for family use. This should not be your job search e-mail address. You need to set up a separate online identity, and maintain it exclusively for your job search.

Privacy Is a Concern for Everyone

Don't include too much personal information in an online resume. It could allow unscrupulous people to use your personal or professional identity for their own purposes. Posting your home phone number or address on the Internet attracts junk mail and telemarketing calls.

Anyone who has an e-mail account is familiar with junk e-mail, commonly called spam. Reverse spamming is when an electronic spider grabs your personal information, e-mail address, or resume then redistributes it to other sites or a third party. An electronic spider is a programmed tool that searches the Internet for certain types of information the "spider owner" specifies. Don't be afraid to use the Internet in your job search, but be aware that the information that you post is readily available to other users. Be careful about the type of information and the amount of personal data you make electronically available.

When using a free e-mail account, handling junk mail is an expected inconvenience you tolerate for the service. Identity fraud, however, is a far more serious complication that can potentially arise in free e-mail usage. You put your professional identity at risk when listing professional licenses or certificate numbers on your resume—so don't do it, ever! Dates of birth, driver's license numbers, and Social Security numbers are other items that should never be included on electronic resumes. With that information alone, someone could steal your identity and ruin your personal or professional credibility.

Rules to Protect Your Online Privacy

Here are some general guidelines for making online job sites and resume banks work for you rather than against you:

- Look at the site's privacy statement. Read it carefully to understand the extent of protection afforded personal information. Even without guarantees, this is a security starting point.
- Only post your resume to sites that password protect their resume bank (this is the best prevention against those pesky spiders). Password protection means that the site electronically screens all visitors. This helps to ensure that only credible employers and recruiters have access to your resume.

- Know who owns and operates the site. The owner's contact information should be available. If they are unwilling to share their identity with you, don't share your identity with them.
- You must be able to update, edit, and remove your posted resume, along with any other personal information whenever you choose.
- Blocked resume bank services are services that supposedly allow you to block access to your information from specifically unwanted viewers, such as a current employer. Do not trust these services to actually do so. These sites are not foolproof, so only post items that you don't need blocked.
- If you decide to build and create your own Web site to post your resume and work samples, password protect it. This type of Internet strategy is really only applicable for job hunters needing to demonstrate an advanced grasp of Internet technology as a part of their professional credentials.
- Never put your social security number, driver's license number, or professional license number on your resume in any format.
- Do not use your company e-mail address, computer, or Internet lines to search for jobs or to access your private e-mail account.

Free E-mail Accounts

There are dozens of sites that offer free e-mail accounts that take only minutes to set up. While many personal interest sites offering free accounts exist, remember that your career e-mail address shouldn't contain any personal information. *Martin@match.com* reveals too much personal information, and isn't appropriate for professional use. You want to create a professional, eye-catching image right from the start; take your time in selecting your professional e-mail service and user name.

As an example of the process, let's create a new identity for a fictional job search candidate, Susan O'Malley. Go to *www.hotmail.com*, and then select the "Sign Up" icon on the front page of the site. That will link you to a page requesting a user profile. When you complete the profile, you will be directed to the site user agreement. This explains user rules and the site's privacy policy. Read this information carefully; you have to accept the terms of the agreement before your address is activated. Stick with the larger, more public firms because they tend to be more reliable and honorable about such terms.

Typically, public sites offer paid upgrades to your new account that allow you more control over your mail address. Upgrades are unnecessary if you limit the number of messages stored in your mailbox at any given time.

Account signup

I chose a professional username for Susan: SOMALLEYHRPRO—this gives her the e-mail address *somalleyhrpro@hotmail.com*. Remember: this account is set up strictly for job search purposes. An appropriately named professional e-mail like this will grab the attention of prospective employers.

Should you run into a situation where the username you want is not available, choose your alternatives wisely. Most sites will make suggestions, usually by adding numbers to the end of the username. This is not appropriate for job-hunting and career management needs. You do not want to be confused with *jsmith118@hotmail.com* when you are assigned the name *jsmith119@hotmail.com*, nor do you want to choose a number that could easily be mistaken for your year of birth. Instead, make it a career-related screen name as we did for Susan.

How to Organize Your Job Hunting E-mail Account

For those of you planning to use public or shared computers, free accounts such as this one offer a nice security feature at the front door—provided you utilize it. Susan activated the highest level of security by clicking on the "Public/shared computer" button. At this increased level of security, Susan will be asked for her user name and password whenever she attempts to enter her account from any computer. If Susan always uses her home or private computer, the "Neither" or the "Keep me signed in" option assumes that every time her Web browser links to HotMail, she is identified as the user and is automatically logged-in. This also allows her to keep her job hunt secure on her family computer. For your own safety, emulate Susan and set your account up at the highest security level possible.

Whether you use HotMail, Yahoo!, Outlook, or some other major e-mail program, all of them allow you to create and manage folders. (see the buttons for "Create Folder" and "Manage Folders" in the screen shots below) Think of these as the electronic equivalent of paper folders and filing cabinets. What folders do you need? Let's start with the two major sites where Susan will be posting her resume and searching for jobs: Monster.com and SHRM.org (the Society for Human Resource Management). Both of these sites offer job delivery service, so when she signs up at either of these sites using her new e-mail account, she is quickly able to review jobs and file those she wants to save.

Susan will also create a folder for leads. As the leads mature into communication and contact with specific companies and recruiters, she can create specific folders for them. To get started, Susan's new e-mail account looks like this:

The new e-mail account

Organization does not end there. It is crucial to your long-term ability to manage your career that you are constantly and consistently building a contact manager for job prospects. This applies both to companies you might want to work for and for contacts within recruiting firms. Follow Susan's example and you will be ten steps ahead of the game when you next need to make a strategic career move.

In creating new address books, you want to organize groups of addresses, and not just add individual ones. Each "group" will contain a separate set or group of addresses, tailored to specific audiences for current or future job searches. Typically, these groups fall into three categories: companies, recruiters, and networking prospects/professional colleagues. By creating an address book group for each of these categories, you create a database for your professional life.

Additions to these groups needn't be based on direct contact, interviews, or job offers. If you see a recruiter within an industry of interest, put that address in the recruiter book. If you find a company in your geographic area or professional field, put that address in the company book. By doing this regularly, you create a vehicle for launching a massive career blitz whenever the need arises. Organize yourself now, and the information you collect along the way can be used throughout your entire professional life. You'll have an enormous database loaded and ready to go!

The Electronic Resume

Your resume is your introduction to prospective employers, and your best tool in landing interviews. While the factual content of an effective resume remains the same, your electronic version requires adaptations for maximum effect. Your electronic resume must include three crucial attributes

1. It must have the proper key words.
2. It must be scannable.
3. It must be Web e-mail ready in multiple formats.

All of these points are critical. Whether electronic or a paper, companies increasingly store resumes received in electronic databases. You need to create a database compatible resume—so that it can be stored in an employer's database, where Human Resources people can have quick access to it.

Due to competition and the growth of the Internet, resume scanning and searching capabilities are now available to virtually all companies and recruiters. When an employer needs to sort through resumes for likely job candidates, they go to the keyboard, type in a job title, and are presented with a list of descriptors. Descriptors are keywords describing different aspects of a particular job that they may need to fill. The software program searches in the company's database and ranks the documents containing any of these keywords. The more keywords your resume matches, the better your chances are of having it read. As you use the Internet to find open positions, pay attention to the keywords that you see repeated. If you see keywords in job descriptions for positions that interest you and fit your qualifications, add these keywords to your resume.

Making Your Resume Scannable

In today's electronic world, you need both a "keyword conscious" paper resume that is scannable as well as an electronic resume that is text-based and can be sent via e-mail. When you mail your resume to a company it is a paper document. In order for a company to quickly and effectively transform your resume to an electronic format they scan, or digitize, it.

Here's what happens behind the scenes: a company receives your paper resume and they place it in a scanner that takes a picture of your resume. When you fax your resume to a company, the fax machine will act just like a scanner and create a file with a picture of your resume. A software program called OCR (optical character recognition) is then applied to that picture of your resume. The OCR software tries to identify parts of that picture that represent letters, numbers, and symbols. Knowing that recruiters and employers use this technology means that you must create your resume to operate within the technical capabilities of the software. Here are some general rules to follow to assure that your resume is indeed scannable:

- Always avoid paper with a dark or even medium color, a colored border, heavy watermark or graining—plain white paper is best.
- Never print a border around a document or around a section of text in the resume. The OCR software could identify the outline as a single character and omit the entire content of that section.
- Do not use columns—when scanned, the order of words will be out of sequence and that could hurt the effectiveness of your keyword sections.

- Do not use fonts smaller than 10 point. If the employer experiences difficulty in scanning your resume you will not receive a polite phone call asking you to resubmit.
- Stay away from excessive use of bolding, italics, underlines and fancy fonts—especially at smaller font sizes. You do not want your resume to look too cluttered or busy.

When Should You Use a Scannable Resume?

Anytime you are mailing or faxing your resume to a company, assume that it will be scanned. Always use the "fine mode" setting when faxing your resume. This will result in better resolution and allows the OCR to optimize the digital conversion. Many companies do not print faxed resumes, but instead, convert them directly to digital. Also, most PC's now come with standard software that allows the user to fax and receive documents without ever having to print them.

The Difference Between Scannable and Electronic Resumes

An electronic resume is one built solely on a computer, sent via e-mail to the recipient, and, once received, usually downloaded directly into an employer's resume database. Whereas an electronic resume is only digital, a scannable resume is a paper resume that is converted to digital. There are three different ways you can send your resume electronically:

1. ASCII or Plain text
2. Formatted, scannable text
3. Web based / HTML

You may not need all three, but you will definitely need at least the first two. Here are descriptions of all three:

1. Plain text or ASCII: This is the simplest version of the three. We're talking just the basics: only text; letters, numbers and a few symbols found on your keyboard. ASCII (American Standard code for Information Exchange) resumes are important because this is the only format that any computer type, whether PC or Macintosh, can read. The reader will not need a word processing program such as Microsoft Word

or Word Perfect, and their software or printer compatibility needn't be considered.

- No fancy formatting.
- No bolded words.
- No bullets.
- No italics.
- No underlining.

An ASCII resume looks like the average e-mail message you receive.

2. Formatted Electronic Resume: This is a resume that is also sent via e-mail, but as an attachment. A formatted electronic resume is still attractive, utilizes many features of your word processing program, and it is scannable. You should only send attachments if the employer has directed you to do so and you're certain that your resume can be downloaded directly by their resume software package.

- You must use a word processing program that is compatible with the employer's.
- You must adhere to the restrictions on scannability—no borders, columns, small or fancy fonts.
- Do not forget about your keywords—formatted electronic resumes are still downloaded into a resume database, so you must be sure to include the appropriate keywords.

3. Web or HTML Resume: A Web resume is not "must have" for everyone. Essentially, a Web resume is an electronically formatted resume housed on the Internet. There are some advantages; you can include audio and video clips, music, and pictures. If you are in a creative profession and would typically have a portfolio, a Web resume can allow access to your work samples. Likewise if you are a Web page design professional or HTML guru, then by all means, use the Internet to show your creative and electronic abilities. I would not recommend that you post a site for all to see, but rather build a password-protected site so that you can approve, track, and have the ability to follow-up with anyone interested in seeing your work.

How to Convert Your Formatted Resume to ASCII

Converting your keyword-packed, formatted, scannable resume into a text or ASCII version is simple. To start the ASCII conversion process, go to your

"My Documents" or "My Briefcase" folders and create a series of new folders to store the various documents you will be creating.

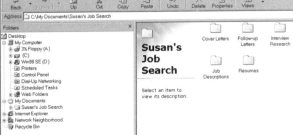

Job search folders

As you can see, Susan has created a section within the "My Documents" folder and then created a series of folders within that to hold her "Resumes," "Cover Letters," "Job Descriptions," etc. Within each of these folders, she will need to name her documents appropriately—even creating additional sub-folders.

Next, open your resume using your word processing program. The most widely used is Microsoft Word, so that's what we'll use in our example. Copy the entire document by choosing "select all" from the "edit" pull-down menu (or Cmd+A for Macintosh) then, by choosing "copy" from the "edit" pull-down menu or Ctrl+C for Windows (Cmd+C for Macintosh).

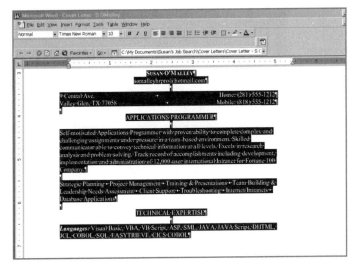

Converting your resume

Then, open a new document in your word processor. Set the margins to 60 characters per line, which equates to margins of about 1.7 to 1.75 inches on both the left and right sides. The number of characters in each line must be limited because electronic screens are restricted to that viewing width; consequently you do not want text to "wrap off the screen."

Setting margins

Next you are going to paste the resume you just copied into this new document. Simply choose "paste" from the "edit" pull-down menu or Ctrl+V for Windows (or Cmd+V for Macintosh). Initially, the document will look very similar to your previous resume, but we will modify it further. Do not panic if your one page resume just became two pages. If you had small margins, the shorter line length will create a longer resume. In this new electronic world of text and ASCII based systems, length does not matter as much as format.

Go to the "edit" pull-down menu and choose "select all" (Cmd+A for Macintosh). Now you are going to change the font type and size. To do this, choose "font" from the "format" pull-down menu and change the font type to Times New Roman or Courier. Change the size to 12 point.

Changing the font

Now, we need to save this new document using the "save as" command. Select the document type as "text only," and rename the document. Let's call it "Text Resume 1" and even put it in a new folder—let's use Susan's resume folder.

Pay attention: you will get a message box saying that you will change your formatting that asks if you want to continue. Answer "yes." An ASCII or text-based resume strips out formatting that could make your document difficult to read. Notice that the file name of the resume no longer ends with *.doc*; it now ends in *.txt*, meaning text-based document.

The document has lost many of its features and "pretty looks." Spacing is also altered considerably. You will want to spend some additional time proofreading this new document. Any tabs, tables, or columns that you used in your formatted version may wreak havoc on your new text version. In order to prevent lines from wrapping or flowing down to the next line, you need to make your document flush left by removing empty spaces and tabs.

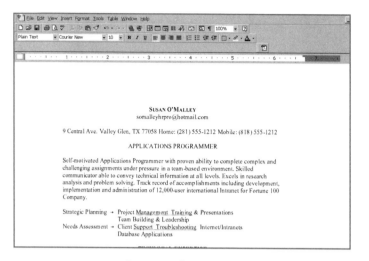

A text-only resume

You will need to use ALL CAPS for section headers and to replace things that were bolded or underlined. Likewise, all of your bullets will be gone and you will have to adjust the spacing to create a new type of emphasis, or use characters on your keyboard such as *. Remember that the goal is to get your resume downloaded into the databases of potential employers and then noticed by them. A better-looking paper resume can be sent after your first electronic contact with the Human Resource professional or recruiter.

Once properly edited, Susan's resume looks like this:

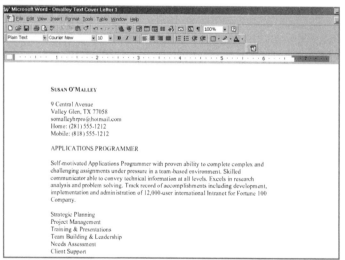

A properly edited text resume

Before you send your resume, take time to save and proofread it carefully. Send your electronic cover letters and resume attachments to yourself, your friends, or your family members. Ask them for printouts of your practice e-mail messages and resumes to ensure that what you intended to send is actually what was received. Often this exercise will help you find any spelling mistakes, bloopers, or larger problems incurred during the conversion process.

Posting Your Resume and Tricks to Online Questionnaires

Career sites have evolved tremendously over the last few years. What was once a collection of help wanted ads has turned into a job-hunting community full of career-related advice and tools. There are literally thousands of job boards on the Internet, from mega sites to very focused sites that cater to a specific geographical location or industry.

Most of the larger sites offer free job delivery and resume posting services. You just select a few criteria, and job listings matching your specifications are automatically sent to your inbox. If you are already employed, these sites allow you to stay on top of your career path and keep abreast of other available opportunities. However, if you are currently in a full-blown job search, spend plenty of time browsing the job site itself. Keep your search criteria broad based, even eliminate salary or geographical requirements. This enables you to uncover companies and recruiters in your industry. Even if the specific job opening isn't a great match or you aren't planning to relocate, you'll become aware of these companies for future reference. Internet posting allows an employer to find you while you are sleeping, playing, or working—it never sleeps. It sounds great and it works—if you understand the rules of the game.

Not all job sites and resume banks work the same way. On some sites, you simply copy and paste your resume like we've done in the prior examples. On other sites, you'll have to complete a proscribed profile or questionnaire that creates your online presence at that site for all who visit it.

These sites are usually free for job hunters, but employers pay them to post job openings. They also pay fees for searching the resume bank on the job site. The job sites work with these prospective employers to develop better screening tools, since they are the paying clients. By making job seekers fill out very specific profiles and questionnaires, these employers screen people in or out—so remember this when you post.

When filling out a profile or questionnaire, keep these two things in mind:

1. What is my audience? Who will be reading this?
2. What are they really asking me?

When a site or a company does not want your resume, but does want you to complete a registration or profile process—they are looking to screen you out. Let's take a closer look at the Monster resume builder because it is a screening tool they have built to assist the employer, not the searcher, despite any Monster protestations to the contrary.

Susan is smart to use the Monster.com site in her online strategy. Once on the site, she follows the buttons for new users, and begins to set up her free "My Monster Account," filling out her name, address, career level, and degree, which are all required fields. When a field is required, it must be completed or your enrollment process stops. These are the hardest fields to complete, as they tend to force you to divulge too much information unless you can find a way to "trick" them.

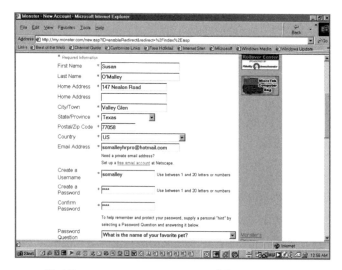

Setting up a new account at Monster.com

As with most "free" sites, Susan is immediately asked to sign up for newsletters and advertisements.

One of the nice features of Monster.com is that it allows you to maintain five different resumes/profiles. Use this opportunity! Make some of your profiles very specific, and make others very broad in order to increase your visibility.

The Monster resume builder is typical in that it breaks up the resume, and, in this case, a profile, into 13 specific topics, to be exact. A few of these topics include Career Objective, Target Job, Target Location, Salary, Work Status, Skills, References, and Education. These are all common topics covered in most online profiles and registrations.

One of the very first screens Susan is asked to complete includes her "Title" and "Career Objective." The site offers examples to help you fill in answers to these questions—but their advice is not in your best interest. Remember, Monster.com is paid by the employer and they are trying to help the employer screen you out. Monster advises you to list a specific position title and, in the "Career Objective" field, write out a short professional profile and list your career goals.

If you want to increase your visibility, then you need to think beyond these questions. This is all about keywords. Instead of completing the "Title" field Susan, noticing that this field holds up to 60 characters, has the opportunity to add another 37 characters besides her actual title. The best way of utilizing that space is to list the computer languages, software, and systems that she knows.

A Monster.com online resume

According to the comments under the "Objective" field, Monster tells us that it holds up to 2000 characters. That's half of Susan's resume! Following the site's examples by listing a two- or three-sentence objective would be wasting an opportunity to inundate employers with favorable keywords. So, from her resume, Susan copied her professional profile, her language, software, and systems expertise into this field, which still had room for a list of all her accomplishments with past employers. When answering these questions, you are building your resume all over again, so use your keywords and highlight past successes that will attract the attention of database search software, and, consequently, prospective employers.

As Susan continues to complete her profile, she comes to a section that breaks down her "target job." The important element to notice here is that you are not always limited to one answer—even in the case of check boxes. Susan can select both employee and contract work, and even intern if she wanted. It's a good idea to test the site to see if you can select more than one answer. Never assume you are limited—not even if the directions on the screen indicate that you are.

Choosing a target job

Susan was also asked about her salary requirements. We all dread this question; in a pre-employment screening profiles, it is the worst. Although the salary question is sandwiched between "required" fields, it is not required. So Suan can, and should leave it blank. In instances where you are forced to answer the question, answer in terms of a range as you would in an interview situation.

The last question on this screen allows Susan 500 characters to describe her ideal job. This is not a space for her to answer that question. These 500 characters offer space for her to inject more keywords. Remember, the screener is searching and retrieving The more keywords that appear in your profile, the higher on the list it will appear; and the more likely it is to be read by a sentient human being.

Now the dreaded relocation question—make sure that this is a required field. If it isn't, don't answer it. If it is, keep your answer broad. Any company or recruiter only interested in local candidates will use the address on your resume as the search parameter.

Choosing a location

Here's the rule: you can always say 'no,' but you can't say 'yes' unless you've been asked. For the right job, the right opportunity, and the right money, we all might move to Timbuktu. Besides, what isn't right for your career today may be tailor made for your future career plans.

Choosing a company

Notice that while the page is optional, the "Company Category" field is designated "required" by the red asterisk. Most people have probably completed this screen assuming that it is required. Read every word to distinguish between what is optional and required and how much information can be included or excluded.

Another common section on the questionnaires is "work experience." Always use these fields to include illustrative stories about what you've done.

You may be given instructions to list every job you've ever had in chronological order. Let's be clear on this issue. You are building your online resume, not writing a testimonial to your work history. Include only those jobs you regularly include in your resume.

You are most likely to come across online questionnaires and profiles in these situations:

- Registering with a job site
- Posting a resume to a job board
- Applying for a job within a company
- Registering with a recruitment firm

In each case, you must always consider who is asking you the question and why. They are trying to screen you in or out, so consider your responses carefully. Always read the instructions, avoid questions on salary and relocation if possible, and add as many keywords as possible. Proofread and spell check everything you enter, and only post to sites that allow editing and updating.

Answering online questionnaires, profiles, and registrations affect your online job-hunting success to such a degree that new career services have been developed. There are a number of companies specializing in optimizing these job sites for the job hunter. For a fee, these companies will post your online profiles for you. Some will even evaluate and edit your online postings. Two firms that have been doing this quite successfully for executives for the last four years are Karrus Evergreen (*www.careerroadblocks.com*) and Career Objectives (*www.getinterviews.com*).

Sending Your Resume Directly to Companies and Recruiters

The third way to distribute your resume via the Internet involves direct contact with companies and recruiters. There are a number of ways to use the Internet to help you locate companies and recruitment firms. Once aware of a company in your industry or a recruitment firm that makes placements within your function or industry—why not make contact? You do not need a help-wanted ad to have a reason to get your credentials in front of hiring eyes.

The Internet is a particularly useful information resource—provided you know where to look. Luckily, sites and services exist to simplify our search.

If a Healthcare/Medical Insurance Sales Manager went to *www.6figurejobs.com* and did a simple search for keyword "insurance" he or she would get hundreds of results. The vast majority of hits would be for jobs of limited interest. Instead of replying directly to the job postings, visit the company Web sites and browse there. Send a letter of introduction and interest to the contact persons you uncover. Add this contact information to your database for future job-hunting efforts.

Many job sites offer pages listing all companies posting jobs with them. Usually, these lists link to those company's job openings, or directly to their home page. Look for this feature on every job site you enter; it will help you quickly build your job search database.

Sound too tough? If currently employed or busy, it could be. There are other ways. Ever been to *www.corporateinformation.com*, Hoovers Online (*www.hoovers.com*), or seen the *www.fortune.com* site where you can access the *Fortune* 500 list? These and dozens of other sites offer you searchable databases of companies. You can purchase mailing and e-mailing lists as well. Companies such as Kennedy Information (*www.kennedyinformation.com*) and USAinfo.com (*www.corporateinformation.com*) offer you the option of purchasing industry lists and other specific criteria lists for this purpose.

Getting your hands on hundreds of recruiter contacts is just as easy. Kennedy Information also sells headhunter lists, as does Your Missing Link (*www.yourmissinglink.com*). Free lists of recruiters can be found at Recruiters Online (*www.recruitersonline.com*) and at i-Recruit.com (*www.i-recruit.com*).

A second, more reasonable use of this data is accumulating e-mail addresses in an address book or even in a Word document. Assemble an electronic cover letter suitable for a mass distribution to go with it, and "blast" your resume out there yourself. By utilizing the bcc (blind copy) feature on your e-mail software, you can e-mail one hundred letters at a time—far more productive than individually.

A third option is hiring a company to do it for you. Several years ago, these resume "blasting services" came into being. Their results are not too bad. Companies like ResumeBlaster (*www.resumeblaster.com*) and Blast My Resume (*www.blastmyresume.com*) will distribute your resume electronically (via e-mail) for about $30 to $100. It is important to receive a copy of this list, even if it adds to the cost of the service. This list allows you to follow up after the "blast," and you can enhance your career management database with it.

Keep in mind that whether you do the research on your own, or purchase it from another company, either process involves time or money—probably a bit of both. Treat it as an investment in your career management.

Internet Job Searching Strategies

The Internet is a powerful job search tool, and your approach in using it will make a difference in your success. No single job search method guarantees this success. The best approach is one that integrates networking, online job searching, newspapers, and the other techniques addressed in *Knock' em Dead*.

Using the Internet in your job search can take many forms; base your choices on the need for confidentiality and the time frame you place on a career move.

The following list is a brief overview of Internet strategies.

- The Blitz—just like in football, send everyone to make the tackle. You are unemployed (or soon to be unemployed or graduating) and need a job ASAP. In this case, you have no concern for confidentiality and want maximum exposure and results. You should visit and post your resume to all of the top job boards. You should "blast out" resumes to all the companies and recruiters on the databases you have accumulated from your research or purchase.
- Focused Attack—a much more focused version of the Blitz. Employed or unemployed, you will want to use a couple of the major job boards with more specialty sites, associations, and specific company site research. The focused attack could be as confidential as you decide to make it. It can also work well for those pursuing multiple potential career paths, or for those interested in a career/industry change. If you are still employed but have informed your employer that you are looking for a change, then this is the perfect strategy for you.
- Stealth Mode—There are two types of job seekers fitting this strategy. The first is the employed seeker who understands the value of keeping a pulse on the job market. Only post confidential resumes, if any, and only utilize sites that deliver jobs to you. The second type of job seeker using this strategy is one who has identified his or her dream company or geographic area to work in. You are employed, and are using the Internet to monitor sites that this dream company posts to, in order to send them confidential resumes, research their executive bios, association members, and like information, to find an open door.

Whichever strategies you use, make the commitment and follow through. Remember, no single strategy is an absolute, sure-fire way to find a suitable job. Always use an integrated approach employing all of your online and offline resources.

Electronic Resume Distribution

You already have your formatted, scannable, keyword-packed resume as well as your ASCII text-based one. You have set up a private, secure, and professional e-mail address. Now, it is time to focus on distribution. The Internet encourages three primary methods of resume distribution:

1. Responding to help-wanted ads (job postings)
2. Posting your resume and credentials
3. Sending your resume directly to companies and recruiters

Any time you can grab human attention before the electronic system takes over, it is to your advantage. Two elements will help to get you there: the ability to use your cover letter and the subject line to garner attention, and circumventing the electronic system to find additional human contacts.

Since all e-mail messages you send are electronic versions of your cover letter, you may want to take a look at the companion book *Cover Letters That Knock 'em Dead*. Electronic cover letters are shorter, more direct versions of paper ones. Just as you would limit a paper cover letter to one page or 3–5 paragraphs, you need to keep your electronic cover letter to one screen view. (Do not make the reader scroll down to see the rest of the letter—chances are they won't do it.)

Use keywords that illustrate your potential and examples of your accomplishments to prospective employers in this document as well. With a little practice, you can write short, powerful sentences, which will get your e-mail messages and attached resumes read. Another useful trick to save time and energy is to create cover letter templates that you can easily customize for each response.

The subject line is your first, and possibly only, chance to interest the initial reader enough to read your resume instead of mechanically uploading it directly into a database. The key is to focus on a clear message stating the nature of your contact, hopefully giving them some incentive for interest. In other words, state the job posting number or job title, but take that extra step to get yourself noticed.

Susan O'Malley has been using the Society for Human Resource Management career site and has found an appealing job posting in California. A vacation resort developer is seeking a Regional Human Resources Manager.

A job posting

This position requires ten years of experience, and the job description indicates that knowledge of employment laws such as EEOC, FLSA and ADA are important. Susan is a good match.

This position has requested that correspondence be sent in the following manner:

> "Candidates may apply by sending their resume to Trendwest Resorts, 9805 Willows Road, Redmond, WA 98052 or by e-mail to *pamelae@trendwestresorts.com*."

Responding by e-mail suggests technological aptitude, while a regular mail response offers another opportunity to get your resume noticed and to the top of the pile. You should do both.

Since the employer did not provide any additional directions, it is best for Susan to attach the electronic resume to her e-mail message, and also paste it into the body of the e-mail.

We want our electronic cover letter example to do three things: identify the purpose of sending this resume; emphasize why it deserves to be read; and get you an interview or next contact. Notice in the next figure how Susan has accomplished these things with her ASCII cover letter.

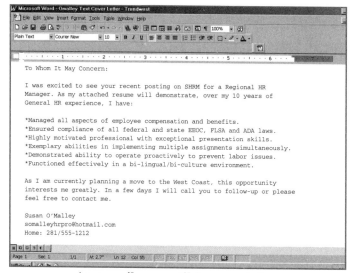

To Whom It May Concern:

I was excited to see your recent posting on SHRM for a Regional HR Manager. As my attached resume will demonstrate, over my 10 years of General HR experience, I have:

*Managed all aspects of employee compensation and benefits.
*Ensured compliance of all federal and state EEOC, FLSA and ADA laws.
*Highly motivated professional with exceptional presentation skills.
*Exemplary abilities in implementing multiple assignments simultaneously.
*Demonstrated ability to operate proactively to prevent labor issues.
*Functioned effectively in a bi-lingual/bi-culture environment.

As I am currently planning a move to the West Coast, this opportunity interests me greatly. In a few days I will call you to follow-up or please feel free to contact me.

Susan O'Malley
somalleyhrpro@hotmail.com
Home: 281/555-1212

An e-mail compatible cover letter

She succinctly stated the purpose of her e-mail, hit her "hot points" to get the reader's attention, and requested the follow-up information. Before closing this document, Susan needs to copy the entire letter. She does this by choosing "select all" from the "edit" pull-down menu (or Cmd+A for Macintosh), then, by choosing "copy" from the "edit" pull-down menu or Ctrl+C for windows (Cmd+C for Macintosh).

The next step is to create the e-mail, insert the cover letter, and attach the resume. From her inbox, Susan will create a new message by choosing "compose" from the tabs along the top of the page. By placing her cursor within the message of the newly created e-mail, Susan can then paste the contents of her custom electronic cover letter in the message box. Simply choose "paste" from the "edit" pull-down menu or Ctrl+V for Windows (or Cmd+V for Macintosh).

With the cover letter safely pasted, turn your attention to addressing the e-mail to the proper recipient and establishing your subject line. From the job posting, you can copy and paste the e-mail to the address provided by the company. The subject line needs to be factual, professional, and intriguing. How about "Your next Reg HR Manager-EEOC, FLSA, & ADA exp" or "Reg HR Candidate-10 yrs exp w/ EEOC, FLSA, & ADA." Remember, the subject line may get your resume an immediate review instead of automatic computer upload. Give it adequate thought.

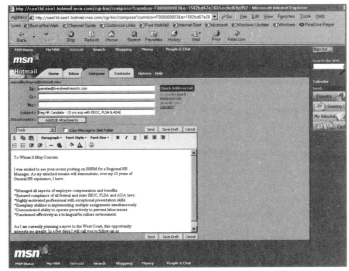

A professional and intriguing subject line

Keep copies of all your correspondence. It's a good idea to keep track of exactly what you've sent out to avoid unnecessary repetitions. It also allows you to move messages from that folder to a more specific folder once you have started a communication stream with an interested party.

Under the subject line of the new e-mail Susan created, there is a button for "Add /Edit Attachments." All programs will have a menu choice to insert documents, for example, in Microsoft Outlook; the paper clip icon designates the button for this function. Once you select this menu choice, you need to find the document that you want to attach. Follow the instructions on the screen. Once you have "browsed" to locate the file, it may have you select "open." In HotMail, once you've browsed and found the file you must then select "attach." The name of your file will appear in the attachment box.

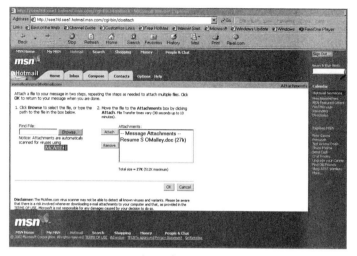

Attachments

Before you send a message, recall the two points made earlier when Susan came across this job posting. First, the employer did offer a suggested resume format. The most popular format is the one we have chosen, but it is not 100% effective if the employer doesn't use Microsoft Word, or cannot open the attachment. A sensible solution is to copy and paste your ASCII resume.

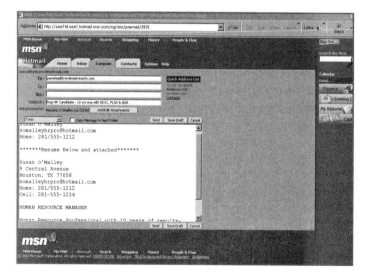

Sending the message

Your goal is not just to get your resume out into cyberspace, but also to get it read by a human being. Often with company e-mail addresses, the Web site of the company is part that comes after the person's username and the "@" symbol. In this case it is safe to assume that if we break up the e-mail address of *pamelae@trendwestresorts.com*, we can probably find the company's home page at *www.trendwestresorts.com*. Knowing that, you can surf the site to look for a company career center, the bios and contacts for company executives, and press releases about their business. Your mission here is finding other potential inroads, other people to whom you can pitch yourself. With a little effort, you could make a direct connection to your next potential boss, gather information that will help you ace an interview, and garner you your dream job. As they say, luck comes to those who make it happen.

 **Cover Letters**

Junk mail. Tons of it have probably made it into your mailbox over the years. Now, what do you do with the stuff marked "Occupant"? Either junk it without reading, or junk it after a quick glance.

The days when you could dash your resume off to "Personnel," with a clear conscience and no personal note, are long gone. Your cover letter is the personalizing factor in the presentation of an otherwise essentially impersonal document—your resume. A good cover letter sets the stage for the reader to accept your resume as something special.

So your first effort with a cover letter is to find an individual to whom you can address it. That shows you have focus, and guarantees that a specific individual will open and read it. It also means you have someone to ask for by name when you do your follow-up—important when you are interview hunting.

Your target is someone who can either hire you or refer you to someone who can—and management rather than personnel offers you a much better chance of achieving that goal.

Your cover letter will either be sent to someone as a result of a prior conversation, or sent "cold"—with no prior conversation. You will see how to handle both these eventualities as we progress through the chapter.

Cover Letter Rules

Cover letters are brief, never more than a page. Write more, and you will be labeled as an unorganized windbag. Space can be at such a premium, however, that you can dispense with the formality and begin with a normal salutation: "Dear _____." Stick with the protocol when you can, ignore it when you have to.

The following four steps will help you create the body of the letter.

Step One

Grab your reader's attention by using quality stationery. If you don't have personal stationery, use some of the sheets you bought for your resume. That way, letter and resume will match. Basic business letters should be laid out according to the accepted standards, like this:

[YOUR ADDRESS/LETTERHEAD
AND TELEPHONE NUMBER]

[DATE]

[ADDRESSEE ADDRESS]
[SALUTATION]

Recently I have been researching the leading local companies in data communications. My search has been for companies that are respected in the field, and who provide ongoing training programs. The name of DataLink Products keeps coming up as a top company.

I am an experienced voice and data communications specialist with a substantial background in IBM environments. If you have an opening for someone in this area you will see that my resume demonstrates a person of unusual dedication, efficiency, and drive.

My experience and achievements include:

- The complete redesign of a data communications network, projected to increase efficiency companywide by some 12 percent.
- The installation and troubleshooting of a Defender II call-back security system for a dial-up network.

I enclose a copy of my resume, and look forward to examining any of the ways you feel my background and skills would benefit DataLink Products. While I prefer not to use my employer's time taking personal calls at work, with discretion you can reach me at (213) 555-5555 to initiate contact. Let's talk!

Yours,

[SIGNATURE]
[TYPED NAME]

Step Two

Generate interest with the content. You do this by addressing the letter to someone by name and quickly explaining what you have to offer: The first sentence grabs attention, the rest of the paragraph gives the reader the old one-two punch. The rule is: Say it strong and say it straight.

A little research, for example, can get your letter off to a fast start.

> I came across the enclosed article in *Newsweek*. It encouraged me to do a little research on your company. The research convinced me of two things: You are the kind of people I want to be associated with, and I have the kind of qualifications you can use.

Of course, in the real world, we don't all apply for jobs with companies that are featured in the big magazines. Here are some other examples:

> I have been following the performance of your fund in *Mutual Funds Newsletter*. The record over the last three years shows strong portfolio management. Considering my experience, I know I could make significant contributions.

> Recently, I have been researching the local _____ industry. My search has been for companies that are respected in the field and that provide ongoing training programs. The name _____ keeps coming up as a top company.

> With the scarcity of qualified and motivated *(your desired job title)* that exists today, I felt sure that it would be valuable for us to communicate.

> I would like the opportunity to put my _____ years of _____ experience to work for _____.

> In three weeks, I will be moving from New York to San Francisco. Having researched the companies in my field in my new hometown, I know that you are the people I want to talk to.

> The state of the art in _____ changes so rapidly that it is tough for most professionals to keep up. I am the exception. I am eager to bring my experience to bear for your company.

I am applying for a position with your company because I know you will find my background and drive interesting.

This letter and the attached resume are in application for employment with _____.

If you are looking for summer jobs:

In six weeks I shall be finishing my second year at John Carroll University. I am interested in working for your firm during the summer because…

As the summer season gets under way, I know you will be looking for extra help.

I am a high school senior looking for some real world experience during the summer break.

I am very interested in becoming one of your summer interns.

If you are writing as the result of a referral, say so and quote the person's name if appropriate:

Our mutual colleague, John Stanovich, felt my skills and abilities would be valuable to your company.

The manager of your San Francisco branch, Pamela Bronson, has suggested I contact you regarding the opening for a _____.

I received your name from Henry Charles last week. I spoke to Mr. Charles regarding career opportunities with _____ and he suggested I contact you. In case the resume he forwarded is caught up in the mail, I enclose another.

Arthur Gold, your office manager and my neighbor, thought I should contact you about the upcoming opening in your accounting department.

If you are writing as the result of an online job posting or a newspaper advertisement, you should mention both the source and the date—and remember not to abbreviate advertisement to "ad."

> I read your advertisement job posting on CareerBrain.com yesterday and, after researching your company, felt I had to write.

> I am responding to your recent job listing on your Web site offering the opportunity to manage accounts receivable.

> In re: Your advertisement in the *Columbus Dispatch* on Sunday, the eighth of November. As you will notice, my entire background matches your requirements.

> This letter and attached resume is in response to your advertisement in the *Boston Globe.*

Note: In a cover letter to executive search firms, unlike any other circumstances, you must mention your salary and, if appropriate, your willingness to relocate. Some example sentences:

> I am forwarding my resume to you because I understand you specialize in representing clients in the _____ field.

> Please find the enclosed resume. As a specialist in the _____ field, I felt you might be interested in the skills of a _____.

> Among your many clients may be one or two who are seeking a candidate for a position as a _____.

> My salary is in the mid-20s, with appropriate benefits. I would be willing to relocate for the right opportunity.

Step Three

Now turn that interest into desire. First, make a bridge that ties you to a general job category or work area. It starts with phrases like:

> I am writing because…

My reason for contacting you is…

This letter is to introduce me and to explore any need you might have in the _____ area.

…should this be the case, you may be interested to know…

If you are seeking a _____, you will be interested to know…

I would like to talk to you about your personnel needs and my ability to contribute to your department's goals.

If you have an opening for someone in this area, you will see that my resume demonstrates a person of unusual dedication, efficiency, and drive.

Then call attention to your merits with a short paragraph that highlights one or two of your special contributions or achievements:

I have an economics background (Columbia) and a strong analytical approach to market fluctuations. This combination has enabled me to consistently pick the new technology flotations that are the backbone of the growth-oriented mutual fund.

Similar statements applicable to your area of expertise will give your letter more personal punch. Include any qualifications and contributions that qualify you as someone with talent to offer. If an advertisement (or a conversation with a potential employer) revealed an aspect of a job opening that is not addressed in your resume, it can easily be covered in the cover letter.

I notice from your advertisement that audio and video training experience would be a plus. In addition to the qualifications stated in my enclosed resume, I have over five years' experience writing and producing sales and management training materials in both these media.

Whether you bullet or list your achievements in short, staccato sentences will be determined in part by the amount of space available to you on the page.

Step Four

Here's where your letter turns that desire into action. You want to make the reader dash straight to your resume, then call you in for an interview. You achieve this with brevity.

Your one-page letter shouldn't be longer than four or five paragraphs, or two hundred words. Leave the reader wanting more. This final step tells the reader when, where, and how you can be contacted. Then tell the reader that you intend to follow up at a certain point in time if contact has not been established by then. This can encourage a decision on the reader's part to initiate action, which is what you want. Useful phrases include:

I look forward to discussing our mutual interests further.

It would be a pleasure to give you more data about my qualifications and experience.

I will be in your area around the 20th, and will call you prior to that date to arrange a meeting.

I hope to speak with you further and will call the week of the 20th to follow up.

The chance to meet with you would be a privilege and a pleasure. To this end I will call you on the 20th.

I look forward to speaking with you further and will call in the next few days to see when our schedules will permit a face-to-face meeting.

My credentials and achievements are a matter of record that I hope you will examine in depth when we meet.

I look forward to examining any of the ways you feel my background and skills would benefit your organization. I look forward to hearing from you.

Resumes help you sort out the probables from the possibles, but they are no way to judge the true caliber of an individual. I should like to meet you and demonstrate that I have the personality that makes for a successful _____.

My resume can highlight my background and accomplishments. My drive, willingness and manageability, however, can come out only during a face-to-face meeting. With this in mind, I shall call you on the 20th, if I don't hear from you before.

After reading my resume, you will know something about my background. Yet you will still need to determine whether I am the one to help with the current challenges. I would like an interview to discuss my ability to contribute.

I am anxious to meet and discuss any potential opportunities further. I will make myself available for an interview at a time convenient to you.

I expect to be in your area on Tuesday and Wednesday of next week and wonder which day would be best for you. I will call to find out.

With my training and hands-on experience, I know I can contribute to your company, and want to speak with you about it in person. When may we meet?

I feel certain that I can contribute and that I can convince you I can. I look forward to a meeting at your convenience.

You can reach me at (202) 555-1212 to arrange an interview. I know that your time investment in meeting with me will be amply repaid.

Thank you for your time and consideration. I hope to hear from you shortly.

I am sure that our mutual interests will be served by speaking further, and am convinced a personal meeting will assure you of my ability, willingness, and manageability. I look forward to meeting with you.

> A brief phone call will establish whether or not we have mutual interest. Recognizing the demands of your schedule, I will make that call within the week.

As many employed people are concerned about their resumes going astray, you may wish to add:

> In the meantime, I would appreciate my application being treated as confidential, as I am currently employed.

Just as you worked to get the opening right, labor over the close. It is the reader's last remembrance of you, so make it strong, make it tight, and make it obvious that you are serious about entering into meaningful conversation.

Writing the Cover Letter

Keep your sentences short—an average of fourteen words per sentence is about right. Likewise, your paragraphs should be concise and to the point. In cover letters, paragraphs can often be a single sentence, and should never be longer than two or three sentences. This makes the page more inviting for the harried reader, by providing adequate white space to ease eye strain.

Short words work best here also. They speak more clearly than those polysyllabic behemoths that say more about your self-image problems than your abilities. A good approach is to think in terms of sending a telegram, where every word must work its hardest.

While abiding by accepted grammatical rules, punctuate for readability rather than strictly following E. B. White or the *Chicago Manual of Style.* Get by on commas, dashes—and periods. And in between the punctuation marks, use the action verbs and phrases that breathe life into your work.

Cover Letter Examples

Notice that the italicized areas come directly from the previous examples. You too can write a dynamite cover letter with the old "cut and paste" technique. Then just make the minor adjustments necessary to personalize your letter.

James Sharpe   November 16, 20__
9 Central Ave
Los Angeles, CA 93876

Dear Mr. Bell,

*Recently I have been researching the leading local companies in
data communications. My search has been for companies that are
respected in the field, and who provide ongoing training programs.
DataLink Products keeps coming up as a top company.*

I am an experienced voice and data communications specialist with
a substantial background in IBM environments. *If you have an opening
for someone in this area you will see that my resume demonstrates a
person of unusual dedication, efficiency, and drive.*

My experience and achievements include:

- Complete redesign of a data communications network, projected
  to increase efficiency companywide some 12 percent;
- The installation and troubleshooting of a Defender II call-back
  security system for a dial-up network.

*I enclose a copy of my resume, and look forward to examining any
of the ways you feel my background and skills would benefit DataLink
Products. While I prefer not to use my employer's time taking personal
calls at work, with discretion I can be reached at (213)555-5555 to
initiate contact. Let's talk!*

Yours truly,

James Sharpe

James Sharpe

In response to an advertisement, here is an example using a different
selection of phrases.

Jane Swift   November 16, 20__
9 Central Ave
Sunnyside, NY 11104

Dear Ms. Pena,

I have always followed the performance of your fund in *Mutual Funds Newsletter.*

Recently, your notice regarding a Market Analyst in Investors Daily *caught my eye—and your company name caught my attention—because your record over the last three years shows exceptional portfolio management. With my experience with one of your competitors, I know I could make significant contributions.*

I would like to talk to you about your personnel needs and how I would be able to contribute to your department's goals.

An experienced market analyst, I have an economics background and a strong analytical approach to market fluctuations. This combination has enabled me to consistently pick the new technology flotations that are the backbone of the growth-oriented mutual fund.

For example, I first recommended Fidelity Magellan six years ago. More recently, my clients have been strongly invested in Pacific Horizon Growth (in the high-risk category), and Fidelity Growth and Income (for the cautious investor).

Those following my advice over the last six years have owned shares in funds which consistently outperformed the market.

I know that resumes help you sort out the probables from the possibles, but they are no way to judge the personal caliber of an individual. I would like to meet with you and demonstrate that, along with the credentials, I have the personality that makes for a successful team player.

Yours faithfully,

Jane Swift

Jane Swift

The Executive Briefing

An executive briefing provides a comprehensive picture of a thorough professional, plus a personalized, fast, and easy-to-read synopsis that details exactly how you can help with an employer's current batch of problems. Behind the executive briefing is the belief that the initial resume screener might have little understanding of the job in question. It looks like this:

EXECUTIVE BRIEFING
for a
CREDIT/LOAN SUPERVISOR
as advertised in the *Gotham Daily News*

Jane Swift   November 16, 20___
9 Central Avenue
Mesa, AZ 85201
(602) 555-5555

To help you evaluate the attached resume and manage your time effectively today, I have prepared this executive briefing. It itemizes your needs on the left and my skills on the right. The attached resume will give you additional details.

Job Title:	My Current Title:
CREDIT AND LOAN SUPERVISOR	CREDIT AND LOAN SUPERVISOR
Required Experience:	Relevant Experience:

- Five years in consumer banking Arizona
- Knowledge of Teller Operations

- Three years Consumer Loans and Mortgage Loans
- Extensive Customer Service experience

- Five years with a major consumer bank
- Four years in Teller Operations, as teller and supervisor
- Five years Consumer & Commercial and Mortgages
- Four years in customer service. Reviewed as "having superior communication skills."

The Broadcast Letter

The broadcast letter is nothing but a simple variation on the cover letter. The information you need is on the achievements section of your questionnaire. It can often get you into a telephone conversation with a potential employer. A broadcast letter might have a place in your campaign, but do not use it as a resume substitute. Here is an example of a broadcast letter sent in response to a blind newspaper advertisement:

Dear Employer,

For the past seven years I have pursued an increasingly successful career in the sales profession. Among my accomplishments I include:

SALES
As a regional representative, I contributed $1,500,000, or 16 percent of my company's annual sales.

MARKETING
My marketing skills (based on a B.S. in Marketing) enabled me to increase sales 25 percent in my economically stressed territory, at a time when colleagues here were striving to maintain flat sales. Repeat business reached an all-time high.

PROJECT MANAGEMENT
Following the above successes, my regional model was adopted by the company. I trained and provided project supervision to the entire sales force. The following year, company sales showed a sales increase 12 percent above projections.

The above was based and achieved on my firmly held zero price discounting philosophy. It is difficult to summarize my work in a letter. The only way I can think of for providing you the opportunity to examine my credentials is to talk with each other. I look forward to hearing from you.

Yours sincerely,

James Sharpe

James Sharpe

Here is an example of a cover letter sent as a result of a conversation.

Dear Ms. _____,

I am writing in response to our telephone conversation on Friday the 10th regarding a new- and used-car sales management position.

With a successful track record in both new- and used-car sales, and as a Sales Manager, I believe I am ideally suited for the position we discussed. My exposure to the different levels of the sales process (I started at the bottom and worked my way up), has enabled me to effectively meet the challenges and display the leadership you require.

I am a competitive person professionally. Having exercised the talents and skills required to exceed goals and set records as a Sales Manager, I believe in measuring performance by results.

I would appreciate a meeting where I could discuss in more detail my sales and management philosophy, and capabilities. Please call me at your earliest convenience to arrange a personal meeting.

Sincerely yours,

James Sharpe

James Sharpe

Here is an example of a cover letter you would send to a headhunter:

Dear Mr. _____,

As you may be aware, the management structure at XYZ Inc. will be reorganized in the near future. While I am enthusiastic about the future of the company under its new leadership, I have elected to make this an opportunity for change and professional growth.

My experience lends itself to a management position in any medium-sized service firm, but I am open to other opportunities. Although I would prefer to remain in Detroit, I would be amenable to relocation if the opportunity warrants it. I am currently earning $65,000 a year.

I have taken the liberty of enclosing my resume for your review. Should you be conducting a search for someone with my background— at the present time or in the near future—I would greatly appreciate your consideration. I would be happy to discuss my background more fully with you on the phone or in a personal interview.

Very truly yours,

James Sharpe

James Sharpe

9 | What Do You Do with It?

Creating one of the best resumes in America is a major part of your job hunt, but nevertheless, only a part.

Companies are always looking for employees. Even a company with no growth rate can still be expected (based on national averages) to experience a 14 percent turnover in staff over the course of a year. In other words, every company has openings. The intelligent job hunter will use a six-pronged approach to cover all the bases. This process incorporates different ways to use:

- Internet distribution
- Resume banks
- Employer Web sites
- Newspapers
- Employment agencies

- Executive recruiters
- College placement offices
- Business and trade publications
- Personal and professional networking

Internet Distribution

If you are not Internet savvy, I cannot urge you strongly enough to take the plunge. It will only take two days (and less if you have a friend who will lend a guiding hand) to learn the ropes and get your resume loaded for distribution. The ease with which you can reach potential employers is just impossible with more traditional methods of distribution.

Your ability to use the Internet for resume distribution sets you apart from other candidates. All employers want technologically adept employees, so approaching them this way immediately makes a point in your favor. There are two principal forms of electronic resume distribution:

- Posting your resume in resume banks, which are in turn searched by corporate recruiters and headhunters.
- Sending your resume directly to an employer's Web site.

Resume Banks

There are literally hundreds of resume banks where you can post your resume for free. Most have resume forms where you fill in the blanks. Have your resume handy; it's easier and more accurate to cut and paste an existing document than starting over every time. Your submission will look more polished (and therefore powerful) and there is less chance of spelling mistakes; with the availability of spell checking, typos are a clear sign of sloppiness.

Sending out 100 resumes used to be a real chore. Now, every time you post a resume it will be seen by thousands of employers . A word of caution here: In an effort to keep these resume banks fresh for the paying customers (employers pay for access to these banks) the administrators typically purge resumes over 90 days old. Every time you post to a new resume bank, make a note of its storage policies. That way you'll know when to repost your resume.

Employer Web Sites

Almost every one of the millions of companies with an Internet presence uses part of their site for recruiting. By delivering your resume directly to the site you will set yourself apart from the resumes coming in from other Internet sources.

All of these sites offer information about the company (history, press clippings, even financial data in the case of public companies) so you can easily customize your cover letter and your resume to fit the company's needs.

To find e-mail addresses you can:

- Type the company name into the search engine of your choice
- Use one of the following electronic yellow pages services, each of which claims listings for over 10 million companies:

    whowhere.com   onvillage.com
    bigbook.com   superpages.gte.net

A potential employer's Web site may allow you to submit a formatted resume, an ASCII version, or you may be required to cut and paste your information into a resume template custom-designed by the company.

If you have an strong interest in a specific company, you can usually keep your resume posted there until the right opportunity comes through. Company databases are managed pretty much the same way as the commercial ones, which means they get purged on a regular basis. Keep a log of the e-mail addresses you've posted to and the corresponding storage policies so that you can repost when the time comes.

Your Privacy

Unfortunately, your privacy becomes more of an issue with electronic distribution. The ease with which electronic resumes are distributed means that many more people are going to see your resume. But once it's available electronically, it also becomes almost effortless to copy or forward it. You'll need to take precautions to protect your anonymity.

First, use your own e-mail, not your employer's. If this is not possible, many resume banks will provide a "blind" account to handle responses from their clients—but that only covers you for that specific bank. Many Internet service providers offer e-mail addresses. If yours doesn't, many resume writers and career counseling firms will furnish you with a numbered account that will protect your privacy in all online job hunting scenarios.

With an electronic resume, your e-mail address can replace most of your other contact information, although you may choose to provide your home telephone number.

Corporate e-mail addresses don't change as often as you might think. Even if the corporation moves from 10 Main Street to 260 Center Street, it usually keeps its "hr@bigcompany.com" (or similar) e-mail address intact. You may find that by keeping a careful log this time, you've saved yourself hours of time in the future.

Newspapers

A first step for many is to go to the want ads and do a mass mailing. But beware. If this is the first idea that comes to *your* mind, hitting the want ads will probably be at the front of everyone else's mind, too. So your approach must be more comprehensive than that of the average applicant. The following tips might be helpful.

- Newspapers tend to have an employment edition every week (usually Sunday, but sometimes midweek), when, in addition to their regular advertising, they have a major drive for help-wanted ads. Make sure you always get this edition of the paper.
- Look for back issues. Just because a company is no longer advertising does not necessarily mean that the slot has been filled. The employer may well have become disillusioned and gone on to hire a professional recruiter to work on the position.
- Cross-check the categories. Don't rely solely on those ads seeking your specific job title. For example, let's say you are a graphic artist looking for a job in advertising. Any advertising or public relations agency with any kind of need should be flagged. On the basis that they are actively hiring at the moment, simple logic leads you to the conclusion that their employment needs are not restricted to that particular title.

Employment Agencies

There are essentially three categories: State employment agencies, private employment agencies, and executive recruiters.

State Employment Agencies

These are funded by the state's labor department and typically carry names like State Employment Security, State Job Service, or Manpower Services. They will make efforts to line you up with appropriate jobs and will mail resumes out on your behalf to interested employers who have jobs listed with them.

If you are moving across the state or across the country, your local employment office can plug you into a computer bank accessing major employers on a national basis (often referred to as a national "job bank"). Insiders agree, however, that it can take up to a month for a particular job from a local office to hit the national system. The most effective way to use the services is to visit your local office and ask for an introduction to the office in your destination area.

Private Employment Agencies

Here we have a definitely for-profit sector of the employment marketplace. There are some major questions that you should get answered before signing up with any agency. Chief among them: Are the fees to be paid by the client or by you as the job candidate? The answer distinguishes employer-paid fee (or EPF) agencies from applicant-paid fee (or APF) agencies. *In all but the most dire emergencies you are strongly recommended to work only with EPF companies.*

Here are some practical ways for you to check on the professional standing of your agent. Be sure to ask:

- When was the firm established? If the company has been in town ever since you were in diapers, the chances are good that it is reputable.
- Is the agency a member of the state employment association? State associations have strict codes of behavior and ethics and provide ongoing training for their members.
- Does your particular agent have a CPC designation? That stands for Certified Personnel Consultant, a title achieved only after considerable time and effort. Employment consultants with this designation are top drawer, so you can trust them and should listen attentively to their advice.
- Is the agency part of a chain or independent network? Both kinds of organizations provide training for their associates, a feature that can enhance the level of service you receive. In addition, other members of the network may have a job for you if the one you've located doesn't.

Finally—don't get intimidated. Remember, you are not obliged to sign anything. Neither are you obliged to guarantee an agency that you will remain in any employment for any specified length of time.

Resources

Executive Recruiters

All the above advice regarding employment agencies applies here, although you can take it for granted that the headhunter will not charge you a fee. He or she will be more interested in your resume than in seeing you right then and there, unless you match a specific job the recruiter is trying to fill for a client. Executive recruiters are far more interested in the employed than in the unemployed. An employed person is less of a risk (headhunters often guarantee their finds to the employer for up to a year) and constitutes a more desirable commodity. Remember, these people are there to serve the client, not to find you a job.

Other Resources

College Placement Offices

If you're leaving school, you should take advantage of this resource. (If you don't, you're crazy.) Many of the larger schools have alumni placement networks, so even if you graduated some time ago, you may want to check with the alma mater and tap into the old-boy and old-girl network.

Business and Trade Publications

Two uses here. The articles about interesting companies can alert you to growth opportunities, and individually can provide neat little entrees in your cover letters. Of course, most of these magazines carry a help-wanted section.

Networking

The Encyclopedia of Associations (published by R.R. Bowker) tells you about associations for your profession. Networking at the meetings and using an association's directory for contacts are wise and accepted uses of membership.

At the Library

The business reference section can give you access to numerous research books that can help, including *Standard and Poor's, The Thomas Register, The National JobBank,* and *The Directory of Directories.*

Follow-Up

Always take five or six copies of your resume with you to interviews. Often you can attach it to those annoying application forms and then just write on the form "See attached resume." You can have one on your lap during the interview to refer to, as the interviewer does.

It is always wise to offer copies to subsequent interviewers—they have very often been inadequately briefed about your background and skills. Also, leave copies with managers for their personal files.

In the job hunt there are only two kinds of "yes" answers: Their "yes-we-want-you-to-work-for-us," and your "yes-I-can-start-on-Monday." Never take rejections of your resume as rejections of yourself. Keep things in perspective. Good luck!

10 | The Resumes

And now, without further ado...the stars of our show.

The resumes on the following pages are based on the genuine articles, the ones that really did the trick for someone who had to translate his or her fantastic skills and background into a single, compelling document.

Whether or not your background is represented in the following sample, use the resumes reproduced here as a starting point for composing your own.

Accounting and Administrative Assistant

Jane Swift
9 Central Avenue, Windsor, Ontario N9V 1V2
Home: (519) 555-1212
Email: jswift@careerbrain.com

Accounting & Administrative Assistant

Accounts Payable & Receivable / Payroll / Computer Systems Expert

Organized and responsible Administrative & Accounting Assistant with more than 12 years of experience across diverse industries. Educated and energetic professional recognized as a quick learner with exceptional computer skills and the unique ability to manage several tasks in a stressful environment. Excellent communicator seeking a challenging position, utilizing current skills and abilities, with the opportunity for professional growth.

- Accounts Payable / Receivable
- Payroll / Payroll Systems
- Employee Scheduling
- Purchasing / Lease Agreements

- Microsoft Windows, Excel, Word
- Daily Ledger / Bookkeeping
- Customer Service
- Database Development

Professional Experience

Manager of Casino Administration / Analyst   1998 - present
   Casino Royale, Windsor, Ontario
- Responsible for tracking, analysis and payment approval of all accounts payable for the department averaging $100,000 monthly.
- Created a computerized daily tracking system utilized by all managers and the casino President due to its flexibility and user friendliness.

Pit Manager   1996 - 1998
   Casino Royale, Windsor, Ontario
- Accepted the challenge to learn the scheduling system for the staff of 1000, during a crisis, allowing payroll to resume uninterrupted for the entire casino.

Floor Supervisor   1994 - 1996
   Casino Royale, Windsor, Ontario
- After just one year as a dealer, was promoted to Floor Supervisor managing up to 300 dealers on a shift.

Agency Office Manager   1987 - 1994
   Gulliver's Travel, Windsor, Ontario
- Managed all day-to-day operations including accounts receivable, accounts payable, bookkeeping, payroll, budgets, employee training and customer service.

Travel Agent   1982 - 1987
   Gulliver's Travel, Windsor, Ontario

Education and Professional Credentials

Computer Programmer Analyst, 3 year business program including accounting
St. Clair College of Applied Arts & Technology, 1983-1986

High School Diploma
Assumption College School, 1978-1982

Microsoft Excel Advanced, *2001*   **Microsoft Access Advanced,** *2001*
Microsoft Excel Intermediate, *2000*   **Microsoft Access Intermediate,** *2000*
Microsoft Excel, *1994*   **Microsoft Word,** *1994*

St. Clair College of Applied Arts & Technology

Accounting Executive

Jane Swift
Lusaka (USAID) PL 100502 Dos
Washington, DC 20521
Residence +260-1-292-4303
Office +260-1-590-847-22/1
albornoz@usaid.gov

SENIOR OPERATING & FINANCE EXECUTIVE

Financial Analysis & Reporting / General Accounting / Operational Analysis & Improvement / Creative Leadership

Astute financial management professional offering expertise in governmental and business accounting principles and their appropriate applications. Expert in evaluating organizational needs and superintending the financial features of development, relief, service, and outreach programs to consistently achieve and surpass operating goals.

- Control Systems Design
- Regulatory Compliance
- Financial Feasibility Analysis
- Budgeting & Forecasting

- Fiscal Management
- Process Redesign
- Resource Allocation
- Payment Services

- Internal / External Auditing
- Staff Training & Development
- Performance Improvement
- Team Building & Leadership

Extensive international experience with excellent knowledge of the political and social cultures, trends, and financial environments in developing countries. Strong and decisive leadership qualifications, with excellent analytical, organizational, and cross-cultural communication skills. Fluent in English and Tagalog. CPA.

PROFESSIONAL EXPERIENCE

USAID/ZAMBIA Lusaka, Zambia   1991 - Present
Since 1977, the United States Agency for International Development providing programs to citizens in Zambia with a staff of eight Americans and 72 Zambians. Annual budget about $37 million.

<u>Chief Accountant</u> 1996 - Present
Presently serving as the principal assistant and advisor to the Controller leading all aspects of the Mission's internal management and technical program activities. Also responsible for managing all project and OE accounting, budgeting, payment services, financial reporting and fiscal management. **Selected Highlights:**

- Simultaneously and successfully served as Chief Accountant, Supervisory Voucher Examiner, and Acting Controller from December 1999 to August 2000.
- Appointed to serve as interim manager in the absence of both a Controller and Chief Accountant for two months in 1996.
- Challenged to revitalize existing office structure, document flow, cuff records, and inter-department relationship management.
- Restructured staff job descriptions, training programs, workload distribution, and accountability protocols; created a performance evaluation system still in use today.
- Experience managing $20M annual program budget, and $2.4M operating budget.
- Reduced outstanding reconciling items by 93% in two years to rank lowest among Regional Financial Management Center client Missions.
- Slashed outstanding advances from $2.4M to $0.3M, leaving none over 180 days old.
- Streamlined existing payment process to ensure proper tracking and aging. Decreased early payments by 98% and late payments by 82%.
- Pioneered the implementation of MACSTRAX and ECS to increase internal efficiency.
- Pinpointed and corrected existing errors and increased collections to reduce the Mission's outstanding advances by 77%.
- Contributed an innovative internal control structure, restructured staff training and development, initiated multiple corrective actions, and facilitated team effort philosophies to earn a Meritorious Award for the office in 1998.

Acting Mission Controller 1999 - 2000

Upon the unexpected departure of the controller, challenged to immediately fulfill all duties and responsibilities of the senior operating post including OE and project accounting/audits, budgeting, financial analysis, payments, and cashier functions.

Participated in the planning, installation and maintenance of internal control systems, administrated outside contract agreements, held full responsibility for maintaining continued regulatory compliance, performed fund prevalidation, and superintended staff of 11 in recruitment, training, development, and performance. **Selected Highlights:**

- Received the *Outstanding Performance as Acting Controller* Award in July 2000.
- Established an Electronic Certification System (ECS), reducing check-processing turnaround by 80% and significantly increasing security.
- Developed the Mission's Y2K contingency plan, increasing the volume of December transactions by 100%. Led the successful transition to 2000 without incident.
- Secured signature of Zambian Government Representative creating a special account for the SPA Trust fund worth $150K to cover USAID administrative costs.
- In a collaborative effort, transferred $1.5M to Central Board of Health for use by Zambian clinics.
- Prepared R4 operating expense budget for 2000-2002 representing $7.4 million.

Senior Financial Analyst 1994 - 1996

Supervised and managed the analysis and application of new and revised procedures issued by USAID/Washington, the IG Office, the Zambian government, and Mission Management. Additionally, acted as Audit Liaison preparing lists of audits to be conducted, performing and supervising audit work, and verifying, analyzing, and communicating the reported results. **Selected Highlights:**

- Commended for superior ability to clearly communicate large amounts highly technical information, recommendations, and regulations to non-technical project officers.
- Restructured code sheet transfer system to increase efficiency and decrease cost.
- Charged with the training and supervision of one financial analyst, who was quickly capable of conducting successful, independent assessments with minimal guidance.
- Identified a $330K erroneous deposit into one of the government's special accounts to save the Zambian Government valuable resources.

Financial Analyst 1991 - 1994

Analyzed and advised on the financial aspects of designing, implementing, and evaluating AID projects. Designed and conducted analyses of various internal operations of the Controller's Office and Host Government institutions. **Selected Highlights:**

- Analyzed and closed 19 unresolved recommendations in less than six months.
- Organized counterpart funds and managed local currency resulting in positive management assessment within the first two months of tenure.
- Developed financial sections of *Democracy & Governance* (total $15M), *HIV/AIDS* ($19.7M), and ZAPTID project extension ($4.6M).
- Supervised Price Waterhouse management of Emergency Relief Funds worth $18M.
- Challenged to organize and conduct an audit certification workshop for the RIG Office, resulting in five additional, fully certified organizations and improved communication between AG and RIG offices.

EDUCATION AND SPECIAL CERTIFICATIONS

University of the East - Manila, Philippines
BS Business Administration / Major: Accounting, Cum Laude Distinction

Certified Public Accountant (CPA)

PROFESSIONAL AFFILIATIONS

Member, Philippine Association of Certified Public Accountants (PICPA)

Applications Programmer

JANE SWIFT
jswift@careerbrain.com

9 Central Avenue
Valley Glen, CA 91405

Residence (818) 555-1234
Mobile (818) 5554321

APPLICATIONS PROGRAMMER

Self-motivated Applications Programmer with proven ability to complete complex and challenging assignments under pressure in a team-based environment. Skilled communicator able to convey technical information at all levels. Excels in research, analysis and problem solving. Track record of accomplishments including development, implementation and administration of 12,000-user international Intranet for Fortune 100 Company.

—Core Competencies—

Strategic Planning • Project Management • Training & Presentations • Team Building & Leadership
Needs Assessment • Client Support • Troubleshooting • Internet / Intranets (Database Applications

TECHNICAL EXPERTISE

Languages: Visual Basic, VBA, VB Script, HTML, ASP, XML, JAVA, JAVA Script, DHTML, JCL, COBOL, SQL, EASYTRIEVE, CICS COBOL

Applications Software: Microsoft Access, Project, Excel, FrontPage, Hummingbird, Visual SourceSafe, Documentum, Cimage, Dream Weaver, Home Site, Image Wave, Lotus Notes

Operating Systems: Windows 3.1 /9x/2000/NT, MSDOS, OS/2, TSO (MVS-390)

PROFESSIONAL EXPERIENCE

SANTA MONICA UTILITY BUSINESS SERVICES, Santa Monica, • 2000 to Present
Achieved Fast-Track Advancement for Fortune 100 International Utility Company

Programmer, Dec. 2000-Present Nov. 2001
Following series of notable achievements, received promotion from entry-level position with full responsibility as Intranet portal administrator. Intranet serves as comprehensive portal through which all company business is transacted—from Web hosted chat rooms to online benefits and bonus enrollment.

- Collaborated with Project Manager on all phases of development and deployment of 12,000-user multinational Intranet, followed by 24/7 support. Assessed needs, established standards and procedures, served as point person, managed change control process, monitored and tested portal.
- Delivered presentations and training to clients, ranging from new hires to senior executives.
- Met critical deadline on time and under budget, receiving widespread recognition for success of project which was rolled out within only seven months.
- Maintained 90% uptime for highly volatile high-profile project demanding 24/7 support.
- Motivated new staff members, improving team morale in highly stressful environment.
- Challenged to organize and manage action response team to combat major computer virus (Nimda), successfully completed project within one week.

SANTA MONICA UTILITY BUSINESS SERVICES, continued
Programmer Associate / Customer Support, May-Dec. 2000
Created Access databases utilizing Visual Basic GUI's. Maintained OSEA database for health and safety department; provided support and updates to existing Visual Basic applications, developed software requirements using SDLC. Provided 24-hour on-call application support. Assisted in recruiting and hiring new team members. Proactively requested and/or assumed additional responsibilities.

- Selected to develop and implement a dynamic ad hoc check writing application for the accounting department. Surveyed clients and researched formats to assess needs and maximize user-friendliness. Successfully built stable and reliable application (using Microsoft Access with Visual Basic code for functionality), reducing work time by 50% and achieving zero downtime.
- Assigned challenging task of developing personnel database to track performance for Corporate VP, managed entire project from needs assessment through successful launch.

UNIVERSITY OF CALIFORNIA, Los Angeles, CA • April to August 1999 (*Concurrent with Studies*)
Programmer
Programmed and supported COBOL and CICS accounting department's mainframe systems. Utilized EASYTRIEVE PLUS to write adhoc queries and update production data.

- Designed, created and maintained documentation including several data dictionaries for each of the VSAM and flat files.
- Analyzed, coded and tested programs for Y2K conversions.

EDUCATION

UNIVERSITY OF CALIFORNIA, Los Angeles, CA; May 2000
Bachelor in Business Administration, Management Information Services

PROFESSIONAL DEVELOPMENT / CONTINUING EDUCATION

Hummingbird Portal Training, 2001
HTML/XML, 2001
Technical Fundamentals/Developing Doc Apps, 2001
Java Script, 2001
Java Programming, 2000
COBOL Programming, 2000

Banking—Customer Management

Jane Swift
9 Central Avenue, Nesconset, NY 11767 ((631) 222-9544

Customer Support Management - Banking

Results-driven, customer support management professional with a steadfast banking career focusing on Customer Service Delivery Operations, Multi-site Care Center Management, Human Resources, Quality Assurance, and Special Events Coordination. Maintain a track record for the successful rollout of company-wide programs and key projects designed to improve performance management, increase employee morale, and launch newly developed customer service initiatives. Select areas of qualifications encompass:

- Program / Project Management
- Customer Loyalty & Retention
- Key Account Management
- Performance Improvement

- In-Service Training / Presentations
- Service Delivery Measurement
- Procedural Development
- Staff Training & Development

- Call Center Operations
- Team Building / Leadership
- Regulatory Compliance
- Budget Control Management

Professional Experience

JP MORGAN CHASE, Hicksville, NY   1988 - 2001

Held management positions of increased and diverse responsibility for this leading banking organization with a global customer base of 20 million accounts. Played a vital role in ensuring the smooth transition and new development of programs and project initiatives throughout all phases of division-wide transitions resulting from corporate mergers with JP Morgan, Chemical Bank, and Manufacturers Hanover Trust.

Communications Manager, Research Department 1996 - 2001

Collaborated with senior management and cross-functional departments on the strategic development and implementation of cost-effective communication programs and action plans designed to improve the morale and performance of more than 500 division-wide staff members.

Program / Project Management

- Worked closely with project team members, and served as Chairman for the Department Communication Task Force to lead discussions on issues, concerns, and proposed plans directly impacting staff morale, communications improvements, and team building efforts.
- Co-led the Research Department's Migration Project in charge of managing the appropriate, cost-effective relocation of employees to Tampa and Delaware site locations in collaboration with Human Resources, managers, relocation specialists, and community representatives during the JP Morgan-Chase merger.
- Selected by Chase's Senior Vice President of Research to launch the Department's call center pilot program in response to a need to update the organization's Platinum MasterCard customer service communications model rolled out to New York, Tampa, and Delaware branch locations.
- Coordinated the logistics of in-house special events providing employees with viable avenues to explore career opportunities, learn about available programs, products, and services, and proactively network internally with all levels of management.
- Planned and developed highly specific agendas and topics based on employee performance and needs assessments, and conducted follow up opinion surveys to measure the effectiveness of programs and events reflected in progress reports deliverable to senior management.

- continued -

JANE SWIFT
Page 2

Professional Experience, continued

Staff Training & Development

- Collaborated with Human Resources on the recruitment of qualified customer service representatives and administrative personnel, and assumed full responsibility for ensuring the fulfillment of employee training and quarterly performance reviews.
- Created and presented visual/verbal communications tools at in-house and off-site staff training classes that illustrated Chase's diversity initiatives, values and brand promise, and encouraged skill improvement.
- Formed an internal Employee Review Committee to address employee relation issues, and published a monthly newsletter to promote interdepartmental achievements and business initiatives.
- Created an ergonomic employee environment through installation of user-friendly keyboards, monitors, and workable cube space that reduced employee stress, increased morale, and improved workflow efficiencies.
- Instituted monetary-based employee incentive plans to support productivity requirements while delivering the highest standards of quality service.

Budget Control Management

- Managed an annual expense control budget of $25,000 for cross-site communication sessions and motivational events, and implemented quarterly incentive and recognition programs, presenting employees with Chase-sponsored monetary awards under an allocated budget of $200,000.
- Reduced overhead expenditures through fundraising campaigns and vendor negotiations to ensure the cost-effective availability of resources and event participants to support the area's objectives and profit plans.
- Collaborated with Management Information Systems teams in tailoring the direct database mechanism to facilitate local and remote viewing capabilities pertaining to customer data and Chase's on-line job postings.

Manager, Inbound / Outbound Call Center Operations, 1992 - 1996

- Managed a specialized call center supporting 400 customer branches in areas of Private Banking, Select Banking, MasterCard/Visa Corporate Card, and consumer products for corporate and high profile accounts.
- Coordinated the recruitment and training of all call center personnel, reducing salary expenditures by $200,000 through implementation of a newly designed staffing structure.
- Achieved customer loyalty and increased customer retention levels through the development and leadership of 30 professional call center representatives, resulting in a cohesive customer service organization recognized for expedient turnaround resolutions.
- Networked with the total Customer Service organization comprised of 2,500 representatives throughout the United States, Europe, and Asia, ensuring open lines of communication and mandatory compliance with MasterCard/Visa Corporate Card regulatory guidelines.
- Traveled extensively to Texas to support Chemical's acquisition of Texas Commerce Bank profiles and to develop a customer retention program that resulted in maintaining an existing accounts base by 70%.

Extensive Listing of Professional Development Workshops Provided Upon Request

Banking—Vice President

James Sharpe
9 Central Avenue, Charlotte, NC 28206
704-558-9245
jsharpe@careerbrain.com

SENIOR LEVEL EXECUTIVE

Wealth Management ... Corporate Management ... Consumer Management ... Risk Management

Talented and visionary leader with a reputation for integrity and ability to influence results. Delivered strong and sustainable gains in revenue, fee income, and asset value within highly competitive and volatile markets. Expert in turnaround management, business development, and wealth management combined with solid P&L, general management, and strategic planning ability. Series 7, 24, and 63 licensed. Areas of expertise include ...

High Level Relationship Management   Team Building & Organizational Leadership
Competitive Market Positioning   Performance Improvement
Multi-State Operations Management   M&A / IPOs / Divestitures

PROFESSIONAL EXPERIENCE

WACHOVIA (formerly First Union) - since 1986
(The fourth largest bank in the United States)

Retained through three mergers (Barnett, First Union, Wachovia). Identified for leadership ability and financial business acumen, and fast-tracked through increasingly responsible management positions.

Senior Vice President, Market Executive, Charlotte, North Carolina - since 1999
(Wealth management for clients with $1+ million in investable assets)
Transferred to revitalize a broken market ranked #11 in business retention out of 11 markets. Challenged to position the organization as a full-service leader providing customized investment management, trust, financial, estate planning, and credit products to the high net-worth market. Lead a 70-person staff with full P&L responsibility for managing $2 billion in AUM, $36 million in annual revenues, and $500 million in outstanding loans; direct a $6 million operations budget. Key member of the senior management team; private banking representative for the North Carolina Management Team.

- Change-managed and revitalized the division, eliminating 25% of the sales staff and implementing "top grading." Replaced non-performing staff with top performers, instituted a customer retention management program, and implemented an aggressive goals program. ***Drove the Charlotte market from last place to #1 in business retention within two years.***
- ***Maintained annual gross revenues despite a 20+% market downturn. One of only two markets in the southeastern United States with positive operating revenue growth in 2001.***
- Key contributor to the organization ***capturing market share leadership*** in North Carolina.
- ***Invited by the Estate Planning Council of the Bar Association to provide the keynote*** on the Private Banking industry.
- ***Championed a performance management program*** that has significantly improved employee morale and contributed to 100% retention of top performers.

Special Assistant to the President of Private Banking, Atlanta, Georgia - 1999
Personally selected to manage two short-term, high profile projects. Revamped the incentive program and directed the team creating the division's sales management program.

- ***Crafted the incentive program*** for relationship managers which was adopted by corporate and implemented nationwide, and ***resulted in an objective, performance-based compensation plan and improved retention of key associates.***
- Led the team effort researching and ***formulating the sales management program that contributed to double-digit revenue growth for two consecutive years and positive revenue growth in 2001.***

James Sharpe   Page 2   704-558-9245

National Manager for Training & Development (Performance Support)
Tampa, Florida - 1994 to 1999
  Recruited to direct the national training program for the commercial, private banking, small business, and premier services divisions. Managed an $8 million operations budget with full P&L responsibility. Led a 120-person staff. Challenged to develop and implement post-merger integration strategies.
  - Served as the *front line executive through three mergers* working with new management to ensure a smooth transition, integrate the cultures, and provide training on systems and procedures.
  - *Conceived the commercial business training program to support the strategic vision and lead the successful conversion from a loan shop to a full-service provider.*
  - Renegotiated favorable contracts with vendors, securing greater cost breaks and *saving more than 15% in annual outsourcing costs.*
  - One of only two executives selected to research and develop a national knowledge channel. *Launched the organization's first-ever satellite training for senior management executives, eliminating millions of dollars in travel expenses and delivering an immediate ROI.*

Manager, Commercial Department, Charlotte, North Carolina - 1991 to 1994
  Promoted to oversee the commercial department with full P&L responsibility. Directed a 15-person staff in managing relationships for companies with revenues up to $250 million.

Commercial Relationship Manager, Charlotte, North Carolina - 1989 to 1991
Banking Center Manager, Charlotte, North Carolina - 1988 to 1989
Assistant Banking Center Manager, Charlotte, North Carolina - 1988
Management Trainee, Charlotte, North Carolina - 1986 - 1987
Customer Service Representative, Charlotte, North Carolina - 1986

LICENSES

(Registered Representative) Series 7, Series 24, and Series 63

EDUCATION

Bachelor of Business Administration - 1987
University of North Carolina, Chapel Hill, North Carolina

Commercial Credit School *(extensive graduate level Accounting & Finance classes, credit analysis, memo writing, and on-the-job training)*

PROFESSIONAL DEVELOPMENT

Selling Managed Investments	Asset Allocation Program
Leading With Advice	Maximizing Call Power
Selling Fiduciary Solutions	Power Coaching / Sales Management

CIVIC AFFILIATIONS

Chairman, Corporate Campaign Committee - Charlotte Museum of History
Board of Directors - Charlotte Museum of History
Board of Directors - Charlotte Performing Arts Center
Volunteer - North Carolina State Mentoring Program

Broadcast Sales

James Sharpe
9 Central Avenue
Tampa Bay, FL 32301
(904) 555-1212
James@careerbrain.com

Profile

Marketing/ Advertising/ Sales/ Corporate Development/ Communications/ Public Affairs/
Promotions/ Non-profit Ventures/ Events/ Sponsorships

- Creative, results-oriented professional with 12 years of experience in broadcast sales, marketing, and corporate development. Strong track record generating revenue from existing partnerships, new customers, and nontraditional sources. Oversee numerous successful promotions, projects, and special events.
- Energetic and resourceful, self-directed and innovative. Highly effective communication skills include demonstrated ability to satisfy client needs through relationship building and creative development. Career-driven, willing to relocate.

Experience

Corporate Development/Account Executive, KTTV, Tampa Bay, Florida, 1992 - present
A leading revenue producer for Fox affiliate in the nation's 34th largest television market.

- Service existing accounts and generate new business. Arrange airtime through quarterly, annual, and specific TV buys.
- Develop television media strategies through qualitative and quantitative research for clients in all categories including retail, business-to-business, and entertainment. Increased existing shares of local direct and agency business. Revenues: Average $2 million account list.
- Recruited BankSouth, MCI Wireless as third-party co-sponsors for the Theater League of Florida. Supported local productions of Broadway musicals and promoted corporate image of sponsors to community. Revenues: $240,000/year (negotiated annually).
- Directed station sponsorship of the Florida Film Festival and the Florida Summer Theater Program. Supervised contracts, promotions, production, tickets, special events, and collateral materials distributions (ads, guides, brochures, posters). Currently negotiating sponsor relationships to underwrite a documentary film on festival for distribution to schools.
- Managed creative development and revenue stream for Drive to Stay Alive, an ongoing public awareness campaign that promotes safe driving issues. Revenues: $50,000/year.
- Helped establish and promote the annual Make a Wish fundraiser and gala event. Generated incremental revenue through corporate sponsorships. Secured news talent as spokespersons and event emcees. Event attendance grew from 75 to 600+ people in 4 years.
- Coordinated station promotion and third-party sponsorship for the Florida Arts Festival, raising money for art supplies and local elementary schools.

Account Executive, KZTV, Albany, New York   1987 - 1992

- Developed new business accounts to generate advertising revenue for NBC affiliate in number 61 television market.

Professional Affiliations

- Florida Advertising Federation, Vice President 1998 - Present, Board of Directors 1995 - 1998, President-Elect 2000 - 2001: Manage public service portfolios; organize social activities; administer student services, internship program, and scholarships; oversee payroll and budgets; frequent public speaker.
- Community Advisory Board, 1999 - Present: Coordinate fundraising and corporate contributions for YMCA.
- Florida Acting Company, Board of Directors 1998 - Present

Education

B.A., Business and Communications, State University of New York at Albany

Brokerage Professional

James Sharpe
9 Central Avenue
Chicago, IL 60625
(312) 555-1212
James@careerbrain.com
Page 1 of 2

Profile

- High energy, hands-on management professional with extensive background blending operations management, high-volume brokerage information distribution, and fast-paced brokerage activities.
- Employ analysis and creativity to form productive systems and interdepartmental partnerships. Cool under pressure with an excellent on-time and on-budget record.
- Hold high personal standards and consistently lead teams to achieve departmental goals. Believe that profitability, customer service, and quality work are primary factors of success in any industry.

Areas of Knowledge and Ability

•stock and brokerage service •brokerage information distribution •proxy processing •
•SEC compliance •stock inventory management •postal rates and requirements •ISO-9002 •
•procedure development •budget development •scheduling •training •departmental supervision •

Career Highlights

- Selected to participate with upper management in steering committee to plan company's ISO 9002 certification process. Project was so successful that company received certification in 6 months against 12 month industry standard.
- Achieved a consistent history of promotions and excellent performance appraisals. Started with Investor Services when division employed 5 permanent operations associates; division's operations department, at peak levels, now employs over 200 associates. Have the longest service in the operations department and have hands-on knowledge of all operational procedures.
- Wrote work instruction manual for department at general level for step-by-step process of informal to formal training. Produced written instructions for training of new associates. Designed contract review process and approval.
- Developed new spreadsheet formats for Central Investments that allowed for faster, more accurate tracking of stock inventory and over-the-counter profit and loss.
- Presented stock information to Central Investments CEO and VP level Trading Department head. Interfaced with controller on a monthly basis to reconcile profit and loss dollars.
- Supported the fast paced activities of 1,000 Central Investments brokers trading with a million plus shares of stock inventory.

Brokerage Services Experience

Investor Services, Chicago, IL	1993 to present
Manager, Data Entry and Process Control	1999 to present
Manager, Receiving	1997 to 1999
Receiving Supervisor	1995 to 1997
Data Entry Clerk	1993 to 1995

- Manage all operations of department processing over 35,000 jobs per year, peaking at more than 300 jobs per day. Mailing consists of dividend checks, monthly brokerage statements, and investor communications for 10,000 companies. Department is the hub of all other peripheral operations.
- Control the movement of sensitive, high-profile, investment-related material. Ensure compliance with SEC, client and postal regulations. Deeply involved in productivity and quality assurance issues.
- High speed operation requires exceptional on-time/on-budget performance. Develop annual budget of $600,000 and schedule staff to cover cyclical highs and lows using historical data to project volume. Determine best postal rates and discount eligibility. Come in on or below budget on a consistent basis.

Brokerage Experience
Central Investments, Chicago, IL   1992 to 1993
Assistant Manager, Trading   1993
Trading Coordinator   1992

- Tracked millions of shares of stock inventory to determine on-demand availability of company supply.
- Notified VP of levels needed for new buy. Tracked over-the-counter traders' purchases/sales and profit/loss on a daily basis.
- Followed and analyzed over-the-counter P&L and daily inventory for next days reporting and selling.

Computer Skills
Word for Windows, Excel, Windows 95/98, industry-specific software

Education
Gold Coast Community College, Chicago, IL, 30 Liberal Arts credits with concentration in math and science.
Professional Development Courses: How to Give Presentations, Fred Pryor Seminars; Business Writing

Business Development Manager/Consultant

Jane Swift
9 Central Avenue
Chicago, IL 60602
(312) 555-1212
Jane@careerbrain.com
Page 1 of 2

Expert in the Telecommunications Industry Through 20 Years Experience

Dynamic, award-winning career reflecting pioneering expertise in consultative sales and marketing of telecommunications network infrastructure equipment and services. Offer a rare combination of superior interpersonal skills coupled with in-depth technical systems understanding. Known for innovation and lateral thinking skills; consistent success in solving a diversity of demanding business problems. Outstanding record of achievement leading to accelerated sales, improved business processes, and optimized market share.

Key Words

Business Development & Marketing
Training Program Development & Management
Strategic & Tactical Sales Planning
Consultative & Solution Sales

Organizational & Process Improvement
Revenue, Profit & Market Share Growth
Staff Mentoring, Training & Coaching
Creative & Resourceful Problem Solving

Professional Experience

Patterson Technology, Rockford, IL   1996 - 2000
   SENIOR SALES TRAINER

- Rejuvenated the sales training department of this $300 million manufacturer of telecommunications switching equipment. Re-engineered methodologies and processes, instituted department goals, and established training certification programs.
- Created a new training methodology that refocused emphasis to build consultative and solution sales competence. Transformed the sales process by empowering account executives with the knowledge and tools to assess customers' business needs and meet requirements through product solutions.
- Encouraged expansion into emerging telecommunications markets worldwide by introducing and familiarizing the sales team with various industry segments including ILEC, CLEC, satellite, and international carriers.
- Designed and developed a critically acclaimed multimedia Web-based sales training module that taught the sales force both basic and advanced selling skills. Delivered the module to the sales team at a national sales conference.

Consulting Partners, Chicago, IL   1992 - 1996
   MARKETING MANAGEMENT CONSULTANT

- Contracted as an interim marketing manager. Led interdepartmental team in the creation and roll out of a precedent-setting sales initiative that drove $9 million in sales the first year and halted the competition, protecting an additional $2 million annual revenue.
- Coordinated with stakeholders to ensure support of a streamlined methodology that cut 50% of the time required to add capacity to the 5ESS Switching system. Managed proposal and pricing development and collaborated in the winning contract negotiations; led on-time implementation.
- Designed and deployed an innovative training program for customer's engineers on the state-of-the-art telecommunications switch. Successfully transferred technical knowledge and established market positioning as a premier and adaptable solution to telecommunications needs.
- Honored with the prestigious "Technology Grows Award" for outstanding contribution. Achieved a feature story in a nationally distributed magazine that highlighted the innovative training program.

Jane Swift (312) 555-1212
page 2 of 2

Telecom Solutions, Chicago, IL   1980 - 1992
    SALES MANAGER (1989 - 1992)
    DISTRICT TECHNICAL MANAGER (1984 - 1989)
    AREA SALES MANAGER (1982 - 1984)
    ACCOUNT EXECUTIVE (1980 - 1982)

- Promoted through a series of progressive positions, selling and supporting fiber optic systems and telecommunications switching equipment. Led teams of up to 15 professionals and coordinated the activities of support personnel in a matrix management environment. Supported up to $250 million in annual sales and personally delivered on sales quotas of up to $50 million.
- Launched the SONET technology, building sales from the ground floor to $9 million within the first year of introduction. Received the "Sales Director's Award" for valuable accomplishments.
- Delivered $50 million in new annual revenue by negotiating and closing a competitive fiber cable contract that displaced a well-entrenched, existing vendor. Recognized for top sales production with the "Regional Vice President's Award."
- Created an annual $9 million revenue stream by leading a team of engineers, product managers, and marketing personnel that designed and brought to market a new fiber optic tie cable product in just 8 months. Honored for achievement with a "Sector Vice President's Award."
- Initiated and acted as a change agent to support a paradigm shift in the role of sales engineers. Transformed the position from that of a "back office" role to a customer-focused, sales support role designed to meet the unique and demanding needs of customers.
- Directed a team comprised of internal staff and customer employees in developing and implementing a new system for engineering and provisioning switching equipment that saved $1.9 million annually. Awarded special appreciation honors by the customer's top management.
- Formulated and executed a strategy that achieved 88% market share for 5ESS Switching systems in spite of a price disadvantage.
- Closed the first commercial sale statewide and managed implementation of the then cutting-edge ISDN service; earned both regional and national sales honors.
- Captured a $15 million account by developing an innovative warehousing service that met the customer's need for "just in time" product delivery.
- Increased market share 50% by closing the first multiyear contract in the company's history; led a team in improving the order realization process to optimize fulfillment times for custom orders.

Education & Training
    DePaul University - Business Administration/English
    Extensive training in:

Telecommunications Engineering & Technology	Sales & Negotiations
Steven Covey Leadership	Quality Management
Process Improvement	MS Office (Word, Excel, PowerPoint, Project)

Community Affiliations
    Board of Directors, County Education Foundation
    Member, County School District Communications Team
    Coach and U.S. Soccer Certified Referee, Mustang Soccer League

Buyer

James Sharpe
9 Central Ave
Manhattan, NY 10012
(212) 555-1212
James@careerbrain.com

EXPERIENCE

3/00 - Present, Ohrbach's (New York, NY), **Buyer,** *Boyswear*

Responsible for purchasing boyswear sold in boys departments at 45 stores chainwide, with yearly sales exceeding $5.5 million. Branch managers report to this position. Visit wholesale showrooms on a weekly basis.

- Analyze daily sales data and inventories to plan promotions and make adjustments.
- Prepare and maintain budgets. Redistribute merchandise between stores.
- Travel to branch stores to direct departmental start-ups and solve problems.
- Train and evaluate assistant buyers.

2/99-3/00 **Assistant Buyer**, Silverware/Cookware/Junior Knits

- Promoted through three different lines. Consistently exceeded quota.
- Assisted buyers in selection of merchandise.
- Prepared orders, budgets, and inventories.
- Planned and created newspaper advertisements.
- Organized and promoted annual Housewares Exposition.

8/97-2/99 **Sales Manager**

- Managed four separate departments in two stores, exceeded projections 14%.
- Trained, scheduled, and supervised salespeople; turnover dropped 20%.
- Met daily sales quotas, handled all merchandising.

EDUCATION

B.A. Merchandising: New York Fashion Institute of Technology (1996)

All education self-financed through working in Manhattan retail outlets throughout college years.

Claims Representative

Jane Swift
9 Central Avenue
Sacramento, CA 95691
(916) 555-1212
Jane@careerbrain.com

Objective: Seeking a position utilizing my extensive knowledge and successful experience in planning, organizing, and following up multi-faceted, complex activities; and a position offering opportunities for personal contribution and professional growth.

SUMMARY OF QUALIFICATIONS

Offering comprehensive experience and expertise in the following areas of responsibility:

- Extensive experience planning, organizing, evaluating, and following up varied responsibilities in a timely and complete manner.
- Proficient in developing excellent relationships with clients and consultants.
- Experienced in knowledge of and in analyzing provisions and exclusions of policies in order to decide eligible benefits.
- Skilled at organizing work and resolving problems that arise in day-to-day activities.

EXPERIENCE HIGHLIGHTS

1991 to Present   **Claims Representative**   *Farmers Fund Insurance Co.*, Sacramento, CA
Responsible for meeting with policyholders, claimants, and attorneys to examine, evaluate, and decide upon claims for property damage and personal injury.

- Planning, organizing, evaluating and approving up to 100 active claims in process.
- Taking statements of witnesses and performing on-site inspections. Analyzing reports and statements of policyholders, witnesses, and claimants.
- Receiving and evaluating medical reports. Performing analytical reports of bodily injury claims.
- Negotiating claims settlements with individuals and attorneys.

1989 to 1990   **Management Trainee**   *PizzaTime Theaters*, Sacramento, CA
Participated in Management Training Program and assisted in interviewing, hiring, training and supervising personnel. Managed operations in absence of Manager.

1988 to 1989   **Administrative Assistant**   *Eastern Illinois University*, Charlestown, IL
Responsible for assisting Alumni Fund Director in fund-raising projects. Maintained daily and monthly reports of fund-raising activities. Organized and coordinated meetings and luncheons.

Education: B.A., Eastern Illinois University, Charleston, IL. 1988. Majored in Speech Communication/Business Management.

Licenses: Casualty License, including Auto Physical Damage and Liability, and General Liability issued by Texas Board of Insurance.

Strengths: Highly motivated, accurate, thorough and precise in attention to details. Excellent analytical and organizational skills. Major strength is completing multi-faceted tasks within time constraints allotted. Skilled in public relations, loyal, dependable, and willing to do whatever is needed to meet established goals.

References furnished upon request

Computer Instructor

James Sharpe, MCSD, MBA, PMP
_____

**9 Central Ave.** ◆ _Portland, OR 97201_ ◆ _503-246-5600_ ◆ _jsharpe@careerbrain.com_

EXPERIENCED COMPUTER INSTRUCTOR

Professional Summary

Success-driven **Computer Educator** with proven record of achievement in instructing the adult learner using unique combination of teaching experience coupled with 10 years' business background and extensive computer skills. Outstanding project management, technical, training, and presentation skills. Expertise in:

• Dynamic Teaching Methods	• Motivational Strategies	• Active Learning Methods
• Curriculum Development	• Internet Research	• Utilization of Technology
• Use of Instructional Aids	• Lecture Preparation	• Student Advising

Education

M.B.A. in Financial Management, Santa Clara University, San Jose, CA, 1998

B.S. in Business Administration, University of California, Sacramento, CA, 1979

Additional Coursework:
Java Programming I, Mt. Hood Community College, Portland, OR, 2001
Advanced VB Programming, Mt. Hood Community College, Portland, OR, 2000
Intermediate VB Programming, Mt. Hood Community College, Portland, OR, 2000
Introduction to VB Programming, Mt. Hood Community College, Portland, OR, 1999
Computer Programmer Certificate, Sacramento Business Institute, Sacramento, CA, 1982

Certifications

Microsoft Certified Solution Developer
Microsoft Certified Professional-Designing and Implementing Databases with SQL Server 7.0
Microsoft Certified Professional-Visual Basic 6.0 for Desktop Applications
Microsoft Certified Professional-Visual Basic 6.0 for Distributed Applications
Microsoft Certified Professional-Analyzing Requirements and Defining Solution Architectures
Certified Project Management Professional

PROFESSIONAL EXPERIENCE

Mt. Hood Community College, Portland, OR   _2001-Present_
PART-TIME INSTRUCTOR
- Developed course materials, syllabi, handouts, quizzes, tests, lectures, and PowerPoint presentations for intermediate VB programming and introductory computer courses.
- Developed VB demos for students to use in learning the course concepts in intermediate visual basic programming classes.
- Created faculty web page (spot.mhcc.edu/~pdarwin) with resources, links, and class syllabus.

James Sharpe

VB Solutions, Inc., Portland, OR   *2000-2001*
VB DEVELOPER
- Designed, developed, and customized software for Solomon accounting using VB 6.0 with heavy use of SQL.
- Created stored procedures and indexes with Query Analyzer and Enterprise Manager. Most projects required the use of custom controls designed for Solomon and heavy use of API functions.

Mortgage Asset Services, Walnut Creek, CA   *1991-1999*
Supervisor Asset Services (1996-1999)
- Managed Asset Services department, which coordinated real estate property valuations nationwide.
- Volume increased from 800 files per month to over 4000.
- Hired, trained, supervised staff of 18 full-time employees.

Systems Operations Analyst (1994-1996)
- Increased operations efficiency with general systems and operations procedure enhancements.
- Acted as liaison to IT department with hardware and software recommendations for upgrades and improvements.
- Coordinated major software operating system upgrade.
- Trained and supported staff on technology issues. Coordinated two office relocations.

REO Coordinator (1991-1994)
- Successfully managed and liquidated bank owned, foreclosed properties.
- Made cost control, marketing and pricing recommendations.
- Screened agents, coordinated escrow.

Walnut Creek Investment Brokerage, Walnut Creek, CA   *1990-1991*
BUSINESS BROKER
- Solicited, listed, and sold business opportunities as commissioned agent.
- Generated 19 listings totaling over $2.7 million.
- Appraised businesses, established buyer qualifications, opened and closed escrow.

SOFTWARE APPLICATION SKILLS

Microsoft Word, Excel, PowerPoint, Access, Publisher, Front Page 2000, Dreamweaver 4, Visual Basic 6.0

PROFESSIONAL AFFILIATIONS

Project Management Institute
Portland Visual Basic Users Group
International Association of Business Communicators

Computer Technician

JANE SWIFT

9 Central Ave. ◆ Rochester, New York 14607 ◆ 585-621-3988 ◆ E-mail: jswift@careerbrain.com

SUMMARY: Computer Technician currently pursuing MCSE certification in Windows NT 4.0. Additional technical experience as Research Chemist, with 20-year track record in academic and industrial research laboratories.

EDUCATION:

Ziff-Davis Education Center; Rochester, New York.
Pursuing Microsoft Certified Systems Engineer (MCSE) - Windows NT 4.0

Coursework:

A+ PC Operating Systems
A+ PC Hardware
Understanding Network Fundamentals

Administering Windows NT 4.0
Supporting Windows NT 4.0 Core Technologies

Bachelor of Science, Chemistry
University of Rochester; Rochester, New York.
With Highest Honors; GPA: 3.88/4.00; Physical Chemistry Award

EXPERIENCE:

6/99 - Present   **PITTSFORD CENTRAL SCHOOL DISTRICT; Pittsford, New York.**
Systems Technician (Volunteer)
- Install and set up new hardware and software.
- Trouble-shoot problems on network and individual PCs.
- Perform routine network maintenance duties.
- Serve in "Help Desk" capacity for network users.

1995 - 1998   **UNIV. OF ROCHESTER CENTER FOR IMAGING SCIENCE; Rochester, New York.**
Staff Scientist
- Participated in privately funded research project investigating silver halide compounds.
- Developed test methodology and designed experiments.
- Supervised graduate students assisting in research.
- Co-authored two papers on experimental results and provided information in support of professional presentations based on research.

1976 - 1992   **POLAROID CORPORATION; Cambridge, Massachusetts**
Environmental Sciences Section   **Jan. 1992 - Aug. 1992**
- Conducted feasibility testing for use of activated carbon to remove impurities from processor overflow.
- Designed laboratory and developed experiments.
- Performed experiments, compiled results, and published internal document on findings.

Consumer Imaging Division   **1986 - 1991**
- Tested potential sensitizing agents for use with photographic papers. Experiments involved chemical and spectral sensitization, spectral sensitivity, elemental analysis and spectroscopy.

Color Paper Group   **1980 - 1986**
Research Laboratory - Photographic Studio   **1978 - 1980**
Research Laboratory - Color Negative - Positive Systems Group   **1976 - 1978**

Consultant

James Sharpe

9 Central Avenue • Novi, Michigan 48374 • Ph: (810) 555-1212 • Pager: (313) 555-1213
James@careerbrain.com

Executive Summary

An innovative and seasoned **Senior Executive** and **Consultant** with a successful background in **crisis resolution, turnaround and start-up situations**. More than 15 years successful, progressive experience in all phases of Strategic Planning, Operations and Financial Management. Recognized as a hands-on, pro-active **troubleshooter** who can rapidly identify business problems, formulate strategic plans, initiate change and implement new processes in challenging and diverse environments. Exceptional ability to **execute income enhancement strategies** and cost control actions.

Areas of Effectiveness

- Capital & Operational Budgeting
- Production & Inventory Management
- Financial & Operational Cost Control
- Business Valuation
- Sales/Marketing Strategies
- Corrective Action Planning
- P&L Responsibility
- Crisis Management
- Liquidation Management

Significant Accomplishments

- Recruited as a **Turnaround Consultant for ROTH,** to create spending accountability in all areas, resulting in cost reductions of $1 million annually. Facilitated successful negotiations with vendors, customers, the Internal Revenue Service, various state authorities and banks for lines of credit.
- As the **President of NoviTechnolgies**, orchestrated the start-up and growth of a subsidiary organization. Within just four years successfully established 18 retail stores, 3 warehousing/distribution locations and sales exceeding $10 million. Additionally created a wholly owned subsidiary for acquisitions and acquired 21 stores through bulk sale and transfer.
- Within 9 months, as the **Divisional Controller for The Electronics Store**, selected and implemented a fully integrated Purchase Order Management Systems enabling the centralization of national purchasing contracts and staff reductions resulting in a cost savings exceeding $2 million.
- Promoted to **Plant Comptroller**, for the **fifth largest facility in the U.S., at Warren Computers** in less than three years (the standard was seven years). Effectively negotiated with and administered 4 unions and 15 different locals. Responsibilities for this 600 employee facility included: standard cost, budgets, sales forecasting, multi-state distribution, and capital projects.
- Developed and implemented internal controls and security measures to successfully resolve an inventory shortage that exceeded $1 million per month. Additional operational improvements resulted in a 25% increase in deliveries as well as a 20% reduction in staff.
- As the **Acquisition Manager**, spearheaded the acquisition of a 95-unit, 350-employee organization. This included the creation of a new company for the bankruptcy purchase, due diligence, negotiations with creditors, inventory valuation, employee termination and selective rehiring.
- Directed the closure of a manufacturing facility: transferred assets, handled MESC, workers' compensation and union issues, dismissed staff, idled plant, absorbed production.

Education

B.B.A., *Business Management & Accounting*
Novi College

Corporate Communications

Jane Swift
9 Central Avenue
Los Angeles, CA 90071
(213) 555-1212
Jane@careerbrain.com
Page 1 of 2

Project Management / Media Research / Client Relations

TOP-FLIGHT MANAGEMENT CAREER building high-profile organizations that have consistently enhanced competitive market positioning, won favorable media and customer recognition, and supported substantial revenue growth. Combine strong planning, organizational leadership, and consensus building qualifications with creative design and writing skills. Proven effectiveness in successfully matching products and services with client needs to ensure consistent repeat business.

Work well under pressure. Thrive in atmosphere of challenge, creativity, and variety. Flexible work style—can adapt quickly to changing work and client needs. Assertive, hands-on leader with extensive publications, audio, video, and broadcast studio experience. Hold B.A. in Communications/Broadcasting and M.A. in Communications Research.

Key Words

Mass media communications	Public affairs	Media relations
Strategic planning	Desktop publishing	Public relations
Video and broadcast technology	Event planning and management	Trade shows
Training and development	New business development	Conference planning
Workflow planning and coordination	Performance and profit improvement	

**Creating High-Impact Images, Concepts, Services, Programs and Opportunities
to Improve Performance and Build Revenues**

OVERVIEW

- Organized, detail-oriented communications professional with demonstrated ability to successfully increase productivity and profitability.
- Versatile, with diversified experience in networking, business development, and training.
- Work well under pressure in demanding, time-sensitive environments.
- Achieved reputation for "getting the job done."
- Highly adept in developing productive internal and external business development and referral channels.

PROFESSIONAL EXPERIENCE

1999 - Present

Takeshima Electronics, Los Angeles, CA   Sales Support Representative
- Furnish product specifications in response to inquiries.
- Achieved reputation for matching product offerings to customer needs.

1994 - 1999

Professional Video, Los Angeles, CA
Fast-track promotions through a series of increasingly responsible positions.

Production & Sales Coordinator / Account Executive   1995 - 1999
- Successfully directed and coordinated high-caliber efforts to both expand and maximize company's market presence while strengthening market awareness.
- Arranged for media coverage in the trade press. Coordinated large mailings to announce acquisition of the latest state-of-the-art technology.
- Posted information to ensure mention in relevant magazine articles.
- Arranged for company presence at important trade shows. Assessed and evaluated new equipment's ability to meet upcoming needs.

- Planned and hosted numerous professional trade organization meetings.
- Developed well-received media kits that included relevant article reprints.
- Effectively surveyed competitor's rates as part of a comprehensive market research project.
- Designated target audience and adapted specialized mailing lists.
- Coordinated studio operations for taping projects.
- Significantly increased repeat business through extensive consultation with clients regarding specialized needs in an effort to successfully meet those needs.
- Participated in trade meetings regarding digital technology.
- Assigned camera and audio crews to optimize resources.
- Surveyed shoot sites to establish camera placements, equipment needs and crew availability.
- Developed logistics and scheduling to maximize budgetary resources and provide maximum value for clients' dollars. Established prices; quoted bids for projects and negotiated consistently favorable terms.
- Conducted production meetings to facilitate crew scheduling.
- Coordinated all facets of on-location shoots including lighting and audio.
- Performed extensive quality checks to ensure equipment's optimal operation
- Provided extensive client follow-up to ensure complete satisfaction and gain repeat business.

Office Manager   1995
- Screened and interviewed employment candidates.
- Effectively trained and supervised office personnel.

Administrative Assistant   1994
- Provided quality support for all office staff including heavy telephone support and client contact.
- Maintained all aspects of accounts payable/receivable.

1992 - 1993
University of Virginia, Charlottesville, VA
Communications Instructor
- Instructed students in Interpersonal, Organizational, and Media Communications.
- Conducted classroom lectures, discussions, and administered tests.
- Evaluated subject-children in a classroom environment.

COMPUTER SKILLS
Highly proficient in utilizing the following software packages:
- Microsoft Word, Excel, Access, FrontPage, and PowerPoint.
- Internet communications packages including leading search engines.
- Leading desktop publishing packages.

EDUCATION
University of Virginia, Charlottesville, VA
Master of Arts: Communications Research   1993
GPA: 3.8
- Research: Media and Its Effect on the Public
- Analytical research on the effects of television on children: feedforward vs. feedback theory.

University of California at Los Angeles, Los Angeles, CA
Bachelor of Arts: Communications / Broadcasting   1992
- Graduated summa cum laude

REFERENCES
Excellent references will be furnished on request.

Corporate Taxation

Jane Swift
9 Central Avenue
Ypsilanti, MI 48187
(734) 555-1212
Jane@careerbrain.com
Page 1 of 2

A highly experienced tax professional with comprehensive skills in corporate taxation. Offers 6 years of combined experience in corporate tax management, tax preparation, and budgeting. Proficient in analyzing complex tax issues, multistate income tax returns, and streamlining effectiveness and efficiency of tax management. Currently manages all state corporate tax functions of a company exceeding $250 million in sales. Reputation of a hard working and dedicated employee.

AREAS OF EXPERTISE

SBT, C-Corporation and S-Corporation State Income Tax Returns • Vehicle Use Tax Returns • State Income Tax Budgeting and Accrual • Multistate Property Tax Returns • Federal, State, and Local Exemption Certificates • State and Local Sales, Use and Excise Tax Management • Tax Audit Management • Tax License and Bonding Maintenance • Certificates of Authority and Annual Report Filing Maintenance • State Sales and Use Tax Assessment • Federal Excise Tax Collection and Deposits • Determination of Nexus • Tax Amnesty Programs

CAREER HIGHLIGHTS AND ACHIEVEMENTS

- Identified double-paid federal excise tax; resulted in federal excise tax refund of $60,000+ and 10,000+ interest
- Reversed $75,000 proposed tax assessment including penalties and interest; provided auditor appropriate documentation necessary to reverse proposed tax assessment
- Saved an estimated $10,000 in interest/penalties by filing for tax amnesty in various states
- Designed database of all applicable federal, state, and local fuel, sales, and environmental taxes— ability to price fuel with all applicable taxes at over 700 locations nationwide
- "Self-disclosed" $200,000+ fuel tax liability to taxing authority; collected 100% of tax from customer and paid tax without penalty and interest
- Manage thousands of federal, state, and local sales, use, and excise tax exemption certificates on products purchased exempt from suppliers and sold exempt to customers
- Implemented new process of filing all property tax returns for fixed assets saving the company $1,500+ in the first year
- Succeeded in creating a comprehensive database detailing multistate S-Corporation income tax filing requirements for federally elected S-Corporation, Qualified Subchapter S Subsidiary (QSSS), and nonresident shareholders

COMPUTER EFFICIENCY

In-depth knowledge of Microsoft Word, Excel, Lotus, various tax and accounting software programs, Macintosh, Internet, and e-mail

PROFESSIONAL EXPERIENCE

Finance Corporation - Ypsilanti, Michigan   1993 - Present
Associate Tax Director (1998 - Present)
- Manage filing of nearly 100 C-Corporations, S-Corporations, and composite returns including nonresident income tax returns for out of state shareholders
- File annual federal excise tax liability between $36 and $40 million
- Execute quarterly federal excise tax refund of nearly $100,000 each quarter
- Budget and accrue state income tax liability (1998: $250,000)
- Assess state sales and use tax of 500+ components of leased equipment nationwide

Tax Coordinator (1994 - 1998)
- Automated billings for parts department to bill correct amount of sales/use tax
- Instructed accounting department on scope of corporate taxation
- Managed 25,000+ client accounts and 500 vendor accounts with appropriate federal, state, and local fuel, sales, use and environmental taxes
- Assessed state sales and use tax on all labor, replacement parts, and freight related to leased equipment

Credit Card Supervisor (1993 - 1994)
- Managed operations and supervised 4 employees within department
- Handled inquiries regarding accounts and assisted clients
- Designed first comprehensive reference manual issued to clients detailing credit card process

OTHER WORK EXPERIENCE (During College)
Financed 100% of Schooling
- Chili's Restaurant - Ypsilanti, Michigan 1991 - 1993
    Waiter/Trainer
- Bill Knapps Restaurant - Ypsilanti, Michigan 1987 - 1991
    Waiter

EDUCATION
Eastern Michigan University - Ypsilanti, Michigan
Bachelor of Business Administration (Double Major) - Accounting, 1993 • Finance, 1991
Master of Business Administration Degree Program in progress

CERTIFICATION
Notary Public - Expiration 2003

Credit Analyst

Jane Swift
9 Central Avenue
Yonkers, NY 10701
(914) 555-1212
Jane@careerbrain.com

Branch Manager
Credit Analyst/Commercial Credit/Consumer Credit/Credit Administration/Credit Management/
Lending Office/Finance and Budgeting/Personnel Manager

Strong commitment to excellence. Dynamic presentation, communication, and marketing skills. Distinguished performance encompassing a steady advancement of increasing accomplishments resulting in fast-track promotion and progressively responsible banking duties. Motivated, results-oriented individual. Excellent planning, organizational, development and leadership qualifications. High-impact negotiator, spokesperson, and client service manager.

Professional Experience
ABC Financial, Regional Credit Manager: Manage 30 employees covering a tri-state region. Analyze competitor programs and develop marketing strategies for competitive market positioning to increase market share. Communicate effectively with dealers to initiate, develop, and maintain customer relationships and client satisfaction. Reporting, record keeping, and documentation of business deals, self audits, and budget control. Manage and track funding goals of credit analysts. Performance management of staff through effective training and evaluations. Conduct regular staff meeting and communicate company policy and procedures. Design, development, and implementation of effective succession plan to reduce staff turnover. (1998 - present)

Regional Branch Manager: Managed 16 employees covering the entire East Coast. Regulated and coordinated all aspects of branch operation to achieve volume and profit goals. Managed branch operation within established guidelines and budget parameters. Scope of responsibilities included lending, collections, marketing and sales, administration and personnel. Hired organized, trained, and evaluated personnel in all phases of branch operations. Motivated production while organizing marketing activities and strategies in a changing market. Facilitated monthly market, projection, and production reports for Senior and Regional Vice Presidents. Generated quality customer service and ongoing customer loyalty. (1997 - 1998)

Assistant Manager: Evaluated and reviewed credit applications submitted by auto dealerships for credit line and contract purchase in accordance with company policy. Supervised office staff to ensure company policy and procedures. Performance management, training, and evaluation of personnel. (1994 - 1997)

Northeast Bank, Loan Officer/Credit Analyst: Conducted all aspects of consumer and commercial lending. Cultivated and maintained customer relationships through quality customer service. Promoted from entry level trainee to Associate Loan Officer to Loan Officer/Credit Analyst within a 2-year period. Scope of responsibilities included cash flow, credit, financial statements, and budget spreadsheet analysis. (1992 - 1994)

Licenses and Education
Licensed Real Estate Agent (1995 - Present), Bachelor of Arts, Economics, University of Texas (1992)

Volunteer Work
Meals on Wheels, Big Sister

Credit and Collections

JAMES SHARPE

9 CENTRAL AVE.
SCOTTSDALE, ARIZONA 85242
602-235-4589
<u>JSHARPE@CAREERBRAIN.COM</u>

PROFESSIONAL OBJECTIVE

Opportunity with a Dallas-based financial services organization where expertise in commercial collections, credit administration, and financial analysis/structuring contributes to increased profits.

PROFILE

- Extensive general business experience in the financial services industry, with credentials in both line and staff positions. Areas of expertise:

  - credit/portfolio administration
  - asset structuring/restructuring
  - commercial collections
  - loan documentation
  - regulatory compliance

  - financial analysis
  - risk assessment/underwriting
  - problem asset resolution/loan work-outs
  - operations/information integration
  - lender liability issues

- Background in diverse environments ranging from major regional financial holding companies to large and small community banks.
- Driving force in the establishment of a newly chartered commercial bank in the Phoenix area.
- Customer-focused professional whose philosophy is to "do it right the first time."
- Viewed by clients as an individual who is worthy of their trust, and who holds their best interests paramount.
- Effective at building sound internal/external relationships to support client and organizational goals.
- Actively involved in leadership roles focused on community development.

EDUCATION

M.B.A.   **Financial Administration**
Northwestern University, Evanston, Illinois, 1979

B.A.   **Business-Economics**
Vanderbilt University, Nashville, Tennessee, 1977

Executive Professional Development Programs:

- Northwestern University - Management School for Corporate Bankers
- University of Texas - National Commercial Lending Schools
- Certified Commercial Lender - American Bankers Association
- Computer School for Executives - Bank Institute of America
- Leadership and Lending - National Credit Executives Association

JAMES SHARPE
PAGE TWO

EXPERIENCE

RIVCOM STATE BANK, Mesa, Arizona   **1995 - Present**

- Founder/Charter Director/Executive Vice President and Senior Lending/Compliance Officer.
- Member of three-person team that founded and organized a new state-chartered FDIC insured commercial bank. Established nine-member Board of Directors.

Key Accomplishments:

- Led efforts in generating $17.2 million in start-up capital.
- Grew bank into a profitable organization with $120 million in assets, while maintaining strong loan quality.
- Personally managed 70% of the bank's borrowing client base and 60% of $72 million in total loans outstanding.

U.S. LEASING COMPANY, Fort Worth, Texas   **1992 - 1995**

- Senior Vice President, Leasing - Managed lease origination process for a national leasing company. Offerings included private label programs for five Fortune 500 companies. Trained, supervised and developed new team members.

Key Accomplishment:

- Introduced commercial bank quality underwriting procedures to correct prior portfolio deficiencies for leases averaging $75,000 per transaction.

STATE BANK AND TRUST, Springfield, Illinois   **1986 - 1992**

- Vice President and Senior Lending Officer - Responsible for bank's credit administration and management of commercial, consumer, and residential lending. Chaired loan and Community Reinvestment Act (CRA) committees.

Key Accomplishment:

- Developed and implemented new credit culture, achieving an all time bank record of 1.12% ROA, from a minus .67%.

COMMERCIAL BANK, Chicago, Illinois   **1980 - 1985**

- Commercial Lending Officer - Special Loan Division - Established and managed new loan workout activity to support the bank's domestic commercial lending group.

Key Accomplishment:

- Directed reduction of internally classified credits and non-performing assets by 70% each.

CIVIC AND PROFESSIONAL ACTIVITIES

- Board of Directors and Past President, Local Chamber of Commerce
- International Association of Bank Executives, Charter Member and Board of Directors
- Senior Board Member, National Banking Institute of Arizona

Customer Service Specialist

JANE SWIFT
9 Central Avenue, Central Islip, New York 11722 (631) 437-0002

Customer Service Specialist / Account Executive

Outgoing, traveled professional with solid experience in areas of customer service, account management, and data processing procedures throughout communications and government organizations. Maintain excellent interpersonal communication, organizational, and time management skills. Equally effective at collaborating with others to achieve established goals. Select skills include:

- CUSTOMER RELATIONS AND SUPPORT
- NEEDS ASSESSMENT AND CONSULTATION
- SALES/ACCOUNT MANAGEMENT
- ACCOUNT COLLECTIONS

- EMPLOYEE/GROUP TRAINING
- DATA CENTER SUPERVISION
- FRAUD INVESTIGATION
- RESEARCH & REPORTING

- LABOR RELATIONS
- QUALITY ASSURANCE
- REGULATORY COMPLIANCE
- VENDOR RELATIONS

Professional Experience

HORIZON COMMUNICATIONS, Bay Shore, New York   8/88 - 7/00

Database Consultant	2/00 - 7/00
Customer Service Representative	7/94 - 9/99
Collections Representative	12/91 - 7/94
Directory Assistance Operator	8/88 - 12/91

Held a progressively responsible tenure with this leading communications company throughout all phases of multiple corporate mergers. Selected for a post-tenure consultant assignment to collaborate with programmers on the development, testing, and rollout of a newly implemented network database.

- Coordinated a matrix of customer support services for residential accounts in areas of telephone line installations, repairs, itemized features, toll free numbers, local and long distance, calling cards, and a broad range of specialized services.
- Expertly utilized a comprehensive network database to access service availability and billing information, and to monitor the occurrence of suspicious activity.
- Notified customers of service cancellations pending fraud investigations, examined all pertinent information to determine the validity of explanations, and established new accounts accordingly.
- Obtained official documentation allowing for expeditious closing and reconciliation of accounts affecting the ledgers of financial and cross-functional service departments.
- Conducted customer needs assessments through illustration of cost-effective benefits and solutions, resulting in increased customer satisfaction and exceeded sales goal levels of up to 175%.
- Coordinated the scheduling, dispatching, and confirmation of field support services.
- Managed a 60-90-120 collections account portfolio with a high record of success for resolving billing disputes through payment negotiations in compliance with FCC and PSC guidelines.

- continued -

JANE SWIFT
Page 2

PROFESSIONAL EXPERIENCE, continued

TAX PREPARATION SERVICES, Howard Beach, New York   3/73 - 8/88
    Data Processing Center Specialist   9/84 - 8/88
    Tax Examiner   3/73 - 9/84

Held a challenging tenure with this tax service in progressively responsible positions. Ensured the integrity of tax returns from point of filing to centralized distribution processes. Recognized by management for performance excellence, knowledge of by-laws and regulations, and ability to train employees on an individual and group basis.

Data Processing Center Specialist
- Coordinated third shift scheduling operations with shared responsibility for master tape runs in collaboration with all levels of management to ensure satisfaction of critical deadlines.
- Directed data collection and storage processes involving mainframe data source tracking, inventory control, and the mandatory back-up and archiving of data tapes, cards, and reels.
- Troubleshot and resolved data integrity problems to ensure the accurate and on-time distribution of data tapes to respective filing office locations for further processing.
- Improved communication levels between shifts and reduced the department's error rate through use of a detail-logging system documenting the process and status of Service Center operations.

Tax Examiner
- Performed a high volume of tax examinations in relation to the review and evaluation of moderate to complex federal tax returns including business, individual, and residual filings.
- Selected by senior management to lead a six-month pilot project resulting in the development and implementation of the division's permanent Collections Department.
- Headed a comprehensive Statistics of Income project designed to evaluate individual, corporate, and pension returns reflected in repots to Washington, DC for use by various government agencies.
- Researched and reported to various levels of management on the weekly error rate, staffing requirements, and billable man hours.
- Ensured regulatory compliance in accordance with the Federal coding system.
- Held interim positions as Union Steward and Safety Inspector with responsibility for representing employees, and ensuring corporate compliance with safety regulations demonstrating excellent negotiation, case development, and presentation skills.

Education

Associates in Applied Science, Business Administration, 1983
NASSAU COUNTY COMMUNITY COLLEGE

Disaster Recovery Planner

JAMES SHARPE
9 Central Avenue
San Jose, California 00000
(555) 555-5555 • jsharpe@careerbrain.com

INFORMATION SYSTEMS CONSULTANT

Experienced Certified Disaster Recovery Planner (CDRP) and Certified Business Continuity Planner (MBCI) serving a diverse client base in finance and banking, health care, telecommunications, insurance, gas, chemicals, publishing, and government. Project management qualifications combine with demonstrated ability to develop and implement technical solutions to meet critical business needs. Outstanding leadership and interpersonal skills resulting in effective working relationships and top performance among staff. An excellent communicator between technical and business units who can translate complex data into easily understood terms.

AREAS of EXPERTISE

Information Systems Integrity • Business Impact Analysis • Systems Applications
Disaster Recovery Planning & Auditing • Technical Support & Training • Compliance
Business Continuity Planning • Information Protection Analysis • Technical Documentation

PROFESSIONAL EXPERIENCE

DEP SOLUTIONS • San Jose, California • 1999-present
Information Systems Consultant
Recruited to manage development, implementation and enhancement of business resumption and computer disaster recovery programs for corporate clients in finance/banking, health care, publishing, insurance, gas/chemicals, telecommunications, and government. Achieved distinction as first recipient of company's recognition award for outstanding performance. **Key Projects:**

- Developed and implemented business recovery program with 5 platforms, data center and complex network at financial services organization with 32 business units at 6 regional sites.
- Created business recovery plans with 2-year maintenance program for 2 major customer service centers supporting client company and its operations globally.
- Designed voice systems disaster recovery plans and models for corporate headquarters/field locations of major telecommunications corporation.

APEX SYSTEMS • San Jose, California • 1993-1999
Manager of Planning Services (1995-1999)
Planned, developed and managed all disaster and business recovery projects for entire company. Functioned as information systems security administrator controlling user identification creation and distribution as well as menu creation and distribution access. Researched, planned and provided technical support for work flow and document management projects. **Key Projects:**

- Performed risk assessment, analyzed business impact and led crisis management team in the development of data and business recovery plan.
- Instrumental in saving $7 million annually through coordination and transition to an in-house claims data processing system.
- Collaborated on the design and implementation of mainframe-based system completed in just 15 months.
- Analyzed workflow procedures and downtime costs for utilization management and provided recommendations to maximize future growth potential.

Manager of Special Projects (1994-1995)

Managed all phases of MIS project planning, development, implementation, and management. Represented MIS Department to all business units and with subcontractors. Initiated and wrote procedures to automate MIS request system increasing efficiency, accountability and control.

- **Strengthened confidence and productivity level of 100+ nontechnical staff through training in microcomputers and software applications.**
- **Created new system to organize and categorize 350 internal/external reports for a state contract.**
- **Provided technical solutions to expedite completion of Medicare contract; company was awarded contract out of 450 bids nationwide.**

Manager of Enrollment Services (1993-1994)

Reorganized and supervised staff in the daily operations of department. Reviewed, developed and implemented new policies and procedures. Involved in the development of system enhancements and participated in the design and implementation of a new automated membership system.

- **Significantly improved productivity through outstanding team-building and leadership skills.**
- **Increased applications processing 25% in just one month by redesigning work flow procedures.**
- **Introduced cross-training program, turning around employee morale and performance.**

RYAN-LANCE CORPORATION • San Jose, California • 1992-1993
Systems Analyst

EDUCATIONAL BACKGROUND

B.S. (Computer Science) New York University, New York, New York

Additional Training

Hewlett Packard Product Support • NEC Product Marketing
UNIX & 3b2 • Development of Disaster Recovery Strategies
Novell Netware Engineer • IBM Business Partner
Voice/Data Telecommunications (ATM, SONET & Frame Relay)
Bell Atlantic Disaster Recovery Institute Training Program

COMPUTER CAPABILITIES

Hardware: IBM 9672 • IBM 9221 • HP 3000-III • AT&T 3b2
Compaq Systempro • HP Vectra • Epson • various PC platforms
Software: Microsoft Windows, Word, Access, Project & Excel • dBASE III

ASSOCIATIONS

Disaster Recovery Institute • Business Continuity Institute
Information Systems Audit & Control Association

Electrical Design Engineer

JAMES SHARPE

9 Central Avenue

Fredericton, ON K5B 8K9

(613) 888-9304   jsharpe@careerbrain.com   (416) 999-9187

RF ■ HARDWARE DESIGN ENGINEER
Superior Expertise within Leading Edge Technology

Focused and high performing engineering professional, offering extensive hands-on expertise working within telecommunications industry. Technical knowledge in the design, development and delivery of cost-effective, high performance technology solutions to meet challenging business demands. Capabilities include:

■ Research & Design Test Fixtures	■ Evaluation & Testing	■ Product Development
■ Problem Resolution	■ IP Telephony & Acoustics	■ Quality Control
■ Client Relations	■ Training & Supervision	■ Internal Consulting

Ability to learn and adapt to meet all expectations

TECHNICAL SKILLS

Superior knowledge and abilities troubleshooting, product verification, and new technology development. Fully versed in the following software applications:

■ C Language ■ Pascal ■ Motorola 68332, 68HC11, 6809 ■ Unix ■ MS-DOS ■ Windows ■

EDUCATION / PROFESSIONAL LICENSES

BEng in Electrical Engineering - St. Geoffrey University, Toronto, ON (1993)
Professional Engineering License - Ontario (1999)

HIGHLIGHTS OF KEY DESIGN PROJECT

Assumed role of supervisor for large design project, utilizing thorough knowledge of test fixture field to ensure success of lifecycle management from conception to completion, initializing improvements at all levels with creative attitude.

Challenge: Charged with overseeing development of $100,000USD automatic acoustic test fixture for Bitel Networks.

Action: Acted as liaison with all stakeholders relaying mechanical design, hardware design, and acoustic design specifications. Instrumental in applying stringent safety features to design.

Result: This test fixture incorporated sophisticated mechanical optical and hardware elements to test Bitel Networks 5305 Conference phone. Completed project within time constraints, exceeding expectations, reducing testing time from 5 minutes to 30 seconds per conference phone.

JAMES SHARPE
PAGE 2

PROFESSIONAL EXPERIENCE

BITEL NETWORKS, Kanata, ON   1997-2001
(Leader in research and design of next generation IP communication solutions employing 2000 employees with annual sales of $600 million USD.)
Test Engineer
Recruited to develop new test equipment for Bitel's new IP telephony, interfacing with all business divisions ensuring meeting of time and quality goals. Instrumental in verifying hardware design prototypes. Provided technical guidance to technicians in troubleshooting a wide range of IP products.
Project Highlights:
- Pioneered the introduction of data collection system allowing the identification of how well equipment was working within established specifications.
- Spearheaded the designing of optical sensor board for test fixture, incorporating p.n. photodiodes and Altera Max 7000 PLD.
- Gained extensive knowledge utilizing Cadence program Concept to create schematic diagrams.
- Designed and supervised production of test fixtures for Bitel Networks 5010 IP phone, 5140 IP Appliance, and 5423 IRDA module.
- Authored and modified test programs for Microtronix M500 and M60 telephone handset tester.
- Configured and tested complex HP VXI telephony test equipment.

GREGORY INC, Scarborough, ON   1993-1997
Failure Analyst
Employed to train and co-ordinate analysts involved in determining root cause of failure on SCSI controller cards using various types of test equipment. Contributing member of weekly production meetings, preparing and presenting all updates.
Selected Accomplishments:
- Created and maintained database containing all defects found on SCSI controller cards.
- Gathered superior knowledge and experience on a variety of test equipment including:
  - *EST emulator for Motorola 68332 microprocessor utilized to single step through C language code.*
  - *Hewlett Packard 3500B logic analyzer for capturing and examining up to 25 signals at a time.*
  - *Thermal cycle stress chamber for inducing failures in temperature sensitive SCSI controller cards.*

Electrician

James Sharpe
9 Central Avenue
Metairie, LA 70002
(504) 555-1212
James@careerbrain.com

SUMMARY

Master Electrician (licensed in Louisiana A-15346). Experienced in all types of electrical work—residential, commercial, industrial, electrical construction, and estimating. Six years' management experience as a Foreman.

EXPERIENCE
1996 to present

Cajun Electric—Metairie, Master Electrician
Responsible for all sales, estimating, work scheduling, billing, ordering of parts and equipment, maintenance of inventories, and customer service. Projects have included complete wiring of a manufacturing business after relocation, new home construction, repair of equipment, building additions. Have worked as a contractor and subcontractor.

1996

Industrial Light—New Orleans. Journeyman Electrician
Foreman on medium-sized projects, with crews of 2 to 10. Scheduled the work, checked quality and productivity, provided layouts and supervision.

1994

Prudhomme & Sons—New Orleans. Journeyman Electrician
Crew member on construction of the New Orleans Sheraton.

1993

Bechte—Saudi Arabia. Journeyman Electrician
Worked on a nuclear power plant (heavy industrial project), where safety and reliability were extremely important.

1991 to 1992

Tujaques—New Orleans. Journeyman Electrician
A variety of commercial and industrial projects (hospital, high-rise condominiums, office-hotel complex).

TRAINING

Louisiana Technical College, New Orleans
Certificate in Completion of Apprenticeship program

PERSONAL

Willing to travel, relocate

References Available

Emerging Technologies

James Sharpe
9 Central Avenue, Charlotte, NC 28799
Email: jsharpe@careerbrain.com
Phone: (828) 555-1234

Emerging Technologies Globalization Executive
Deal Maker / Market & Product Strategist / Business Developer / Negotiator

Results-driven and innovative Telecommunications Industry Executive with a 20+ year successful track record driving revenue growth and winning market share primarily in turnaround, start-up and high growth situations. Consistently delivers strong and sustainable revenue gains through combined expertise in Strategic Business Planning, Product Management, Market Strategy, Contract Negotiations, and Customer Relationship Management. Recognized for exceptional ability to assess business unit capabilities, identify and implement appropriate business and product re-engineering measures thus assuring bottom line growth. Rare ability to establish the organization's vision, develop "C" level relationships and negotiate the deals that guarantee success.

Key Accomplishments

- "C" level relationship builder with a track record personally negotiating contracts with companies such as Xerox, Lockheed Martin, Bank of America, Morgan Stanley, EDS, Visa, Oracle, Microsoft, Nortel, Boeing, Nordstrom and The Gap.
- Consistent track record developing contracts and terms that utilized company capabilities and met customer needs, including the first pre-paid international contract. This allowed the company to accelerate into the international market achieving $1+ billion in revenue. This approach became the industry standard.
- Turned-around an under-performing business unit lacking leadership by redesigning and motivating the sales and services teams, successfully recovering 60% of the lost accounts and adding new business to increase revenues to $5+ million annually in the first 12 months.
- Conceived and coordinated the global account management process; identified customer needs and product capabilities, spearheaded product and service level agreement changes to win the first global contract. Not only did this grow market share from 7% to 100% and revenue from $330,000 to $6 million per month, it set new industry standards in global business practices.
- Revitalized a product offering by identifying and implementing an International Reseller Channel, re-engineering the existing product through the addition of a conversion process adding packaging enhancements and aligning a service / support structure extending the product life by 2 years and capturing a potential revenue of $10 million annually.
- Within 45 days, conceived and implemented a National Accounts Program, establishing pricing model, sales organization structure and customer service delivery format, successfully increasing revenue from $12 million to $27 million per month. This program became the standard for the entire company.
- Led the company's new technologies market development (VPN, Web Hosting, co-locating Internet) securing sales in excess of $15 million within 6 months.

Employment Summary

Software Company, Inc.   **2001 - Present**
Vice President, Business Development and Alliances, Philadelphia, PA
Recruited to drive the product development process and expand market reach through the implementation of an international reseller channel and strategic business alliances.

- Negotiated contracts with Fuji Xerox, Xerox, Accenture and Lockheed Martin capturing $10 million in potential revenue.
- Managed the re-negotiation of two existing alliances that will net the company at least $2M over the next 12 months.
- Established a new technology relationship with Open Text extending the company's reach in the Life Sciences market.

James Sharpe, page 2   Ph: (828) 555-1234

International Telecom, Inc.   1994 - 2001
Regional Vice President National Accounts, Nashville, TN
Recruited to develop a major account program and subsequently developed a national account program.
Responsibilities included full P&L, $20 million operational budget and more than 250 personnel.
- During a 15-company acquisition period, including the ITI acquisition, (the largest in Telecomm history), consistently exceeded all business objectives.
- Managed the best corporate AR and bad debt levels, achieved outstanding customer retention level of 94% and managed corporation's lowest employee turnover rate of 10%.
- Developed and implemented a National Account Program expanding revenues within the first year from $180 million to $260 million and achieved Top Regional Vice President award for outstanding revenue increase.
- Post ITI merger, expanded account base from $300 million for Fortune 1000 to $456.
- Averaged a 21% annual internal revenue growth and was selected to the President's Club from 1995 through 2000 by continually identifying new business opportunities and establishing the right teams, resources and support to grow the organization and meet the customer's expectations.

ABC Telecom, Inc.   1992 - 1994
Executive Director - Global Accounts, California
Promoted to manage the Western US team of 139 sales and support staff, 5 direct reports and to oversee 35 national accounts.
- Managed and negotiated $750 million in contracts with "C" level players including BOA, Visa Microsoft, The Gap, Sun Apple, Oracle, AMD and Nordstrom. Grew market share from less than 15% to 48% in two years.
- Averaged 122% of revenue target every year.

ABC Telecom, Inc.   1989 - 1992
Branch Manager, California
Recruited to grow and manage the Bank of America account successfully leading a team of 39 cross-functional members.
- Grew annual sales and revenue from $3.6 million to $80 million within two years, attaining 100% market share.
- Spearheaded largest commercial sale in ABC history, valued at $400 million, successfully converting the entire Bank of America network to ABC in less than 6 months while maintaining 100% customer satisfaction.

BS&S   1983 - 1989
Field District Manager, San Francisco, CA
- Consistently exceeded quota averaging 112% and made President's Club every year while in sales/sales management positions.
- As staff member for the President of BS&S Information Systems, was responsible for revenue and issues for all national accounts west of the Mississippi, approximately 200 accounts, achieving 109% of the revenue quota.

BS&S   1980 - 1983
National Account Management, BS&S Headquarters, New York, NY
- Negotiated and implemented the largest state government equipment contract, valued at $20 million.
- Key member of the Organization Design Committee responsible for re-integrating BS&SIS and BS&S sales organizations.
- Named to Management Development Program (top 2% of all management personnel) recognized for superior executive and leadership potential.

Education

Bachelor of Arts, New York University

Career Development: Intensive 18-week BS&S account management and product training

Entrepreneurial

Jane Swift

9 Central Avenue   Yardley, Pennsylvania 19067   (H) (215) 555-1212   (O) (215) 555-1213
Jane@careerbrain.com

QUALIFICATIONS SUMMARY
Human Resource Management
Program Development, Recruitment, Training, Quality Process Management

EXPERIENCE

Philadelphia College of Textiles and Science, Philadelphia, Pennsylvania   1993 to Present

Director, Career Planning and Placement   1998 to Present
Liaison between college and industry, building international reputation through development of the following support and services:

- Direct professional staff of three, semi-professional staff of 10 and $175,000 operating budget in providing comprehensive placement service for 3,000 BS students, 250 MBA students, and alumni.
- Develop network of corporate and government employers within Business, High Tech, Creative, and Science areas.
- Annually achieve 90% placement of graduates, and hundreds of alumni at management level.
- Market on-campus recruiting program resulting in over 200 companies visiting each season.
- Host VIP campus visits and receptions.
- Extensive travel includes organizing and supervising trade shows, attending conferences, visiting industry.
- Provide input for academic program development through analysis of industry trends.
- Initiated seminar and workshop programs covering all aspects of career planning and search.
- Publish bi-monthly nationally circulated Job Opportunities Bulletin, Annual Placement and Salary Survey, Resume Book, and Student Handbook on Placement.
- Supervise internship and summer job programs for undergraduates.
- Directed software development and computerization of department, 1993.

Assistant Director, Placement Office   1993 to 1998

INVOLVEMENTS

- Selected for Task Force, Middle States evaluation for college accreditation, 2000.
- Visited/consulted with South African organizations on recruitment program development, 1999.
- Member, College Placement Council.
- Member, Middle Atlantic Placement Association.
- Past Chairman of Membership, Publicity and Office Training Committees.
- Published articles for trade journals, appear on media, conference speaker.
- Volunteer, Freedoms Foundation of America at Valley Forge.
- Member, Toastmasters International.
- Member, Colony Civic Organization, West Norriton, Pennsylvania.
- Accomplished photographer, enjoy painting.

EDUCATION
PHILADELPHIA COLLEGE OF TEXTILES AND SCIENCE
Evening Division, 1993 to 1998, Marketing/Management
Numerous Technical and Business Seminars
Executive Management Program
Werner Management Consultants, 2000

Entry-Level Advertising Sales

Jane Swift
9 Central Avenue
Akron, OH 44303
(216) 555-1212
Jane@careerbrain.com

Strengths: Enthusiastic, creative, and hard working advertising major with demonstrated successful sales experience. Reputation for providing excellent customer service resulting in increased sales and improved customer retention. Eager to translate solid classroom and internship experience in advertising sales into bottom-line revenues in the radio/television industry.

Education: B.S. in Advertising, Case Western Reserve University, Cleveland, OH - May, 2000. Coursework included advertising research & strategy, design & graphics, media planning, ad sales & campaigns.

Senior Project

- *Challenge:* Create an advertising campaign for the Ohio Hospice Group.
- *Action:* As key member of a 6-person team, performed demographics survey, developed campaign strategies, created logo and slogan, authored and designed bilingual brochures, and created media kit within $250,000 budget.
- *Result:* After presenting project to 11-person panel, won first place out of 12 teams. The Ohio Hospice Group implemented the slogan and several campaign strategies.

Internships

Advertising Sales Representative, Great Lakes Advertising, Cleveland, OH, Sept. - Dec. 1999
- Sold print advertising to local businesses using cold calling techniques.

Production Assistant, TV5 (NBC affiliate), Akron, OH, Jan. - May 1999
- Assisted with production of 2 to 3 commercials a week. Accountable for delivering all technical equipment to the site and pre-production set up of lights, monitors, microphones, and cameras. Worked closely with sales department and producer, learning both the technical side of commercial production as well as sales and customer service issues.
- Handled pre-production and on-air tasks for the noon news, including studio set up, script delivery, running pre-taped segments during the news, operating on-air cameras and soundboards.

Sales/Customer Service Experience

Sales/Wait Staff, Great Lakes Brewpub, Cleveland, OH
- Consistently generate additional revenues utilizing thorough product knowledge and friendly sales technique to up sell house specials and add-on items. Contender for the "$1,000 Night" sales award.

Host/Wait Staff, Jack's Seafood, Mentor, OH
- Developed repeat business by providing excellent customer service in fast-paced environment.

Awards/Memberships

- Won Silver Addy, an annual award for college students, 1999
- Served as Co-Director of Adwerks, developing ads for nonprofit organizations, 1998
- Member and committee chairperson of the Ad Society, a college professional organization, 1998 - 2000

Event Planner

James Sharpe
9 Central Avenue
Arlington, Virginia 22201
Home - (703) 654-8403   Work - (301) 871-3976

PROFILE SUMMARY

Meeting Planning ◆ Conferences ◆ International Events ◆ Fund-raising ◆ Golf Tournaments

Creative professional with expertise in all aspects of successful event / program planning, development, and management. Excel in managing multiple projects concurrently with strong detail, problem solving and follow-through capabilities. Demonstrated ability to manage, motivate and build cohesive teams that achieve results. Sourced vendor, negotiated contracts and managed budgets. Superb written communications, interpersonal and organizational skills. First-class client relation and teaming skills. Proficient in Access, Excel, PowerPoint, Outlook, MS Project, Publisher, MeetingTrak and Corel WordPerfect.

PROFESSIONAL EXPERIENCE

Meeting Planning Management

Planned and coordinated government, association and private conferences, meetings, events and fund-raisers. Coordinated all conference activities, workshops, meetings, tours, and special events. Trained, directed, and supervised teams to accomplish goals. **Saved $72,000 on most recent meeting**.

- Team Leader coordinated 10-26 annual workshops for Centers for Disease Control and Prevention.
- Coordinated 2001 National Conference on Smoking and Health. (2000 participants)
- Organized 6,000 participant national annual conferences.
- Coordinated Global Scholarship Pre-Conference Training for 200 third world participants.
- Developed and supervised education sessions at CSI's 1998 National Convention.
- Directed CSI's National Seminar Series.

Meeting Coordination

Team leader coordinated production, distribution, and grading of exam materials. Supervised registration and tracking of continuing education units. Negotiated hotel and vendor contracts. Prepared and administered budgets. Arranged all on-site logistics, including transportation, accommodations, meals, guest speakers and audiovisual support. **Consistently come under budget for each meeting planned.**

- Developed and maintained 5,000-person database.
- Developed, promoted, and implemented CSI's National Certification Program.
- Managed logistics for a Regional Pacific Training in Guam.

Fund-Raising

Team player in the development, promotion and implementation of membership and retention programs for BUILD-PAC. Coordinated PAC fundraising events. Supervised high-donor club fulfillment benefits. Provided updated donor reports.

- Coordinated 2 PAC fundraising golf tournaments.

James Sharpe

EVENTS MANAGEMENT EXPERIENCE

Conferences / Meetings / Program Coordinator   1994-Present

- Centers for Disease Control and Prevention/Office on Smoking & Health
- Tobacco Control Training & Technical Assistance Project
- Health & Human Services Department's Administration on Children, Youth and Families Grant Review Contract
- Food and Drug Administration
- Centers for Disease Control and Prevention/National Center for Health Statistics
- National Library of Medicine
- Housing & Urban Development Grant Review Contract
- CSI National Seminar Series
- CSI 1995 & 1996 National Conventions and Exhibits

PROFESSIONAL EMPLOYMENT

CORPORATE SCIENCES ◆ Rockville, Maryland   2000-Present
Senior Conference Specialist

ROCKVILLE CONSULTING GROUP ◆ Arlington, Virginia   1997-2000
Logistics Manager
Senior Conference Coordinator

CONSTRUCTION SPECIALISTS ASSOCIATION ◆ Arlington, Virginia   1994-1996
Assistant Coordinator of Education Programs

NATIONAL ASSOCIATION OF PIPE WELDERS ◆ Washington, D.C.   1994
Assistant Director, Fundraising

EDUCATION & CERTIFICATIONS

VIRGINIA POLYTECHNIC INSTITUTE & STATE UNIVERSITY ◆ Blacksburg, VA
B.S. Exercise Physiology ◆ 1993
Minor Psychology

Go Members Inc. MeetingTrak Certification ◆ 2001

Certified Meeting Professional (CMP) - Pending Jan. 2002

PROFESSIONAL AFFILIATIONS

- Meeting Professionals International - Annandale Chapter (AMPI)
  - Logistical Committee
  - Educational Retreat Committee
  - Member Services Committee
  - Community Outreach Committee
- Connected International Meeting Professionals Association (CIMPA)
- DC Special Olympics - Volunteer
- Hands On DC - Volunteer
- SPCA of Northern Virginia - Volunteer

Executive Marketing/Sales

JAMES SHARPE

9 Central Avenue • Venetia, Pennsylvania 15367 • (412) 555-1212 • James@careerbrain.com

Executive Summary

A fast-track, highly motivated, team oriented executive with a successful background in **turnaround situations.** *More than 8 years progressive experience in all phases of* **HMO Market Development** *and* **Regional Sales Management.** *Recognized for exceptional ability to develop specialized marketing stratagems, sales methods, and training procedures. Effectively motivates others on all levels in the achievement of individual and organizational goals.*

- P & L Responsibility
- Sales Management
- Market Optimization
- Marketing/Advertising Strategy
- Training Module Development
- Benefits Program Development
- Operations Management
- Interpersonal Relations
- Provider Contracting

Selected Achievements

- *Orchestrated the turnaround of the Pittsburgh region through the creation and introduction of a prototype Medicare Risk Marketing Program which set the standard for all other* **Health Associates** *Regions.*
- *Developed and implemented sales management and advertising/marketing strategies resulting in a 260% increase in sales, from $71 million to $185 million in 1995, thus tripling profitability.*
- *Facilitated successful negotiations with Key Providers & Hospitals increasing the Primary Physician Network from 225 to 700.*
- *In just one year boosted* **Health Associates** *net membership from 40,000 to 80,000 and Medicare net membership from 2,200 to 17,000, achieving 100% and 775% increases, respectively.*
- *Developed and implemented competitive training modules ultimately utilized company-wide. Initiated the management team's supervision of all marketing and sales representatives thus assuring full compliance and a successful continuing educational process.*
- *Spearheaded new business development in Boston, a highly penetrated managed care market, and increased regional sales from $9 million to $90 million as well as net membership from 5,000 to 50,000.*

Employment History

Regional Vice President   *1998 to Present*
    Health Associates, Pittsburgh, Pennsylvania

District New Business Sales Manager   *1993 to 1998*
    Health Associates, Boston, Massachusetts

Account Executive   *1991 to 1993*
    Health Associates, New York, New York

Education

Bachelor of Science, Education/Mathematics, 1990
Cortland State College, Cortland, New York

Finance Executive

James Sharpe
9 Central Avenue
New York, New York 00000
(555) 555-5555

FINANCE EXECUTIVE
Finance & Accounting Management ... Banking & Cash Management ... Budgeting
Insurance & Risk Management ... Tax & Regulatory Compliance ... Information Systems

Finance, public accounting and administration executive with diverse industry experience in retail/wholesale distribution, financial services and manufacturing. Proven ability to improve operations, impact business growth and maximize profits through achievements in finance management, cost reductions, internal controls, and productivity/ efficiency improvements. Strong qualifications in general management, business planning, systems technology design and implementation, and staff development/leadership.

PROFESSIONAL EXPERIENCE

SOUTHINGTON COMPANY • New York, New York • 1991-2001
Treasurer/Senior Controller • 1993-2001
Corporate Controller • 1991-1993
Chief financial officer appointed to treasurer and Executive Committee member directing $500M international consumer products company. Accountable for strategic planning, development and leadership of entire finance function as well as day-to-day operations management of company's largest domestic division. Recruited, developed and managed team of finance professionals, managers and support staff.

Operations Achievements

- Instrumental in improving operating profits from less than $400K to over $4M, equity from $8.6M to $13.6M and assets from $29.7M to $44.4M.
- Boosted market penetration by 27% which increased gross sales 32% through acquisition of 25 operating units as key member of due diligence team.
- Initiated strategies to redeploy company resources, resulting in 54% increase in gross margin by partial withdrawal from high-risk/low-margin product lines.
- Directed annual plan review process and strengthened accountability by partnering with senior-level department and district managers in all business units.

Financial Achievements

- Cut receivable write-offs $440K by developing credit policies, instituting aggressive collection strategies and establishing constructive dialogue with delinquent accounts.
- Negotiated and structured financing agreements, resulting in basis point reductions, easing/more favorable covenant restrictions and simplification of borrowing process.
- Saved over $2M through self-insurance strategy and an estimated $200K annually by positioning company to qualify to self-insure future workers' compensation claims.
- Designed executive and management reporting systems and tailored financial and operating reporting system to meet requirements of 100+ business units.

Southington Company continued...

Technology Achievements

- Turned around organization-wide resistance toward automation and streamlined procedures that significantly improved efficiency while reducing costs.
- Championed installation of leading-edge systems technology resolving long-standing profit measurement problems and created infrastructure to support corporate growth.
- Implemented automated cash management system in over 100 business unit locations and reduced daily idle cash by 50% ($750K).
- Recognized critical need and upgraded automated systems to track long-term assets which had increased from $28M to $48.8M in 5 years.

HAMDEN COMPANY • New York, New York • 1987-1991
Chief Financial Officer
Recruited for 3-year executive assignment to assume key role in building solid management infrastructure and positioning $15M company for its profitable sale in 1991. Directed general accounting, cash management, financial and tax reporting, banking relations, credit and collections, data processing, employee benefits, and administration. Managed and developed staff.

- Converted company to small business corporation saving $450K in taxes over 3-year period.
- Realized $195K in accumulated tax savings through strategies adopting LIFO inventory method, minimizing taxes on a continual basis.
- Secured 25% of company's major client base (50% of total sales volume) by leading design, installation and administration of computer-based EDI program.
- Reduced collection period from 3 weeks to 5 days by initiating new policies and procedures.

MADISON COMPANY • New York, New York • 1981-1987
Partner
Jointly acquired and managed public accounting firm serving privately held companies (up to $200M in revenues) in wholesale distribution, financial services and manufacturing industries. Concurrent responsibility for practice administration and providing accounting, business and MIS consulting services to corporate clients.

EDUCATION

B.S. in Accounting
New York University • New York, New York

Certified Public Accountant - New York

Financial Consultant

JAMES SHARPE
36 Alexander Avenue
Southport, CT 06490
(203) 259-1234
jsharpe@optonline.net

OBJECTIVE   **Proprietary Trader / Hedge Fund Manager** position continuing a successful record of profit generation.

PROFILE
- 12 years of high-performance in financial investment. Past 10 years as a Market Maker on the floor of the Pacific Stock Exchange with a consistent, verifiable record of achievement in competitive and volatile environments. Traded futures, options, equities, bonds and derivatives.
- Licensed Broker Dealer - American and Pacific Stock Exchanges.
- Demonstrated competencies in creative problem solving, decision making, negotiating and utilization of computer trading applications.
- Noted for options trading expertise, vision, initiative and ethics.

EXPERIENCE   **Market Maker**   1991-Present
JMS Trading, San Francisco, CA

- Earned over $10,000,000 in profits starting with $40,000 in equity. Reversed initial client investment within six months.
- Achieved strong and sustainable gains each year, regardless of market conditions, through a conservative trading approach.
- Acquired Lead Market Maker (one of three) designation for equity options traded on Microsoft and JDS Uniphase.
- Invested in and coached five novice traders-on Amex, PSE and CBOE-securing a $500,000 return within three years.

Financial Consultant   1989-1991
Morgan Stanley, Los Angeles, CA

- Cultivated and managed a base of 300+ clients (retail and institutions) with speculative investments, mutual funds, insurance, stocks, bonds, futures and options.
- Led the account development and service of a $24+ million portfolio in collaboration with management.
- Performed personal financial analysis including net worth, cash flow, income tax situation, investment portfolio analysis, insurance detail, retirement outlook and estate planning.

EDUCATION   **B.A., Business Administration - Finance**   1989
University of Southern California, Los Angeles, CA
- Co-created an options trading computer program that funded 1.5 years of education.

Finance Trust Administration

James Sharpe
9 Central Avenue
Madison, WI 53708
(608) 555-1212
James@careerbrain.com

Career Summary

A dedicated finance professional with 17 years experience in trust administration and operations. Expert analytical and technical skills. Continually monitor, update skills and maintain compliance with industry and government regulations. Highly efficient, able to read and understand complex legal documents while quickly determining most important details. Strong customer relationship management skills, driven to provide same day, high-quality service.

Experience

First National Trust, Princeton, New Jersey   1986 - Present
Assistant Vice President, Corporate Trust Bond Administration (1993 - Present)
Administer, according to governing documents, a broad portfolio of corporate trust appointments including bond trusteeships, municipal bonds, and corporate escrows. Properly invest $100 million in assets and maintain $1 billion in debt issues. Consult and work closely with bond counsels, financial advisors, and underwriters. Review and execute agreements; represent First National at closing. Develop new business and maintain strong relationships with existing clientele.

  Achievements
- Successfully managed transfers of 4,000+ accounts when First National acquired another trust organization.
- Headed up 3-person departmental restructure that transferred responsibility along functional rather than product lines, resulting in increased efficiencies and cost savings.
- Developed strong industry network, allowing for timely responses to customers' inquiries.

Systems Administrator (1988 - 1993)
Oversaw all bond and stock processing for the Corporate Trust Department including administration of entire bondholders' database. Identified and solved process problems and conducted meetings to improve operational efficiency. Hired, trained, and supervised staff. Developed job standards, action plans, and goals and objectives. Fielded and researched complex investor service inquiries.

  Achievements
- Handled conversion to Sunstar bond processing system including vendor research, vendor negotiation, and implementation.
- Participated in nationwide user action committees to evaluate software and recommend enhancements.

Security Processing Clerk (1987 - 1988)
Accountant (1986 - 1987)
Operations Clerk (1986 - 1986)

Education

Bachelor of Business Administration in Finance, Rutgers University (1986)

Computer Skills

Sunstar, SEI, Microsoft Word, Lotus 123, Lotus Approach, Lotus WordPro

Community Service

Appointee to Community Development Authority for Princeton, New Jersey (1999)

Health Care Program Administration

Jane Swift
9 Central Avenue
Clifton, NJ 07013
(201) 555-1212
Jane@careerbrain.com

Qualifications

- Medicaid Programs Administrator offers successful experience and up-to-date, comprehensive knowledge of Medicaid services and limitations, and New Jersey Medicaid Management Information System. Broad scope of expertise in key areas such as:
  - Medicaid policies and procedures
  - Hospital, physician, and pharmacy billing
  - Claims troubleshooting and problem resolution
  - Case management and utilization review
  - Medicaid prescribed drug program
  - Centralized, electronic, and DUE claims processing
  - Social service and counseling programs
  - Coding and medical terminology
- Demonstrated ability to provide extensive technical support for pharmacies, hospitals, and physicians.
- Sound judgement across a wide spectrum of programs and applications, demonstrating an analytical approach to problem solving.
- Able to develop and deliver in-depth, hands-on training for Medicaid claims processing and billing programs.
- Exceptional interpersonal and communication skills, particularly in the areas of presentations, management reporting, people development, team building, research, negotiations, and management information systems.
- Adapts to new situations and requirements easily; quickly able to develop a productive rapport with diverse populations.
- Resourceful and creative; skilled in the planning and execution of programs and projects for optimum results.
- Recognized as a focused, practical thinker who is willing to devote the time and energy, as well as take reasonable risks, to accomplish outstanding results.

Professional Experience

State of New Jersey   *1987 - Present*
Program Specialist, Health Care Administration Agency (1994 - Present)
Coordinate and implement policy and procedures to insure Medicaid program compliance and consistency. Provide technical support for providers and assist with written and verbal inquiries for health care and pharmacy billing and claims issues. Supervise two staff members handling provider inquiries and research requests. Maintain open communications with providers and recipients alike.

Counselor II - HCA (1993 - 1994)
Directed the effective provision of counseling services for Medicaid clients relevant to established policies and procedures of the program, eligibility and scope of services available. Worked closely with staff and community agencies to interpret Medicaid policies and resolve problems. Served as Acting Supervisor as needed.

Counselor II - HRS (1987 - 1993)
Maintained an active case management of 200+ clients. Extensive field work including client home visits. Provided educational and counseling to insure that children were receiving physical examinations, dental care, and eye examinations on a regular basis. Maintained up-to-date client and approved providers record. Promoted from Counselor I in 1988.

Education

Masters candidate, Social Work, Rutgers University
B.S. General Studies, Western Kentucky University

Affiliations

American Business Woman's Association (ABWA) 1999
Who's Who in the Northeast, 1993-1994

Health Care Sales

Jane Swift
9 Central Avenue
Dallas, TX 75379
(214) 555-1212
Jane@careerbrain.com

Top Performing Sales/Marketing Professional/Health Care Industry

- A natural communicator who excels in relationship building and business development. Possesses excellent presentation and public speaking abilities.
- Skilled in problem solving with an ability to learn quickly, providing a foundation for success in any organization.
- Well organized with attention to detail and accuracy in a high-pressure, fast-paced environment.
- Track record of consistently exceeding company goals.

Professional Experience

Independent Broker - Medicare Risk Sales 1998 to Present
Achieved high volume of sales, representing several major insurance companies. Optimized self-generated business by developing and maintaining strategic alliances with MDs and key decision-makers at medical groups.

Individual Specialist, Texas Medical 1996 to 1998
Consistent top producer for leading Medicare contracting organization. Successfully built and nurtured relationships with IPAs and their office staffs. Maximized exposure through skill in community-based marketing. Performed extensive follow-up and public relations to encourage member retention. Diligently monitored competition and industry trends.
- Special achievements included:
  Outstanding Sales Achievement Award in 1997 for top production in area;
  Top Sales Production Award 9 out of 12 months, 1997 - 1998;
  Leadership Award, Nov. 1996; Rookie of the Month, Jan. 1997.
- Consistently exceeded all goals with average monthly closing rate in excess of 90%.
- Selected to train new representatives.

Assistant Manager, Lone Star Drug Stores, 1990 to 1994
Promoted to Assistant Manager after 2.5 months employment—company average is 9 to 12 months.
- Assisted in overseeing all day-to-day operations of second highest grossing store in chain with weekly sales of $325,000. Supervised and managed support staff of up to 65 employees.
- Identified sales trends; implemented innovative marketing strategies, maximizing sales results. Developed monthly, quarterly, and annual budget projections.

Education
Bachelor of Arts in Psychology, Texas A&M University, 1989

Human Resources Professional

JANE SWIFT
9 Central Ave.
Point Pleasant, NJ 08742

(732) 753-8859
jswift@careerbrain.com

HUMAN RESOURCES EXECUTIVE / BENEFITS ADMINISTRATION SPECIALIST
Global Corporations . . . Multi-Site Locations . . . Union and Non-Union Workforces

Senior-level HR Executive with a strong record of achievement in global, Fortune 500 companies. Expert in managing projects and implementing benefits administration policies that streamline procedures and deliver bottom line results. Experienced in employee benefit plan audits.

- PeopleSoft
- SPD Writing
- IRS 5500
- COBRA / HIPPA compliance
- EGTTRA
- Health and Welfare Plans

- FMLA
- Retirement Planning
- 401K Training
- Department of Labor Regulations
- Vendor Management
- Rollouts and Renewals

Career History
Bloomberg L.P., New York, NY (6/99-Present)
Benefits Specialist
Direct a benefits administration program for a 7,600 non-union employee, informative services, news, and media company with global market presence in 108 offices worldwide. Workforce is comprised of sales staff, reporters, news writers, editors, and multimedia, video and radio professionals, as well as programmers, financial analysts, technicians, translators, warehouse workers, and operations / administration professionals. The company serves interests throughout Latin America, Asia Pacific, and Europe.

- Manage domestic and international health and welfare, disability, worker's compensation, and retirement saving plans. Coordinate annual renewals, ensure corporate tax reporting compliance, and administer annual enrollments.
- Ensure utilization, efficacy, and cost-competitive edge of benefits programs. Manage vendor relationships to ensure compliance with corporate goals and objectives.
- Control costs and drive corporate revenues by reducing role of consultants. Cut budget in half by assuming the functions of SPD and retirement booklet writing and health insurance plan renewal management.
- Meet stringent deadlines in implementing and rolling out retirement plans. Delegate duties to global HR representatives and oversee project from conception to completion. Currently working with global vendors to duplicate and make equitable on a global basis existing domestic tax issues and plan provisions.
- Achieved the successful rollout of retirement plans and supplemental benefit programs in Singapore and Australia. Currently working with vendors in Japan to accomplish the same.
- Work hand-in-hand with HRIS department to globally enhance PeopleSoft skills and extend PeopleSoft usage. Initiate the process by determining how programs should be customized to best meet global user needs.
- Conduct 401K benefit presentations, new hire orientations, and benefits refresher courses to 1,000 employees in New York office and via teleconferencing to overseas and other off-site domestic locations.

(Page 1 of 2)

Career History Company (Continued)

National Starch and Chemical Company, Bridgewater, NJ (4/89-6/99)
Benefits Assistant
Reporting to the Director of Benefits, administered this global chemical company's domestic retirement plan program. Workforce was comprised of 3,000 union and non-union, salaried and hourly employees, encompassing sales representatives, chemists, R&D professionals, and systems and operations personnel in such multi site locations as California, Missouri, Wisconsin, Pennsylvania, Ohio and Tennessee.

- Coordinated annual open enrollments, conducted benefit presentations, and compiled and dispersed employee informational packets.
- Prepared the filing of legal documents, comprised of Form 5500, PBGC, and SARs., compliance paperwork relating to ERISA reporting and disclosure requirements, and annual PBGC and IRS filings.
- Prepared disclosure to plan participants for company's welfare, pension, profit sharing savings, and 401K plans.
- Ensured compliance with QDROs and pension plan minimum distribution requirements; formulated annual pension plan valuations.
- Provided assistance in conducting annual employee benefit plan audits.
- Responded to employee benefit inquiries and provided pension benefit counseling to employees, retirees, and survivors.
- Calculated retirement packages and prepared retirement profiles.

Huffman-Koos, Inc. , Riveredge, NJ (8/87-4/89)
Benefits Coordinator
Administered the corporate benefits program for 850 non-union sales and operations employees.

Purolator Products, Inc., Edison, NJ (11/86-8/87)
Benefits Coordinator
Administered the corporate benefits program for 1,000 salaried employees.

Hudson City Savings Bank, Paramus, NJ (1/85-11/86)
Benefits Coordinator
Assisted in the administration of the benefits program for 850 salaried and non-union salaried employees.

Education / Professional Training
- **BA**, Psychology, College of Staten Island, Staten Island, NY
- Currently pursuing Certified Employee Benefits Specialist designation (CEBS)

Professional Affiliations
- New York Chapter of the Risk and Insurance Management Society, Inc.
- International Foundation of Employee Benefit Plans

Computer Skills
Word, Excel, PowerPoint, PeopleSoft

Human Resources Recruiter

Jane Swift
9 Central Avenue
Salt Lake City, UT 84106
(801) 555-1212
Jane@careerbrain.com

Dynamic Human Resources Professional with a proven record of top performance in recruiting, screening, and placing professional, managerial, and technical candidates. Committed to exceeding performance expectation. Excellent communication and problem resolution skills; energetic motivator. Computer proficient. Expertise in:

- recruitment/hiring
- training and assessment
- benefits administration
- compensation package negotiations
- employee relations
- policies and procedures

Selected Highlights

- Recognized as a Top Producer in 1998 and 1999 by filling an average of 37 positions monthly
- Appointed to serve on the task force charged with developing and implementing regional recruiting and transfer policies and procedures; selected as chairperson for the non-nursing task force
- Spearheaded use of Internet recruiting methods, significantly reducing print advertising costs and increasing candidate pool

Relevant Career Experience

Summit Health System, Salt Lake City, Utah
Recruiter/Employment Coordinator (since 1997), *Benefits Specialist* (1996 - 1997)

Promoted to employment coordinator and charged with recruiting non-nursing personnel for a 9-hospital health system alliance. Create advertising copy, attend trade shows, develop recruiting campaigns, screen and evaluate prospects, conduct interviews, and negotiate compensation packages. Worked with cross-functional teams to administer flexible benefits plans including COBRA and HIPPA. Background in HRIS/DBS. Knowledgeable in FSA, DCA, FMLA, disability, medical, dental, 403(B), and life insurance plans.

Smith Communications, Salt Lake City, Utah
Marketing Coordinator (1995 - 1996)

Recruited to launch training and employee learning division; reported to COO of division. Scheduled training with top executives of companies; managed lead processing/tracking database; recruited and trained new hires.

Utah Outdoors Corporation, Orem, Utah
Sales and Marketing Manager (1991 - 1994)

Professional Memberships
Society for Human Resource Management & HR Salt Lake City, Utah Health Recruiters Assoc.

Education
B.A., Business Administration, Brigham Young University

Information Security

JAMES SHARPE

9 Central Avenue
Augusta, Ontario A2A 3B3

Phone: (905) 888-7777
Email: jsharpe@careerbrain.com

PROFESSIONAL PROFILE
★ *Recipient of the highest corporate distinction for commitment to excellence* ★

Award-winning professional combining top quality strategic, operational, and management expertise. Distinguished 20+ year career providing high-level information security solutions designed to safeguard technology investments, services, facilities, and databases. Dynamic and results-oriented leader with outstanding communication, consulting, and team building skills. Recipient of distinguished Wall of Winners Award for excellence.

Information Security & Disaster Recovery
- Expert in Information Security, Disaster Recovery, and Business Continuity
- 20+ years expertise planning and implementing enterprise-class security and recovery solutions to ensure integrity and protection of all critical corporate data and technology services
- Expert in mainframe and enterprise LAN/WAN technologies (Alpha, VAX, HP, Novell, and Unix)

Vendor Management & Contract Negotiations
- Outstanding contract procurement and negotiation skills - proven ability to secure comprehensive, top-quality, cost-effective vendor agreements
- Particularly skilled in managing long-term vendor relationships in a consistent and professional manner

Team Leadership & People Management
- Reputation for building and leading strong high-performance teams
- Ability to create high team morale, and motivate teams to consistently meet and exceed corporate and departmental objectives
- Recognized for ability to create a positive and productive environment that effectively reduces staff turnover

PROFESSIONAL EXPERIENCE

ALPHA RETAIL CORPORATION, Toronto, Ontario
Rapid advancement through senior technology and information security positions on the strength of advanced strategic planning, team leadership, process improvement, cost control, and vendor negotiation and relationship management capabilities.

CHIEF INFORMATION SECURITY OFFICER   1997 - 2000
Senior technology position charged with the strategic planning, maintenance, implementation, administration, and interpretation of all Information Security policies, standards, guidelines, and procedures across the organization to safeguard the corporation's vital technology services, facilities, and databases. Concurrently tasked with managing key technology projects and vendor negotiations. *Achievements include:*
- Revitalized the integrity of all security privileges, and established comprehensive security and disaster recovery protocols that exceeded all audit security recommendations.
- Mandated disaster recovery procedures and offsite storage solutions for the midrange and distributed systems (Alpha, VAX, HP, Novell, and Unix).
- Successfully renegotiated major outsource printing contract with Xerox Canada, securing over $725,000 in savings for Alpha Retail over the term of the agreement, and further identifying a $100,000 cost avoidance opportunity for Xerox.
- Renegotiated critical Comdisco disaster recovery contracts resulting in cost savings of over $700,000, improved client coverage, and the additional elimination of all 6% annual contract increases.

MANAGER -

Disaster Recovery, Data Centre Security, Facilities Management, and Health & Safety   1995 - 1997

Challenged with safeguarding all enterprise technology services, security, and data in the event of a physical disaster. Included comprehensive planning and coordination of all network and mainframe recovery testing, physical security of computing facilities, environmental controls, and executive transportation to recovery site.

- Established infrastructure and procedures to ensure network connectivity to all business clients within 48 hours of disaster, and relocation of corporate executive to recovery site in Bergen, NJ within 3 hours.
- Spearheaded implementation of SAE, effectively reducing erase time by 66% and resolving outstanding issues.
- Successful audited five corporate computing facilities to ensure integrity of environmental and employee safety controls, including fire alarm systems, air conditioning, environmental alerts, and use of UPS/diesel generators.
- Re-evaluated and/or eliminated card access to secured areas, and initiated weekly and monthly audits, reporting, and procedures to ensure security issues.

MANAGER - Program Delivery   1993 - 1995

Selected to build and manage key Project Management Team and coordinate multiple ongoing enterprise initiatives on time and within budget. Direct management of five Project Managers and resource pool of 40 technical specialists.

- Built and maintained an efficient and highly regarded professional unit through solid team leadership, process improvement, priority management skills.
- Effectively controlled staffing costs through judicious training and redeployment within the resource pool.

MANAGER - Network Planning and Support Data & Voice   1992 - 1993

Coordinated all planning, support, and applicable outsourcing for enterprise telecommunications, voice (BPX), and WAN services across the corporation.

- Recommended technology improvements and outsourcing opportunities that allowed for significant cost savings while improving level of service.
- Effectively managed seamless crossover to outsourced voice services.
- Managed ongoing support of newly implemented Spacepac satellite communications system throughout all Associate stores and Express Auto Parts facilities.

MANAGER - Spacepac Satellite Information Systems   1990 - 1992

Concurrently seconded by Senior Technology Team to lead strategic planning and implementation of Spacepac satellite system across 400+ Associate Dealer network. Challenged to establish entire infrastructure and manage cycle through pre-installation, installation, training, and ongoing support.

- Doubled senior management mandate by signing all 400+ Corporate Associate Dealers in first year (met expectation of 200 signed orders within 6 months).
- Successfully managed all hardware and software installations without disruption to day-to-day operations.

MANAGER - Computer Operations / Disaster Recovery   1985 - 1990

Coordinated all online computer services, computer planning, disaster recovery, and system development throughout the organization. Additionally accountable for all negotiation and relationship management with 3rd party vendors and technology partners. Managed 42-person team with 7 direct reports.

- Successfully instituted a number of industry and corporation firsts, including the first online automated cartridge system in Canada, the largest Amdahl single image processor in Ontario, and a new Data Centre Help Desk.
- Replaced and renegotiated over 50% of current vendor relationships unable to meet business needs, resulting in significant cost savings and service improvements.
- Renegotiated all Micrographics contracts to reduce annual costs and turnaround first profit of $500,000.

EDUCATION

Business Administration - Marketing, Centennial College, Toronto, Ontario

Information Technology Consultant

James Sharpe
9 Central Avenue
Dayton, OH 45401
(513) 555-1212
James@careerbrain.com
Page 1 of 2

Summary

Talented, profit-driven professional qualified by nearly 10 years of visible achievements in leading-edge information technologies. Expertise in high-volume territory sales management, demonstrating skills in maintenance of revenue-generating accounts in highly competitive markets. Areas of strength include: key account management, staff recruiting/development, strategic business planning, product presentation, technical staff management, relationship building, client consulting, value-added selling, contract negotiation, project management. Technically proficient in Win95, Win98, Windows NT Workstation, Windows NT server, Novell 3.x and 4.x, SMS, SQL, TCP/IP, cc:Mail, Microsoft Exchange and most Microsoft applications; trained in CISCO and Synoptics Design and Diagnostics.

Recent Consulting Projects

Lloyd Corporation. Orchestrated marketing and configuration of Compaq servers and all peripherals valued at $5 million annually; successfully sold and managed company-wide roll-out of new computer and software encompassing over 7,000 desktops, valued at $1 million in four states. Accountability for placement and management of 10 technical service professionals generating $624,000 annually.

Royal Uniforms of America. Cooperatively secured $2.5+ million nationwide contract for full inventory of desktops, servers, laptops, and peripherals with services including setup/configurations, depot repair, and on-site support at 500 locations.

Dayton School Board. Provided expertise in $1.2 million sale consisting of 550 computers with complete setup and configuration to desktop; successfully negotiated service agreements valued at $325,000 annually.

United States Department of Defense. Participated in sale of over 600 machines valued at $1.5 million with four technical professionals generating $625,000 annually.

Western Hospital. Key player in successful marketing complete Intranet and online policy manual ($60,000), total help desk solutions ($89,000), various service agreements ($50,000 annually), and technical personnel ($120,000 annually).

Navy Technology Center. Successfully directed installation and configuration of all LAN/WAN equipment (3Com) purchased for two-story building and valued at $250,000.

Garcia Industries, LTD. Placement and management of four technical professionals generating $350,000 annually.

Professional Experience

United Technologies, 1996 - Present
Director of Technical Service & Sales

- Manage $3.2 million full-service profit center supporting business development and technical service efforts for computer reseller/integrator generating $12 million in annual revenues.
- Direct workflow of 12 in-house and 30 on-site technical associates involved in repair and service of hardware from all major manufacturers in addition to LAN/WAN network design, support, and maintenance.
- Key member of sales function focused on new business development, client needs analysis, product/service presentation, suggestive/strategic selling, and extensive ongoing value-added selling, customer service, and problem resolution.

- Oversee special projects, workflow management, quality assurance, and technical troubleshooting; significant achievements managing priorities under pressure while maintaining positive client relations.
- Credited with increasing number of technicians from 17 to 42, doubling service department revenues within two years while increasing response time to fewer than eight business hours and maintaining less than 15 percent employee turnover.

Southeastern Capital, 1992 - 1996
Senior Engineer
- Orchestrated on-site technical services at corporate headquarters for four years; instrumental in placement and management of 11 on-site technicians; spearheaded numerous special projects to assure quality and efficient information management for all accounts.
- Supported 1,200 PCs, 300 printers, 14 NT file servers, and 12 Novell servers and provided support on Windows 3.x, Win95, Windows NT Workstation, Windows NT server, Novell 3.x SMS 1.1, SQL, TCP/IP, cc:Mail, and all Microsoft applications.
- Managed entire quick response team for headquarters and several remote sites including all desktop and server-related hardware or software problems.
- Project manager of NT roll-out team, responsible for converting over 1,200 PCs to Windows NT 3.51 workstation and 12 NT servers with back-office products.

Helwett-Packard, 1990 - 1992
Technical Services Manager/Sales Representative
- Directed daily shop operations, sales, inventory control, call dispatching and weekly reporting for small organization offering full line of information technology solutions; instrumental in increasing annual revenues from $500,000 to $1.5 million.
- Gained valuable background in troubleshooting, maintenance and repair of all types of computer systems, printers, monitors; setup, supported, and administered several Netware servers and supported Windows and DOS applications.

Education/Certification
Dayton University, Dayton, OH, BS in Computer Information Technology
Certified in MCP, NT Workstation, NT Server

Information Technology Instructor

Jane Swift
9 Central Avenue
Sterling Heights, Michigan 48310
(810) 555-1212
Jane@careerbrain.com

Qualified computer training specialist and information technology instructor. Trained and instructed numerous accounts for Fortune 500 companies. Known for compliance and clarity; regarded for competence and creativity. Areas of expertise include:

computer training and coaching	technical writing	presentations/demonstrations
syllabus composition	resource documentation	technology instruction
Internet/e-mail	Microsoft certified	

Career Summary

Computer Trainer - certified in Microsoft products; competent in numerous Windows applications.

Technical Writer - developed user manuals, technical documentation, classroom syllabus design, presentations, and demonstrations.

Freelance Employment Columnist - for the *Business News.*

Employment Specialist - trained, evaluated, and interviewed prospective employees; effectively matched qualified candidates with positions.

Guest Speaker/Facilitator - speak for various groups and organizations; facilitate job search and career enhancement workshops.

Memberships - American Society for Training and Development (ASTD), National Association for Job Search Training (NAJST).

Computer Expertise

Word Processing: Microsoft Word, AmiPro
Operating Systems: Windows 3.1/95/98, OS/2
Graphics: PowerPoint, Harvard Graphics
Spreadsheets: Microsoft Excel, Lotus 1-2-3
Database Management: Microsoft Access
Other: E-mail/Internet, PROFS

Experience

Chicago Medical Center, Information Analyst	1999 - Present
Remote Solutions, Information Technology Trainer/Consultant	1997 - 1999
Offsite Resources and Services, Trainer/Staffing Specialist	1995 - 1997
Career Counseling Services, Owner	1995 - Present
Chicago Business Center, Word Processing Specialist	1993 - 1995

Education and Professional Development

University of Michigan, BA
Oakland Tech, AAS

Information Technology Management

Jane Swift
28 Lochnivar Lane
Rochester, New York 14611
585-258-2196 • E-mail: janeswift@aol.com

IT PROJECT MANAGEMENT / BUSINESS PLANNING / MANAGEMENT CONSULTING

Dynamic professional with demonstrated capacity to effectively manage a variety of IT consulting projects. Excellent ability to develop client rapport and assess client needs. Experience defining project specifications, establishing project goals and deliverables, and communicating objectives to inter-disciplinary project teams. Experience participating on management teams for multi-million dollar projects and supervising the activities of up to 25 IT professionals, as part of a larger project team. Additional capabilities in the areas of marketing, sales support, and business planning.

PROFESSIONAL EXPERIENCE

Project Manager, Salient Design Corporation; Chicago, Illinois   **May 1999 - Jan. 2003**
Managed projects that defined client needs and developed technology solutions to meet clients' business objectives in the areas of e-commerce solutions, website development and implementation, network and Client Server applications, and user-friendly front-end systems.

- Met with clients to assess needs, identify key challenges, and define project scope and deliverables.
- Facilitated client workshops to gather critical information and establish strategic vision as it related to technology projects.
- Developed project specifications and communicated project goals to technology teams.
- Provided leadership to cross-functional teams encompassing software developers, systems engineers, web designers, and graphic artists.
- Directed testing and evaluation of projects at established integration points to assess progress and identify key functionality issues.
- Reported to clients on project status and served as liaison to key customer contacts.
- Conducted User Acceptance Testing (UAT) at key points in application development to ensure clients' requirements were being met.
- Supported sales team in responding to Requests for Proposal (RFP) and Requests for Information (RFI), and preparing presentations to prospective clients.

Significant Projects:

Played an integral role in team management of $12 million project to develop web-based applications for The American Diabetes Association. Managed activities of inter-disciplinary team, including six representatives of client organization. Tested applications and developed text scripts to meet client's needs.

Supervised testing during implementation phase of project that used Visual Basic and MS Sequel Server to develop a front-end system that improved end-user efficiency by over 90% for Foundation Life Insurance Company.

Directed the activities of 20-person team charged with building a complex Website for Voyageur Unlimited, an Internet-based travel agency. Interdisciplinary project team included website developers, graphic artists, engineers, and programmers. This $2.2 million project was delivered ahead of schedule and on budget.

Led team that conducted technology assessment for INVESTCO, a consortium of five multi-national banks providing 50% of ATM services in Costa Rica and Argentina. Assessed existing systems and networks, and collected information necessary to develop proposals for migration of this business to the Internet.

Served in project leadership roles for engagements with various US and international firms, including Agilent, Sun Oil, Hurst Interactive Radionet, and PRA Rio (Brazilian on-line grocer).

ADDITIONAL EXPERIENCE

Office Manager / Sales Agent, Redmond & Sons Insurance Brokerage; Brooklyn, New York   **1995 - 1999**
Fulfilled a broad array of operations management, customer service, and strategic planning functions for this insurance firm writing property and casualty policies for small businesses and individuals.
- Assisted agency owner/manager in developing marketing strategies for new and existing products.
- Developed new business through field sales calls to automotive dealerships.
- Addressed client concerns and functioned as liaison between insurance companies and clients.
- Implemented office procedures and performed general office duties, as required.

Special Project:

Played an integral role in developing new line of business and establishing separate operating entity to offer lines of personal auto insurance to brokerages at the wholesale level. Researched and established contacts with potential strategic partners and designed marketing plan for this new business venture. Selected site for new offices, procured furniture and equipment, and developed operating procedures. Defined staffing needs and interviewed, hired, and trained office employees.

EDUCATION

Bachelor of Arts, Sociology   **June 1995**
(Minors in Business Administration, Philosophy, and Socio-Legal Studies)
State University of New York at Stonybrook; Stonybrook, New York
GPA: 3.7/4.0; Dean's List; Student Mentor; Special Olympics volunteer coach

PROFESSIONAL DEVELOPMENT

Project Management Training (Salient Development Corporation)
Seven Habits of Highly Effective People (seminar)

TECHNICAL KNOWLEDGE

Working Knowledge of:
Windows 2000, Windows 95/98, Windows NT, MS Office, MS Project,
Visio, Sequel Server (7.0 / 2000), HTML, Cold Fusion, Sequel, Tracker.

Exposure to:
JAVA Script, ASP Script, Visual Basic, E-prise, Blue Martini, Visual Source Safe,
Mercury WinRunner, plus various other web application testing and automation tools,
configuration management tools, telecommunications applications.

LANGUAGE SKILLS

Conversational Spanish and Portuguese

References Available Upon Request

Insurance Claims

Jane Swift
9 Central Avenue
Yonkers, NY 10701

(914) 555-1212
Jane@careerbrain.com

Career Profile

High-energy, cross-functional background as resourceful fast-track insurance claims specialist with an outstanding record of success in winning settlements and reducing claims payouts to acceptable and just amounts. Investigate, negotiate, and settle complex claims, from beginning stages up to trial, for Hartford and Aetna.

Areas of Expertise

Administration

- organized and effective performance in high-pressure environments
- presentation development and delivery
- heavy phones/switchboard
- word processing and spreadsheet development (type 60 words per minute)
- Microsoft Office, Internet, and Intranet proficiency
- claims investigation with meticulous documentation
- skilled customer care

Insurance Claims

- commercial and personal lines liability
- property damage and bodily injury claims
- claimant, attorney, and litigation representation
- settlement and target value range setting
- general liability, auto, homeowners, and products liability
- injury exposure values
- complex arbitration and mediation negotiation
- medical and liability evaluation

Highlights

- Handle case load of up to 230 pending commercial and personal lines claims. Establish contact within 24 hours, maintain impeccable documentation, and determine value of case based on liability/injury. Decide claim values up to $50,000. Negotiate/settle cases in mediation, arbitration, or litigation. Productive in judge's chambers, courtroom, or at mediation table.
- Delivered a $15,000 saving to Hartford by obtaining a defense verdict on a case that a judge suggested Hartford "buy out" for $15,000. Communicated with attorneys, evaluated liability/facts and determined feasibility for trial. Case went to trial and Hartford paid nothing but legal costs.
- Saved Aetna $40,000 on complex $100,000 second-degree burn claim by determining case's suitability for mediation, and meeting with judge and plaintiff's attorneys. Case was settled for a fair $60,000 without incurring major legal costs for Aetna.
- Promoted onto Aetna fast-track after only one year; became the youngest adjuster in company history. Track record of positive mediation, arbitration, and litigation outcomes is equal to or better than that of more senior professionals.
- Possess outstanding administrative/organizational skills, superior presentation and negotiation abilities, a passion for excellence, and a contagious enthusiasm. Work well in independent or team environments. Tenacious, with the stamina needed to function in high-pressure environments.

Employment

Hartford Insurance Corp., Claims Representative	1998 to Present
Aetna Claims Services	
Claims Specialist	1997 to 1998
Fast-track Representative	1995 to 1997
Claims Assistant	1994 to 1995

Education and Professional Development

A.A.S. in Business, Insurance, and Real Estate, Bronxville Community College
Pepperdine Law University: Two-day Negotiation Seminar
Industry Courses: Commercial General Liability, Claims Statements, Property Casualty Principles, Litigation Guidelines, Medical Terminology and Treatment, How to Handle Cases to Avoid Litigation, Accurate Reserving

Insurance Executive

James Sharpe
9 Central Avenue
Memphis, TN 38137
(901) 555-1212
James@careerbrain.com
Page 1 of 2

Career Profile

- Over ten years background in casualty insurance.
- Key player in the building of one of the nation's top ten insurers.
- Senior Vice President and Core Management Team member of Casualty Insurance. Recognized as an astute visionary, delivering fresh perspectives and keen assessments using intellect, judgement, and character. Known for making and upholding tough decisions.

Areas of Expertise

Management Skills:

- program creation/strategic planning
- resource development
- multimillion-dollar budget creation
- budget management/cost controls
- corporate restructuring
- relationship and team building
- boardroom-level presentations

Insurance Experience:

- loss development and analysis
- high-level claims analysis and resolution
- high exposure claims
- severe injury and multiple policy management
- complex litigation management
- medical profession liability policies
- reserving and settlement authority

Executive Highlights

- *Accelerated Growth*
  During senior management tenure, helped to grow company from 3,000 to 7,500 policyholders, adding a wide range of clients. Growth exploded business and caused expansion of department from 15 to 50 employees.
- *Financial Analysis and Cost Improvement*
  Handled complex financial analysis and legal cost containment. Reduced litigation costs by 15% to 20%. Streamlined claims handling process by enabling claims examiners to handle larger caseloads through realignment of custodial tasks to clerical staff. Collaborated with company actuaries to interpret and act upon loss trends and developments.
- *Profit and Loss*
  Developed highly accurate, multimillion dollar budgets. In addition, effective personal handling of reserving and settlement authority, legal cost containment, favorable trial results, and efficiency measures directly affected corporate bottom line.
- *New Systems and Technology*
  Significantly reduced legal costs through research, development, and implementation of innovative automated legal processing and auditing program.
- *Business Reorganization*
  Following CI's recent acquisition, collaborated as key member of transition team to develop and implement efficient reorganization plan to achieve efficiency gains.
- *Career Advancement*
  Fast-tracked from claims representative to vice president in four years. Was handpicked, recruited, and mentored by CEO during CI's initial period of accelerated growth.

Employment

Casualty Insurance (CI), Memphis, TN

• Senior Vice President	1999 to present
• Vice President	1993 to 1998
• Claims Manager	1992 to 1993
• Claims Supervisor	1991 to 1992
• Claims Representative	1990 to 1991

- *Management Summary*

  Report directly to the CEO and Board of Directors. Oversee two direct reports administering activities over 60 headquarters and branch staff members. Direct and manage claims reserved in excess of $900 million, handling reserving and settlement of individual claims of up to $1 million.

  Daily functions include $4 million budget development and management, staffing, cost control, appointment of legal counsel, policy creation, determination of complex coverage issues, high-exposure claims monitoring, and interface with re-insurers/excess insurers.

- *Significant Achievements*

  Track record of wide ranging contributions in systems development, cost containment, and claims management. Maintained severity at flat levels for the past five years, reduced litigation costs, and improved beneficial trial results. Fast-tracked from claims representative to VP in four years.

Professional Development

American Management Association continuing professional development courses include annual seminars on insurance issues, Accounting for Non-Financial Executives, Managing Conflict, Interpersonal Skills, Management of Reciprocals and Mutuals.

Education

Bachelor of Science in Biology, Memphis State University, Pre-Med Program

Internet Technology Consultant

James Sharpe

9 Central Avenue
Yonkers, NY 10708

Page One of Two

(914) 961-8844
jsharpe@careerbrainl.com

Internet Technology and eBusiness Consultant

- Contributed to launch of hundreds of Web sites including large-scale, multi-million dollar initiatives.
- Skilled at analyzing struggling projects, creating new action plans and prototypes, obtaining stakeholder buy-in, managing design and programming staff to meet goals, and testing.
- Won new business through participation in presentations and pitches and client relationship management.
- Employed hands-on technical experience and broad-based knowledge of information systems to discover solutions to organizational challenges.
- Transformed business processes, utilizing Internet technologies, to improve sales, customer relations, and internal communication.
- Demonstrated competencies: Project Management, Application Development, Information Architecture, Team Building, Leadership, Resource Management, Analytical Thinking, Prototyping, Writing, Presentations, Client Service, Problem Solving, and Employee Training & Development.
- Willing to travel and relocate.

Technical Skills

Web Languages	HTML, DHTML, JavaScript, Cascading Style Sheets, XML/XSL
Server-Side Scripting Languages	Cold Fusion, PHP, ASP
Operating Systems	Unix/Linux, Windows 95/98/NT
Internet Applications	Macromedia Homesite, Cold Fusion Studio, Netscape Navigator, Internet Explorer, DSM (content management), FTP, shell clients, email
Applications	Adobe PhotoShop, MS Office, Adobe Illustrator, MS Project
Database	Oracle

Experience

WebServices Corporation (www.webservices.com), New York, NY   1998-2002
Manager, Site Building (8/00-2/02)
Senior Site Builder (6/99-8/00)
Site Builder (1/99-6/99)
Production Specialist (6/98-1/99)
Assumed increasingly responsible positions for this start-up product and service Web development company with 80 employees. Managed up to 12 staff to translate graphic designs into Web sites and ensure quality/integrity of the client-side code. Accountable for hiring, training, reviews, termination, resource allocation, budget management, and client service. Augmented sales force in scoping new business, writing proposals, and delivering pitches.
Highlights:

- Increased team's ability to meet project objectives by introducing development methodologies.
- Envisioned and implemented a Quality Assurance and documentation process to track approvals and notes at each stage of a project, resulting in increased controls and easier project reviews.
- Initiated and developed a departmental intranet, decreasing the need for meetings and increasing understanding of relation of projects to events and directions in the industry.
- Developed a process that reduced project estimation and pricing time by approximately 50%.

James Sharpe

WebServices Corporation (Continued)
- Prevented loss of millions of dollars of business from two clients through meetings and training.
- Spearheaded company's policy for supporting Netscape Navigator 6 and other Web technologies.
- Turned around a struggling multi-vendor, multi-million dollar project to build a loan trading application. Built a prototype which was referenced by the client as "what they want" throughout the project life-cycle.
- Completed Hard Rock Cafe Web site and reservation system in four weeks after assuming leadership of this project, which was six months overdue and approximately $50,000 over budget. Results: Full payment of fees and client received in excess of ten times their ROI in first year.
- Trained Fortune 100 clients in Hong Kong, Tokyo, and London before launching their global intranet. Wrote training documents and scheduled live, online training sessions at night to accommodate time differences.
- Developed a prototype, new screen plan, and templates for AIG to convert a traditional desktop application plan into a Web application for trade credit insurance.
- Built an eCommerce application, enabling customers to order consumer research data reports online. This application automatically featured the current month's highlighted reports.
- Designed and implemented an interface that translated a dot-com CD warehouse's transaction data into a variety of daily financial reports.
- Collaborated with graphic designers to devise one of the first "email style" Web message boards for an online learning application.
- Authored an in-house, company-wide training program to integrate a large number of new employees and facilitate an understanding of how roles fit together for project success.

Computer Development Center, New York, NY   1996-1998
Studio Director
Launched multiple, small Web sites for this retail operation. Accountable for client consulting, user-interface development, and Web site design / production.
Highlights:
- Devised a series of questions to help define project requirements.
- Implemented one of the first Amazon.com Associates bookstores for a fiction author.

Education

Bachelor of Arts, Vassar College (www.vassar.edu)
Concentration in Mathematics (including Computer Science) and History

Investment Banking Executive

James Sharpe
9 Central Avenue
Fox Hills, CA 90230

(310) 555-1212
James@careerbrain.com
Page 1 of 2

Investment Banking/Telecommunications/Media

- Fast-track and comprehensive career path to Vice President in Investment Banking for Wells Fargo Securities. Wide experience in media and telecommunications industries.
- Originate, execute, and close deals representing a career total of $5.6 billion. Author and deliver dynamic Board of Director-level presentations, achieving bottom-line results through a blending of financial acuity, industry knowledge, and humor. Proactively originated and managed 18 months of VP-level projects as an associate. Accomplished in M&A cost analysis, valuation, and due diligence.

Areas of Knowledge and Expertise

● Telecommunications	● Media/entertainment	● Equity
● Equity-linked	● Fixed income	● IPOs and secondaries
● Mergers/acquisitions	● Private placements	● Debt financing
● Corporate finance	● Origination	● Fairness opinions
● M&A cost analysis	● Valuation	● Due diligence
● Client presentations	● Team building	● Research
● Internet	● MS Office Suite	

Career Highlights

- Originated and closed a $15 million convertible mandate for MANEX (revenue: $4 million). Managed origination effort, wrote and led all presentations, partnered with team to execute transaction, and coordinated with CEO of investment banking. Created road slide shows, wrote valuation, and performed due diligence.
- Originated and currently executing a $10 million private placement mandate for an Internet retailer of collectibles (anticipated revenue: $700,000). Created and co-led all presentations. Currently working with team to execute transaction. Presently writing valuation and projections.
- Originated research relationship with the Houston Group (revenue: $50,000). Persistently contacted client to originate relationship. Authored and led all presentations. Officially commended for presentation's hard facts, energy, and humor.
- Originated $100 million IPO mandate for XTR Pacific. Managed origination effort with head of global equity underwriting. Wrote and delivered all presentations, valuation, and performed due diligence. Effort established quality of presentation skills and precipitated fast-track career path.
- Assisted origination and closing of $100 million sell-side M&A mandate for NuevoTel (revenue: $1 million). Participated in strategic buyer solicitation and closing while an associate. Performed all valuation work, conducted due diligence in Latin America, and co-authored selling memorandum.
- Assisted origination of $350 million IPO mandate for TTI International. Performed all valuation work. Co-wrote and attended presentations.

Career Development

Wells Fargo Investment Banking
Vice President   1998 to present
Senior Associate   1996 to 1998

Developed relationship and led team effort that won and closed a lead-managed, $15 million convertible issue for small cap MANEX. Currently executing a personally originated $10 million private placement mandate for Internet retailer of collectibles. Originated co-managed mandate for $100 million IPO of Pacific Rim communications company (XTR Pacific). Originated research relationship with satellite communications operator (Houston Group). Advised privately held Latin American communications company (NuevoTel) on $100 million strategic sale.

James Sharpe (310) 555-1212
page 2 of 2

Conglomerate Media
Corporate Consultant   1996
  Assisted in evaluation of offering memoranda and investment banking proposals. Advised Conglomerate
  Media on entry options into textbook publishing, focusing on strategic fit, cross licensing opportunities, and
  return on invested capital.

Price Waterhouse
Senior Investment Banking Associate   1994 to 1996
  Won $350 million IPO mandate for global communications firm (TTI International). Delivered fairness
  opinions for sale of publishing companies.

First Houston Corp.
Associate in Investment Banking   1990 to 1994
  Assisted in start-to-finish origination and closing of buy-side mandate for Casualty Underwriters Insurance
  Corp. Co-wrote fairness opinion. Co-authored valuation models and performed due diligence. Involved in
  capital markets transactions for large cap clients. Total capital raised: $500 million.

Education, Certification, and Registrations
M.B.A. Northwestern University
B.A. University of Houston
Certificate: Investment Banking, University of California, Berkeley
  Series 63, 7

Law Enforcement

James Sharpe

9 Central Avenue
Kansas City, Missouri 64141

jsharpe@careerbrain.com

Home: 913.565.8521
Cell: 913.375.3211

LAW ENFORCEMENT PROFESSIONAL

SUMMARY OF QUALIFICATIONS

- Competent disciplined Military Police Officer who demonstrates high standards of professional conduct. Self-starter with strong planning, organizing, coordinating and leadership skills. Consistently meet deadlines and objectives; work well under pressure.
- Possess the knowledge and experience required for managers, administrators, and supervisors to function more effectively in all types of organizations.
- Articulate and effective communicator, proven ability to work with diverse population of people regardless of race, gender, religion or ethnicity. Consistently maintain excellent relationships with superiors, subordinates, staff, directors and military families. Work well as part of the team or independently.
- Over 15 years of successful experience in law enforcement and corrections activities such as:
    - Planning and execution of law enforcement and crime prevention operations to include undercover and drug suppression activities, traffic control operations, and protective services for dignitaries.
    - Development and establishment of physical security standard operating procedures in the area of law enforcement operations, security and control of maximum custody inmates, and inventory and preservation of evidence.
    - Direct support coordination with local and federal law enforcement agencies.
- Track record for identifying complex administrative problems; resourceful in developing and implementing creative solutions resulting in increased productivity with enhanced sensitivity to safety, cost and efficiency.
- Devised and prepared lesson plans, materials, training aids and demonstrations to effectively convey critical concepts and factual knowledge in law enforcement activities and maximum custody operations.
- Fluent in English and Polish.

PROFESSIONAL SKILLS

Leadership

- Professional achievements and ability to lead, in any organizational environment, contributed immeasurably to sustained superior performance. Effectively led and managed organizations ranging in size from 30 to 300 military and civilian personnel in a wide range of missions.
- Personal time management concepts and leadership abilities resulted in exceptional performance by subordinates. Awarded the Army Meritorious Service Medal for exceptional service in training and leadership.
- Inspired successful team effort to exceed US Army recruiting program and retention goals by 30%.

Training

- Developed and implemented training activities to achieve mission requirements in a comfortable and secure atmosphere. Conceptualized a certification program for new soldiers assigned to the Special Housing Unit that was emulated throughout the institution.
- Within the confines of safety and common sense, provided challenging training that inspired excellence, initiative, enthusiasm and eagerness to learn. Recognized with the Army Commendation Medal for exceptional service while performing duties as the Battalion Training Officer.
- Developed engaging daily classroom presentations; reviewed and discussed lesson objectives and after action performances. Provided clear explanation, creative approaches and extra tutoring as needed.

James Sharpe   page 2

Analytical

- Innovative problem solver who draws upon in-depth knowledge and experience while supervising control and security of maximum custody inmates.
- Initiated new programs in response to identified deficiencies and training needs that resulted in a safer environment for both inmates and staff alike.
- Unique ability to coordinate group efforts toward attainment of common goals. Exceeded requirements of assigned duties and position resulting in special recognition.

Decision-Making

- Most capable of making independent judgements and decisions required to run highly effective organizations.
- Experienced in the reorganization of administrative and operation structure to include development and implementation of new policies and procedures. Developed and implemented the system integration, training and operation of the National Criminal Investigation Center (NCIC) into daily law enforcement operations.
- Consistently demonstrated outstanding professional and supervisory ability, and unwavering self-reliance in daily performance of duties.

Planning

- Strong planning and negotiating skills resulted in a $30,000 budget increase in support of criminal investigations throughout the battalion area of operation. Recognized with the Army Commendation medal for exceptional commendatory service while performing duties as the Criminal Investigation Planning Officer.
- Designed and implemented US Army and US Army Reserve recruiting programs for high schools, colleges and universities that assisted recruiters and staff in building and maintaining an effective school recruiting program.
- Spearheaded the first proclamation signed by the governor of Kansas in an effort to support the administration of the Armed Services Vocational Aptitude Battery (ASVAB) test for all high schools in the State of Kansas.

Supervision

- Know and understand worth and dignity of subordinates and successfully integrate this human element in daily leadership. Advised and counseled individual soldiers in military qualification skills and on aspects of military and civilian life.
- Worked on human relations problems arising with the introduction of newly establish standards and work procedures.
- Genuine desire to be of service to people.

Computers

- Experienced with spreadsheet inventory management in Microsoft Excel and Microsoft Access.
- Proficient in several windows-based programs, including Microsoft Word, Outlook Express, and PowerPoint.
- Coordinated the complete automation, integration and training for all recruiters assigned to the unit increasing productivity by 60%.

WORK EXPERIENCE

Military Police Officer, U.S. Army, 1990 - Present

EDUCATION

Master of Science, Public Administration, Central Michigan University, Fort Leavenworth, Kansas, 2001
Bachelor of Arts, Political Science, University of Warsaw, Warsaw, Poland, 1989
Combined Arms and Services Staff School, Fort Leavenworth, Kansas, 1996
Military Police Officer Advance Course, Fort McClellan, Alabama, 1995
Military Police Officer Basic Course, Fort McClellan, Alabama, 1990

Law Firm Internship

Jane Swift
9 Central Avenue
Columbus, OH 43215

(614) 555-1212
Jane@careerbrain.com

OBJECTIVE

A LAW FIRM INTERNSHIP which will utilize strong organizational skills, effective research skills, and the proven ability to get the job done.

OVERVIEW

- Organized, highly-trained individual with exceptional follow-through abilities and excellent management skills, able to plan and oversee projects from concept to successful conclusion.
- Strong interpersonal skills; proven ability to work well with individuals on all levels.
- Possess strong problem resolution skills.
- Dedicated individual; achieved reputation for consistently going beyond what is required.
- Proven ability to gather, extract, identify, and effectively utilize data.
- Computer literate; proficient in using current business software; exposure to legal packages: West Law and Lexus Nexus.

EDUCATION

OHIO STATE UNIVERSITY SCHOOL OF LAW, Columbus, OH
- Juris Doctor candidate, May 2001
- Current course work: Contracts, Property, Administrative Law, Torts, Constitutional Law, American Legal History, Civil Procedure, Criminal Law

OHIO UNIVERSITY, Athens, OH
Bachelor of Science in Language: German   May 1998
- Concentration: International Business
- GPA: 3.67   • Honors: *cum laude*
- Volunteer Tutor: tutored disadvantaged children, three times per week as part of the Athens Schools project. Taught English, Reading, and Math one-to-one. Also taught foreign-born students with limited English proficiency.

UNIVERSITY OF TUEBINGEN, Tuebingen, Germany
Semester Abroad: Full Matriculation into a German speaking university.   January - July 1997

ACHIEVEMENTS

- Achieved superior score on the PWD business German test developed by the Goethe Institute and the Association of German Chambers of Industry and Commerce, signifying an advanced level of German language proficiency in a business environment.
- Recognized for outstanding achievement by the German Department; First Honors once; Second Honors twice; Dean's List twice.

EMPLOYMENT

Summer 1998, CAMP NITTANY, Mohawk, PA   Head Counselor
- Supervised two assistant counselors in servicing 20 eight-year-old campers.
- Recognized for achieving excellent rapport with both campers and parents.

1996 - 1998, ACCESS SERVICES; OHIO UNIVERSITY LIBRARY, Athens, OH   Security Manager
- Supervised staff of three in maintaining security and order during late hours.
- Controlled access to the Library.

Summers 1996 & 1997, CERTIFIED TAX CONSULTANTS, New York, NY   Accounting Assistant
- Interviewed clients to gather information for tax returns.
- Maintained organized flow.
- Utilized computer software to produce final documents.

Lawyer (Entry-Level)

JAMES SHARPE

9 Central Avenue, Chicago, IL 60606 (312) 555-1212, James@careerbrain.com

Page 1 of 2

OBJECTIVE

A position as an Associate in a Law Firm where I can expand my knowledge and gain experience and expertise in the area of Corporate and Transitional Law.

SELECTED REFERENCES

- "…professional in manner, dress and approach…well-educated, articulate and well prepared…passionate, committed and focused on a goal-or goals…ethical and honest…will make a difference wherever (he) goes…," John Bryant, Chairman, Founder and CEO, OPERATION HOPE.
- "…outstanding young man, intelligent, capable and hard-working…well respected by his peers, a team member, a natural leader that I recommend for scholarship…," Marc Massout, Accounting Professor, Claremont McKenna College.

EDUCATION

UNIVERSITY OF CHICAGO LAW SCHOOL, Chicago, IL.

J.D. Degree, to be awarded June, 2000
- **Student Lawyer**, University of Chicago Mandel Legal Aid Clinic
  Member, Employment Discrimination Project, 1999 to Present
- **Member & Prospective Student Host Coordinator**, Student Admissions Committee, 1997 to 1998
- **Treasurer**, Black Law Students Association, 1998 to 1999

CLAREMONT McKENNA COLLEGE, Claremont, CA
- **B.A. Degree, Dual Major, Government & Economics/Accounting**
- **Graduated with Honors**, May 1997
- **Awarded "Claremont McKenna College Scholar"**
- **Appointed Member of Student Board,** Academic & Student Affairs Committee
- **Awarded 4-Year Merit Scholarship**
- **Senior Thesis:** "The Nature and Extent of Police Power in the United States" (Tracing Evolution from Plato, Socrates, Machiavelli to Current Community-Based Policing)

PROFESSIONAL EXPERIENCE

Legal Experience

1998 to present   **UNIVERSITY OF CHICAGO MANDEL LEGAL AID CLINIC**, Chicago, IL
Student Lawyer. Member of Employment Discrimination Project. Appeared in Federal Court and State Administrative Court; co-authored a brief submitted to Illinois State Appellate Court. Certified to practice as a Senior Law Student under Illinois Supreme Court Rule 711. Research issues regarding handicapped discrimination, racial discrimination, and procedural issues. Develop legal theories; interview prospective clients; negotiate and opposing counsel; prepare briefs and argumentative memoranda.

1998   **KIRKLAND & ELLIS**, Law Firm, Los Angeles, CA
Summer Associate. Participated in Kirkland & Ellis Institute of Trial Advocacy. Researched and produced memos, gave oral presentations regarding a wide range of legal issues, i.e., real property, trade libel, procedural issues, employment law, environmental matters, white-collar crime.

PROFESSIONAL EXPERIENCE (Continued)

Business Experience

1997   **OPERATION HOPE**, Los Angeles, CA
Summer Intern. Selected to intern directly for the CEO of Organization. Created and reviewed proposals to the Department of Commerce.

Drafted a general framework of proposal and created a condensed synopsis of a specific proposal to operate a Minority Business Development Center in Los Angeles. Contributed promotional ideas and support to launch of Operation Hope Banking Center.

1992 to present   **"REAL MEN COOK" FOUNDATION**, Fundraising Organization, Marina Del Ray, CA
Board Member, 1995 to present, **Executive Administrative Assistant**, Summers, 1990 to 1993 in conjunction with major pharmaceutical company, key member of team to plan, promote, and implement annual fund-raisers for 600 to 800 guests. Funds raised have supported 4 minority medical schools and increased awareness and prevention measures for prostate cancer. Additionally, prepare in-house financial reports for the Program Director.

Government Experience

1996   **U.S. DEPARTMENT OF COMMERCE** (California Task Force), Washington, DC
Summer Intern, researched to assure acquisition of funds and grants allocated for California. Worked directly with Office of Management of Budget as well as HUD. Prepared and delivered oral reports directly to Task Force Director. Helped to evaluate the potential of grants to foster recovery and economic growth in California cities formerly engaged in the defense industry.

1995   **OFFICE OF CONGRESSMAN CRAIG WASHINGTON**, Washington, DC
Summer Intern. Attended committee hearings, researched issues and bills, and corresponded with constituents regarding legislation.

ADDITIONAL REFERENCES AND RELATED DATA AVAILABLE UPON REQUEST

Management Consultant

James Sharpe

9 Central Avenue • Centreville, Virginia 20121 • Phone: (703) 555-1212 • James@careerbrain.com

Professional Profile

A seasoned, highly motivated senior executive with a successful track record in international operations and project management. Recognized for exceptional problem solving and motivational skills as well as the ability to **negotiate, deal, and close successfully across cultural barriers**. Extensive experience in management consulting in diverse industries, ranging from unit construction and mining/drilling operations to industrial equipment procurement, sales and distribution. **Bilingual with extensive international experience**, including Africa, the Middle East, South Asia, and Western Europe.

Areas of Impact

- International Conflict Resolution
- Operation and Project Management
- Global Emergency Planning

- Worldwide Corporate Security
- New Business Development
- International Public Relations

- Risk Assessment
- International Law
- Recruitment/Training

Career Highlights

- Successfully provided diplomatic, risk management, and crisis resolution services to a broad range of Fortune 100 companies, Ambassadors, Heads of State, cabinet ministers, and senior government officials, U.S. and foreign.
- Successfully negotiated, on behalf of Pete's Oil, with an east African government to resolve a cross-cultural crisis and avoid closure of a $1 billion distribution facility.
- Developed and implemented logistics and training programs involving several thousand U.S. and foreign personnel and a $40 million annual budget. Effectively achieved all objectives with a budget savings of 12%.
- Directed Jones & Jones, Big Truck Co., and Movers International in the successful negotiation of more than $15 million of capital equipment sales to a west African government.
- Conducted numerous feasibility studies and risk assessments, both political and economic forecasts, for a variety of projects including gold, platinum and diamond mining, nuclear energy development, port, railroad and packaging facilities.

Employment History

International Affairs Consultant

Professional Services Provided to: Whitman International, Virginia Properties International, Pete's Oil, Tall Trees, Inc., Rothstein's Petroleum, Movers International, Jones & Jones, Big Truck Company, Top Flight Airlines, Technology USA, PTR International, Ltd., National Telecommunications Foundation, Master Technologies.

National Security Agency

Near East and Africa Referent…Chief of Station…Chief of Operations…Chief of Branch, Counterterrorism…Deputy/Chief of Station.

Education

Juris Doctorate, *International Law*, University of Denver, Denver, CO
Master of Arts, *History*, University of Denver, Denver, CO
Bachelor of Arts, *History*, New College, Sarasota, FL

Marketing Analyst

JANE SWIFT
9 Central Avenue
DEARBORN, MI 48126
(313) 555-1212
Jane@careerbrain.com

EXPERIENCE:

Daytons, Inc. (Detroit, MI)   July 1998 to Present
MARKETING ANALYST - Provide a broad-based flow of data for merchandisers, buyers, Catalog Distribution Center associates, and management to assure continuing high-level profitability of the company's catalog sales. Access all databases by CRT terminal using CRIMS, an on-line system interfacing with ISA, IDB, and MIDB. Computer Analyses focus on:

- Historical applications, such as impact of season, media ads, space, price, and color changes
- Reliable pre-season forecasts of catalog demand patterns and in-season revisions where necessary to maintain inventory control
- Study of inventory turnover in relation to buying estimates, commitments, and quality of merchandise
- Choice of models and development of new ones for item estimating
- Identification of systems problems in estimates above or below plan
- Establishment of recommendations for inventory surplus solutions
- Decision-marketing, planning, scheduling to meet data deadlines

Zachary & Front Advertising, Inc.   New York, NY Summer 1997
OFFICE MANAGER - Arranged for in-house weekly newsletter and biweekly policy memos for new agency. Developed billing system, dealt with clients, and managed clerical staffing.

Tisch Properties   New York, NY Winter 1997
ASSISTANT BOOKKEEPER - Worked with accounts receivable/payable, bank reconciliations

EDUCATION:

State University of Ohio
B.S., Business Administration, 1998
Concentration: Marketing and Management Information Systems

COMPUTER SKILLS:
Visual Basic, C++, FCS-EPS, and SPSS software package

References Available Upon Request

Marketing—Entry Level

Jane Swift

9 Central Avenue (Through May, 1999)
Lexington, Kentucky 40508
(606) 233-5181
jswift@careerbrain.com

(Permanent) 18 Central Park Avenue
Cincinnati, Ohio 45242
(513) 236-0289
jswift@msn.com

PROFILE
Energetic, dedicated Business / Marketing graduate with a proven ability to organize, motivate and contribute quickly and positively to the organization. Looking for the opportunity to join an established, forward thinking team in an entry level capacity with emphasis on marketing, advertising, public relations, or a related field. Strengths and accomplishments include:

- Earned two scholarships to Transylvania University in Lexington, Kentucky.
- Selected to participate in an International Study Program in Costa Rica, 1997.
- Consistently included on Dean's List for high academic achievement.
- Exceptional leadership ability; able to motivate others to appropriate action.
- Self motivated and detail oriented, functioning well in fast paced environments.
- Comfortable and effective handling multiple tasks simultaneously.
- Superior work ethic with the self discipline, focus, and desire to succeed.
- Equally effective working independently or as part of a team.
- Confident and articulate during oral presentation.
- Not bound by geographic region; willing both to travel and relocate.

TRANSFERABLE SKILLS

- Accomplished in base level use and understanding of conversational Spanish.
- Proficient in Microsoft Word, Word Perfect, Excel, Windows 95 and the Internet.
- Strength and experience in artistic design, including brochures and other marketing and communication tools.
- Expertise in planning and executing programmed events.
- Experienced in research and market development planning and implementation.
- Seasoned organizer; participant and leader of many campus groups and activities.
- Committed to volunteer work both on campus and in the community.

INTERNSHIPS
1999 - Greater Lexington Chamber of Commerce, Government Division.
Assisted in conducting research of business-related issues and drafting position and policy statements; attended and reported on meetings of state and local governments; advocate for statutory and regulatory change; reported progress of programs and initiatives; administrative functions as required.

1998 - Preston-Osborne Group, Campaign Central Division.
Researched and compiled background information on clientele for marketing executives within the firm; assembled promotional artwork into presentation portfolio for client education; composed entry for national public relations contest; courier service, data entry, and secretarial duties as required.

EDUCATION
Transylvania University, Lexington, Kentucky
BA Business Administration with Marketing emphasis
Minor in Studio Art
Anticipated graduation date: May, 1999

ACTIVITIES
Delta Delta Delta Sorority member, Officers Council, various chairs, 1995-99
Student Activities Board, Promotion Committee, 1996-97
Transylvania Dance Team, 1996-99
Exhibitor in juried Transylvania art shows, 1998-99

Marketing Management

Jane Swift
9 Central Avenue
Lexington, KY 40579

(606) 555-1212
Jane@careerbrain.com

Profile

Marketing Management ● Promotions Management ● Sales Management

A goal-oriented, decisive manager with 10+ years experience in a corporate sales and marketing environment. Exceptionally creative with effective organizational abilities and interpersonal skills. Powerful leadership and management expertise with especially strong planning, coordinating, and delegating capacities. Solid problem solving abilities. Demonstrated capacity to successfully manage multiple projects and deadlines, coming in on time and within budget.

Demonstrated Strengths

- key account development and relations
- new product introduction
- sales and trend analysis
- target market development
- software proficiency with PowerPoint, Excel, Word, and FM Pro
- presentation development and delivery

- creative purchase incentives and promotions
- sales management
- distributor management
- project management

Selected Achievements

- Received Achievement Award 2 years in a row for double-digit increases in sales and development of promotional strategies and programs.
- Selected as one of 19 managers nationwide to participate in pilot program to restore positive sales growth in Southwest market areas.
- Developed numerous creative merchandising pieces throughout career that increased visibility and sales.
- Key player in several marketing initiatives such as a marketing partnership that brought several major companies together in a massive merchandising program. Effectively managed essential initiatives that positioned Pepsi very competitively.
- Guided distributors to improve sales and marketing figures.
- Increased sales figures 50% in one year in a targeted segment. Increased sales in key accounts an average of 5% and improved feature activity and display performance from 50% to 80%.
- Counseled sales representatives and helped one improve performance from marginal to outstanding in one year.
- Met project deadlines (average lead time 4 - 6 weeks) 98% of the time.

Professional Experience

Pepsi Cola Bottling Company
Promotions Manager, Lexington, KY
1998 to Present

Assist National Sales Manager and key accounts by developing customized, value-added promotions that drive volume and gain ad and display activity. Manager over 150 programs annually. Purchase incentives include cross-merchandising programs with other vendors, coupons, rebates, liquidators, and sweepstakes. Coordinate promotional ideas and programs with creative agencies, sports marketing, and legal departments. Manage project costs and a budget of over $4 million.

Sales and Merchandising Manager, Boston, MA
1997 to 1998

Supervise a team of sales and marketing specialists to increase sales in the Boston/New England markets. Develop distributor incentives. Work alongside distributors and corporate personnel to cultivate key retail accounts, sell product and displays, increase cooler space, and improve merchandising.

Jane Swift
page 2 of 2

Marketing Manager, Chicago, IL   1995 to 1997
Manage territory that generates sales of 40+ million cases of Pepsi products annually--
the region's largest in terms of volume and budget. Work closely with media partners to
foster awareness and develop promotional lineup. Integrate regional marketing efforts
with national brand strategies. Directly accountable for $600,000 budget.

Sales Manager, Phoenix, AZ   1994 to 1995
Aggressively lead targeted incentive programs and promotions. Improve distributor sales
by conducting surveys and developing action plans to capitalize on sales opportunities.
Make frequent calls on buyers. Increase company awareness through development of a
monthly newsletter.

Sales and Marketing Planner, Lexington, KY   1992 to 1994
Assist Regional Manager in managing sales/marketing activities. Develop "how to"
promotional manual for field personnel. Improve media support of promotions in 3 states.
Administer a $200,000 budget.

Education
BS in Business Administration, Major: Marketing, University of Kentucky, Lexington, KY

*"Jane has the unique
ability to motivate a
diverse group to work
together."*
*– Tracy Dodd, President
Delta Delta Delta
Sorority
1997-98*

*"Jane is a team player
and a finisher. She
also possesses strong
individual initiative as
well as creative
project approaches."*
*– Dr. Catherine Crosby,
Professor of Marketing
Transylvania University*

*"Jane shows a strong
desire to learn and to
succeed. The
Chamber is grateful to
have her, and she will
truly be an asset to all
future employers."*
*– William Peterson,
Senior Vice President
Greater Lex Chamber of
Commerce*

Medical Technology Sales

JANE SWIFT
9 Central Avenue
Newport Beach, California 92660

Jswift@careerbrain.com   949-555-1212

MEDICAL INDUSTRY PROFESSIONAL
Training Specialist / Pharmaceutical Sales / Medical Software Support

Radiologic Technology graduate integrating work and education to achieve career goal. Ability to communicate highly technical medical information to professionals, as well as to patients and their families. Persuasive public speaker delivering high-impact presentations to diverse audiences including board of instructors. Expert time manager with tenacity and perseverance to handle rejection without taking it personally. AART License. PC Proficient in MS Office, Lotus and industry-specific software.

EDUCATION

BS in Radiologic Technology with minor in Biology, Orange College, Santa Ana, California, 2002
- Magna Cum Laude Candidate; Deans List, 4 years
- GPA 3.7 / 4.0; Multiple scholarship recipient
- Selective Courses: Medical Terminology, Physics, Microbiology, Human Anatomy and Physiology

Radiologic Internship, Chapman General Hospital, Orange, California
Studied all Radiology modalities by rotating through areas of CV, Mammography, CAT Scan, Special Procedures, Ultrasound, Radiation Oncology, Diagnostic, Surgery, Nuclear Medicine and Patient Care. Observed procedures and participated in hands-on training; completed detailed patient histories.
- Established network of physician contacts by demonstrating exemplary performance and proving competency / reliability in the operating room and at clinical sites.

Associate of Arts, Santa Ana Junior College, Santa Ana, California, 1997
- GPA 3.2 / 4.0
- Selective Courses: Sociology, Psychology, Microbiology

CONTINUING PROFESSIONAL DEVELOPMENT
- Emergency and Triage Seminar, Chapman General Hospital, Orange, California, 10/01
- Trauma Seminar, Chapman General Hospital, Orange, California, 7/01
- Caring for Customer Service, A. D. Banker & Company (8-week course), Tustin, California, 8/90

PROFESSIONAL EXPERIENCE

CHAPMAN GENERAL HOSPITAL, Orange, California   2/01 to Present
CAT Scan Technician (Part time)
Administer quality CAT Scans for outpatients and inpatients, plus emergency and trauma patients, while pinpointing immediate problems to provide patient care. Trained on operation of G.E. and Phillips machines, acquiring knowledge of physics principles. Assess and triage patients according to procedural priorities. Facilitate communication between doctors and patients. Interact with patients' families in crisis situations. Delegate tasks, as necessary, to maintain homeostasis.
- Dispense correct patient contrast and radiation dosage to prevent contraindications.
- React quickly and accurately in trauma situations utilizing critical thinking and reasoning.

Continued on Page 2

ADDITIONAL EXPERIENCE

Accounting Clerk, LEWIS, RYAN & FESTER, Tustin, California   6/96 to 1/00
- Performed general accounting functions for tax and litigation law firm.

Office Manager / Secretary, AUTO SUPPLY OUTLET, Tustin, California   4/96 to 6/96
- Supported six outside account representatives, assisting with direct sales and customer service.

Accounting / Shipping / Line Manager, C&B EMBROIDERY, Tustin, California 11/94 to 4/96
- Supervised quality control and resolved problems as liaison between employees and owners.

Data Entry Clerk, BANK OF AMERICA, Santa Ana, California   2/94 to 11/94
- Rewarded several times for speed and accuracy with large dollar return items.

Office Manager, DELANEY CONSTRUCTION, Santa Ana, California   11/91 to 9/93
- Established business relationships with vendors, Labor Department and OSHA.

Accounting Clerk, CPA FIRM, INC., Anaheim, California   5/90 to 11/91
- Assisted Department Supervisor in this CPA firm; performed A/P, A/R and data entry.

Customer Service Manager, BANKS & COMPANY, INC., Orange, California   6/88 to 5/90
- Delivered train-the-trainer presentations on customer service techniques.

EARLY POSITIONS
Accounting Assistant / Secretary to Owner, 3/88 to 6/88
Reproduction Department Head / Relief Receptionist, 6/87 to 3/88
Rental Store Manager, 8/86 to 6/87
Dental Assistant, 6/85 to 8/86

PROFESSIONAL AFFILIATIONS / CERTIFICATIONS

AART License, 2002; American Registered Radiologic Technologists, Member, 2 years
CPR and Advanced Lifesaving Certifications, 1999
Radiologic Science Club, Charitable Volunteer Coordinator, Member, 2 years

COMMUNITY INVOLVEMENT

Ronald McDonald House: Prepared and served dinner to families through class project, 2001.
Hope House: Collected and delivered clothing and home products through class project, 2000.
Angel Tree: Collected gifts for children of incarcerated parents through church project, 2000.

Military

JAMES SHARPE

9 Central Avenue
Sarasota, FL 34239
(555) 941-1222

OBJECTIVE

To provide leadership and guidance as an *Airport Fire Chief* utilizing extensive training, distinguished service, and experience in the field.

PROFILE

Decorated military Fire Chief with 25+ years of experience in all aspects of fire fighting operations. Consistent record of exceeding standards and expectations by choosing the most challenging assignments that were above and beyond the call of duty. Highly motivated and organized, with a documented ability to motivate and train units and subordinates. Areas of expertise include:

- Fire, Rescue & Recovery
- Emergency Medical Services
- Hazardous Materials

- Politically Sensitive Operations
- Safety Regulations/Standards & Inspections
- Curriculum Development & Instruction

CREDENTIALS

- National Fire Academy Incident Command System Training
- Fire Protection Internships at Skilled, Advanced, and Superintendent Levels
- Fire Protection Management Applications
- On-Scene Commander's Course

- Fire Investigation
- Fire Prevention Technician Course
- Ranger Propane Fire Safety School
- Leadership for Mid-Level & Senior Managers
- Principles of Instructional Systems
- Development

RECORD OF EXPERIENCE

UNITED STATES AIR FORCE   **1967-Present**

Randolph Air Force Base - Texas
Fire Chief, Hazardous Materials Program Manager, and Safety Design Review Authority
- Management of fire fighting teams with a record of encountering numerous fires and medical incidents without injuries and minimal loss.
- Initiated and implemented changes within six fire fighting companies advancing a "satisfactory" inspection rating to an "outstanding" rating by headquarter experts.
- Secured initial accreditation for the Department of Defense from the International Fire Safety Accreditation Council.
- Directed childcare center staff toward flawless fire safety certification.
- Reduced construction costs by $2.5 million, utilizing lower cost materials and procedures.
- Increased OSHA compliance.
- Received an Air Force Achievement Medal for solving problems with the P-23 Fire Vehicle.

Ramstein Air Base - Germany
- Fire Chief, Hazardous Materials Program Manager, and Safety Design Review Authority
- Supervised a department of 95 personnel.
- Directed all operations as "On-Scene Commander" during major aircraft incidents, resulting in zero injuries and minimal damage.
- Presided as final review authority for fire safety designs and installations.

Andrews Air Force Base - Maryland
Fire Chief
- Served as main contact for fire, rescue, and emergency medical services for 234 Air Force families.
- Decreased base fires by 88%.
- Ensured highly visible fire protection for the President, visiting heads of state, and high-ranking dignitaries.
- Created a hazardous material program in a record six-month period.
- Passed OSHA inspection without a single discrepancy.

Eglin Air Force Base - Florida
Deputy Fire Chief
- Led and motivated unit of command from a "barely acceptable" inspection rating to an "excellent" rating by the Air Force Inspector General in only 100 days.
- Pioneered new standards for airfield barrier operations currently used in the United States and six other nations.
- Controlled politically sensitive operations in foreign territory.

Langley Air Force Base - Virginia
Shift Supervisor
- Acted as deputy fire chief in absence of fire chief; supervised 12 fire fighters.
- Participated in a cardiovascular study conducted by the Air Force, which set fitness standards for all active-duty members worldwide.

Los Angeles Air Force Station - California
Station Fire Chief
- Qualified as the youngest person to hold position within the previous 10-year period.
- Oversaw all fire fighting operations for Space Command Tracking Facility.
- Worked with Air Force civil engineers to ensure compliance of all buildings with OSHA safety regulations.

Robins Air Force Base - Georgia
Instructor
- Composed and facilitated curriculum to entry-level USAF fire fighters.
- Initiated and launched new course on the correct handling of toxic materials.
- Recognized as "Instructor of the Year."

Langley Air Force Base - Virginia
Fire Fighter
- Helped direct rescue and recovery missions at air crash sites.
- Awarded "Airman of the Quarter."

Edwards Air Force Base - California
Fire Fighter

Robins Air Force Base - Georgia
Student, United States Air Force Fire Fighting School

HONORS

- Air Force Commendation Medal with Two Oak Leaf Clusters (End of Tour Decoration)
- Meritorious Service Medal with One Oak Leaf Cluster (End of Tour Decoration)
- John P. Morely Memorial Award for Heroism in Lifesaving Operations

MIS Administrator

James Sharpe

9 Central Avenue
Ashburn, VA 20148

(703) 777-7070
Email: jsharpe@careerbrain.com

SUMMARY OF QUALIFICATIONS

Skilled Customer Care Representative/Help Desk Administrator with seven years experience diagnosing and resolving technical/customer inquiries. MCSE Certified. Proficient in Windows-based environments, Internet, and MS Office applications. Strong working knowledge of Telecommunications Products and Services. Able to clearly understand problems and find positive solutions through use of troubleshooting, problem solving, teaming and communication skills. Bilingual English/Russian.

TECHNICAL TRAINING

Strayer College   Falls Church, VA   1998-1999
Diploma of Enterprise Network Professional
- Install and configure MS DOS 6.22, Windows 95/ 98 and Windows NT 4.0 Server and Workstation
- Create and manage user accounts/Establish security policies for accounts
- Configure user/system-specific settings
- Design and implement single and multiple master NT domain models
- Use Windows NT Diagnostics, Event Viewer, and Server Manager for troubleshooting

RELATED WORK EXPERIENCE

Net2000 Communications, Inc.   Herndon, VA   1998-2001
Order Administrator
- Reviewed all paperwork for new and existing orders to ensure accuracy and completeness
- Created new orders in TBS for voice and data services
- Researched customer's accounts utilizing Telecom Business Solutions Software Version 5.0, Saville Billing System, and Sales On-Line database
- Made changes to existing customer accounts, enforced process flows for Revisions, Expedites, and Cancellations
- Maintained Access database regarding order status to ensure accurate reporting
- Trained and mentored new employees
- Contributed to Siebel-TBS Order Integration Project implemented by Net2000 EAI Team
- Recognized as the **Top Producer** in Technical Administration Team

SITEL Corporation   Herndon, VA   1998-1998
Associate Support Engineer
- Provided technical support of HotSync synchronization between Palm personal organizers and desktop PC
- Responded to requests regarding Palm personal organizers hardware/OS software and HotSync conduit data synchronization technology
- Responded to customer calls within designated timeframes

MCI Telecommunications Corporation   Arlington, VA   1996-1997
Customer Service Representative
- Provided superior customer care service while maintaining company objectives
- Researched and updated computerized accounts of MCI customers utilizing the OS/2 IBM database

EDUCATION

Bachelor of Arts, Moscow University, Moscow, Russia, 1981, Major: International Relations

Network Architecture Specialist

Technical Expertise

Applications
Adaptec Easy CD Creator
Adaptec Direct CD
Carbon Copy
Cc Mail
Clarify
HP Colorado Backup
MS Active Sync
MS Office Professional
MS Outlook 98 and 2000
MS Internet Explorer
NetAccess Internet
Netscape
Norton Ghost
Partition Magic
PC Anywhere
Rainbow
Reflection 1
Reflection X
Remedy-ARS
Symantec Norton Antivirus
Visio
Windows CE

Operating Systems
Microsoft Windows 2000
Microsoft Windows NT 4.0
Workstation and Server
Microsoft Windows ME
Microsoft Windows 95, 98
Cisco Router/Switch IOS
MS-DOS
Unix

Hardware
Intel-based Desktops
Intel-based Mobile
  Computers
HP Colorado Tape Backup
Cisco 2500 Series Router
Hewlett Packard Pro Curve
Switches
CD Writer

Protocols & Services
TCP/IP
DHCP
DNS
NetBEUI
Remote Access Service
WINS

Networking
Ethernet
Token Ring
Microsoft Networking

James Sharpe
9 Central Avenue, Denver, CO 8000 • Phone 555.555.1234 • E-mail jsharpe@careerbrain.com

Network Architecture Specialist
Cisco Certified Network Associate

Results-driven, self-motivated professional with solid experience supporting hundreds of users in multiple departments in the corporate environment. Recognized for outstanding support and services, process development, and project management. Able to manage multiple projects simultaneously and to move quickly among projects. Capable of leading or collaborating. Areas of expertise include:

- Network architectures and networking components
- Software and operating system deployment in corporate environments
- PC hardware installation/repair and disk imaging
- Troubleshoot complex operating system problems
- Call tracking, case management, solution integration

Accomplishments

- Reduced help desk calls by developing end-user training and knowledge database.
- Led migration for 3000+ client/server email accounts from HP Open Mail to MS Exchange.
- Developed data collection protocol for BLM Natural Resource Inventory.
- Mentored teammates on technical materials and procedures.
- Built relationships to quickly resolve business critical issues.

Certifications

Technical Certification for MS Network Support Program, 9/99
CCNA - Cisco Certified Network Associate, 8/99

Work History

Technical Support Engineer, ABC Technologies (Holt Services), 4/00 - Present
E-mail Migration Specialist, ABC Technologies (Holt Services), 11/99 - 4/00
PC Technician, RBM (The Cameo Group) 5/99 - 11/99
Customer Support Specialist, Center Partners, 9/98 - 5/99
Recycle Technician, RBM (WasteNot Recycling) 2/98 - 9/98
Soil Scientist, Bureau of Land Management, 5/97 - 10/97

Education

Pacific Institute Workshop - Goal Setting, Achievement, Motivation, 1/98
B.S., Soil Science: Environmental Mgt. - CA Polytechnic State University, 12/97
A.A., Mathematics, Mira Costa College, 7/94

Awards and Honors

ABC Shining Star Award for Outstanding Customer Service, October '01
Outstanding Services to Technical Services Division, January '00
High Quality Customer Service Award, RBM Technical Support March & April '99

Nurse

JANE SWIFT
813-428-3333

1345 Orange Circle, Tampa, FL 33602

NURSING PROFESSIONAL
Legal Nurse Consultant ... Registered Nurse

QUALIFICATIONS SUMMARY

Competent and knowledgeable medical professional with more than 10 years of increasingly responsible experience. Effective critical thinking, problem solving, and interpersonal skills.

EXPERTISE

Legal Nurse Consultant

- Direct initial client assessments to identify potential liability
- Organize and review medical charts and records
- Review surgeon and expert witness depositions

Nursing Expertise

- Direct patient care and advocacy
- Triage
- Intubation and airway management
- Medication administration
- Cardiac monitoring and EKG rhythm interpretation
- Conscious sedation
- Counseling and education
- Chart review quality assurance

EDUCATION

Legal Nurse Consultant Certification Program - Current
Kaplan College, West Palm Beach, Florida

Associate in Science in Nursing (R.N.) - 1997
St. Petersburg Community College, St. Petersburg, Florida

Associate in Science in EMS Management - 1992
EMT and Paramedic Certification Program
St. Petersburg Community College, St. Petersburg, Florida

CERTIFICATIONS / TRAINING

Advanced Cardiac Life Support (ACLS)
Pediatric Advanced Life Support (PALS)
EMT-Tactical, Counter-Narcotics Tactical Operations
Introduction to Chemical, Biological, & Radiological Defense

PROFESSIONAL EXPERIENCE

Registered Nurse, - Emergency Room, Radiology Specialist
MEASE HOSPITAL, Clearwater, Florida
Current
General nursing duties within a critical care setting.

Rescue Lieutenant - Firefighter - SWAT Paramedic
PINELLAS COUNTY FIRE RESCUE, Tampa, Florida
1990 to 2000
Directed field medical patient care and supervision.

Hospital Corpsman, 2nd Class, Fleet Marine Force
UNITED STATES NAVAL RESERVE, Jacksonville, Florida
1991 to 1999
Provided field medical patient care and coordinated urinalysis, immunization, and annual medical/dental screening programs.

Emergency Medical Services Lab Supervisor
HILLSBOROUGH COUMMUNITY COLLEGE, Tampa, Florida
1996 to 1999
Monitored and assessed student progress.

Office Manager

JANE SWIFT
9 Central Avenue
Jefferson, Maryland 21755
(301) 743-9009
jswift@careerbrain.com

OFFICE MANAGEMENT - OFFICE ADMINISTRATION - OFFICE AUTOMATION

Summary of Qualifications

- ❖ Recent college graduate - Summa Cum Laude.
- ❖ Organized, efficient, and precise with strong communication and liaison skills.
- ❖ Skilled in planning and execution of special projects during time-critical environments.
- ❖ Decisive and direct, yet flexible in responding to constantly changing assignments.
- ❖ Enthusiastic, creative and willing to assume increased responsibility.
- ❖ Able to coordinate multiple projects and meet deadlines under pressure.
- ❖ Proven ability to adapt quickly to challenges and changing environments.
- ❖ Highly skilled at solving customer relations problems.
- ❖ Effectively able to communicate with customers, staff and management.
- ❖ High initiative with strong self-management skills.

Relevant Skills

- ❖ PC proficiency in MS Office applications, Corel WP, Adobe
- ❖ Basic Web page design and update
- ❖ Basic accounting and finance
- ❖ Library / File / Internet research
- ❖ Travel planning and coordination
- ❖ Collecting and recording statistical and confidential information
- ❖ Assembling and organizing bulk mailings and marketing materials
- ❖ Data entry and correspondence preparation

Relevant Professional Experience

ADMINISTRATIVE ASSISTANT - NCC GME OFFICES
Uniformed Services University, Bethesda, Maryland

PROGRAM COORDINATOR - NCC FACULTY DEVELOPMENT COURSE
Uniformed Services University, Bethesda, Maryland

PROGRAM SUPPORT ASSISTANT - NCC GME PEDIATRIC RESIDENCY PROGRAM
Uniformed Services University, Bethesda, Maryland

Education

- ❖ Bachelor of Arts - Marywood University
- ❖ Major: Communication Arts Specialization Theater
- ❖ Minor: Business
- ❖ Graduated Summa Cum Laude
- ❖ Member Delta Epsilon Sigma, Catholic College Honor Society
- ❖ Mentioned in 2000 Edition of Who's Who in American Colleges and Universities
- ❖ George Perry Award for Academic Achievement in Major
- ❖ St. Genesius Medal for hours accumulated in practicum

References available upon request.

Operations and Executive Project Management

James Sharpe

9 Central Avenue • White Sulphur Springs MT 59645 • Ph. (406) 555-1212 • Fax (406) 555-1213
James@careerbrain.com

Executive Summary

A seasoned, team-oriented business executive with a highly successful track record with start-up and turnaround situations. More than 15 years progressive experience in all phases of **Operations and Project Management** *with particular strength in feasibility analysis. Recognized for exceptional organization building skills as well as the ability to motivate others on all levels in the achievement of individual and organizational goals.*

• *Business Process Re-engineering*	• *Project Management*	• *Business Valuation*
• *Feasibility Analysis/Projections*	• *Crisis Resolution*	• *Liquidation Management*
• *Negotiation and Arbitration*	• *Start-up Management*	• *P&L Responsibility*

Selected Achievements

- Successfully administered a portfolio of contracts with a value exceeding $10 million. The average income of each client **increased by 15%, a gain of more than $1.5 million.**
- Provided consulting services to more than 1,090 clients from numerous parts of the U.S. and Latin America as well as conducted numerous feasibility studies for projects valued at up to **$100,000,000.**
- Orchestrated a successful start-up company with responsibilities including site selection and acquisition through P&L accountability; **annual sales exceeded $50 million within ten years.**
- Aggressively negotiated, supervised, or advised in the negotiation of several contracts totaling in excess of $68 million, **savings clients at least $6.5 million.** Recent negotiations resulted in a verifiable return of **40% over current market value, a total gain of $520,000.**
- Pioneered state-of-the-art plant expansion that involved a capital investment of $500,000 and realized a **50% increase in plant capacity.**
- Successfully restarted an organization that had been shut down due to severe labor-management and production problems. Through various management techniques and styles that motivated the employees, **production increased by nearly 50% while operating costs stayed constant.**

Consulting Highlights

Wright and Holmes, Inc., *White Sulphur Springs, MT*   *Since 1992*
   President

Representative List of Clients

Dodson & Mark	*The Life Insurance Co.*	*Ambrose Technologies*
Montana Trust	*Sulphur Springs Real Estate*	*Pacific Northwest Financial*
Horn Communications	*Jervais Investments*	*UpStart USA*
Jones Timber	*Mountain Hydraulics*	*National Research Foundation*

Education

Bachelor of Science, Business Administration
University of Montana, Missoula MT

Interim assignments and consulting projects preferred. Available for extensive travel in U.S. and abroad.
Undeterred by the most arduous conditions.

Operations Management Investment / Securities Industry

Jane Swift
9 Central Avenue
Nyack, NY 10960
(914) 555-1212
Jane@careerbrain.com
Page 1 of 2

Expert in Process Redesign, Performance Reengineering & Productivity/Performance Improvement

RESULTS-DRIVEN PROFESSIONAL with 13+ years experience in leading-edge investment industry research production systems. Excellent analytical and problem-solving skills. Able to work under pressure in fast-paced, time-sensitive environments. Experienced in analyzing and streamlining systems and operations to increase productivity, quality, and efficiency. Proven ability to manage projects from planning through execution. Strong contributions in driving organizational change and improvement. Highly experienced in using spreadsheet, database, and word processing applications. Additional expertise includes:

- Strategic Planning
- Team Building and Leadership
- Financial Models
- Financial Analysis
- Operational Benchmarking
- Systems Administration

PROFILE

- Organized, enthusiastic management professional; willing to hear new ideas and go the extra mile to improve performance.
- Possess strong interpersonal skills; able to work effectively with individuals on all levels.
- Demonstrated ability to develop and maintain sound business relationships with clients, anticipating their needs.
- Strong problem resolution skills; able to efficiently and effectively prioritize a broad range of responsibilities to consistently meet deadlines.
- Hold both Series 7 and 63 licenses.
- Catalyst for change, transformation, and performance improvement.
- Achieved reputation as a resource person, problem solver, troubleshooter, and creative turnaround manager.

PROFESSIONAL EXPERIENCE

Dulce & True, New York, NY
Senior Business Analyst - Fixed Income Pricing Group

October 1989 - Present
May 1998 - Present

- Currently developing the tactical capability to reprice over 3,000 issues in the Salomon Corporate Bond Index on a daily basis and package these prices for sale to buy-side investment companies.
- Designed and implemented Web-based data verification process, improving the quality of Salomon's corporate bond pricing data to the point where customers want to purchase the data to compute daily NAVs.
- Innovated pricing system on the High Yield trading desk, providing sales staff access to valuable pricing data used to generate increased trading with customers.
- Recognized for the ability to work with many areas of the firm, bridging the gap between competing and sometimes adversarial departments to create business opportunities.

Manager - Fixed Income Index Production Group

May 1994 - May 1998

- Streamlined the index production process, responding to customer requests for earlier publication and also allowing index production personnel more time to get involved in more challenging, productive, and profitable projects.
- Effectively implemented several new systems versions and processes without any disruption to our business, our customers, or the business of other areas of the firm.
- Built and maintained strong relationships with customers, ensuring their continued business with the firm.

- Implemented verification processes to prevent the publication of inaccurate data, thereby avoiding strained relationships with customers.
- Improved accuracy of index products, generating greater market share, and confirming our position as market leaders in the fixed income index business.
- Assumed responsibility for the Index Production Group at a very crucial time in the development of indexing as a primary portfolio management strategy. Managed staff of eight responsible for the timely and accurate production of the Aggregate, Global, and Eurobond Indices.
- Improvised in the event of system failures or other problems and made quick firm decisions directing subordinates to focus on the solution or their part of the plan of action.
- Successfully introduced Eurobond Index providing the foundation for subsequent European Fixed Income Indices.
- Directed the conversion to SUN based pricing system for over 5,000 corporate and high-yield bonds from a clumsy and inefficient paper based system eliminating the need for data to be handled twice.
- Researched accuracy problems, reorganized and restructured verification procedures surrounding the Salomon Indices, significantly enhancing the accuracy and reliability of published numbers.
- Reduced production time by more than 60% while increasing quality standards.
- Never had to republish or restate monthly index results.

Portfolio Strategist - Fixed Income Strategy Group   July 1992 - May 1994
- Formed constructive ongoing relationships with several clients around structuring their fixed income portfolios, which generated increased trading with the firm and an additional communication link to the customer.
- Trained customers with respect to the workings of the index and our analytics, increasing their comfort level and willingness to do business with Salomon.

Analyst - Fixed Income Index Production Group   October 1989 - July 1992
- Organized and streamlined the production of the Daily Treasury Index leading to daily publication in the *Wall Street Journal*.
- Designed and implemented all data verification and distribution procedures.
- Published hourly U.S. Treasury market commentary on Telerate News Service.

Hartford Life - Hartford, CT   February 1987 - October 1989
Regional Accounting and Coordinating Divisions

COMMUNITY INVOLVEMENT
CENTRE COLLEGE ALUMNI CLUB, Danville, KY
    President (1997 - 1999), Executive Committee Member (1992 - 1999) for College Alumni Organization committed to supporting college athletic programs.
 LACROSSE CLUB, Hartford County, CT
    Member (1987 - 1994) and Coach (1993 - 1994)
SPORTS FITNESS CLUB, Greenwich, CT
    Yoga Instructor (1995 - 1998)

EDUCATION
CENTRE COLLEGE, Danville, KY
    Bachelor of Arts: Economics
                                                                             May 1987

REFERENCES
Will be furnished on request.

Organizational Management

Jane Swift
9 Central Avenue
Arlington, MA 02174
(617) 555-1212
Jane@careerbrain.com

Organizational Manager/Program Coordinator/Turnaround Strategist

Career Profile
Accomplished administrator with over ten years of experience in cost-effective program development and revitalization. Work with large not-for-profit entities providing therapeutic and preventive services focusing on restoration of families to productive employment and societal relationships. Run programs with a social worker's compassion blended with a corporate manager's productivity, fiscal responsibility, and results.

Areas of Expertise
- Total program administration
- Cost-effective management
- Long-term strategic planning
- Team building and leadership
- Staff training and mentoring
- Fundraising and grant writing
- Multimillion dollar budget oversight
- Program start-ups and turnarounds
- Program development/enhancement
- Crisis intervention
- Public speaking and education
- Windows 98, Microsoft Word, Internet

Career Highlights
- **Instrumental in start-up of association formed to assist former inmates with re-establishment of family units, drug-free living, and employment.** Hired to aid in the From Prison to Paycheck start-up. Created "preventive" element of program, hired professional staff, constructed organizational structure, planned services, trained staff, and authored treatment plans. Ensured retention of funding by meticulous following of state mandates.
- **Revitalized and dramatically expanded youth program slated for closure.** The Dorchester Foster Home for very troubled children was running at less than half capacity. Immediately strengthened referring relationships and implemented new policies and procedures. Increased to 24-resident capacity within first year. Now, after five consecutive successful years, have a $6 million budget, over 80 children in program, and substantial government funding. Program is community-based and more cost effective than treating children in a facility.
- **Received Best Site award for successful revamping of poorly run teen group home.** Created general structure, daily living schedule, and boundaries; revised mental attitudes; established consequences; and instituted a reward system. Retrained staff and reduced turnover. Changes precipitated a stronger sense of self esteem, instilled a sense of home in the residents, reduced AWOL rate, decreased school absenteeism, and raised residents' grades.
- **Restored program suffering from lack of proper casework processing.** Recruited as Supervisor to resolve near-crisis situation. Mandated monitoring and tracking was not being performed to standard. Department was overwhelmed with new daily cases and over 100 ongoing cases requiring (by mandate) 24 hours to investigate, 7 days to recommend, and 30 days to refer. Took over, cleaned up unit, saved funding, and prevented closure of vital program.
- **Addressed Fortune 500 CEOs as keynote speaker at the Athenaeum.** Presented an informative presentation about the day-to-day operations of a successful therapeutic foster care program, an overview of its management, and a perspective on its bottom-line value.

Education and Certification
M.S.W. Harvard University; B.S.W. Boston University; C.S.W. University of Massachusetts

Professional Development

Dorchester Foster Home: Program Director, Program Coordinator   1998 to present

    Recruited to revive ailing program and prevent closure. Have tripled enrollment, expanded to multiple locations, and obtained needed government funding. Manage overall administration and $5 million budget. supervise 32 staff members in 3 offices. Coordinate referral intake process and recruitment/training of therapeutic foster parents. Liaison with all relevant government and community agencies. Provide 24/7 crisis intervention coverage.

From Prison to Paycheck: Start-up Consultant, Case Work Supervisor   1997 to 1998

    Oversaw 70 preventive cases of people involved with the criminal justice system. Supervised staff. Monitored all mandated paperwork. Coordinated workshops. Obtained linkages with community organizations. Provided emergency beeper coverage.

Family Crisis Foundation: Site Supervisor, Case Manager   1990 to 1997

    Revitalized ailing group home for troubled youth, creating a model that received Best Site of the Year award. Managed total operation of home including hiring, budgetary, physical site, casework, staff oversight, and intensive casework. Oversaw 100 active crisis and long-term cases. Supervised child protective workers and case workers. Consulted with agency attorneys. Provided 24/7 emergency coverage. Developed goals for a caseload of 33 families, utilizing direct services, advocacy, and referrals. Supervised visitation. Responded to crisis situations.

Awards and Service

- Mayor's Award for Outstanding Service
- Distinguished Service Award
- Best Site of Year Award

Outside Sales/Account Manger/Customer Service

Jane Swift
9 Central Avenue
Wilmington, DE 19801
(302) 555-1212
Jane@careerbrain.com

Energetic and goal-focused sales professional with solid qualifications in large account management and customer relationship building/maintenance. Proven ability to develop new business and increase sales within established accounts and mature territories. Self confident and poised in interactions across all business hierarchies; a persuasive communicator and assertive negotiator with strong deal closing abilities. Excellent time management skills; computer literate. Areas of demonstrated value include:

- Sales Growth / Account Development
- Commercial Account Management
- Prospecting & Business Development
- Customer Liaison & Service
- Consultative Sales / Needs Assessment
- Territory Management & Growth

PROFESSIONAL EXPERIENCE

Morris Mtr. Co., Wilmington, DE   1995 - Present
    SALES EXECUTIVE (1997 - Present)
    Promoted and challenged to revitalize a large metropolitan territory plagued by poor performance. Manage, service, and build existing accounts; develop new business, establishing both regional and national accounts. Serve as key liaison for all customers and work as the only outside sales representative in the company. Produce monthly reports for major national accounts.
    <u>Selected Results</u>

- Reversed a history of stagnant sales; delivered consistent growth and built territory sales 22%, to $4.75 million annually, in less than 2 years.
- Surpassed quota by a minimum of 20% for 14 consecutive months.
- Personally deliver 95% of all sales generated for the company's main site.
- Prospected aggressively and presented products to key decision-makers during cold calls; opened more than 60 new commercial accounts.
- Improved account service and applied consultative sales techniques; grew sales in every established account a minimum of 15%.

    MANAGER, Harrisburg Store (1995 - 1997)
    MANAGER TRAINEE, Wilmington Store (1995)
    Initially recruited as a management trainee and rapidly advanced to management of a retail location generating $1 million annually. Supervised and scheduled 12 employees. Budgeted and produced advertising, oversaw bookkeeping, and set/managed sales projections and growth objectives.

EDUCATION AND CREDENTIALS

B.S., BUSINESS MANAGEMENT, 1995
Wilmington College, New Castle, DE

Additional Training

- Building Sales Relationships, 1998
- Problem Solving Skills, 1998

Professional & Community Associations

- Member, Chamber of Commerce, 1996 - Present
- Member, Country Club and Women's Golf Association, 1996 - Present
- Youth Soccer Coach and FIFA Certified Referee, 1999 - Present

Paralegal

JANE SWIFT
9 Central Avenue
Greenville, South Carolina 29607
Mobile (828) 516-4548 • Residence (828) 236-9925

PARALEGAL / LEGAL SECRETARY

Dedicated to providing superior, uninterrupted administrative support to legal and non-legal staff.

Confident, articulate and results-oriented legal support professional offering a strong foundation of education and experience. Creative and enthusiastic with proven record of success in prioritizing and processing heavy workflow without supervision. Superior organization and communication skills, committed to personal and professional growth. Looking to join an established team that rewards hard work and personal achievement with stability and the opportunity for increased responsibility.

IMMEDIATE VALUES OFFERED

- Highly proficient in word processing, data entry, and Dictaphone transcription using Microsoft application software; noticed for maintaining consistently superior levels of accuracy.
- Organized, efficient, and thorough; maintains flexibility in changing work assignments.
- Performs well under stress, taking pressure off superiors and peers.
- Proficient in the planning and execution of projects in time-critical environments.
- Dependable and successful problem resolution and time-management solutions.
- Creative and cooperative, works equally well individually or as part of a team.
- Outstanding record of performance, reliability, confidentiality and ethical business standards.
- Computer skills include Microsoft Word 97, 2000, Windows 95, 98, Word Perfect; familiarity with Excel, PowerPoint, and Access. Typing rate is approximately 80 WPM.

LEGAL EXPERIENCE

Criminal / Civil	Powers of Attorney	Complaints
Domestic Relations	Divorce	Exhibits / Witness Lists
Affidavits	Adoption	QDRO
Subpoenas	Probate	Personal Injury
Motions	Wills	Client Interviewing
Orders	Estates	Real Estate
Research	Workers Compensation	Mortgages / Deeds

SUMMER INTERNSHIP EXPERIENCE

Paralegal, **Tranter & Tranter, Attorneys and Counselors at Law** Greenville, SC - 2001
(Temporary Replacement) Legal Secretary, **Elmer George, Attorney At Law** Spartanburg, SC - 2000 - 01

EDUCATION AND SPECIAL CERTIFICATIONS

Associate of Science Degree, Paralegal Studies - Sullivan College, Greenville, SC
Magna Cum Laude Distinction, Dean's List
Degree Awarded 1/2002

Attended South Carolina Business College, 19 credit hours accumulated, Legal Writing
Attended Hutchinson Community College, 24 credit hours accumulated, Criminal Justice

Commissioned Notary Public, South Carolina State-at-Large - Status, current

Pharmaceutical Sales

Jane Swift

4040 East 50th Street
Austin, IL 60000

janeswift@hotmail.com

☎ [312] 555-5555 (Office)
☎ [312] 555-6666 (Home)

WHAT I CAN OFFER **CROSLEY** AS YOUR NEWEST **PHARMACEUTICAL SALES REPRESENTATIVE**

- Meeting demanding customers' needs • "Selling" ideas to doctors • Communicating to get results under tough conditions • Using creative ideas to solve problems on my own

RECENT WORK HISTORY WITH EXAMPLES OF PROBLEMS SOLVED

- Investigator *promoted from six eligibles to* **Hospital Liaison** *promoted to* Training Supervisor *and* Hiring Manager, Illinois Department of Protective and Regulatory Service, Austin, IL

  97 - Present

  CAPABILITY: Well informed, senior, busy judges and **doctors usually approve my recommendations quickly because I've built their trust** without the benefit of formal training.
  CAPABILITY: Regularly **win the day** with my ideas, even **after** penetrating **cross examination** by some of the best attorneys in the business.
  CAPABILITY: Persuaded senior decision makers to help us deliver better quality, reduce turnover, and make our employees more effective. Our **clients were served even better.**
  CAPABILITY: My new training program lowers **costs, despite our diverse workforce. Team members** now **master training** that once intimidated them.

- Child Specialist, State of Missouri, Division of Family Services, Kansas City, MO   96 -97

  CAPABILITY: Convinced a decision maker that **my plan would help his patient stay with a demanding treatment protocol.** Patient and her unborn child protected.

- Account Manager, Dunhill Staffing, Austin, IL   95 -96
  Dunhill provided temporary clerical and light industrial workers to local employers.
  CAPABILITY: Boosted our client's productivity and made us more productive at the same time. **Complaints fell to zero** and stayed there.

EDUCATION

- B.S., University of Illinois, Austin,   94
  Earned this degree while working up to 20 hours a week. GPA: 3.2.

COMPUTER SKILLS

- Expert in Word and Excel; proficient in proprietary customer information software suite and Outlook; familiar with Internet search protocols

Project Coordinator

Jane Swift

9 Central Avenue
Silver Spring, MD 20904

jswift@careerbraincom

(301) 555-7809 - Home
(301) 712-9744 - Mobile

PROJECT COORDINATOR - STAFF ASSISTANT - DATA ANALYST - MEMBERSHIP MANAGER

Summary of Qualifications
- Organized, efficient, and precise with strong communication and liaison skills
- Skilled in planning and execution of special projects during time-critical assignment
- Decisive and direct, yet flexible in responding to constantly changing assignments
- Able to coordinate multiple projects and meet deadlines under pressure
- Enthusiastic, creative and willing to assume increased responsibility
- Attention to details and strong follow through

Special Skills
- Language - Fluent in Spanish
- Computer - UNIX, VMA, Lotus Notes, MS Office, Word Perfect, SPSS 8.0, ESRI
- Certified in radiation safety
- Experience with medical terminology
- Database development

Relevant Skills
Office Administration
- Collecting and recording statistical and confidential information
- Assembling and organizing bulk mailing and marketing materials
- Data entry, with exceptionally fast typing and related Office Administration activities
- Organization specialist, able to ensure smooth and efficient flow of functions
- Progressive experience in office management, scheduling, and support services, data analysis, and research collection

Customer Service
- Extremely sociable and able to put visitors at ease
- Excellent verbal and written communication skills
- Highly skilled at solving customer relations problems

Education
- Masters in Public Administration, George Washington University, Washington, DC
- BA, Sociology, Concentration in Spanish, University of Pennsylvania, Allentown, PA

Relevant Professional Experience
PUBLIC HEALTH DATA ANALYST/NHMA MEMBERSHIP COORDINATOR
The National Hispanic Medical Association Washington, DC

ADMINISTRATIVE PRACTICUM
The VA Healthcare System, West Haven, CT

GRADUATE ASSISTANT IN CONTINUING EDUCATION
The G.W. University, Washington, DC

POLO RL SPECIALIST
Hecht's Company Department Store, Pittsburgh, PA

LAW CLERK
Patton & Page Law Firm, Pittsburgh, PA

Project Manager/Programmer Analyst

James Sharpe
321-855-7996 • jsharpe@careerbrain.com
9 Central Avenue • Chicago • IL • 60012

PROJECT MANAGER

Systems Engineering and Design ... Internet Technology & E-commerce ... Relational Database
Technology Solutions and Integration ... Cross Functional Technology Teams ... Process Reengineering

Fast-track management career; combine visionary leadership with technology expertise to analyze needs, define parameters, and lead cross-functional teams in the development of cost-effective solutions. Excel at assessing and proactively responding to changing organizational needs. Excellent communication, troubleshooting, and interpersonal skills; diligent and detail-oriented. Strong commitment to deliver timely, accurate, and quality work.

TECHNICAL EXPERTISE

Microsoft
Windows 2000 Directory Services Infrastructure • NT Server 4.0 • Enterprise Technologies
TCP/IP on Windows NT 4.0 • Internet Information Server • SQL Servers 6.5 and 7.0
Networking • Visual Basic 6.0 for Applications • Project 98

E-business
Internet Access • Collocation • E-mail Hosting • Net News Access • Content Hosting
Network Management • Video Conferencing • Automated Disaster Recovery
E-commerce • Reliable Trading Platforms • Security

Virtual ISP
Modem Access • E-mail Service Access • Web Hosting • Customer Billing
Customer Care • 1st and 2nd Level Technical Support • Server Management
"Plug and Play" E-commerce Services • Internet Security

Networking
Interconnecting Cisco Network Devices (ICND)

NOTEWORTHY CAREER HIGHLIGHTS

Challenge: Automate and streamline the vote history research process. **Action**: Led a cross-functional team in re-engineering the existing flat-file system to a relational database with a Web-based interface allowing for execution of queries and drill-down reports.

> **Result: Realized annual savings of more than $240,000 and increased reporting accuracy to almost 100%.**

Challenge: Distribute timely corporate communications to targeted interest groups and constituencies. **Action**: Drove the compilation of a 2.5 million record database, automating the transmission process through integration with fax and email servers.

> **Result: Instant transmission of corporate message to targeted audiences, which significantly expanded constituent and interest group awareness. Increased published news stories by 800% within first year of launch.**

Challenge: Automate administrative tasks and accelerate approval process. **Action**: Conceptualized, planned, designed, and coordinated a secure, confidential corporate Intranet.

> **Result: Reduced administrative staff time by 50 hours per month; cut management approval processes in half; and saved more than $6,000 in paper costs within the first year.**

Challenge: Create a database solution providing shared access to multiple customers while decreasing customer cost and increasing profitability. **Action**: Designed and implemented a shared SQL server database providing access via ODBC from a customer web server.

> **Result: Significantly reduced capital costs and increased monthly profits from $8,500 to $25,000 - over 300%.**

Challenge: Unite a sales department floundering from a lack of direction and product knowledge, and reduce 3 to 5-month delivery time. **Action**: Created a sales and marketing plan clearly defining products and services.

> **Result: Addressed all potential problems up-front through a new business prospect review meeting, and reduced product and service delivery time to less than 30 days**.

PROFESSIONAL EXPERIENCE

FINITE TELECOMMUNICATIONS, Chicago, Illinois - since 2000
(World class facilities-based provider of managed data services for Internet-centric businesses)

Senior Technical Project Manager -Product Integration Group

Challenged to conduct customer needs assessments; analyze feasibility and impact; and develop technical solutions. Develop work breakdown structures for implementation.

- Representative clients include Foodvision.com; Synergex, and InformedInvestors.com.

ILLINOIS STATE ASSEMBLY, Chicago, Illinois - 1995 to 2000

Senior Technical Project Manager / Director of IT - 1997-2000
Deputy Director of IT - 1996
Network Administrator - 1996
Systems Engineer - 1995

Hired as a systems engineer and fast-tracked into a management position within one year. Developed strategic IT objectives and directed a $7 million computer services operating budget. Provided visionary leadership to cross-functional teams to ensure cost-effective business solutions were delivered to customers on time and within budget.

EDUCATION / TRAINING

Completed all MCSE coursework

Associate of Arts - 1999
Crystal Lake Community College, Chicago, Illinois

Property Management

Jane Swift
9 Central Avenue
Omaha, NE 68106
(402) 555-1212
Jane@careerbrain.com

OBJECTIVE
Position in Property Management.

QUALIFICATION HIGHLIGHTS
- More than six years of experience assisting in the management of multiple rental properties.
- Thoroughly familiar with both tenant and landlord laws and guidelines; experienced in collections and municipal court procedures.
- Extensive business background in general management, customer service and support, and subcontractor supervision.
- Advanced computer skills and demonstrated proficiency in streamlining administrative tasks through the application of technology.
- Resourceful and innovative in problem solving; adapt quickly to a challenge. Strong prioritization, delegation, and planning skills.
- Relate warmly to diverse individuals at all levels; respectful yet assertive communication style.

KEY SKILLS & ABILITIES
- Perform background, reference, and credit checks; select quality tenants and maintain high occupancy rates.
- Show available properties to prospective tenants; negotiate lease and rental agreements.
- Handle tenant communications; respond to requests for maintenance and answer questions.
- Troubleshoot and resolve disputes, including evictions and cleaning/damage deposits.
- Research legal issues utilizing Nolo Press publications, file court documents, and represent property owner in court.
- Schedule and supervise subcontractors; oversee upgrades, maintenance, and renovations.
- Plan and manage budgets; execute general accounting functions.
- Set up and maintain computerized property management systems.
- Coordinate and track rent collection, maintenance, and repairs. Proactively address security issues.

CAREER HISTORY
Assistant Property Manager (1998 - Present)
       Smith's Realty, Omaha, NE
             Assist in the management and oversight of multiple residential rental properties. Set up efficient administrative systems, coordinate rent collection, handle tenant disputes, and resolve legal issues.

Owner-Manager (1986 - 1998)
       Computer Works, Omaha, NE
             Founded and managed this micro/mini-computer sales and systems integration company. Achieved status as a Southwestern Bell Master Vendor.

EDUCATION
Metropolitan Technical Community College (1985 - 1986)
Emphasis in Business Administration

Public Relations/Media Spokesperson

JANE SWIFT
9 Central Avenue
Phoenix, AZ 85016
(602) 555-1212
Jane@careerbrain.com

OBJECTIVE:

A position in Public Relations where I can utilize my skills as a media spokesperson and my ability to execute a variety of projects simultaneously.

EXPERIENCE:

Public Relations Associate/Media
ADRIENNE ARPEL. Phoenix, AZ. 1992 to Present

- Media spokesperson for 12 western states: Interviewed and trained personnel for TV, radio and print
- Established contacts with producers and editors
- Wrote press releases
- Developed media and promotional packages
- Booked interviews with press

District Sales Manager
ADRIENNE ARPEL. Phoenix, AZ. 1989 - 1992

- Supervised 169 representatives with a $500,000 sales volume

Account Executive/Radio Reporter
KTUV RADIO. Phoenix, AZ. 1986 - 1989

- Designed and sold advertising for KTUV Radio
- Developed a $9,000 account list in the Phoenix metro market
- Sports and news announcer (included in-studio as well as location)
- Traffic reporter

Assistant Editor
Daily Argus Observer, Ontario, OR, Summers 1984/1985

- Feature writer, reporter, photographer, layouts and design

EDUCATION:

B.S., Speech Communications, University of Arizona, 1986

AWARDS:

1994 Arizona Business and Professional Women's "Young Careerist" Annual Award

OTHER FACTS:

Experience as a Public Relations Seminar Leader

References/Portfolio/Video and Cassette Tapes available upon request

Publishing/Marketing Professional

Jane Swift
9 Central Avenue
Seacliff, NY 11579
(516) 555-1212
Jane@careerbrain.com

PROFESSIONAL *A New York Publisher of trade and scholarly books*
EXPERIENCE: **DIRECTOR OF ADVERTISING AND PROMOTION (March 1998-Present)**

Key responsibilities include: managing advertising/promotion department with staff of four; overseeing and actively engaging in all aspects of promotion, advertising, and publicity. I have established and am maintaining a 22-person national sales force and make seasonal visits to the nation's two largest bookstore chains.

Active in negotiating special sales and acquiring new titles, and as liaison with domestic and foreign rights agents. In 1998 I traveled to England, visited several publishers, bought and sold rights.

Frequently arrange author appearances on television and radio talk shows. As a company spokesperson, I have been interviewed numerous times by newspapers, magazines, syndicates, and radio stations.

ADVERTISING AND PROMOTION MANAGER (1996-1998)

Advertising and Direct Mail: Created, designed, and wrote copy for brochures, flyers, and display ads; created direct-mail campaigns; represented company at publisher's book exhibits.

Publicity: Wrote news releases, selected media, made follow-up calls, arranged author media appearances.

ASSISTANT EDITOR (1994-1996)

Responsibilities included reading authors' manuscripts, copyediting, proofreading; writing jacket copy, coordinating and writing copy for catalog. Some editing and proofreading was done on a freelance basis.

Compton Burnett (New York, NY) ADVERTISING COPYWRITER (1992-1994)

Responsible for designing and writing copy for bimonthly catalog and supplementary flyers. Created ads and brochures; wrote sales letters and edited and rewrote direct-mail pieces.

EDUCATION: State University of New York at Buffalo
Degree: B.A. in English, 1992
Minor: Social Sciences

SKILLS: Word processing, working knowledge of typography, research proficiency.

REFERENCES: Will be provided on request.

Purchasing Manager

James Sharpe
226 Valley Canyon
Hambone, WA 88000
(888) 888-8888
Jsharpe@email.net

Results-oriented **FINANCE PROFESSIONAL**. Consistently successful in controlling costs and improving net profitability while continuing to support critical operations. Background includes procurement responsibility up to $5 million annually. Excellent communicator with a good attitude and sense of humor. Tenacious negotiator with keen vendor management skills. Strong research and analysis, organization, and decision-making abilities. PC proficient with Word, Excel, and MainSaver.

CAREER SUMMARY

Purchasing / Maintenance Assistant, NAES Energy Services, Hambone, WA, 1994-present
Progressed from Purchasing Assistant to Maintenance Assistant. Selected by upper management to train as Assistant Plant Operator.

- Conducted and oversaw all procurement operations-requisitions, purchase orders, price negotiation, receiving, delivery verification. Commodities consisted of chemicals, hardware, consumables, office supplies, and maintenance equipment.
- Prepared weekly and monthly reports of dollars committed and delivery status. Ensured inventory was current and needs were met. Performed preventive maintenance and assisted mechanic with machinery repairs.

Subcontract Administrator, Huge Aircraft Company, Second, CA, 1984-1993
- Administered yearly government subcontract purchases of $1+ million. Solicited bids, negotiated prices, awarded jobs. Interfaced with representatives of many different organizations. Coordinated with Engineering, Program, Quality, Price, and Cost Analysis staff through completion.

Received High Achiever Award for saving over $100,000 annually.

Purchasing Manager, Electro-Line, Mainstream, OH, 1981-1983

- Procured electronic components of purchases in excess of $5 million annually, including price negotiation, and delivery. Ensured compliance with applicable Government Procurement Regulations.

Buyer, Huge Aircraft Company, Second, CA, 1977-1981

- Placed purchase orders for computer and test equipment, electronic hardware, optics, and other commodities.

Received Corporate Superior Performance Award for
outstanding attitude and work performance.

EDUCATION / ADDITIONAL TRAINING
B.S., General Business Administration, University of Arizona
CPR / First Aid Certification - Licensed Forklift Driver
Continuing Education includes Teaming Techniques, Negotiation Skills, and other relevant classes.

Real Estate Development

James Sharpe
9 Central Avenue
Overland Park, KS 66210

(913) 555-1212
James@careerbrain.com
Page 1 of 2

OBJECTIVE

A position in REAL ESTATE DEVELOPMENT that will utilize strong analytical skills, knowledge of marketplace trends and practices, and benefit from my legal background.

OVERVIEW

- Organized, take-charge professional with exceptional follow-through abilities and detail orientation; able to plan and oversee a full range of events from concept to successful conclusion.
- Demonstrated ability to efficiently prioritize a broad range of responsibilities in order to consistently meet deadlines.
- Dynamic negotiator; effective in achieving positive results. Licensed Mediator in NJ.
- Demonstrated capability to anticipate and resolve problems swiftly and independently.
- Possess strong interpersonal skills; proven ability to develop and maintain sound business relationships with clients, anticipating their needs.
- Highly articulate, effective communicator, experienced presenter: possess excellent platform skills.
- Highly adept in utilizing state-of-the-art software packages for industry-related functions, from data and finance management to CADD. Hands-on experience with Argus and Project.
- Currently completing Master's Degree in Real Estate Development at NYU.
- Demonstrated skills in:

• Research	• Mediation	• Mergers & Acquisitions
• Urban Development	• Legal Writing	• Real Estate Tax Issues
• Accounting	• Analytical Writing	• Corporate Finance
• Bankruptcy	• Financial Analysis	• Administrative System Design
• Small Business Planning	• Small Business Development	• Foreclosure

PROFESSIONAL EXPERIENCE

May 1999 - Present
SMITH & ASSOCIATES, Overland Park, KS

Special Projects Consultant for well-respected communications consulting firm. Firm's principal authored two critically acclaimed standards in the marketing/business field: *The New Positioning* and *The Power of Simplicity.*

- Perform directed Internet and other research in preparation for an upcoming book.
- Analyze research and draft description for inclusion in articles and future book.
- Specifically recruited for special projects on basis of past performance.

September 1998 - Present
RIVERVIEW ARTISANS INC., Overland Park, KS

Assistant Manager for firm affiliated with the Mapleridge Design Center.

- Collaborate with decorative artist on projects in the $75K range, custom building business furniture, conference rooms, mahogany libraries, etc.
- Perform multitude of skilled operations from rough milling to fine detail finishing and veneer application.
- Assist in project estimates and sales proposals.

June 1997 - December 1997
WALTERS, JUSTA & MILLSTEIN, Kansas City, KS
    Law Clerk
- Gained valuable experience in bankruptcy proceedings.

January 1997 - May 1997
HONORABLE HENRY MARGOLIS, Kansas City, KS
    Judicial Internship
- Legal research and writing on legalities relating to general equity matters.

September 1996 - December 1996
HONORABLE ROSE GIARDELA, Kansas City, KS
    Judicial Internship

Summer 1996
STRATTON, BRIGGS & ROTHMAN, Overland Park, KS
    Law Clerk

January 1994 - June 1994
UNITED STATES DEPARTMENT OF JUSTICE, Washington, DC
    Intern

EDUCATION

UNIVERSITY OF MISSOURI, KANSAS CITY, Kansas City, MO
Master of Science: Real Estate Development   May 2000

UNIVERSITY OF KANSAS SCHOOL OF LAW, Lawrence, KS
Juris Doctor   June 1998
Admitted to Kansas Bar 1998
Honors and Activities:
- Seton Hall Constitutional Law Journal - NOTES & COMMENTS EDITOR (1997-98)
- Who's Who: American Law Students - 16th Edition (1997)
- Tax Law Society

KANSAS WESLYAN UNIVERSITY, Salinas, KS
Bachelor of Arts, Political Science   August 1995
Honors and Activities:
- Dean's List
- Pi Sigma Alpha Honor Society (for outstanding Political Science Majors)

REFERENCES
Excellent references will be furnished on request.

Retail District Manager

James Sharpe
9 Central Avenue
Metairie, LA 70002
(504) 555-1212
James@careerbrain.com

Profile
Highly focused, enthusiastic and goal-driven professional with solid experience in marketing, management, sales, operations, and training. Demonstrated success in implementing test marketing programs and promoting products that consistently increase sales. Reputation for innovative problem solving, organization, and professionalism.

Employment History
Stop & Go Convenience   1996 - Present
District Manager - Louisiana
> Recruited to provide leadership and management for stores with high employee turnover and lagging sales. Supervise day-to-day operations of 6 retail stores with full responsibility for P&L. Hire, train, and manage 60 to 70 employees. Develop and maintain vendor relations. Introduce new products and plan marketing strategies for all stores. Plan and conduct area training meetings.

> Selected Accomplishments:
> - Increased inside sales 15–20% over a year, and total sales by 10%, through improved management techniques, attention to detail, inventory control, and developing good relationships with vendors.
> - Reduced employee turnover 50% by fostering a team atmosphere through improved training, communication, and motivation.
> - Received five merit-based salary increases.
> - The second most senior (and youngest) supervisor in Texas.
> - Won sales award for increased profits per store.
> - Selected out of 80 people by the VP of Operations to attend National Association of Convenience Stores (NACS) to lobby congressmen in Washington D.C. along with the CEO and president.

District Manager - Texas
> Promoted from Manager. Recruited from Alabama to work with 3 stores to improve management, decrease turnover, and increase sales. Ran several successful pilot/test programs that were implemented throughout the company.

Manager - Birmingham, Alabama:
> Promoted from Management Trainee.

Computer Skills
PowerPoint, MS Word, Excel, Lotus, Internet (PC and Mac)

Education
Auburn University, B.A. in Communications. Courses included marketing, publicity, media, group dynamics, speech writing. Paid for 100% of college through employment.

Retail Management

Jane Swift
9 Central Avenue
New York, NY 10017
(212) 555-1212
Jane@careerbrain.com

Profile

Accomplished manager with more than 15 years experience managing high-profile, upscale operations, leading teams, and consistently delivering sales, profit, and organizational improvements. Recognized for ability to achieve results through leadership, teamwork, and exceptional customer service.

~Operations Management~Business Analysis & Planning~Expense Control~
~Inventory Management~Human Resources (interviewing, evaluating, scheduling, counseling, coaching, and developing)~Buying and Merchandising (maximizing sales volume and profitability)~

Selected Achievements

Management/Leadership

- Currently managing the largest branch store with 40 executive reports and 600 staff associates.
- Brought in to turn around an underperforming back-of-house operation that was impacting negatively on profitability of entire operation. Reorganization showed immediate improvement and brought store back on plan.
- Drove sales and profits at Galleria store despite mall renovations and store's own 30,000 square foot expansion and renovation.
- Opened three new multilevel stores in major malls from the ground up. All stores exceeded plan.
- General Manager of the Year (1997) for the entire company.

Merchandising/Customer Service

- Won CEO's Cup for sales/profitability and excellence in customer service. Shared award with 4 others out of 70 general managers.
- Took Miami Beach store to Top Ten status in customer service throughout chain.
- Led Scarsdale store to Top Ten in customer service
- Drove Albany store to Number One in customer service
- Selected to pioneer a pilot project for a Selling Skills Training Program for all stores nationwide. Resulted in target stores all ranking highest in chain.
- Instrumental in company's customer service program. Consistent top ten producer.
- Worked with Hub Merchandising Organization to restructure merchandise mix to better serve South Florida market.
- As buyer, increased department 14% in first year and by 23% in second. Expanded private label program in Orient, increasing gross margins and upgrading fashion image.

Career History

Saks Fifth Avenue, New York, NY (1990 - Present)
    Vice President and General Manager (1999 - Present)
        General Manager Divisional Vice President (1994 - 1998)
        General Manager (1992 - 1994)
        Buyer (1990 - 1992)
Lord & Taylor, New York, NY
        Assistant Buyer (1985 - 1990)

Education

AAS in Fashion Buying and Merchandising, Fashion Institute of San Francisco

References upon request.

Sales/Account Manager

JANE SWIFT
9 Central Avenue • Dunwoody, Georgia
(770) 555-5555 Residence • (770) 555-5555 Mobile
jswift@careerbrain.com

SALES / MARKETING / CUSTOMER SUPPORT REPRESENTATIVE

Proven top performer with records for new account development, account retention, and increase in sales to existing accounts. Confident communicator with a professional image offering high caliber presentation, negotiation, and closing skills. Special ability to relate warmly with people, easily generating trust and rapport that translates into a high rate of closings. Looking to join with an established organization that rewards hard work and personal dedication with competitive compensation and opportunities for advancement. Immediate values offered include:

- Advanced skills in relationship building, outside sales, PR, and account management.
- Strongly motivated to succeed; enthusiastic and committed to personal and professional excellence.
- Consistently proven ability to gain participation of others to benefit company projects.
- Extensive experience planning and executing professional sales campaigns and trade show exhibits.
- Noticed for the ability to diffuse and reverse potentially volatile situations utilizing well-developed conflict resolution and interpersonal skills.
- Uncompromising consideration for customer retention and service.
- Equally comfortable and effective in self-managed or collaborative projects.
- Solid track record for upholding fiscal efficiencies; particularly skilled in organization and time management.
- Computer literacy includes knowledge of Word, Word Perfect, Excel, Windows, and the Internet.
- Embodiment of the highest levels of business ethics and performance standards.

PROFESSIONAL EXPERIENCE

1999 - Present   **LEXMARK INTERNATIONAL, INC. - Atlanta, GA**
Global developer, manufacturer and supplier of printing solutions and products for the office and home markets.
Senior Account Manager. Challenged to research market trends and create effective sales strategies for 33 Fortune 500 accounts. Conduct customer needs assessment, develop creative presentation of products, and initiate / nurture productive relationships with target companies. Goal: To deliver substantial and sustained revenue gains to Lexmark's Retail and Hospitality Industry Team. Highlights: After completing a period of comprehensive, in-house training, was promoted before peers from Account Executive to Senior Account Manager. Typical sales $500K to $1 million. Noticed by senior management for maintaining corporate objectives in the face of over-saturated sales force and diminishing market share.

EDUCATION AND PROFESSIONAL DEVELOPMENT

Transylvania University - Lexington, Kentucky
Bachelor of Arts, Business Administration with Marketing emphasis, minor in Studio Art
Degree awarded 1999

Completed the following Lexmark-sponsored programs:
Printer University, IBM Sales Training, IBM Presentation Training, Product Update Training, Bill Kovac's Presentation Performance Class, and Consultative Selling Techniques.

CIVIC ACTIVITIES AND COMMUNITY SERVICE

Member, Atlanta Junior Chamber of Commerce
Volunteer, Atlanta Day Shelter for Women and Children

Excellent personal and professional referrals are available on your request.

Sales and Marketing Executive

JANE SWIFT

9 Central Avenue
Rogers, Arkansas 72756

501-545-1223 Residence
501-327-7441 Cellular

PROFESSIONAL FOCUS

Opportunity to join the leadership team of a forward-thinking organization where successful experience in sales, marketing, and operations management contributes to increased profits and growth, workforce stability and continuous improvement.

PROFESSIONAL PROFILE

- Senior level executive with proven performance in building a professional sales organization.
- Profit-driven manager who effectively manages resources to maximize return on investments.
- Trusted leader in sharing vision, defining goals and developing strategies to achieve profits.
- Proactive approach to business, aggressively pursuing new opportunities and exceeding customers' expectations in a highly competitive market place.
- Results-oriented coach/mentor who leads by example, challenges people's thinking and maximizes the potential of others.
- Initiates and supports positive change to ensure profitable, competitive market position.

EXPERIENCE

JN DISTRIBUTORS, INC., Fayetteville, Arkansas　　　　　　　　　　　**1991 - Present**
Distributor of commercial/industrial construction products.

- Vice President of Sales and Marketing, 1997 - Present
- Vice President, Southeast Region, 1993 - 1997
- Field Sales Manager, 1991 - 1993

Key Results

Growth:

- Integral part of business development and growth; in 1991, JN had 9 employees and a single facility. In 10 year period, expanded operations to 350 employees in 12 midwestern locations.

Profits:

- Directly involved in achieving 850% profit increase, 1991 to date.
- Guided investment decisions to maximize continued growth opportunities.

People:

- Recruited, developed and built a successful, loyal and trusting employee network.
- Maintained strong focus on employees' professional growth and development.
- Respected team members, valuing each as the company's most valuable asset.

Quality:

- Consistently supported and embraced the concept of continuous improvement, adhering to corporate philosophy of "the only way to coast is downhill."
- Initiated efforts to implement TQM programs company wide.

EDUCATION

Bachelor of Science - University of Arkansas, Fayetteville, Arkansas - Top 1% of class, 1990.

* * * * * * * *

Security/Operations Management

James Sharpe
9 Central Avenue
San Francisco, CA 94124
(415) 555-1212
James@careerbrain.com

Career Profile

- Over 14 years of management and leadership experience in security operations and related functions with prominent hotels, retailers, and security providers.
- Currently functions as Director of Security for a prestigious four star/four diamond hotel, earning the highest performance ranking in the company in 1998. Have directed up to 200 officers and developed/managed $500,000+ budgets. Possess an extensive knowledge of security industry standards.
- Develop and lead effective and united teams, transforming fragmented factions into a cohesive alliance of professionals producing exceptional results and adhering to strict codes of conduct. Employ a dedicated hands-on management style that has dramatically increased effectiveness and reduced turnover,
- Certified in Lodging Security Directorship, Hospitality Law, Hotel Security Management, Disaster Preparedness and Emergency Response, Threat Management, Workplace Violence, and OSHA Regulations. Member of the American Society for Industrial Security and the Northern California Security Chiefs Association.

Areas of Expertise

- Security industry standards
- Budget creation and management
- Human Resources management functions
- Recruiting, training, and development
- Coaching, counseling, and motivation

- Departmental turnarounds
- Program and procedures development
- Motivational team leadership
- Interviewing, selection, performance evaluations

Career Development

Director of Security Operations, Four Star Hotel, San Francisco, California　　　　1994 to Present

- Manage all aspects of the security operation of this prestigious, top rated, 600,00 square foot luxury hotel with 300 rooms, a daily roster of 1,000 employees/guests, and 14 full-time security officers.
- Dramatically reversed poor performance history of key hotel departments, achieving ranking of first in the company in 1998
  - Decreased number of security-related incidents by 30%, the lowest in hotel's history.
  - Lowered workers' compensation injuries to 7 cases (of 300 workers), the smallest in the company's history.
  - Raised quality/efficiency while reducing overtime by 65%, the lowest rate in the department's history.
  - Instituted standards that did not allow a single successful safety or security litigation in five years.
  - Earned top ranking as company's best managed department.
  - Achieved lowest employee turnover rate in the entire company.

Produced these results by creating and implementing leading-edge programs including... Innovative training, evaluation, and TQM programs that produced employee motivation, attention, interest, cooperation, and desired response... Standard operating procedures for crisis management, disaster prevention and recovery, risk management, emergency response, incident investigation, and report writing... Detailed investigation standards for all security and safety incidents, including policy violations, and guest or employee injuries.

Chief of Security, DeLuxe Hotel, San Francisco, California　　　　1993 to 1995
Directed security operations of this three star/ four diamond national chain hotel with 200 guest rooms, 200 employees, and 6 security officers, devising effective security policies and procedures, and budgeting and monitoring department's expenditures.

- Produced a 20% decrease in security-related incidents.
- Reduced employee turnover by 50%.

Established new standard operating procedures. Developed and implemented emergency action plans. Contributed to creation of multiple departments' security and safety requirement training programs. Cooperated closely with the Human Resources department on OSHA, workers' compensation, and other industrial safety matters to ensure state and federal compliance.

Operations Manager, Redwood Security, San Francisco, California — 1990 to 1992

Managed over 200 plainclothes and uniform contract security officers in multiple facilities, including defense contractors and film studios. Developed and promoted a proactive culture of risk management and prevention. Promoted through the ranks from Field Officer to Operations Manager, the highest rank within the division.

- Implemented new rewards and recognition programs that raised morale and provided continuous feedback.
- Frequently volunteered extended hours to meet clients' needs and critical project deadlines.

Acted as client liaison to develop partnerships and strategic loss prevention and asset protection programs. Oversaw Human Resources operations including officer selection, field deployment, training, scheduling, inspections, evaluations, and disciplinary actions. Established professional ties with local police authorities.

Loss Prevention Manager, Nordstrom's, Thousand Oaks, California — 1987 to 1990

Oversaw security staff and operations at this upscale retailer.

- Protected assets and reduced legal liability by creating ongoing prioritized loss prevention initiatives.
- Developed effective loss countermeasure strategies and prevention awareness training programs.
- Conducted comprehensive internal audits and investigations for external/internal sources of loss and employee misconduct.
- Minimized accidents and injuries by managing effective safety programs.

Technology Skills

- Proficient in Microsoft Word, Excel, IRIMS, and PPM2000.
- PC proficient in Windows 98/95/3.1
- Extensive knowledge of computer-based, audio/visual, and access control systems.

Education and Certification

Bachelor of Science in Political Science, University of Southern California
Certifications:

- Lodging Security Director (CLSD), American Hotel & Motel Association
- Hospitality Law, AH&MA Educational Institute
- Hotel Security Management, AH&MA
- Disaster Preparedness and Emergency Response, City of San Francisco Fire Department
- Threat Management and Workplace Violence, City of San Francisco Fire Department
- OSHA Regulations and Workplace Violence, California Hotel & Motel Association
- Food Handler, San Jose County Department of Health

Security Services Sales

Jane Swift
9 Central Avenue
Raleigh, NC 27612
(919) 555-1212
Jane@careerbrain.com

Professional Profile

Sales • Account Management • New Business Development Professional

Sales and Account Management Development professional with expert qualifications in identifying and capturing market opportunities to accelerate expansion, increase revenues, and improve profit contributions in highly competitive industries. Outstanding record of achievement in complex account and contract negotiations.

Key Strengths:

- Account development/management
- Customer service/satisfaction
- Bilingual English/Spanish
- Customer needs assessment
- PC proficient

- Consultative/solutions sales
- New market development
- Account retention
- Presentation and negotiations skills

Professional Experience

Key Account Executive, 1996 - Present

American Security Services, Largest privately held security company in the nation with annual sales over $400 million.

Recruited to start up and oversee the market development of contract security services in North Carolina. Conduct in-depth client need assessments and develop technology-based security strategies to ensure maximum efficiency.

- Achieve consistent annual sales production in excess of $2.5 million
- Built territory from ground zero capturing 55% of market share in region
- Expanded annual billable hours from 300 to more than 5,000, fostering a rapid growth in staffing from 30 to more than 300 employees in Raleigh branch
- Successfully negotiated and secured sales ranging from $300K to $1.2 million
- Earned several national and local awards for top sales performance, including the prestigious "Rookie of the Year" award

Account Executive/Loan Officer, 1995 - 1996

Equity Finance, Inc., Nation's oldest finance company, a division of a Fortune 500 company.

Generated and sold bill consolidation loans through telemarketing.

- Consistently exceeded monthly sales objectives
- Received national recognition as one of the Top 10 salespeople in the nation, and Number 1 salesperson in Raleigh branch.

Education

Bachelor of Arts, Business Administration/Finance (GPA 3.8) 1994
University of North Carolina, Chapel Hill

Senior Account Executive

Jane Swift

9 Central Avenue
New York, NY 10012
(212) 555-1212
Jane@careerbrain.com

- 15+ years' experience building partnerships with leading corporations to develop consumer packaging, sales promotions, and collateral to strengthen brand identity and awareness. In-depth understanding of technology, household products, personal care, liquor, and food categories.
- Account management capabilities enhanced by professional design, production, printing, and technical background. Formal design education and commitment to ongoing professional development.
- Adept in Macintosh and Windows applications for graphic design, desktop publishing, word processing, spreadsheets, email, database management, Web site development, and multimedia presentations.

Key Words

Consultative Sales	High-Impact Presentations
Customer Service	Problem Solving & Decision Making
Project Management	Sales Closing & Negotiating
Design Process	Team Building & Leadership

Achievements

- Generated nearly a million dollars in annual sales for packaging design firm by winning key accounts and cultivating relationships.
- Won four Package Design Council (PDC) Gold Awards for package design in personal care and household appliances categories.
- Won account with major multinational corporation and developed packaging, promotional displays, trade, and consumer collateral material. Facilitated the national redesign (60 SKU's) in order to establish products as the technologically superior brand within the category.
- Collaborated on the national implementation of a "company first" branding strategy. Key objective: to reinforce the brand name, weakened by a four-year trend of sub-branding. Brainstormed with marketing and creative executives to create a set of graphic standards to communicate the essence of the brand. Applied this branding system to the entire product line.
- Increased sales and distribution through development of innovative club-store packaging and promotions for a leading liquor supplier.
- Guided design and production of packaging and product launch materials for a 30 SKU line of household products. Product was picked up nationally by Wal-Mart and sales jumped 19% in an introductory period.
- Worked with a leading cereal maker to develop promotional back panel games, sweepstakes, and in-pack offers.
- Directed development of displays, brochures, and merchandising materials for Certs Candy and Ocean Spray Fruit Waves (created through licensing agreement).
- Introduced multimedia capability to firm's new business presentations. Created Web site content including a company tour, an interactive portfolio, and a creative access section—allowing clients online, confidential access to view work.

Career Chronology

Senior Account Executive—1998 - Present
Leading Package Design Firm, Fort Lee, NJ
- Hired as a junior account executive to assist in all aspects of client services. Within seven months, promoted to account executive to develop new business in the consumer electronics category. Established key contacts with industry leaders through cold calling, direct marketing and client presentations. Consulted with clients to determine marketing objectives, packaging requirements and budgetary limitations. Directed numerous packaging, promotion, trade and consumer collateral material projects. Managed staff of five to implement the electronic design and production process.

Computer Graphics Artist—1995 - 1998
Big Design Firm, New York, NY
- Worked with designers and art directors to take concepts through to highly refined computer based production. Trained members of the design and production department in the use of Adobe Illustrator. Setup a high-speed remote viewing network enabling select clients to simultaneously view design concepts.

Account Executive—1991 - 1995
Freelance Placement Agency, New York, NY
- Instrumental in establishing a lucrative desktop publishing placement division. Identified and cultivated profitable markets. Managed and art directed freelancers and worked with clients through all project stages.

Graphic Designer—1985 - 1990
ABC Marketing & Communications, New York, NY
- Accountable for all stages of the design and production of consumer packaging. Participated in beta testing of proprietary graphics software and various high-end peripherals, giving product reviews to manufacturers.

Education
BFA: Graphic Design, Industrial Design, Computer Graphics and Marketing - 1985
New York University

Ongoing Professional Development
- Earned Certificate in Sales Promotion - St. John's University
- Intensive seminars in Web site design, multimedia, and advertising - Brown University

Senior International Marketing and Business Development Executive

Jane Swift   Page 1 of 2
9 Zentral Strasse
Dusseldorf, Germany
Jane@careerbrain.com

Expertise in Product Development • Commercialization & Global Market Expansion
Telecoms • Consumer Electronics • Sports & Leisure Industries

Dynamic management career leading turnaround and high-growth organizations through unprecedented profitability and explosive market growth worldwide. Combine extensive strategic planning, competitive positioning, life cycle management, channel management and product development/management qualifications with strong general management, P&L management, organizational development, workforce management, and multicultural communication skills. MBA; multilingual - fluent German, English, Italian, intermediate Japanese.

PROFESSIONAL EXPERIENCE
MAJOR ELECTRONICS COMPANY, Dusseldorf, Germany   1992 to 2000
    The second largest electronics company worldwide ranking #15 in the Global Fortune 500 ratings.
Senior Vice President Marketing
        Executive Board Member recruited to design marketing strategies and implement systems/processes to lead a worldwide marketing function as part of the business group's aggressive turnaround program.
        Accountable for a $250 million marketing budget. Oversee worldwide marketing operations including business strategy and benchmarking, technology strategy, market research, consumer marketing, regional marketing (EMEA, Asia, U.S.), marketing communications, new media including Internet, intranet, and extranet, and business-to-consumer e-commerce. Manage a staff of 77 through 10 direct reports.

- Led the marketing initiatives for the successful launch of two mobile phone product lines transitioning losses of $200 million in 97/98 to profits of $30 million in 98/99 and doubling world market share to approximately 8%.
- Delivered a 5-point improvement in brand awareness, and 50% relevant set improvement for mobile and cordless phones throughout China and Europe.
- Introduced a worldwide marketing communications spending performance initiative slashing communication costs by $10 million.
- Identified and initiated business development strategies and technology vehicles instrumental in developing international marketing partnerships and equity investments.
- Established a price/value-based market analysis instrument together with the market research and consumer marketing groups to develop pricing accuracy generating revenue increases exceeding $20 million.
- Directed e-commerce marketing initiatives leading to the development of 7 operational online stores in 5 European countries generating 4 million contacts with CAGR of 20% per week, followed by development of a virtual Customer Care Center.
- Conceived and initiated PR strategies for a new product launch generating over 130 million contracts within a few months.
- Led improvements in competitive market intelligence through enhancements to statistical reports and customer satisfaction surveys.

ELECTRONICS COMPANY, Bonn, Germany   1987 to 1992
> A leading European high-end TV, audio and consumer electronics company.

Marketing Director
> Joined this privately held company to improve product life cycle management and channel marketing initiatives. Oversaw budget administration, strategic planning and market research, international communications, training and product management. Directed a staff of 21.

- Instituted a series of channel management and segmentation improvements to correct market planning and positioning initiatives and reduce price erosion throughout retail distribution channels.
- Led development of product definition, life cycle management, and market launch strategies positioning company as the value-based market leader of high-end TV sets in Germany with market share exceeding 14%.

ABC BICYCLE COMPANY, Berlin, Germany   1983 to 1987
> A global leading automotive, motorcycle and bicycle component equipment manufacturer.

Director of Marketing International
> Led transition from an engineering-driven traditional gear hub manufacturer to a market-oriented competitor in the sport and leisure industry. Reported to Division President.

- Established a marketing department, devised strategies for over 1,000 SKUs within 6 product lines, delivered a profit for the first time in 8 years, and boosted new product sales ratios from 10% to 40%.
- Headed up a special internal R&D audit and restructuring project leading to the creation of marketing-driven product development teams. Replaced 15% of R&D personnel, established R&D controls, reduced R&D costs by $500,000, and earned a $30,000 project completion bonus.

ABC AUTOMOTIVE, Wolfsburg, Germany   1980 to 1983
> Leading automotive and home appliance manufacturer.

Product Group Manager
> Oversaw European product management and marketing initiatives for the $500 million Electronic Division. Successfully introduced brands in France, Italy, and England.

EDUCATION

M.B.A., University of California, Berkeley
Diplome d'enseignement Supérieur Europeen de Management, Centre d'Etudes Européennes Supérieures de Management (CESEM), France
Diplom-Betriebswirt (FH), Business Administration, Europäisches Studienprogramm für Betriebswirtschaft (ESB)

INTERNSHIPS

Country Chamber of Commerce, Osaka, Japan, Oskar Duisberg Society Scholarship
> Counseled German and Japanese firms in all aspects of business for their respective countries.

Kornwestheim Club Vertrieb GmbH, Kornwestheim, Germany, Marketing concepts in direct sales.

Senior Management Executive

Jane Swift
9 Central Avenue
San Diego, CA 92109
(619) 555-1212
Jane@careerbrain.com

New Business Development • Strategic Partnerships • Product Marketing

Accomplished Senior Executive with a strong affinity for technology and a keen business sense for the application of emerging products to add value and expand markets. Proven talent for identifying core business needs and translating into technical deliverables. Launched and managed cutting-edge Internet programs and services to win new customers, generate revenue gains, and increase brand value.

Unique combination of technical and business/sales experience. Articulate and persuasive in explaining the benefits of e-commerce technologies and how they add value, differentiate offerings, and increase customer retention. Highly self-motivated, enthusiastic, and profit oriented.

*Expertise in Internet services, emerging payment products,
secure electronic commerce, smart card technology, and Java.*

AREAS OF QUALIFICATION

Business

- Sales & Marketing
- Business Planning
- Business & Technical Requirements
- Contract Negotiations

- Business Development
- Project Management

- Strategic Initiatives
- Strategic Partnerships
- Revenue Generation
- Relationship Management

Technical

- Electronic Commerce
- Public Key Infrastructure
- Stored Value
- Complex Financial Systems

- Encryption Technology
- Firewalls
- Digital Certificates
- Authorization, Clearing, Settlement

- Key Management
- Smart Cards
- Internet & Network Security
- Dual and Single Message

PROFESSIONAL EXPERIENCE

ABC Credit Card Corp., San Diego, CA   *1999 to Present*
E-COMMERCE AND SMART CARD CONSULTANT

- Developed strategic e-commerce marketing plans for large and small merchants involving Web purchases and retail transactions using a multifunctional, microcontroller smart card for both secure Internet online commerce and point-of-sale offline commerce.
- Combined multiple software products for Internet and non-Internet applications: home banking, stored value, digital certificates, key management, rewards & loyalty program, PCS/GSM cell phone, and contactless microcontroller with RF communications without direct POS contact.
- Consulted on business and technical requirements to define new e-commerce products and essential deliverables for ABC Credit Card, valued at $2.5 MM, supporting and enhancing Internet transactions.
- Analyzed systems relating to the point of sale environment in the physical world and at the merchant server via the Internet for real-time authorization, clearing, and settlement.
- Managed projects including the requirements management system for electronic commerce products affecting core systems: authorization, clearing, and settlement. Provided expertise about business and technical issues regarding SET and the Credit Card Payment Gateway Service.

Communications Technology Corporation, Miami, FL   *1994 to 1999*
MANAGER OF WESTERN REGION CHANNEL PARTNER PROGRAM
- Developed and maintained business relationships with large Fortune 500 customers and partners that use or resell client-server software for applications and contracts involving e-commerce and smart card technology for a variety of Internet/Intranet products: home banking, EDI, stored value, digital certificates, key management, perimeter defense with proxy firewalls, secure remote access.
- Negotiated an exclusive contract with one of the largest government and commercial contractors in the industry, projected to generate $2–4 million over a 24–36 month period. Contract includes secure remote access, telecommuting, secure health care applications.

Avanta Corp., Miami, FL   *1990 to 1994*
SENIOR SOFTWARE ENGINEER / SOFTWARE INSTRUCTOR
- Designed new programs and trained software engineers in object oriented analysis and design using UML. Solutions that were implemented in C++ in a UNIX environment.
- Managed a software engineering group of 53 individuals. Developed in-house program that saved over $150,000 in training costs for state-of-the-art communications system software development.
- Received Peer Award for outstanding performance; earned a performance evaluation rating of 4.2/5.0.
- Developed and maintained C and C++ communication software in a UNIX environment.
- Created curriculum and course materials that reduced overall training costs by more than $150,000. Coordinated and presented software training programs.

EDUCATION AND CREDENTIALS
- B.S., Electrical Engineering, University of Miami, Emphasis: software engineering, Minor: Psychology, President of the Sigma Sigma Fraternity
- Top Secret Security Clearance with Polygraph

Senior Sales and Marketing Manager

JAMES SHARPE
9 Central Avenue
Atlantic City, NJ 08404
(609) 555-1212
James@careerbrain.com
Page 1 of 2

Top-producing sales and marketing professional with nine years of management experience in world-class organizations. Consistently successful in developing new markets, penetrating new territories, identifying and capturing new business, and managing large-scale events for Fortune 500 companies worldwide. Goal-driven manager committed to developing outcomes mutually benefiting the company and the client. Excellent qualifications in building corporate relationships with industry leaders.

Areas of expertise include:

- New Account Development
- Key Account Management
- Client Needs Assessment
- Contract Negotiations
- Competitive / Strategic Planning

- Large-Scale Meeting / Event Planning
- Catering Planning / Management
- Co-Marketing Partnerships
- Relationship Management
- Customer Service / Satisfaction

PROFESSIONAL EXPERIENCE

EXQUISITE RESORT SUITES, Atlantic City, NJ   1996 to 2000
Senior Sales Manager

Joined company to lead market entry/penetration initiatives throughout the Northeast Region of the U.S. for this privately-held exclusive resort with 800 suites, a 60,000 sq. ft. conference center, and a full range of guest amenities. Managed business growth among Fortune 500 corporate accounts and national association accounts.

- Developed and maintained relationships with corporate meeting planners of major accounts including IBM, AT&T, Ralston Purina, Bell South, AT&T, Siemens, Medtronic, and others to develop custom-tailored business meeting packages.
- Worked closely with corporate planners throughout all phases of strategic and tactical planning, coordination, and execution of major events to insure superior service and guest relations.
- Captured national association accounts including American Cancer Society, American Heart Association, New York Bar Association, and New Jersey Institute of CPAs.
- Sold and orchestrated multiyear bookings to numerous associations and corporate accounts.
  Achievements
  - Built territory and increased revenues from $1 million to over $7 million within first year.
  - Achieved 157% of annual booking goals (2500 room nights per month).

BUSCH GARDENS, Tampa, Florida   1993 to 1996
Catering Sales Manager

Challenged to develop new markets and products for multicultural groups visiting Walt Disney World.

- Identified target market, initiated contact with prospects, developed proposals, and forged major account relationships.
- Worked closely with corporate planners at Exxon, Compaq, IBM, Frito Lay, McDonald's, and others to create unique and extravagant parties and events ranging up to $2 million per event.
- Sold, planned, and coordinated catered group events for corporate accounts and private parties ranging from 2 to 19,000 guests.
- Developed comprehensive strategic and tactical plans for every phase of event including logistics, transportation, food and beverage, entertainment, and gifts to create a memorable occasion.

- Oversaw scheduled events and served as troubleshooter and liaison between park operators, managers, and corporate clients to resolve issues and insure guest satisfaction and loyalty.
- Compiled planning, tracking, and forecasting reports using proprietary computer system.
    Achievements
    - Achieved 130% of Catering Sales & Service Team Goals, 199X.
    - Consistently exceeded individual annual sales goals.

INTERNATIONAL HOTEL, Tampa, Florida   1985 to 1993
Fast track promotions through a series of increasingly responsible positions based on business growth and improved sales revenues for this high-volume airport property.
Sales Manager-Midwest   (1992 to 1993)
Sales Manager-Orlando   (1989 to 1992)
Associate Director of Catering   (1985 to 1988)
Catering Manager   (1985)

- Created innovative guest packages for corporate accounts locally and nationally for this first-rate property with 300 rooms, a 12,000 sq. ft. conference center, and several guest services facilities.
- Developed corporate and professional relationships throughout the industry and coordinated with other properties to accommodate extremely large groups.
- Identified target accounts and consistently developed new business driving increased revenues.
- Promoted property through trade show and convention participation, including public speaking engagements for large groups.
- Planned and coordinated exclusive large-scale intimate client events for the affluent.
    Achievement
    - Achieved 131% of sales goals throughout the Midwest Region, 1993

CHINESE COURT RESTAURANT, Orlando, Florida   1983 to 1985
Catering/Sales Manager
Successfully sold Chinese themed parties to international wholesale and corporate convention groups.

EDUCATION
B.S., Marketing - University of Nevada at Las Vegas, 1982
B.S., Multinational Business Operations - University of Nevada at Las Vegas, 1982
Diploma, Certificat de Langue Francaise, Institut Catholique De Paris, 1983 (Study Abroad Program)

PROFESSIONAL DEVELOPMENT
Sales Training:
International Hotel, BEST Programs (Building Effective Sales Techniques), Top Achiever Sales, Travel Management Companies, Best Practices
Designation
Certified Meeting Professional (CMP)
Affiliations
Meeting Planners International, Member
American Society of Association Executives, Member

Senior Technology Executive

James Sharpe
9 Central Avenue
Charleston, WV 25301
(304) 555-1212
James@careerbrain.com

Page 1 of 2

Accomplished Management Executive with 15+ years of experience and a verifiable record of delivering enhanced productivity, streamlined operations, and improved financial performance. Natural leader with strong entrepreneurial spirit and a special talent for transitioning strategy into action and achievement. Highly effective team building and motivational skills.

Multifunctional expertise includes:

- Corporate Information Technology
- Staffing & Management Development
- Quality & Productivity Improvement
- Marketing Strategy & Management

- Strategic & Business Planning
- Customer Service & Satisfaction
- Operations Management
- Team Building & Leadership

PROFESSIONAL EXPERIENCE

Roberts Company   1992 - Present
CHIEF INFORMATION OFFICER, Roberts Co., Charleston, WV (1997 - Present)
PRESIDENT, Martins Systems (Roberts Co. subsidiary), Elmview, WV (1997 - Present)

Appointed to these dual senior-level positions and challenged to create and execute technology strategy for Roberts Co. and subsidiaries of the $700 million Roberts Information Services Corporation. Concurrently provide executive oversight for the development and deployment of software products/services and MIS solutions for Martins Systems, affiliate offices, and 3,900 independent agents.

Provide leadership for a team of 200 management and support personnel. Administer a $16 million annual budget. Scope of accountabilities is expansive and includes planning and strategy, operations management, human resource affairs, customer service, marketing, management reporting, and communications.

Key Management Achievements

- Built the complete corporate technology infrastructure from the ground up. Developed technology strategies and tactical plans mapped to align with corporate goals.
- Serve as a member of the corporate Leadership Council. Define corporate vision; develop business plans, create strategies, and establish tactical goals for all business units.
- Established a high-performance management staff and created a team-based work atmosphere that promotes cooperation to achieve common corporate objectives. Instituted a series of initiatives that substantially improved communications between staff and management.
- Developed and integrated programs to maximize productive and efficient use of technology throughout the corporation. Instituted "user champions" to serve as technical experts within each business unit, launched executive "boot camps" to train management in aggressive computer use, and built responsive help centers for technical support.
- Spearheaded creation and implementation of a customer information and marketing team responsible for developing an award-winning marketing program, promotions, direct-mail campaigns, and demonstrations and tours.
- Created innovative processes utilizing product specialists for management of sales leads and distributor networks, resolution of customer escalated issues, and provision of work-flow and engineering consulting for company offices and agents.

James Sharpe (304) 555-1212
page 2 of 2

Key Technical Achievements
- Led implementation of client/server software suite that won the industry's 1996 and 1998 Title Tech Discovery Award for best and most innovative title industry software.
- Spearheaded development of numerous technical infrastructure projects including the corporate Internet presence, corporate intranet, Web hosting solutions for independent agents, and electronic commerce solutions for offices, agents, and service providers in the real estate industry.
- Orchestrated development of an award-winning marketing program, Power Tools for the Modern World, that won the local and district GOLD ADDY awards for best overall marketing program.
- Guided development and implementation of a title industry software suite installed in 400 systems throughout the distributor network. Designed and deployed training programs to insure high quality service levels.
- Managed creation of an Electronic Underwriting Manual that was selected as best policies and procedures implementation in the National Folio Awards competition, 1996.
- Led design and implementation of a 1,200-user corporate WAN, a centralized help desk, a 2000-user corporate e-mail system, and a comprehensive training center for desktop applications.

PRESIDENT, Roberts Gilday, Gilday, FL (1988 - 1992)
Promoted to manage all operations for this Roberts Company subsidiary. Took over leadership for a staff of 25 and recruited/built to 90+ personnel. Oversaw all management reporting, finances, marketing, product delivery, and closing services.

Key Management Achievements
- Delivered profits throughout a severe recession that crashed the local real estate market.
- Maintained a consistent 15% market share despite a tripling in the local competition.
- Achieved standing in the top 15% in profitability and revenues across all company offices nationwide.
- Created and deployed a realtor marketing program including a series of 20 seminars; built strong industry relationships and established a reputation as the area's premier experts.
- Pioneered innovative marketing strategies to reach new markets and build a network of industry professionals.

COMMERCIAL CLOSER, Roberts Gilday, Gilday, FL (1985 - 1988)
Hired to develop and manage a commercial closing division. Achieved the highest market share of commercial closings in the local market.

EDUCATION
Juris Doctor, West Virginia University (1985)
Bachelor of Arts, Business, West Virginia University (1982)

PROFESSIONAL ACTIVITIES
Frequent Lecturer, Title Tech Technology Conferences, 1995 - Present
Member, Systems Committee, American Land Title Association, 1994 - Present
Member, "Technology 2000" Planning Committee, American Land Title Association, 1994 - Present

Senior Technology Executive

Jane Swift
9 Central Avenue
Los Angeles, CA 90071
(213) 555-1212
Jane@careerbrain.com

SENIOR TECHNOLOGY EXECUTIVE

Project Management ● *Multimedia Communications & Production* ● *MIS Management*

Exceptionally creative management executive uniquely qualified for a digital media technical production position by a distinctive blend of hands-on technical, project management, and advertising/communications experience. Offer a background that spans broadcast, radio, and print media; fully fluent and proficient in interactive and Internet technologies and tools.

Proven leader with a strength for identifying talent, building and motivating creative teams that work cooperatively to achieve goals. Highly articulate with excellent interpersonal skills and a sincere passion for blending communications with technology. Capabilities include:

- Project Planning & Management
- Account Management & Client Relations
- Multimedia Communications & Production
- Information Systems & Networking
- Conceptual & Creative Design
- Work Plans, Budgets & Resource Planning
- Department Management
- Interactive / Internet Technologies
- Technology Needs Assessment & Solutions
- Team Building & Leadership

PROFESSIONAL EXPERIENCE

LaRoche Investments, Inc., Los Angeles, CA   *1986 - Present*
VICE PRESIDENT OF MIS (1997 - Present)
ASSISTANT VICE PRESIDENT OF IT/CORPORATE COMMUNICATIONS (1992 - 1997)
CORPORATE COMMUNICATIONS OFFICER (1988 - 1992)
ASSOCIATE (1986 - 1988)

Advanced rapidly through a series of increasingly responsible positions with this U.S. based, European investment group. Initially hired to manage market research projects, advanced to plan and execute corporate communications projects, and in 1992, assumed responsibility for spearheading the introduction of emerging technologies to automate the entire company.

Current scope of responsibility is expansive and focuses on strategic planning, implementation, and administration of all information systems and technology. Lead technical staff members, manage budgets, select and oversee vendors, define business requirements, and produce deliverables through formal project plans. Manage systems configuration and maintenance, troubleshoot problems, plan and direct upgrades, and test operations to ensure optimum systems functionality and availability.

Technical Contributions

- Pioneered the company's computerization from the ground floor; led the installation and integration of a state-of-the-art and highly secure network involving 50+ workstations running on 6 LANs interconnected by V-LAN switching technology.
- Defined requirements; planned and accelerated the implementation of advanced technology solutions, deployed on a calculated timeframe, to meet the short and long-term needs of the organization.
- Orchestrated the introduction of sophisticated applications and multimedia technology to streamline workflow processes, expand presentation capabilities, and keep pace with the competition.
- Administered the life cycle of multiple projects from initial systems/network planning and technology acquisition through installation, training, and operation. Saved hundreds of thousands in consulting fees by managing IS and telecommunication issues in-house.

Business Contributions

- Created and produced high-impact multimedia presentations to communicate the value and benefits of individual investment projects to top-level company executives. Tailored presentations to appeal to highly sophisticated, multicultural audiences.
- Assembled and directed exceptionally well qualified project teams from diverse creative disciplines; collaborated with and guided photographers, videographers, copywriters, script writers, graphic designers, and artists to produce innovative presentations and special events.
- Performed market research and analyses to determine risks and feasibility of multiple investment projects valued at up to $150 million. Developed and recommended tactical plans to transform vision into achievement.

Broadcast, Print, and Radio Advertising & Production   *1971 - 1985*

DIRECTOR OF ADVERTISING, Schwarzer Advertising Associates, New York, NY (1983 - 1985)
ADVERTISING ACCOUNT EXECUTIVE, Schoppe, New York, NY (1984) / Rainbow Advertising, Brooklyn, NY
   (1981 - 1983) / Marcus Advertising, Phoenix, AZ (1980 - 1981) / WCHN, WTYR, AND WSCZ, Boston, MA (1979 - 1980) / WFDX-TV, WFDX-FM, WKLU, WERS, WQRT, Lehigh Valley, PA (1971 - 1978)
WRITER/PRODUCER, RADIO PROGRAMMING, WPTR, Detroit, MI (1971)

   Early career involved a series of progressive creative and account management positions spanning all advertising mediums: multimedia, television, radio, and print. Worked directly with clients to assess complex and often obscure needs; conceptualized and developed advertising campaigns to communicate the desired message in an influential manner.

Achievement Highlights

- Designed, wrote, produced, and launched advertising campaigns that consistently positioned clients with a competitive distinction. Developed a reputation for ability to accurately intuit and interpret clients' desires and produce deliverables that achieved results.
- Hand-selected and led creative teams consisting of graphic designers, artists, musicians, talent, cartoonists, animators, videographers, photographers, and other freelancers and third-party creative services to develop and produce multimillion dollar advertising campaigns.
- Won accolades for the creation, production, and launch of a 4-color fractional-page advertisement that generated the greatest response in the history of the publication. Honored with a featured personal profile recognizing achievements.
- Developed and applied a unique style and advertising philosophy that accounted for the nuances of human psychology and utilized innovative, brainy, and sometimes startling techniques to capture attention and influence the target market.

EDUCATION & TRAINING

A.A.S, Broadcast Production, Russ Junior College, Boston, MA, 1971
Continuing education in Marketing Research and Broadcast Production, 1981 - 1983
The School of Visual Arts, New York, NY

TECHNICAL QUALIFICATIONS

Innate technical abilities and interest in emerging technologies and digital communications. Trained and fully versed in all aspects of network design, implementation, installation, and maintenance. Advanced skill in the installation, configuration, customization, and troubleshooting of software suites and applications, hardware, and peripherals within the Windows environment (3.x, 95, 98, NT 3.5, NT 3.51, NT 4). Proficient with most Web development, multimedia, word processing, spreadsheet, graphic/presentation, and database tools and applications.

Software Development

James Sharpe
9 Central Avenue
White Sulphur Springs, MT 59645
(406) 555-1212
James@careerbrain.com

Summary

IS professional recognized for broad-based skills encompassing Web, hardware and software solutions. Move effortlessly through and adapt readily to ever changing technologies. Areas of expertise encompass: project management, team leadership, staff supervision, coding, design, testing, user training/support, troubleshooting, customer relations.

Technical Skills

Software: MS Office Suite, Quattro Pro, DacEasy, Act!, Premier, Avid Cinema, Authorware, Director, PhotoShop, CorelDraw, VoicePad, Naturally Speaking, Impromptu, PowerPlay, Visio

Hardware: SCSI, RAID Systems, IDE, NIC's, video/audio network hubs, switches, and routers

Web/Internet: Netscape Commerce Server, MS IIS, HTML, CGI, ISAPI

Databases & Technologies: Dbase, Paradox, MS Access, MS SQL Server, Progress, DDE, OLE, OLE2, ActiveX, Automations Servers (in and out of process), Active Forms, DCOM, Memory Mapped Files, Compound Files, MS Transaction Server (version 1.0), NT Services, Named Pipes, Thunking, Multithreaded applications and libraries (Win32), WinSock, mail services, HTTP, FTP, NNTP, TCP, UDP, SMTP, POP3

Operating Systems/Services: MS DOS, MS Windows 3.11, 95, 98, NT Server/Workstation, UNIX, MS Exchange, MS SQL Server, WINS, RAS, DHCP, IIS

Programming Languages: Delphi, Pascal, Progress, C/C++, VB, Fortran, PowerBuilder, Perl, Assembly

Career Highlights

- Recruited to manage several major projects at Technical Services (TS):
    - Reconfigured entire IS department. Developed specifications for new servers for file sharing, Web, and database. Redesigned network 100 Base T; installed T1; and enables WINS, DHCP, Exchange Server, MS SQL Server and IIS.
    - Revamped networks, servers, and internet connections to resolve the weekly, sometimes daily, crashing of network.
    - Project manager for medical/Internet project that was designed to provide continuing education courses online.
    - Supervised two professionals in IS and Web development.
    - Wrote several interfaces for authorware, I.E. 4.0 and Exchange, and created Intranet as dynamic pages from MSQL database.

- Founded Holbrook Software, with sole responsibility for account development, project planning, staffing, and customer relations. Developed software solutions for several public agencies and private firms:
    - Created an employee scheduling software, Illinois married filing status software with yearly upgrades and conversion program
    - Developed a criminal history database, investigation and complaint software packages for City of Missoula, Montana Police Department.
    - Developed a UCR (uniform criminal reporting) software package for state of Ohio. Program enables small cities, villages, and townships to participate in computerized national UCR.
    - Created software to accommodate membership database, account histories, invoices, membership functions, bank deposits, reports, and rosters for the Joliet Brokers Association.

- Designed Vesex Computer Systems Web site, applying knowledge of HTML/CGI, security, and interactive pages, among other functions
  - Developed user-defined help feature for online help
  - Provided HTML CGI and Winhelp training
  - Created interfaces to third-party products
  - Gained extensive expertise with large relational databases

Professional Experience

Holbrook Software   *1997 - Present*
Software Developer/Proprietor

Electronic Systems   *1994 - 1996*
Director of IS, Programming and Web Development

MIC   *1992 - 1993*
Software Developer

Vesex Computer Systems   *1990 - 1991*
Interface Developer/Web Programmer/Webmaster; Online Help Programmer

B. Hevers & Co.   *1985 - 1990*
Regional Computer Coordinator

CompuStat   *1984 - 1985*
Customer Service Representative

Professional Development
Coursework in Advanced Programming, Pascal, and Fortran

Store Manager

James Sharpe
9 Central Avenue
Oldsmar, FL 33557
(813) 555-1212
James@careerbrain.com

WORK EXPERIENCE

Manager, A National Kitchen Utensil Retailer. 1997-present
Manage daily operations of a $2-million annual business. Staff of 12 people. Responsible for increasing sales and profitability and decreasing expenses.

Increased gross margin by 25% and net contribution by 105% on a 3% sales increase.

Senior Assistant Buyer, Stern's, Oldsmar, FL. 1993-1997
Controlled open to buy purchase journal, profitability reports, weekly three month estimate of sales, stocks, and markdown dollars. Planned and negotiated sales promotions, advertising, and special purchases.

Coordinated training and teamwork with managers and merchants in the 22 stores.

Increased department sales 18% more than the Division's increase.

Assistant Buyer. Assisted selection and distribution of merchandise. Managed all buying office functions while learning to plan sales, control stocks, and markdown dollars. Created weekly, monthly, and seasonal financial plans.

Developed all systems to support the growth of the branch from a $1-million volume to a $4-million annual volume.

Buyer/Manager, Gulf Gifts, FL. 1990-1993

Bought merchandise for two different gift stores. Directed daily store operations and sales. Directed merchandise presentation, inventory control, and customer service. Scheduled and supervised a 7-person staff.

Increased sales volume 22% more than corporate projection.

Manager, Willis & Geiger, New York, NY. 1987-1990

Direct daily store operations. Analyzed trends in fashion, merchandise, and consumer needs. Planned effective marketing strategy, displays, advertising, and an employee sales program.

Increased annual net sales volume by 33%.

EDUCATION   Fashion Institute of Technology, New York, NY. B.A. Merchandising, 1986

Systems and Network Manager

James Sharpe
9 Central Avenue
Syracuse, NY 12345
(315) 555-1212
James@careerbrain.com

Profile
- 15 years of management and hands-on background working in IT infrastructure.
- Experience with world-class banks and financial institutions in New York, London, Paris.
- Hold MBA in Banking and Finance.
- Chosen for the 2000 International Who's Who in Information Technology.

Areas of Expertise

network design • systems management • LAN administration • strategic planning • team formation and leadership • budget preparation • project planning and management • presentation • business writing • resource management • product and design research • vendor interface and negotiation • systems conversion • computer operations • systems implementation • branch start-ups and automation • disaster recovery • system migrations • data center overhauls and moves • applications support

Executive Development
A Fortune 100 Company, Syracuse, NY
Vice President and Manager of Network Operations   1998 to present
Control $1 million budget and oversee five technicians in the design, implementation, and support of company's WAN and LAN infrastructure. Handle heavy resource management and coordination with internal departments, vendors, and network integration companies to define scopes of work, technical designs, product selection, required resources, schedules, and price negotiation. Budget resources and prepare reports. Hire, schedule, and review technicians.

Projects
AT&T frame relay and Cisco router implementation, TCP/IP address conversion, Compuserve RAS implementation, Cisco switched Ethernet 100mb/1 gb Catalyst implementation, HP Open View and Cisco Works implementation, MS DHCP and proxy server implementation. Managed project teams at remote sites to implement NT servers, routers, PC hardware upgrades, and Windows 95/NT images. Co-managed 1,100-user move.

A Major Investment Bank, London   1995 to 1998
Network Manager
Managed WAN daily support, hardware installation/configurations, and network changes. Monitored/configured private frame relay voice and data network. Monitored ACC routers and NT servers. Performed Windows NT 3.51 server and workstation installations. Configured ACC routers, Adtran CSU's, and Newbridge 3612 and 3606 multiplexors for remote site installations.

A Large Multinational Bank, Paris   1992 to 1995
Network Operations Supervisor
Managed all network and computer operations for the international hub site, reporting directly to the Technology Manager and supervising a team of technicians and computer operators. Supervised three direct reports, supported traders, reviewed/upgraded operations, handled troubleshooting, researched products and interfaced/negotiated with vendors.

James Sharpe (315) 555-1212

- Completed full office start-up in Luxembourg in three months. Implemented LAN, voice, data, and video capabilities. Hired and trained computer operator to support local users. Implemented support procedures and documentation.
- Saved company over $50,000 annually: Migrated video conferencing from leased lines to ISDN, cleaned up multiplexor maintenance contracts, discovered overpayment on WAN lines. Set up a new process to review all invoices and pre-approved all purchases and communications costs before forwarding to Technology Manager.

Technology Expertise

Hardware: Cisco 7206/4700/25XX, Cisco PIX firewall, Cabletron MMAC+/Smart Switch 6000's/MMAC8, Newbridge 46020/36XX, IDNX 20/12, CYLINK link encryptors, Paradyne CSU's, ACC routers, Northern Telecom Option 11, PictureTel 4000/M8000, VAX 4000/6310/8000, HSC50, RA60/80/82/90 disk drives, MTI disks in DSSI architecture, HP 9000 K100, Sun Ultra 10, HP Laserjet 3/4/5 and QMS laser printers, Dell/Digital/AST/IBM PC hardware, Intel/3Com NIC cards, Cabling knowledge includes category 3/5, IBM Type 1, fiber optic multimode, v.35, x.21, RS232.

Software: SWIFT Alliance v3.0, IBIS, ST400, Montran (CHIPS), Reuters, Telerate, ADP Executive Quotes, IFSL Green Bar Viewer, Euroclear, Tracs, Soar, MS Project 95, VISIO, MS Word/Excel/PowerPoint, Lotus Notes v4.6, MS Mail, Ami-Pro, Lotus 1-2-3, DOS, Chameleon v4.6, Sybase v11, COBOL, Pascal, BASIC.

Protocols/Operating Systems: Cisco IOS version 11.x, TCP/IP, IPX, frame relay, EIGRP, OSPF, RIP, PPP, ISDN, SNMP, DHCP, WINS/DNS, Netbeui, NetBIOS, DECnet, LAT, VAX/VMS v5.5-2, Pathworks v4.1/5.0, Windows NT Server 3.51 and 4.0, Netware 3.12, HP-UX v10.2, Solaris v2.6.1, OS/400 v2.3.

Education and Professional Development

M.B.A. in Banking and Finance, Syracuse University, Syracuse, New York

B.S. in Interdisciplinary Studies, Rensselaer Polytechnical Institute, Rensselaer, New York

Computer Operations Diploma (500 hour program), Institute for Data Systems, Mahopac, New York.

Additional technology courses: Network Design and Performance, Advanced Cisco Router Configuration, Microsoft Project 95. SYBASE SQL Server Administration, SYBASE Fast Track to SQL Server, Fundamentals of the HP UNIX System, Pathworks V5 Migration Planning, RDB Database Administration, Pathworks Tuning and Troubleshooting, PC Architecture and Troubleshooting.

Teacher (Entry-Level)

190-34 Nassau Boulevard
Brittonwoods, NY 11787 **James Sharpe**

(631) 555-3000
JSTeacher @hostmail.com

GOAL To secure a Social Studies teaching position at the secondary education level, 7-12

CERTIFICATIONS New York State Provisional Certification in Social Studies, 7-12, December 2001

EDUCATION STATE UNIVERSITY OF NEW YORK AT FARMINGVILLE, Farmingville, NY
Currently pursuing Masters of Arts in Teaching Social Studies
Anticipated May 2002 - Overall GPA 3.8

Bachelor of Science, Business and Economics, concentration in History
Graduated May 1999 - Overall GPA 3.8

Honors

Graduated Magna Cum Laude
Dean's List, 1995 - 1999, consecutively
Golden Key National Honor Society

Phi Alpha Theta National Historical Society
Sigma Beta National Honor Society
Phi Beta Kappa National Honor Society

Appointments **Teaching Assistant**, State University of New York at Farmingville, 2/98 - 5/99
- Selected to teach Advanced Labor Theory and Microeconomics curriculums.
- Collaborated on the development/implementation of challenging undergraduate lectures.

Internships **Financial Analyst,** Strategic Systems, The Banker, New York, NY, 6/97 - 9/97

Activities **Co-founder/Captain,** Farmingville University's Men's Club Volleyball Team, 9/95 - 5/99
- Planned and coordinated off-site tournaments, handled group transportation and lodging arrangements, and resourcefully managed an annual budget of $10,000.

**STUDENT
TEACHING**
11/01 - 6/02
9/01 - 10/01

BRITTONWOODS SCHOOL DISTRICT, Brittonwoods, NY
Combined knowledge and experience in the following positions:
Brittonwoods High School, Twelfth Grade
Brittonwoods Junior High School, Seventh Grade

Twelfth Grade
- Team teach and observe the instruction of Advanced Placement students, as well as class discussions on current events presented by community leaders Steve Israel and scheduled guest, Rick Lazzio, centered on terrorism and related issues.
- Foster a stimulating learning environment that integrates cooperative learning, role-playing, critical debates, graphic organizers, primary sources, and lesson review.
- Promote higher-level thinking skills through development of reinforcement-based mastery learning techniques modeled for students' individual learning styles.

Seventh Grade
- Held full responsibility for all aspects of instruction and classroom management activities for five daily Social Studies classes over a one-month period.
- Taught comprehensive Social Studies units on Ancient Americans, Anthropology, Archeology, Economics, and Political Science, providing students with an understanding of past civilizations' traditions, religions, agriculture, technology, military, government, and social structures.
- Formulated, administered, and graded lesson-specific tests.
- Participated in weekly Parent-Teacher conferences.

1/01 - 5/01
WESTFIELD SCHOOL DISTRICT, Westfield, NY
Per-diem Substitute Teacher, Grades Seventh - Twelfth
- Effectively taught regular and special education while demonstrating an ability to manage classroom responsibilities and easily establish rapport with students.

WORK HISTORY **Customer Relations Manager,** Food & Country Magazine, Mineola, NY, 6/96 - 5/00

Teacher [Experienced]

JAMES SHARPE

9 Central Avenue
Brentwood, NY 11717
(631) 412-7560

OBJECTIVE
To secure a position teaching English at the secondary education level, 7-12

EDUCATION
SAINT JOHN'S UNIVERSITY, Jamaica, NY
Bachelor of Arts in English, 2001
Minor: Secondary Education

SELDEN COMMUNITY COLLEGE, Selden, NY
Associates in Applied Science, Liberal Arts, 1997

CERTIFICATIONS
New York State Provisional Certification in English, 7-12
CPR / First Aid for Adults and Children

TEACHING EXPERIENCE
The following represents combined experience within the Calverton School District . . .
CALVERTON MIDDLE SCHOOL, Brentwood, NY

4/01 - present
Leave Replacement Computer Lab Teacher, Sixth Grade
- Facilitate the interactive learning process in a virtual classroom setting, utilizing the School Vista program to teach lessons and basic Internet navigation/keyboarding skills
- Implemented an English/Social Studies interdisciplinary unit incorporating the use of the Internet, spreadsheets, Web diagrams, and creative writing exercises to research, organize, and depict their understanding of King Arthur and the Middle Ages

11/00 - 4/01
Permanent Substitute Teacher, Sixth through Eighth Grades
- Managed classroom responsibilities and maintained continuity of the learning process
- Incorporated cooperative education and role playing activities to establish a relationship between course material and students' life experiences
- Devised a mock English Language Arts (ELA) test based on previous testing methodologies and content-specific rubrics; co-selected multiple choice questions for short stories; administered and proctored ELA standardized/mock tests
- Encouraged critical thinking skills through the use of challenging debate

9/00 - 11/00
Leave Replacement English Teacher, Seventh Grade
- Worked collaboratively with English, Science, Math and History teachers to implement an interdisciplinary unit on heritage, incorporating the use of essay writing, laboratory experiments, graphing, and historical research on family roots
- Taught students to formulate DBQs, enabling students to develop an understanding of diversify, individualism, and creativity through short story multicultural literature:
  - "Aida," authored by Leontyne Price (Egyptian and Ethiopian)
  - "The First Flute," authored by Dorothy Sharp Carter (Central American)
  - "L.A.F.F.," authored by Lense Nemioka (Asian-American)
- In participation with the cooperating Social Studies teacher, implemented an interdisciplinary poetry unit on Veteran's Day to develop students' creative/critical thinking skills, and an appreciation for the causes/effects of war through the use of personification, simile, and metaphors illustrated in war-related poetry
- Assisted in the planning and coordination of the 2000 Year Book, providing consultation on layout, and supervised the collection of student photographs, poetry, and song lyrics
- Interfaced with Guidance Counselors, Teachers and Parents at BPST and Parent/Teacher meetings to discuss and review curriculum development and student progress

4/00 - 6/00
2/00 - 4/00
WESTFIELD SCHOOL DISTRICT, Westfield, NY
Substitute Teacher, Grades K-12; Student Teacher, Tenth and Eleventh Grades

CAMP DIRECTOR
SAINT JOHN'S SUMMER CAMP, Jamaica, NY, 1995 - present

SKILLS
Windows 95; MS Word/Excel 97; Word Perfect 6.0; School Vista; Claris Works; Internet

Teacher [Specialist]

Jane Swift
9 Central Avenue, Findlay, OH 45840
(419) 422-1390
jswift@careerbrain.com

PROFILE

A detail-oriented, high-energy ART TEACHER with the ability to motivate students to work at optimum levels while maintaining a comfortable, creative environment, and keeping a clear perspective of goals to be accomplished. Extensive experience in helping students broaden perspectives for personal expression through visual artistry. Qualified by:

Technical Skills	Self-Management & Transferable Skills	
Ceramics/Handbuilding	Resourcefulness	Perception & Enthusiasm
Collage	Creativity & Flexibility	Personal Expression
Paintings/Oils	Productive Competence	Artistic Impact

PROFESSIONAL EXPERIENCE

LIBERTY-BENTON ELEMENTARY SCHOOL, *Art Teacher*   Findlay, OH

2000 - 2002   Instructed grades K-4 at Liberty Benton Elementary in Art Studio and Art History; created
1998 - 1999   weekly art lessons with a variety of subject matter and mediums in both two-dimensional and three-dimensional projects. Instructed a small group of students in a gifted art program; selected artwork throughout the year and facilitated the annual student art show.

1999 - 2000   DELAWARE CITY SCHOOLS, *Art Teacher*   Delaware, OH
Full-time substitute for grades K-12 in the Delaware City School district; part-time art teacher for grades 1-5 at Woodward Elementary.

COMMUNITY INVOLVEMENT

SUMMER 1999   ARTS FESTIVAL, **Table Leader**   Findlay, OH
Collaborated in meetings throughout the year to organize an art activity table.
Recruited community volunteers to assist children with art projects.

FALL 2000   ARTS PARTNERSHIP   Findlay, OH
Bank One Student Art Exhibit,
Entered 5 students' artwork: 4 students received honorable mentions and 1 student received third place.

SUMMER 1999   Summer Arts Camp, **Head Instructor.** Assisted in recruiting volunteers for art, dance and theatre for one-week camp.

2000 - 2002   RIGHT TO READ, **Committee Member**   Findlay, OH
Helped organize a week of activities to promote the importance of reading.
Designed theme T-shirts worn throughout Right-to-Read Week.

2002   MOTHER HUBBARD'S LEARNING CUPBOARD   Findlay, OH
Commissioned by local store to design logo "character" to be imprinted on bags, checks, bookmarks, and signs.

EDUCATION

BOWLING GREEN STATE UNIVERSITY, Bowling Green, OH
Bachelor of Science in Education Degree, 1997
Major: Art Education, K-12 with emphasis in Painting
Minor: Psychology   GPA: 3.3

> "Choose a job you love,
> and you will never have to work
> another day in your life."
> – Confucius

International Scholarship Recipient to SACI School of Art in Florence, Italy, 1996

Telecommunications/Information Systems Management

James Sharpe
9 Central Avenue
San Francisco, CA 94127
(415) 555-1212
James@careerbrain.com

**Voice & Data Communications, Information Technology,
Project/Budget Management, Strategic Planning**

Expert in the design, development, and delivery of cost-effective, high-performance technology and communication solutions to meet challenging business demands. Extensive qualifications in all facets of projects from initial feasibility analysis and conceptual design through implementation, training, and enhancement. Excellent organizational, budget management, leadership, team building, negotiation, and project management qualifications.

Professional Experience

Food Systems International, San Francisco, CA   *1995 - Present*

Achieved fast-track promotion through positions of increasing responsibility for multibillion dollar international company with 30,000 employees worldwide.

Telecommunications Manager   *1998 - Present*

Responsible for management of $15 million department budget. Fully accountable for overall strategy for telecommunications technology acquisition and integration, vendor selection and negotiation, usage forecasting, workload planning, project budgeting, and administration. Plan and direct implementation of emerging telecommunications solutions at all domestic locations consisting of 125 facilities. Provide direction regarding telecommunications technology to affiliates throughout U.S. Lead cross-functional project teams; supervise technical and administrative staff with 20 direct reports. Fully accountable for department's strategic vision and leadership. Representative achievements include:

- Directed $40 million annual MCI network conversion at 200 locations within six months, saving company $15 million over three years.
- Designed and managed implementation of network utilizing Lucent and Octel at more than 100 locations in 12 months, realizing annual cost savings of $1 million.
- Served as technical project director for $12 million consolidation of East Coast headquarters with West Coast location.
- Facilitated move of corporate headquarters involving 3,000 employees over a four-day weekend.
- Implemented video conferencing technology at more than 60 sites.
- Built a four-digit dialing network for Food Systems locations within a four-month period.

Assistant Manager of Telecommunications   *1996 - 1998*

Management Trainee   *1995*

Education
BS in Political Science, Northwestern University, Chicago, IL
Professional Development/Continuing Education: Various American Management Association workshops and courses; BCR technical/technical management courses.

Telemarketing Professional

James Sharpe
9 Central Avenue
Waterbury, VT 05676
(802) 555-1212
James@careerbrain.com

Profile

Telemarketing Specialist/Sales Manager/Team Leader with proven ability to lead sales teams in fast-paced, high-volume environments. Able to coordinate multiple projects and meet deadlines under pressure. Outstanding record in training, motivating, and retaining employees. Knowledgeable in telemarketing business methods and applicable laws.

Telemarketing Experience

Telephone Sales Representative, United States Telemarketing, Waterbury, Vermont, 1999 - Present

Management Trainer, AT&T Net, Burlington, Vermont, 1998 - 1999
Directed performance, training, and recruiting for 13- to 15-person bay marketing long distance and wireless services by telephone to prospective customers across the country.

- Implemented creative sales contests and incentive programs that increased revenues, boosted morale, and minimized employee turnover.
- Trained top-performing sales teams on effective telephone sales and closing techniques.
- Supervised team performance through call splitting and statistical reporting. Maintained target levels for quality management.
- Exceeded corporate goals for team sales per hour and sales hours fulfillment. Consistently ranked in top three of 32 bays.

Team Leader, Domestic Features, Burlington, Vermont, 1997 - 1998
Managed 9-person telemarketing team marketing family-friendly videos for privately owned international film production company with $60 million in annual revenues.

- Led successful teams recognized for commitment to company cause of promoting nonviolent films with no sexual content or innuendo, and influencing the film industry to offer more films of this nature.

Sales Experience

Independent Sales Professional/Certified Flooring Inspector, Burlington, Vermont, 1996 - 1997

Store Manager, Stickly Carpets, Burlington, Vermont, 1994 - 1996
Managed sales and operations for retail flooring business. Directed sales teams, scheduling, goal setting, and motivational seminars. Purchased merchandise from mills, negotiated contracts, and administered promotions and product merchandising.

- Achieved annual retail sales averaging $0.5 million with a gross profit margin of 35%.
- Hired, trained, and managed goal-oriented sales teams with below average turnover.
- Conducted in-service training seminars for sales representatives teaching detailed product information and sales techniques.

Training

B.A. in Human Services, University of Vermont, Burlington, Vermont, 1994
Ongoing Professional Development: sales training and motivational seminars with Anthony Robbins, Tommy Hopkins, Zig Ziglar, Stephen Covey

Trader

JAMES SHARPE

10 Madison Drive
Tarrytown, New York

(555) 555-5555
JSExecutive@hostmail.com

FINANCIAL SERVICES / BANKING EXECUTIVE
Sales ♦ Proprietary Trading ♦ Investment Banking

Consistent top performer with a track record of successive advancement achieved through proactive leadership, generating revenues and producing bottom-line results for global leaders in the financial services/banking industry.

Expertise in the origination, investment and sales of emerging markets fixed income securities for U.S. and European institutional investors with highly profitable results that outperform emerging market equity indices. Proficient in electronic trading.

Solid network of senior-level contacts in banks, corporations and government and originated debt capital markets transactions.

SELECTED ACHIEVEMENTS

- **Delivered $30 million in net profits for the Proprietary Trading Division of Hammond Bank Securities in 2000 and 2001 as the top contributor to the special situation equity and financing books. Instrumental in division's ranking #1 in profitability during 2001.**
- **Originated and managed several debt Private Placements for Hammond Bank's position and for clients of the financing book.**
- **Achieved top ranking in the division at Hammond Bank Securities for 3 consecutive years: #1 producer in emerging markets institutional fixed income sales, #1 producer of derivatives sales, #1 producer in Eurobond sales and #1 in structured financing. Generated $15 million in annual profits.**
- **Produced $45 million in profits over 3-year period for First Bank's Emerging Markets Division, recognized as the most profitable division within the organization.**
- **Spearheaded Eurobond syndication activity for First Bank, which became the #1 European bank involved in Eurobond underwriting over 2-year period. Participated in the syndication of 30% of all new issues - the Bank's first-ever participation in international new issues.**
- **Initiated the entire distribution of Eurobonds for First Bank, successfully cultivating relationships with over 40 institutional investors in Eurobonds and emerging markets fixed income securities.**

PROFESSIONAL EXPERIENCE

HAMMOND BANK SECURITIES, New York, New York (1993-present)
Senior Associate Director & Proprietary Trader (1997-present)
Selected to join the senior executive team in the emerging markets Proprietary Trading Division that managed U.S. $3+ billion in Bank capital. Originate and manage investments for several books: debt, equity, local currency and structured financing with a primary focus on equity investments and structured financing. Co-manage U.S. $1 billion financing book of emerging markets fixed income securities as well as U.S. $100 million equity special situation book.

Associate Director - Emerging Markets Institutional Fixed Income Sales (1993-1997)
Managed relationships with U.S. and Latin American institutional investors and sold Brady Bonds, eurobonds, derivatives, local currency products and structured financing.

continued...

JAMES SHARPE - PAGE 2

FIRST BANK, New York, New York (1987-1993)
Emerging Markets - Senior Proprietary Trader / Head of Capital Markets (1990-1993)
Sovereign Debt Proprietary Trader (1989-1990)
International Banking Officer - Emerging Markets Desk (1987-1989)
Advanced rapidly through progressively responsible positions; traded Eurobonds, Brady Bonds and loans for Bank's proprietary account and Private Banking Division; negotiated sovereign debt swaps. Managed US $10 million Proprietary trading line. Trained and mentored professionals new to the emerging markets desk. Established, developed and managed syndication and distribution of Brazilian eurobonds for the Bank. Built a strong distribution network with Swiss, Brazilian and U.S. institutional investors.

PRIOR ASSIGNMENTS
Consulting assignment with **LaRiviere & Company**, Paris, France, assisting with information technology and retail distribution projects for client companies. Subsequently trained in the International Trade Financing Division; participated in several European trade finance and loan syndication deals.

EDUCATION
B.S. in Financial Management
New York University (New York, New York
NASD licenses: Series 7 and 63

Traffic Control (Shipping and Receiving)

JANE SWIFT

9 Central Avenue • Greenwich, CT 06830 • (203) 555-1212 • Jane@careerbrain.com

SUMMARY OF QUALIFICATIONS

- Extensive, large volume *Traffic Control, Shipping & Receiving* knowledge; strong leadership abilities.
- Solid record of promotions based on performance. Insightful commitment to positive communication.
- Willing to take on new challenges within demanding deadlines utilizing progressive, results-oriented performance style.
- Strong time management and interpersonal skills. Extremely organized.
- Self-motivated, adaptable, loyal team player. Impeccable work ethic.
- Competent blueprint reading capabilities. Computer literate—proficient with spreadsheets.

EXPERIENCE

ABC EXTRUSION, Division of General Corporation • Greenwich, CT   1992 to 2000
Manufacturer of machinery for the rubber & plastic industry. Company name changed several times due to new ownership. Retained as a valuable employee through each transfer.

- **Traffic Control Manager**—Facilitated all shipments of large machinery and spare parts. Coordinated all paperwork and documentation including Bill of Lading, Certificate of Origin and Customs documents. Entered applicable data into computer system.
- **Receiving Manager**—Handled all receiving and stockroom department responsibilities. Identified, tagged and located parts in stock area. Retrieved components and piece parts for assembly floor personnel. Skilled using Federal Express Powership & Pitney Bowes shipping equipment.
- **Receiving**—Supported all receiving department functions. Identified, verified and received parts optimizing the computerized database.
- **Stockroom**—Stocked parts; recorded and cataloged items in database. Assisted in retrieving parts for assembly floor work orders.
- **Shipping**—Prepared and arranged U.P.S. shipments and packing of parts. Operated U.P.S. equipment documenting size, weight and type of cargo. Typed Bills of Lading and Customs forms. Recorded all shipping data.
- **Data Entry**—Logged all new parts and stockroom locations into database.
- **Expediter**—Identified, traced and accelerated parts in process to the next manufacturing operation. Directed finished parts to appropriate assembly areas. Tracked and updated shortage lists.
- **Licensed**—to operate overhead crane, forklift and overhead lifts.

HOMETOWN MARKET • Greenwich, CT   1975 to 1992
Produce Market

- **Owner/Manager**—Directed and oversaw daily store operations. Supervised up to ten employees. Facilitated operational performance of store, implemented all phases of management functions inclusive of inventory, presentations, display, advertising, customer and employee relations, all accounting/bookkeeping, payroll and receivables. Generated and maintained reports, spreadsheets and mailing lists of over 10,000 people.

CONTINUING EDUCATION

- Blueprint Reading Certification, ABC
- Forklift Operation, ABC
- Crane Operation, ABC
- Accounting I, II, Connecticut State University

References Available Upon Request

VP of Operations

Jane Swift	Page 1 of 2

Jane Swift
9 Central Avenue
Houston, TX 77002
(713) 555-1212
Jane@careerbrain.com

SUMMARY OF QUALIFICATIONS

Vice President of Operations, Manufacturing. 20+ years experience in the creative leadership of multisite manufacturing operations to improve productivity, quality, and efficiency. Facilitated significant cost savings through expertise in:

- Operations Systems
- Strategic Planning
- Cost Management
- Facilities Design
- Offshore Production

- Manufacturing Process
- Quality Control
- Supplier Partnership
- Human Resources/Labor Relations
- Compliance

PROFESSIONAL EXPERIENCE

Acme Automotive Products, Houston, Texas   *1989 - 1999*

  A national leader in the manufacturing of automotive water pumps with annual sales of $380 million and 1,500 employees.

   Vice President of Operations

- Managed the company's two plants in Texas and Mexico. Directly supervised two plant managers, a materials manager, advanced manufacturing systems manager, distribution manager, manager for special projects, and training and a Quality Control Division.
- Initiated and secured ISO9002 certification in two plants on the first application.
- Reorganized preventative maintenance schedules that decreased scrap rates by 50% and virtually eliminated rework rates.
- Orchestrated teamwork and communication between marketing and production to ensure customers received precise delivery dates and improved quality.
- Guided efforts with a major supplier to turnaround its sub-quality standards. Avoided a change to the competition's vendors that could have been costly. Result: vendor achieved ISO9000 certification and is now rated top in field.

A1 Heating Corporation   *1979 - 1989*

  A residential and industrial water heater manufacturing company.

Vice President of Mexican Operations, Bordertown, Texas	1985 - 1989
Plant Manager/Director of Operations, Portland, Oregon	1981 - 1985
Manager of Manufacturing, Milwaukee, WI	1979 - 1981

- Instituted a quality control system in Mexican operation that resulted in highest product quality in industry. Responded to suspicions from customers and suppliers about quality of Mexican-produced goods by arranging for decision-makers to see plant in operation.
- Reduced accident rate 200% and turnover rate (from 12% to 3% per month in four years) in Mexican operations by implementing unilateral training programs (e.g., skills, teamwork, supervisory).
- Negotiated commitments from vendors to ensure JIT system.
- Established a 50,000 sq. foot distribution center to improve service to mid-continent customers.
- Prevented theft of valuable copper shipments by working with Mexican police.
- Selected by senior management to solve problems in Canadian plant, which resulted in opening on schedule. Efforts led to promotion to Vice President of Mexican Operations.

- Improved Portland plant operations efficiencies as a result of executing a comprehensive study. In four years increased output significantly and profits by 200% by optimizing space, decreasing product damage during production, and consolidating shipments.
- Oversaw Milwaukee plant closing and transfer to modern facilities. Responsibilities included identification of most economical way to equip new plant, comprehensive study on disposal of buildings, and employee transition management. Production levels remained stable and efforts led to promotion to Director of Operations.

Hillcrest Water Products, Inc., Dayton, Ohio   *1974 - 1979*
       Manufacturing Engineer

EDUCATION
MBA, Apex School of Management, University of Dayton, Dayton, Ohio
Bachelor of Science (Mechanical Engineering), University of Wisconsin, Madison, Wisconsin

ONGOING PROFESSIONAL DEVELOPMENT
- Strategic Planning Seminar, Columbia University Executive Program
- Leadership at the Peak, Center for Creative Leadership
- World Class Manufacturing & Process Capability Studies, K. W. Farn & Associates
- Human Resources Seminar, American Manufacturing Association
- The Employee Team Concept, The Center for Productivity
- MRP II, Oliver Wight
- Understanding Border Culture, Maquiladora Associates

Visual Merchandising Specialist

Jane Swift
9 Central Avenue
Manhasset, NY 11575
(516) 555-1212
Jane@careerbrain.com

With fifteen years' experience in Visual Merchandising Management, I have successfully:

- Coordinated all Visual Merchandising in Macy's third-most-profitable store.
- Supervised visual aspects of a successful $3 million store renovation with responsibility for new fixturing and merchandising.
- Conducted seminar in Visual Merchandising for all new department managers in Macy's eastern region.
- Utilized innovative image control techniques that contributed to a new high-fashion store's becoming the volume leader for its entire chain in one year.

RECENT ACCOMPLISHMENTS

Visual Merchandising Manager of a Macy's store with a $40 million sales volume, I coordinated fixturing, merchandising, and seasonal changes for all twelve departments, along with responsibility for overall store image.

- Analyzed stock levels to determine new fixture needs, prepared requirement reports, and coordinated on-time deliveries of all fixtures.
- Reporting directly to the Vice President for Corporate Visual Merchandising, I supervised five Visual Merchandising Managers brought in from other stores to assist in the project.
- Interfaced with both union and non-union construction personnel while directing movement of departments under construction.
- Guiding all Department Managers through renovation and construction, I familiarized them with new fixturing and applicable merchandising techniques.

EARLIER ACCOMPLISHMENTS

As District Display Director for Laura Ashley Inc., a 100-store specialty women's ready-to-wear chain, I developed fashion awareness, coordinated displays, and trained staff, including new District Display Directors throughout the country. Reporting directly to the Corporate Display Director, I was:

- Given responsibility for image control at the company's new flagship store on 57th St, where fashion image was crucial. My innovative merchandising and display techniques contributed to this store's becoming the number-one-volume store for the entire company by its first anniversary.
- Recognized for my planning, organizing, and coordinating abilities, I was involved in several new store openings throughout the U.S. and Canada.

As Display Coordinator/Visual Merchandising Manager with ESPRIT, Inc., I progressed to having a five-store responsibility. Developing my functional skills, I was promoted to Visual Display troubleshooter for a multi-state region.

Jane Swift (516) 555-1212   page 2 of 2

EMPLOYMENT

MACY'S, 1987 - Present
LAURA ASHLEY, 1983 - 1987
ESPRIT DE CORPS, 1979 - 1983

EDUCATION

A graduate of Harper College, Palatine, Illinois, with a specialty in Fashion Design, I have also completed intensive course work in Architectural Technology which has significantly contributed to my expertise in store renovation and floor plan know-how. Course work in photography has rounded out my background.

PERSONAL

Interests include apparel design and construction, sketching, and free-hand drawing.

Web Site Designer

Jane Swift
9 Central Avenue
Seattle, WA 98102
(206) 555-1212
Jane@careerbrain.com

Areas of Effectiveness

Professional Web Site Design   Site Planning & Renovation
Marketing & Maintenance   Business Solutions
Quality Custom Programming   Graphic Design

Experience

Web Site Designer, Co-Owner. Rainier Software 1999 - Present
Senior Researcher. University of Washington 1997 - 1999

Career Highlights

- Designed and implemented Web site for Mount Rainier Methodist Church (*www.mumc.com*)
- Created Web site for Ultimate Typographical Services based on client design and content specifications
- Stress user-friendly design, emphasizing ease of navigation, quick download times, and appealing graphics
- Maintain clients' Web site registration with Internet search engines; include HTML meta tags to ensure high ranking
- Advise clients on effective marketing techniques to increase Web site traffic

Technical Expertise

HTML   Javascript   Macromedia Fireworks
Dreamweaver   FTP protocols   Search engine submittals
Adobe Photoshop   Microsoft Access, Word, and Excel.

Education

University of Washington, BS (Biology) 1995, MS (Biology) 1997

Appendix

Resumes for Special Situations

These are resumes that performed above and beyond the call of duty for job seekers whose background didn't "fit the mold." They're invaluable guideposts in presenting your own experiences in the most flattering light.

James is leaving the military for a Finance Executive position.

James Sharpe
9 Central Avenue
Indianapolis, IN 46206

(317) 555-1212
James@careerbrain.com

Profile

Confident, dependable, versatile management professional with extensive and diverse experience in the areas of budget management, personnel management, and customer service. Global perspective based upon assignments and travel abroad. Articulate problem solver with superior analytical and communication skills. Organized, meticulous, and methodical; particularly adept in problem identification, research, analysis, and resolution.

Qualifications

- An established record of progressively responsible positions of trust at the highest levels of government.
- A proven history of success in the administrative management of military units
- An innate ability to develop loyal and cohesive staffs dedicated to the task at hand.

Competencies

- communications skills
- top secret security clearance
- training and development
- human resources

- long- and short-range planning
- leadership and supervision
- computer systems
- customer relations

- budget analysis/management
- senior staff coordination
- project management
- organizational skills

Experience

United States Navy, Worldwide Assignments — 1990 - Present
Program Director, Naval Artillery School, San Diego, California — 1998 - 2000
Oversaw operation of largest training complex in the U.S. Navy, with an operating budget over $2.5 million and $100 million in real property listing.

- Supervised 150 military and civilian personnel with 6 direct reports.
- Developed comprehensive 5-year development plan, resulting in $500K funding for improvements.
- Formulated, planned, and implemented $1 million in capital improvements. Actively participated in contract negotiations with vendors and coordinated projects.
- Overcame $400K budget shortfall through budget analysis and cost control.
- Developed organizational vision, goals, and key business drivers.

Program Manager, Eighth Fleet, Southeast Asia — 1996 - 1998
Program and budget manager for large organization with annual budget over $800 million.

- Supervised 20 personnel with 3 direct reports.
- Funded $2.5 million in out-of-cycle, high priority projects.
- Overcame 10% funding decrement through analysis of congressional appropriation bills, identifying shortfall and authoring letters of justification.
- Developed and presented plan to reorganized budget analysts, streamlining executing by 40 - 50% and resulting in annual savings of more than $200K.

Senior Budget Analyst, Oostende, Belgium — 1994 - 1996
Budget and Funds Manager for the acquisition, operation, and maintenance of communications and information systems.

- Prepared, presented, defended, and managed an $11 million budget.
- Generated $1.4 million savings in 1996 budget through analysis and tracking expenditures.

Project Officer/Instructor, Bellevue, Washington — 1990 - 1993
Developed students for leadership and management responsibilities.

- Served as instructor, counselor, and mentor for 12 students during a 20-week course. Led 8 groups in four years.
- Redesigned core curriculum and introduced building block type of instruction.

Education

Bachelor of Business Administration, University of Washington, Seattle, Washington
Graduate--Senior Level Management/Leadership School, U.S. Naval Command College

Jane is changing careers.

Jane Swift
9 Central Avenue
Calabasas, California 91301
(818) 555-1212
Jane@careerbrain.com

OBJECTIVE

A responsible and challenging entry-level position that will utilize my education and background, expand my knowledge, and offer opportunities for personal and professional growth.

SUMMARY OF KNOWLEDGE AND EXPERIENCE

- CUSTOMER SERVICE
- INTERFACE WELL WITH THE PUBLIC
- EXCELLENT COMMUNICATION SKILLS
- SET, MEET DEADLINES/GOALS
- CASHIERING
- MARKETING
- INVENTORY CONTROL
- KNOWLEDGE OF WORDPERFECT

- HIGHLY ORGANIZED
- KNOWLEDGE OF SPANISH
- DETAIL/EFFICIENCY ORIENTED
- RECORD KEEPING
- TROUBLESHOOTING
- TUTORING
- COORDINATION
- PUBLIC RELATIONS

EDUCATIONAL HISTORY

California State University, Northridge
Los Angeles Valley College, Van Nuys

B.A. Psychology - 3.8 GPA - 1995
A.A. General Education

ACCOMPLISHMENTS AND ACHIEVEMENTS

- Awarded Recognition Certificate for achieving 100% on Shoppers Report Evaluation for food service performance, salesmanship, and hospitality at Marie Callender.
- PSYCHI - National Honor Society for Psychology
- Golden Key Honor Society - National Honor Society

EMPLOYMENT HISTORY

4/99 - Present   **WAITRESS**
Marie Callender, Sherman Oaks, California

2/97 - 3/99   **CASHIER / WAITRESS**
Denny's Restaurant, Northridge, California

9/94 - 12/96   **MARKET RESEARCHER**
Suburban Associates, Sherman Oaks, California

9/93 - 6/95   **ASSISTANT TO TEACHER / ART DIRECTOR**
Temple Beth Hillel

VOLUNTEER/COMMUNITY SERVICE

San Fernando Valley Child Guidance Clinic - Tutoring

REFERENCES FURNISHED UPON REQUEST

James is changing careers to Human Resources.

James Sharpe
9 Central Avenue
New York, NY 10012
(212) 555-1212
James@careerbrain.com

Objective

Key member of a human resources consulting team utilizing communication, organizational, and collaborative skills in a challenging environment.

Related Skills and Career Achievements

Project Management

- Led a project team for the successful launch of the Absolut bottle series.
- Managed the Absolut licensing program and facilitated the negotiation of a license agreement that generated significant incremental exposure and sales.

Presentation

- Taught English to 5th graders and gave American Culture lectures to high school students in Thailand for two months.
- Provided orientations to AFS teachers from China and Thailand upon their arrival in the United States.
- Presented regular Absolut marketing updates to staff.
- Contributed to the production of the winning Honda pitch at Saatchi & Saatchi Advertising.

Writing & Editing

- Launched a career services business to help clients define marketable skills and create results-oriented resumes.
- Developed three issues of a 10-page brand newsletter that promoted successful marketing concepts and international brand identity.
- Wrote legal correspondence to ensure adherence to brand license agreements.

Computer Applications

- Extensive knowledge of Windows and Macintosh applications for word processing, desktop publishing, spreadsheets, presentation, database management and Internet navigation.
- Developed contact databases for *House and Garden*'s advertising department.

Career Chronology

Career Marketing Consultant, Self-Employed, New York, NY	1999-2000
Contract Worker/Marketing, Lee Hecht Harrison, New York, NY	1998
Absolut Brand Coordinator, Allied Domecq Intl., Los Angeles, CA	1992-1997
Freelancer, *House and Garden* magazine, New York, NY	1991
Administrative Assistant, Saatchi & Saatchi, New York, NY	1990
Program Assistant, AFS Intercultural Programs, New York, NY	Summers 1988-1990

Education

Bachelor of Arts, 1990
Hunter College, New York, NY

James is a minister seeking a corporate position.

JAMES SHARPE
9 Central Avenue, Arlington, VA 22303
Phone: (703) 555-1231 (Fax: (703) 555-1232 (E-mail: jsharpe@careerbrain.com

---

OBJECTIVE: Administrative position with a privately held hospice services provider.

QUALIFICATIONS SUMMARY

Service-oriented individual with more than 25 years of diverse experience ranging from providing pastoral care and spiritual direction to serving in top administration positions for large institutions. Demonstrated history of success in reengineering problematic and under-performing organizations to be self-supporting and operationally efficient. Adept at caring for people under duress and in extreme circumstances, which includes working with post-traumatic stress disorder patients and their caregivers. Accustomed to working with various community-based organizations.

AREAS OF STRENGTH:

Project Facilitation   Grant Writing   Crisis Intervention
Pastoral Care/Ministry   Bereavement Support   Staff Development
Partnership Building   Information Dissemination   Organizational Restructuring

---

PROFESSIONAL EXPERIENCE

DIRECTOR, Pastoral and Spirituality Ministries, Society of Jesus, Philadelphia, PA   1999 to 2001
Selected to establish this position to administer national planning and development for Pastoral and Spirituality ministries, which involve 25% of the working Jesuits. Collaborated with the 10 Regional Provincial Assistants for Pastoral Ministries to create and implement national spirituality and parish work projects.

- Administered a comprehensive survey of the Jesuit Retreat Houses in the United States.
- Consulted with the Catholic Research Association to create a written survey for broad distribution.
- Profiled Spirituality Houses and Retreat Centers to evaluate their current procedures and operations.
- Identified the desired qualities for young Jesuits and defined necessary training for performing parish work.
- Established the structure for a mentoring and training program for those transitioning into parish work.
- Assisted the Retreat Centers in establishing financial stability and targeting populations.
- Developed training programs for lay people and retired Jesuits to participate in retreat work.
- Served as a liaison to the 10 Regional Provincials to make decisions on Spirituality and Pastoral ministries.

Earned **Spiritual Direction and Counseling Certificate,** Jesuit School of Theology, Berkeley, CA   1999
Academic Sabbatical, Jesuit School of Theology, Berkeley, CA   1997 to 1998
REGIONAL SUPERIOR (Equivalent to CEO), Society of Jesus, San Juan, Puerto Rico   1991 to 1997
Responsible for national planning and development for the Society of Jesus in Puerto Rico.

- Restructured finances and communications and reconfigured the works and communities programs.
- Streamlined the recruitment and assignment of directors of works and communities.
- Transitioned the corporation to complete financial independence and long-term growth by establishing a self-perpetuating endowment of $45 million.
- Procured new equipment and refurbished existing assets valued at more than $65 million.
- Established successful new ministries and works in the areas of parish, education, recruitment and training, and social work.

Continued

James Sharpe
Page 2

EXECUTIVE CHAIRMAN, St. Theresa's Secondary School, San Juan, Puerto Rico   1995 to 1997
Reported to the Ministry of Education and the administration's Board regarding the institution's financial stability, staffing, curriculum, and programming.
- Restructured financial procedures for accountability, recording, reporting, and receiving and banking funds.
- Reengineered administration and staff responsibilities for finances, support staff, and canteen.
- Collaborated with professionals to develop and implement therapeutic programs for faculty suffering from post-traumatic stress disorder resulting from invasive gang violence.
- Established community partnerships in order to integrate the school within the larger community.
- Obtained a $2.3 million grant to establish a computer center and other technical programs.

PRESIDENT, St. Peter's College, San Juan, Puerto Rico   1986 to 1996
Presided over two inner-city institutions - the day school and the evening division - sharing one campus on 18 acres.
     (The day school consisted of 1,300 students, 50 faculty members, five administrators, and 35 support staff
     members; the evening division consisted of 2,200 students, 45 faculty members, and five administrators.)
Reported to the Board and the Ministry of Education for the full operation of both institutions, including planning and development, organizational vision and mission, staff hiring, financial stability, curricula, and administration.
- Revised curricula to encourage academic achievement and improved academic ratings.
- Transitioned the institutions from near bankruptcy to a $12 million annual operating budget with surpluses.
- Established a perpetual endowment, raising $25 million within one year.
- Administered U.S. Government grants to construct an auditorium, computer center, library, and classrooms.
- Raised funds and restored the campus, within 18 months, after it incurred $4 million in hurricane damage.

PREVIOUS EXPERIENCE:
Chaplain and Teacher, St. Peter's College, San Juan, Puerto Rico   1985 to 1986
Vice Principal and Chaplain, Paul VI High School, Bridgeport, CT   1980 to 1984
Chaplain, Daylight Community, Toronto, Canada   1979 to 1980
Teacher and Assistant Chaplain, Connor High School, Toms River, NJ   1974 to 1976

EDUCATION

Master of Divinity, Jesuit School of Theology, Cambridge, MA, 1979
(Concentration on the question of Science and Religious faith.)

MS, Engineering, Bentley College, Waltham, MA, 1974

BS, Physics, Bentley College, Waltham, MA, 1970

James is an Educator in transition.

James Sharpe
9 Central Avenue
Lancaster, PA 17601

(717) 555-1212
James@careerbrain.com

SUMMARY

Skilled educator with 20+ years experience creating curricula and delivering instruction, evaluating students, developing and implementing strategic plans, and managing projects. Seeking opportunity to transition existing instructional, organizational, and human relations skills into a training or human resource position in a corporate environment.

QUALIFICATIONS

Instruction
- State Permanent Teaching Certification (N - 6)
- Prepare lesson plans in Social Studies, Science, Math, and Language Arts.
- Instruct 25 elementary students, addressing individual needs and learning styles.
- Evaluate students' performance and implement plans for improvement, as appropriate.
- Train students, parents, and staff in the use of computer systems.
- Fulfill on-site "Help Desk" role for students and staff using computers.

Planning
- Serve on numerous District Planning and Building Planning Committees that address ongoing concerns of staff and the community, identifying problems and solutions.
- Chair Positive School Climate Committee that promotes a comfortable learning environment and workplace for students and staff, respectively.
- Participated in developing five-year technology plan for Newark district.
- Wrote technology plan for Suburb School District and monitored implementation.
- Implemented computers in the classroom for Rural School District.
- Chaired committee that pioneered school yearbook at a time when the district had none.

Additional Skills
- Wrote grant proposal that resulted in $7,000 in funding from state government for purchase of capital equipment (computers) at Rural Central School.
- Proficient in Windows 95, Microsoft Office / Mac, ClarisWorks, Word Processing, Spreadsheets, and the Internet.
- Coached Soccer at Suburb Central School; Ski Club Advisor (Rural).

PROFESSIONAL EXPERIENCE

1989 - Present   Elementary Teacher, Rural Central School District, New Holland, PA
1976 - 1989   Elementary Teacher, Suburb Central School District, Lewisburg, PA

EDUCATION

1981   Master of Science, Education
       Pennsylvania State University, State College, PA
          GPA: 3.77 / 4.00
1976   Bachelor of Science, Education
       Pennsylvania State University, State College, PA
          Dean's List

PROFESSIONAL ENRICHMENT

Creative Learning Styles   Portfolio Assessment
Cooperative Learning   Gender Equity
Annual Computer Conference   Grant Writing
Essential Elements of Instruction

James is an Electrician changing to a career in sales & promotion.

James Sharpe
9 Central Avenue
Ferndale, MI 48220
(313) 555-1212
James@careerbrain.com

CAREER OBJECTIVE

To support the growth and profitability of an organization that provides challenge, encourages advancement, and rewards achievement with the opportunity to utilize my substantial experience, skills, and proven abilities in a position involving Sales and Promotion within the Consumer Goods industry.

STRENGTHS

- Skilled in motivating and interacting with the public.
- Disciplined and well organized in work habits, with ability to function smoothly in pressure situations.
- Ability to identify problems and implement effective solutions.
- Possess a "pro" company attitude dedicated to the growth and profitability of the company.

EMPLOYMENT HISTORY

McMURRAY ELECTRIC, 22036 Woodward, Ferndale, MI 48220
Journeyman Electrician - April 1997 to Present
Responsible for the installation and servicing of commercial, residential, and industrial accounts. In my current position as Foreman Leader, I supervise the activities of four to five electricians/helpers and have been responsible for as many as thirteen employees.

- Ability to read and effectively implement blueprints, along with extensive layout skills.
- Because of vast knowledge of jobs performed for the company and ability to deal effectively with people, was selected by management to train new employees.

POWERS DISTRIBUTING COMPANY, INC., 2000 Pontiac Dr., Pontiac, MI 48053
On-Premise Promotions - August 1999 to Present
Responsible for representing Miller Brewing Company at promotional functions in on-premise accounts situated in Oakland and Macomb Counties.

- I possessed the energy, enthusiasm, and poise necessary for implementing successful brewery promotions, was selected for newly created position.
- Have acquired extensive knowledge of motivating/sales techniques, which has contributed substantially to increased sales at brewery promotions.
- Active in the development and coordination of brewery promotions.

EDUCATION

Associated Builders and Contractors, Inc. - Graduated June 1998
Course of Study: Electrical
Oakland Community College - Courses relating to Electronics Field (Attended 1989 and 1990)
Ferndale High School - Graduated June 1988

REFERENCES FURNISHED UPON REQUEST

Jane is changing careers after a period of self-employment.

Jane Swift
9 Central Avenue
Burlingame, CA 94010
(415) 555-1212

Jane@careerbrain.com

Objective   Sales representative or showroom position in the fashion industry

Summary of Qualifications

- Five years' experience in design and manufacture of Women's Wear
- Extensive production management and operations experience
- Fifteen years' sales experience in inside sales, showrooms, and tradeshows
- Expertise in conducting tradeshows, designing booths, and managing customers
- Capable and flexible self-starter who is able to travel for trade shows

Work Experience

1994 to 2000   **Owner/Designer**
Gene Sims Designs
Design and manufacture of Womens' Wear accessories, earrings, hair clips, purses, and pins. Extensive experience in buying, trade shows (Canada and Washington state), payroll, collections, billing. Hired 22 sales reps throughout the U.S. and Puerto Rico. Employed 12 people to make accessories.

1990 to 1994   **Outside Sales and Trainer**
West Coast Financial Services
Extensive selling experience cold-calling, canvassing, and prospecting to corporations for medical insurance plans. Organized and set up an entire department and trained department staff.

1984 to 1990   **Personnel and Collections Manager**
Physio-Control
Interviewed potential employees for several department heads. Managed credit and collections. Trained managers on how to interview and hire the right person.

1978 to 1984   **Office Manager/Executive Recruiter**
Betty White Employment Agency
Interviewed prospective employees for professional and clerical positions with corporations.

James has changed careers many times.

James Sharpe
9 Central Avenue
Aurora, CO 80014
(303) 555-1212
James@careerbrain.com

OBJECTIVE   A challenging position providing an opportunity to apply broad Management experience.

EDUCATION   University of Colorado
MBA program—presently enrolled
B.S. Public Administration, Colorado College

QUALIFICATIONS   Progressively responsible management background in a large medical facility, with successful experience in the following areas:

Staff Supervision—presently responsible for 30 skilled, semi-skilled, unskilled, and managerial employees. Hire, train, direct, and evaluate the staff. Responsible for their output and the quality of their work. Maintain morale, motivation, and positive employee relations. Solve problems, take corrective action, apply company policy.

Operations Management—direct staff and activities in several support departments, including maintenance, grounds and buildings, laundry, housekeeping. Manage a budget of nearly a half million dollars. Schedule all departments for the most effective use of manpower, equipment, and facilities.

Inventory Control/Purchasing—maintain an inventory control system for non-medical supplies and food.

Other—frequent involvement in customer and public relations, promoting the facility; work with other staff to prepare for licensing, compliance reviews; involved in Real Estate Management—buying, renovating, and maintaining rental properties; licensed in real estate sales.

As public administration Intern at both the state and federal levels, involved in labor relations activities, legislative actions, communications.

EMPLOYMENT   Aurora Rest Home, Aurora, CO
1999 to present   Supervisor—promoted from Assistant

1995 to 1999   Coors Brewery, Golden, CO
Construction Worker

1993 to 1995   Intern—federal and state

Jane is a handicapped worker who wants to change careers.

Jane Swift
9 Central Avenue
Monroe, WI 53566
(608) 555-1212
Jane@careerbrain.com

OBJECTIVE   Seeking a challenging position in Customer Service.

SUMMARY

- Possess a combined Customer Service and Financial background. Responsible for administering several aspects of pension plans. Significant customer service responsibilities as Office Manager and Credit Coordinator.

QUALIFICATION

- Present position requires accuracy and efficiency in creation of files, calculation of benefits and options, analysis of IRS qualification, preparation of tax forms, and other similar activities.
- Effective verbal and written negotiations with agents, attorneys, plan participants, accountants, and others. Good communications skills are necessary for confidential interdepartmental communications.
- Experience includes Credit and Office Management. My responsibilities in credit include taking applications, securing credit approvals, ordering products, and arranging for delivery. I also calculated salespeople's commissions. As Office Manager, I handled customer service duties, accepted and booked payments, maintained inventories, and performed other functions associated with keeping the office running smoothly.

EXPERIENCE
1999 to present   BC/BC
Pension Technical Specialist

Sears
Credit Coordinator—for major appliance

3M Products
Office Manager

Big Brothers/Big Sisters; United Cerebral Palsy Assoc.
(6 years, part-time)
Office Manager/Clerical

James is a Technology Expert changing to Web Development.

James Sharpe
9 Central Avenue
Pittsburgh, PA 15222

(412) 555-1212
James@careerbrain.com

GOAL

To contribute to a Web development team where my strong technical and business skills and personal passion for computer technology will be of value.

PROFESSIONAL PROFILE

- 10+ years' experience working in cross-functional teams as a technical expert. Oversaw multiyear, multimillion dollar development programs. Produced proposals resulting in new work for organization totaling nearly $500,000.
- Achieved numerous official commendations during tenure for exceptional performance and special acts of service. Consistently received highly favorable customer feedback and successfully developed business relationships with the technical community.
- Enhanced personal productivity and contributions to team through initiative to learn MS Project, MS Office, MS FrontPage, basic HTML, Internet-related applications, and information technology trends.

Demonstrated competencies in:

Technical Analysis	System Design & Information Architecture
Strategic Planning & Problem Solving	Project & Budget Management
Research, Writing, & Presentations	Customer Focus

CAREER HIGHLIGHTS

- Challenged to create a Web site for the Joint Service Small Arms Program Office to increase awareness of their programs for Armed Services customers and to conduct management committee business. Within 3 months, learned basics of Web site design and programming, planned information architecture, and launched the site to positive reviews from customers and other external government agencies.
- Developed a business plan for the Power Sources Base Assessment program (a survey of batteries as power sources for ammunition systems) that was approved by the customer without changes after a competitive selection process. Team awarded $144,000 for the first year's work with potential for another $250,000 in the second year.
- Authored a 250-page technical report on the state of the art in laser technology that was the culmination of a 1-year independent research project. The study was approved and published in 1998 and is used in strategic planning by the Joint Services Committee. Selected to present conclusions to technical community at NDIA Infantry Symposium.
- Introduced a logical strategic planning tool that was used to overhaul several programs in order to meet new timelines for success required by the Pentagon and adopted office wide.
- Devised an innovative method for monitoring a system contractor's cost performance in 5 areas on a $15 million contract. Technical Director mandated that this method be management's standard for analysis of contractor performance in order to spot potentially dangerous trends early.
- Managed development of program's portion of a Department of Defense Master Plan required by the Pentagon. After Congressional Committee review, the program continued to receive financial and political backing.
- Spearheaded review process leading to the successful type classification and on-schedule deployment of mortar weapon systems. Required intense coordination with numerous support organizations and government agencies to produce documents and presentations for material release boards.

CAREER HISTORY

U.S. Army Engineering Facility, Pittsburgh, PA
Mechanical Engineer: First Division - 1999 - Present
Program Management Engineer: Second Division - 1996 - 1999
Systems Engineer: Support Center - 1992 - 1995

EDUCATION

MBA, 1989: University of Pittsburgh, Pittsburgh, PA - Dean's List Honors
BS, 1987: State University of New York at Brockport, Brockport, NY

James is a blue-collar worker and wants a white-collar job.

James Sharpe
9 Central Avenue
Claremont, NC 28610
(704) 555-1212
James@careerbrain.com

OBJECTIVE   An opportunity to apply technical skills and communications ability in a Sales or Customer Service position.

SKILLS SUMMARY   Thoroughly familiar with the process of quoting and producing industrial products for a wide range of customer applications. Work with customers' specifications, ideas, or blueprints to produce parts on a special or stock basis. Call on accounts to assist with product development, to provide service in the event of discrepancies or quality questions. Duties require the ability to communicate effectively on technical problems, and to establish rapport.

In a retail setting, have held major responsibility for staff supervision and customer service, managing several functions with high customer and employee contact.

As a supervisor, held responsibility for training, scheduling, directing, and evaluating the work of skilled machinists. Keep areas of responsibility supplied with tooling, materials, and equipment to ensure the most effective use of manpower and machinery.

Acted as buyer of industrial products: drills, reamers, slotting saws, collects, high-speed carbide steels, ceramics, lubricants, and NC screw machine programs, among others.

Operated and troubleshot sophisticated machine shop equipment, including Swiss screw machines, grinders, lathes, milling machines, drill presses. Able to program CNC equipment. Conversant with the full range of machine shop practices, as well as quality and production control procedures.

EXPERIENCE
1998 to present   **Jig Tools, Claremont, NC**
Supervisor, Quality Control Inspector
Production Machinist

1994 to 1998   **Finest Foods, Raleigh, NC**
Front End Manager, supervising an evening shift.
Involved in cashiering, packing, credit voucher cashing.

1989 to 1994   **Atlas Moving Co., Raleigh, NC**
Truck Driver, Mechanic

PERSONAL   References available upon request.

Jane has had multiple jobs and needs to combine her experience.

Jane Swift
9 Central Avenue
Kenner, LA 70062
(504) 555-1212
Jane@careerbrain.com

OBJECTIVE   A challenging Sales or Sales Management position, providing an opportunity to apply broad experience and a record of success in marketing a variety of products and services.

QUALIFICATIONS   *Sales*—Thoroughly familiar with techniques for generating new business in industrial, commercial, and consumer markets. Employed cold call, referral, and other prospecting techniques. Skilled at assessing client needs and making effective sales presentations, often involving technical product details.

Have regularly exceeded sales quotas.

Sales Management—Responsibilities included selecting, training, motivating, and supervising professionals in sales, service, and other operations.

Performed market research and promotions, forecasting, the development of distribution systems, and other marketing administration functions.

Developed marketing plans, arranged financing, helped establish distribution networks.

EMPLOYMENT   ADT Systems—Worcester, MA
Commercial Sales Representative   1995 to present

Patriot Marketing—Worcester, MA
Owner/Consultant   1993 to 1995

Maxxum Industries, Inc.   1980-1990
Self-Employed Restaurateur
Cherry Buick
Goodnick Miller
International Harvester

TRAINING   Studied Business Administration, Management, and Marketing at Louisiana Institute of Technology, the University of Texas, and Kenner Junior College. Have received technical product and sales training in numerous courses and seminars throughout my career.

PERSONAL   U.S. Navy—honorably discharged
References available upon request

Jane is changing careers to become a Salesperson.

Jane Swift
9 Central Avenue
Utica, MI 48087
(313) 555-1212
Jane@careerbrain.com

OBJECTIVE
An opportunity to apply Medical Technological background in a challenging Sales or Marketing position.

QUALIFICATIONS

- Over six years' experience in Medical Technology in hospital laboratory and outpatient settings. Have worked successfully with physicians in a number of disciplines, including pathology, geriatrics, oncology, other areas; interact daily with laboratory staff (supervisory and technical), patients, and other people throughout the hospital.
- Thoroughly familiar with complex, sophisticated laboratory equipment, such as Coulter S plus IV, Coulter 550, MLA 700, Fibrometer. Provide technical training to other operators and to medical technology students. Accountable for the accurate calibration of equipment, basic troubleshooting, and maintenance.
- Maintenance of inventory, purchase of supplies, and quality control procedures in general.
- These duties require a person who is thoroughly knowledgeable about laboratory and highly technical equipment and associated procedures, is familiar with materials, and is precise in performance of duties.

EMPLOYMENT

1992 to present
Utica Family Hospital—Utica, Michigan
Special Hematology Laboratory Technologist, promoted from Laboratory Technologist

EDUCATION
B.S. Medical Technology, 1992
Detroit State College (Detroit, Michigan)

Registry eligible in Hematology

Additional training by laboratory equipment manufacturers

REFERENCES
Excellent professional references are available upon request.

Jane is a recently divorced homemaker reentering the workforce.

Jane Swift
9 Central Avenue
Wichita, KS 67218
(316) 555-1212
Jane@careerbrain.com

OBJECTIVE
An entry position in Personnel or Human Resources Management, providing an opportunity to apply formal education in the field, and business experience.

EDUCATION
Anna Maria College—Paxton, Massachusetts
B.A. Psychology
Graduated *magna cum laude*

SUMMARY
OF SKILLS
Studies have included courses in Industrial Psychology, Personnel Management, Marketing, Management, Accounting, other Psychology and Liberal Arts courses.

Experience in *Interviewing/Communications*, gained from extensive dealings with customers, clients, students, and peers in the organization. Capable of effective written and oral communication where the ability to gather precisely and act on it is critical.

Background in *Counseling*, with both adults and students in academic and professional settings. Assisted with *Career Counseling* and other forms of personal assistance.

Experience includes work as a *Telemarketing Representative* and as an Administrative Assistant. Have held leadership positions in volunteer organizations, including *Chairperson, Fundraiser, Advisory Board Member,* and *Counselor*. Duties have required the ability to organize, set up, and implement systems for getting tasks completed, as well as the ability to be persuasive and obtain cooperation.

EXPERIENCE
Wichita Employment Services
Telemarketing Representative. Working from research, leads, and cold calls, identifying target markets and make over 500 sales calls per month. Provide quotes, and refer results of research for further action. Set up relevant sales administration systems.

1998 to 2000
Kansas State University
Worked part and full time while attending college.
Assignments included:
Secretary in the Graduate Office, in the Development Office, and to the Director of the Nursing Program.

ACTIVITIES
Chairperson, Boy Scout Troop Committee; Member, Advisory Board; Fundraiser, Counselor, Navy Officers' Wives Association; Fundraiser, Library Committee.

PERSONAL
Health: excellent
Willing to travel/relocate

Jane is a homemaker looking to reenter the workforce.

Jane Swift

9 Central Ave.
Silver Spring, MD 20904

Jswift@careerbrain.com

(301) 555-1254 - Home
(301) 430-0021 - Mobile

Summary of Qualifications

Professional homemaker and activities director with strong organizational skills and proven ability to effectively handle multiple tasks simultaneously. Ten years experience providing creative solutions and resolving conflict to achieve results. Track record of negotiating win-win solutions and fine attention to details. Areas of expertise include:

FINANCE AND BUDGETING: Analyze and implement effective annual, monthly, and weekly budgets. Compile and record all financial activities and records of receipts. Plan and achieve individual and team savings and investment portfolios.

COMMUNICATIONS: Motivate team members to achieve goals, resolve interpersonal conflicts, create positive learning environment. Proven effective written and oral communications including ability to address large groups.

ORGANIZATIONAL SKILLS: Track record of efficient time management techniques including planning, scheduling and delegating. Created and implemented improved workflow processes that expedited and enhanced services, eliminated redundancy, and reduced time to completion.

CUSTOMER SERVICE: Extremely sociable and able to put visitors at ease. Ability to negotiate and persuade to achieve desired results.

COMPUTER SKILLS: Proficient in MS Office including desktop publishing, Internet research, and Email communications.

Education

BA, Sociology, University of Virginia, Charlottesville, VA

Volunteer Positions

Edgewood PTA	1999 - 2001	President
Edgewood PTA	1998 - 1999	Treasurer
Leesburg News	1995 - Present	Contributing Writer

Relevant Professional Experience

Professional Homemaker	1995 - Present	Nicholas Household
Project Manager	1987 - 1995	AT&T
Administrative Office	1984 - 1987	AT&T
Secretary	1980 - 1984	AT&T
Secretary	1978 - 1980	Vienna Glass Company

Professional Resume Writing Services

I am a strong believer in using the services of resume writers who belong to the field's professional associations. They tend to be more committed, have more field experience, and have an all-around higher standard of performance, partly because their membership demonstrates their commitment to the field and partly from the ongoing educational programs that these associations offer to their members.

Remember that a resume isn't just a piece of paper that gets your foot in the door. It also sits on every interviewer's desk as a road map to your professional background, giving them some guidance for the direction your interviews will take. It also works on your behalf long after you have left the interview, and it is probably the last document an employer will consider before making the final decision between candidates.

I am including a list of professional resume writers and professional colleagues, who generously helped me locate some excellent job hunting letters. If you need help in this area, these are all people for whom I can vouch. They all have impeccable credentials. To help you understand those credentials I'll give you a quick overview of the dominant professional associations in the field. They are: the Professional Association of Resume Writers (PARW, *www.parw.com*), the National Resume Writers Association (NRWA, *www.nrwa.com*), and Career Masters Institute (CMI).

Both PARW and NRWA have hundreds of members and provide ongoing opportunities for members to gain mentoring experience and additional training. Both offer resume-writing certification and operate e-mail list servers. The professional training programs range from how to handle specific resume challenges to issues related to running a resume service. The associations build camaraderie between members and offer them access to the expertise of hundreds of other professional resume writers. Both offer an annual convention with workshops on industry issues. PARW offers training seminars several times a year throughout the country. NRWA offers its members a Web-based training program.

Members of the CMI tend to be serious tenured professionals. Almost all (about 95 percent) are Certified Professional Resume Writers (CPRW), a distinction that sets them apart and clearly validates their capabilities. Many (approximately 30–40) have also earned their Job & Career Transition Coach (JCTC) certification. Several (about 10–15—and as a member, I'm one of them) are nationally published authors on resume writing, job search, coaching, and related career topics. Most CMI members offer more than just resume writing services.

The following are some of the members of these three estimable associations who have contributed resumes and valuable insights to the book (with a special thanks to Wendy Enelow and Gwen Harrison).

Abilities Enhanced
PO Box 9667
Kansas City, MO 64134
tel: (816) 767-1196
E-mail: M7125@aol.com
Web: www.abilitiesenhanced.com

Elizabeth J. Axnix, CPRW, IJCTC
Quality Word Processing
329 East Court Street
Iowa City, IA 52240-4914
tel: (800) 359-7822 or (319) 354-7822
Fax: (319) 354-2220
E-mail: axnix@earthlink.net

Ann Baehr
Best Resumes
122 Sheridan Street
Brentwood, NY 11717
tel: (631) 435-1879
fax: (631) 435-3655
E-mail: resumebest@earthlink.net
Web: www.e-bestresumes.com

Certified Professional Resume Writer
Susan Barens, CPRW, IJCTC
Career Dynamics
5932 Wilson Mills Road
Highland Heights, OH
tel/fax: (440) 720-0945 (call before
sending fax)
E-mail: careerdynamics@aol.com
Member, PARWCC
Member, Career Masters Institute

Jacqui D. Barrett, CPRW, CEIP
Career Trend
7501 College Boulevard, Suite 175
Overland Park, KS 66210
tel: (913) 451-1313
fax: (913) 451-3242
E-mail: jacqui@careertrend.net
Web: www.careertrend.net

Kim Batson, CCMC
Netconnect Associates
704 228th Ave NE, PMB 234
Redmond, WA 98074
tel: (425) 836-2910
Toll free: (800) 756-7836
fax: (425) 836-0824
E-mail:
kim@netconnectassociates.com
Web: www.netconnectassociates.com

Kathy Black
Career Recipes
P.O. Box 3686

Evergreen, CO 80437
tel: (303) 679-1519
Fax: (303) 670-4414
E-mail: kathyjane@earthlink.net
Web: www.careerrecipes.com

Arnold G. Boldt, CPRW, JCTC
Arnold-Smith Associates
625 Panorama Trail, Building Two,
Suite 200
Rochester, NY 14625
tel: (585) 383-0350
fax: (585) 387-0516
E-mail: Arnie@ResumeSOS.com
Web: www.ResumeSOS.com
Member, Career Masters Institute
Member, Professional Association of
Resume Writers & Career Coaches
Member, National Association of
Resume Writers

Tracy A. Bumpus, CPRW, JCTC
Executive Director
RezAMAZE.com
1807 Slaughter Lane #200-366
Austin, TX 78760-4270
tel: (512) 291-1404 or
(888) 277-4270
Fax: 208-247-2542
Web: www.rezamaze.com

Diane Burns, CPRW, IJCTC, CCM
President
Career Marketing Techniques
5219 Thunder Hill Road
Columbia, MD 21045
tel: (410) 884-0213
E-mail: DianeCPRW@aol.com
Web: www.polishedresumes.com

Career Advantage
5536 Longview Circle
El Paso, TX 79924
tel: (915) 821-1036
Fax: (915) 822-8146
E-mail: jmoore@dzn.com
CMI, CPPRW

Career Counsel
11 Hillside Place
Chappaqua, NY 10514
tel: (914) 238-1065
E-mail: LinZlev@aol.com

Career Development Resources
1312 Walter Road
Yorktown Heights, NY 10598
tel: (914) 962-1548

Fax: (914) 962-0325
E-mail: cardev@aol.com
Contact: Mark Berkowitz
CMI, CPRW,NCCC, International
Certified Job & Career Transition
Coach

A CareerPro Inc.
201 North Federal Highway, Suite 108
Deerfield Beach, Florida 33441
tel: (954) 428-4935
Fax: (954) 428-0965
E-mail: careerpro@mindspring.com
Web: www.faxrecruiters.com/
amme.html

Career Solutions, LLC
Trenton, MI 48183
tel: (734) 676-9170 or
(877) 777-7242
Fax: (734) 676-9487 or (877) 777-7307

(Ms.) Freddie Cheek, MS Ed., CPRW,
CWDP
Cheek & Cristan Phonelo Career
Connections
4511 Harlem Road, Suite 3
Amherst, NY 14226
tel: (716) 839-3635
fax: (716) 831-9320
E-mail: fscheek@adelphia.net

Comprehensive Resume Services
5300 Spring Mountain Road,
Suite 212-D
Las Vegas, NV 89102
tel: (702) 222-9411

Norine T. Dagliano, CPRW
Inspirations
616 Highland Way
Hagerstown, MD 21740
tel: (301) 766-2032
fax: (301) 745-5700
E-mail: ndagliano@yahoo.com

Lori Davila, Career Coach
LJD Consulting, Inc.
1483 North Springs Drive
Atlanta, GA 30338
tel: (770) 392-1139
E-mail: loritil@aol.com

Deborah Wile Dib, NCRW, CPRW, JCTC
President
Advantage Resumes of New York
tel/fax: (631) 475-8513
Web: www.advantageresumes.com

Member, NRWA, PARW, AJST, CPADN, CMI

Kirsten Dixson, JCTC, CPRW, CEIP
New Leaf Career Solutions
tel: (866) NEW-LEAF (639-5323)
Toll free: (914) 961-9779
Web: www.newleafcareer.com
Certified Career Coach and Resume Writer
Certified Employment Interview Professional
Career Planning & Development Certificate from NYU
Strategies To Recession-Proof Your Career (2002, McGraw-Hill)
Member, PARW/CC, NRWA and IACMP

Jacqui Barrett Dodson, CPRW
Career Trend
7501 College Boulevard, Suite 175
Overland Park, KS 66210
tel: (913) 451-1313
Fax: (913) 451-3242
E-mail: dodson@careertrend.net

Terra L. Dourlain
Executive Career Coach and Resume Writer
Karrus Evergreen, Inc.
318 Cherry Street, Suite 101
Jamestown NY 14701;
tel: (716) 661-9036
E-mail: Terra@netsync.net

Nina K. Ebert, CPRW
A Word's Worth Resume and Writing Service
25 Oakwood Drive
New Egypt, NJ 08533;
tel: (609) 758-7799
fax: (609) 758-7799
Web: www.keytosuccessresumes.com

Cory Edwards, CRW
Partnering For Success
109 Country Road
Sterling, VA 20165;
tel/fax: (703) 444-7835
E-mail: ResumeWriter@aol.com
Web: www.Resumes4Results.com

Debbie Ellis, CPRW
President, Phoenix Career Group, LLC
"Fax your résumé for a professional evaluation!"

(800) 876-5506 (Toll Free Voice Inside U.S.)
(888) 329-5409 (Toll Free 24-Hour Fax Inside U.S.)
(859) 236-4001 (Worldwide Voice)
(859) 236-4001 (Worldwide 24-Hour Fax)
Web: www.phoenixcareergroup.com
Certified Professional Résumé Writer (CPRW)
Resume Expert for www.CareerFolios.com
Member, Professional Association of Résumé Writers (PARW)
Member, International Certification Board, PARW

Wendy S. Enelow, CPRW, JCTC, CCM
President
Career Masters Institute
119 Old Stable Road
Lynchburg, VA 24503
tel: (804) 386-3100
E-mail: wendyenelow@cminstitute.com
Web: www.cminstitute.com
Past President, The Advantage Executive Resume & Career Marketing Service

Dayna Feist, CPRW, JCTC
Gatehouse Business Services
265 Charlotte Street
Asheville, NC 28801
tel: (828) 254-7893
Fax: (828) 254-7894
E-mail: Gatehous@aol.com
Member, Certification Board, PARW65
Member, Career Masters Institute

A First Impression
www.resumewriter.com
Successful job search and career management for professionals, highly effective resumes, coaching, consulting, Internet job exploration and more. Professionally speaking...we have a way with words.

Joyce Fortier, CCM
Create Your Own Career
23871 W. Lebost
Novi, MI 48375
tel: (248) 478-5662
Fax: (248) 426-9974

careerist@aol.com
www.careerist.com

Fox Resume & Career Resources
24242 S. Navajo Drive
Channahon, IL 60410
tel: (815) 467-6153
E-mail: pfoxhr@aol.com
Contact: Patty Fox

Roberta Gamza, JCTC, CEIP, JST
Career Ink
Louisville, CO
tel: (888) 581-6063
fax: (303) 955-3065
E-mail: roberta@careerink.com
Web: www.careerink.ocm

Louise Garver, CMP, JCTC, CPRW
Career Directions
115 Elm Street, Suite 203
Enfield, CT 06082
tel: (888) 222-3731
fax: (860) 623-9473
Web: www.resumeimpact.com

Gatehouse Business Services
265 Charlotte Street
Asheville, NC 28801
tel: (828) 254-7893
Fax: (828) 254-7894
E-mail: Gatehous@aol.com

Wayne M. Gonyea, MS, CCM
President
Gonyea Career Marketing, Inc.
1810 Arturus Lane
New Port Richey, FL 34655
tel: (727) 375-0489
E-mail: online@resumexpress.com
Web: www.resumexpress.com
Founding Member, Career Masters Institute

Michele J. Haffner, CPRW, JCTC
Managing Director
Advanced Resume Services
1314 W. Paradise Ct.
Glendale, WI 53209
tel: (877) 247-1677
fax: (414) 247-1808
Web: www.resumeservices.com

Cheryl Ann Harland, CPRW, JCTC
Resumes By Design
25227 Grogan's Mill Road
The Woodlands, TX 77380

tel: (281) 296-1659
fax: (888) 213-1650
E-mail: cah@resumesbydesign.com
Web: www.resumesbydesign.com

Gwen Harrison
Advanced Resumes
438 Shearwater Drive
Fortson, GA 31808
tel: (877) 353-0025
Fax: (888) 811-3241
Gwen@advancedresumes.com

E. Rene Hart, CPRW
Executive Career Solutions
5337 North Socrum Loop Rd., Box 116
Lakeland, FL 33809;
tel: (888) 522-6121
fax: (509) 277-0892
Web: www.ExecutiveCareerSolutions.com

Beverly Harvey, CPRW, JCTC, CCM
Beverly Harvey Resume & Career
Services
PO Box 750
Pierson, FL
tel: (386) 749-3111; toll free: (888)
775-0916
fax: (386) 749-4881
E-mail: Beverly@harveycareers.com
Web: www.harveycareers.com

Maria E. Hebda, CPRW
Managing Executive - Career
Solutions, LLC
tel: (734) 676-9170
fax: (734) 676-9487
Web: www.WritingResumes.com
Professional Association of Resume
Writers & Career Coaches
National Resume Writers' Association
Professional Resume Writers Research
Association
Career Masters Institute

Lynn Hughes, MA, CEIP, CPRW
A Resume and Career Service, Inc.
P.O. Box 6911
Lubbock, TX 79493
tel: (806) 785-9800
fax: (806) 785-2711
E-mail: lynn@aresumeservice.com
Web: www.aresumeservice.com

Marcy Johnson, CPRW, CEIP
First Impression Resume and Job
Readiness
11805 U.S. Hwy. 69
Story City, IA 50248;

tel: (515) 733-4998
fax: (515) 733-4681
E-mail: Firstimpression@prairieinet.net
Web: www.resume-job-readiness.com

Nancy Karvonen, CPRW, IJCTC
Executive Director
A Better Word & Resume
Galt, CA
tel: (209) 744-8203
Fax: (209) 745-7114
Voice Mail/Pager: (888) 598-1995
E-mail: careers@aresumecoach.com
Web: www.aresumecoach.com
Certified Professional Resume Writer
(CPRW)
Internationally Certified Job and Career
Transition Coach (JCTC)
Member, Career Masters Institute
Member, PARW Certification
Committee

Fran Kelley, MA, CPRW, SPHR,
JCTC
The Résumé Works (a division of Two
Free Spirits Enterprises, Inc.)
Waldwick, NJ
tel: (201) 670-9643
fax: (201) 251-2885
E-mail: twofreespirits@att.net
Web: www.careermuse.com
Certified Professional Résumé Writer
Certified Job & Career Transition
Coach
Certified Senior Professional in Human
Resources

Shanna Kemp
Kemp Career Services
2105 Via Del Norte
Carrollton, Texas 75006
tel: (972) 416-9089 or
(877) 367-5367
Fax: (972) 478-2890
E-mail: respro@aresumepro.com

Bill Kinser, CPRW, CEIP, JCTC
To The Point Resumes, Inc.
Fairfax, VA
tel: (703) 352-8969
Toll free: (866) RESUME1 (866-737-
8631)
Web: www.tothepointresumes.com

Cindy Kraft, CPRW, JCTC, CCM
Executive Essentials
"Helping clients achieve career
success"
Toll free: (888) 221-0441
tel: (813) 655-0658

fax: (813) 653-4513
Web: www.exec-essentials.com
Credentialed Career Master

Bonnie Kurka, CPRW
Resume Suite
85B Schofield Circle
Fort Riley, KS 66442
tel: (785) 375-6981
fax: (785) 717-3289
Web: www.resumesuite.com

Louise Kursmark, CPRW, JCTC
Best Impression Career Services, Inc.
Cincinnati, Ohio
tel: (513) 792-0030
Web: www.yourbestimpression.com

Richard A. Lanham, CCM, M. Div.,
MRE, and MA
RL Stevens and Associates
Indiana Region- General Manager
8888 Keystone Crossing Blvd. Suite
950
Indianapolis, IN 46240;
tel: (888) 806-7313
E-mail: rlanham@rlstevens.com
Web: www.interviewing.com
Career Masters Institute
Professional Resume Writers and
Research Association

Rolande L. La Pointe, CPC, CIPC,
CPRW, IJCTC, CCM
President/Founder
RO-LAN Associates, Inc.
725 Sabattus Street
Lewiston, ME 04240;
tel: (207) 784-1010
fax: (207) 782-3446
E-mail RLapointe@aol.com

Denise M. Larkin, CPRW, CEIP, CHT
ResumeRighter.com
PO Box 10944
Oakland CA 94610;
tel: (510) 891-0200
fax: (510) 891-0157
E-mail: denise@resumerighter.com
Web: www.resumerighter.com

Mary Laske, MS, CPRW
ExecPro Resume Service
1713 Park Blvd.
Fargo, ND 58103
tel: (866) 232-0239
fax: (707) 760-3951
Web: www.execproresumes.com

Diana C. Le Gere
Executive Final Copy
PO Box 171311
Salt Lake City, UT 84117
tel: (866) 754-5465
fax: (626) 602-8715
Web: www.executivefinalcopy.com

Lisa C. LeVerrier, President
Competitive Advantage Resumes
& Career Coaching
5523 N. Military Trail Suite #1212
Boca Raton, FL 33496
433 Plaza Real, Suite 275
Boca Raton, FL 33432
tel: (561) 982-9573 or
(800) 750-5690
Fax: (561) 982-7312
E-mail: gethired@earthlink.net OR
lisalev@earthlink.net
Web: www.jobcoaching.com

Ross Macpherson, CPRW, CJST, CEIP
Career Quest
1586 Major Oaks Road
Pickering, ON, Canada
tel: (877) 426-8548
fax: (905) 426-4274
Web: www.yourcareerquest.com

Christine Magnus
Business Services Plus
tel: (718) 519-0477
Fax: (718) 405-9894
E-mail: BizServ@aol.com
Member, PARW, Career Masters Institute

Linda Matias
34 East Main Street #276
Smithtown, NY 11787
tel/fax: (631) 382-2425
E-mail: careerstrides@bigfoot.com
Web: www.careerstrides.com

Chandra C. May
ACCESS RESUME
Chillicothe, OH
tel: 740-772-6240
E-mail: ccmay@webtv.net

Nicole Miller, CRW, IJCTC, RRP
Mil-Roy Consultants
1729 Hunter's Run Drive
Ottawa, ON K1C-6W2, Canada
tel: (613) 834-4031
E-mail:
resumesbymilroy@hotmail.com

Meg Montford, CCM, CCC, CPRW
Certified Career Coach

Abilities Enhanced
Kansas City, MO
tel: (816) 767-1196
E-mail: meg@abilitiesenhanced.com
Web: www.abilitiesenhanced.com

Doug Morrison, CPRW
Career Power (a division of Career
Planners)
2915 Providence Road, Suite 250-B
Charlotte, NC 28211
tel: (800) 711-0773
fax: (704) 365-3411
Web: www.careerpowerresumes.com

JoAnn Nix, CPRW
Beaumont Resume Service
tel: (800) 265-6901
Fax: (409) 924-0019 or (419) 781-2971
E-mail: info@agreatresume.com
Web: www.agreatresume.com

Debra O'Reilly, CPRW, JCTC
Resumewriter.com
16 Terryville Avenue
Bristol, CT 06010
tel: 860-583-7500
Fax: 860-585-9611
E-mail: debra@resumewriter.com
Web: www.resumewriter.com
Charter Member, Career Masters Institute
Member, Professional Association of
Resume Writers
Member, National Resume Writers
Association

Don Orlando, MBA, CPRW, JCTC,
CCM
The McLean Group
640 South McDonough
Montgomery, AL 36104;
tel: (334) 264-2020
fax: (334) 264-9227
E-mail: yourcareercoach@aol.com

Judith Price, MS, CDFI, IJCTC, CCM
Berke and Price Associates
Skills for Career Success
6 Newtowne Way, Ste. 6
Chelmsford, MA 01824
tel: (978) 256-0482
fax: (978) 259-0787
E-mail: salprice@aol.com
Web: www.careercampaign.com

Professional Resume Services
1214 East Fenway Avenue
Salt Lake City, Utah 84102
tel: (801) 883-2011

Fax: (801) 582-8862
E-mail: resumes@tacisp.com
Web: www.MyCareerResource.com
PARW, CMI, CPRW

A Resume Coach
www.aresumecoach.com
tel: (209) 744-8203
Voice Mail/Pager: (888) 598-1995
Fax: (209) 745-7114
e-fax (801) 650-8140
Certified Professional Resume Writer
(CPRW)
Internationally Certified Job and Career
Transition Coach (JCTC)
Member, Career Masters Institute

Jane Roqueplot
JaneCo's Sensible Solutions
194 North Oakland Ave
Sharon, PA 16146;
tel: (888) 526-3267
E-mail: info@janecos.com

Nadine Rubin
Adam-Bryce, Inc.
77 Maple Avenue
New City, NY 10956
tel: (914) 634-1772 or
(845) 634-1772
Fax: (914) 634-1772 or (845) 634-1772
Web: www.adambryce.com

Jennifer Rydell, CPRW, CCM
Simplify Your Life Career Services
6327-C SW Capitol Hwy. PMB 243
Portland, OR 97201-1937
tel: (503) 977-1955
fax: (503) 245-4212
E-mail: simplify@spiritone.com
Web: www.simplifyyourliferesumes.com

Janice M. Shepherd, CPRW, JCTC,
CEIP
Write On Career Keys
Top of Alabama Hill
Bellingham, WA 98226-4260;
tel: (360) 738-7958
fax: (360) 738-1189
E-mail: Janice@writeoncareerkeys.com

Karen M. Silins, CRW, CTAC, CCA
A+ Career & Resume
Kansas City, MO
tel: (816) 942-3019
fax: (816) 942-1505
Web: www.careerandresume.com

Kelley Smith, CPRW
Advantage Resume Services
P.O. Box 391
Sugar Land, Texas 77487
tel: (281) 494-3330 or
(877) 478-4999
Fax: (281) 494-0173
E-mail: info@advantage-resume.com
or kands@concentric.net
Web: www.advantage-resume.com
Career Masters, PARW, NRWA

Rebecca Stokes, CPRW
President
The Advantage, Inc.
401 Mill Lane
Lynchburg, VA 24503
tel: (800) 922-5353
Fax: (804) 384-4700
E-mail: advresume@aol.com
Web: www.advantageresume.com

Billie Ruth Sucher, MS, President
Billie Ruth Sucher & Associates
7177 Hickman Road, Suite 10
Urbandale, IA 50322
tel: (515) 276-0061
fax: (515) 334-8076
E-mail: betwnjobs@aol.com

Gina Taylor, CPRW
Gina Taylor & Associates, Inc.
1111 W. 77th Terrace
Kansas City, Missouri 64114
tel: (816) 523-9100
E-mail: ginaresume @aol.com

Patricia A. Traina, CPRW, CRW, CEIP
The Resume Writer
P.O. Box 46
Port Reading, NJ 07064;
tel: (732) 500-6330
fax: (800) 887-3467
Web: www.theresumewriter.com

Ilona Vanderwoude
The Vanderwoude Advantage
"Expert Résumés"
Riverdale, NY
tel: (914) 376-4217
fax: (646) 349-2218
E-mail: info@YourResumeWriter.com

Vivian Van Lier, CPRW, JCTC, CEIP
Advantage Resume & Career Services
(Los Angeles, CA)
CuttingEdgeResumes.com
tel: (818) 994-6655
fax: (818) 994-6620
E-mail:
Vivian@CuttingEdgeResumes.com

Web: www.cuttingedegeresumes.com
Certified Professional Resume Writer
Internationally Certified Job & Career
Transition Coach
Certified Employment Interview
Professional

Julie Walraven
Design Resumes
1202 Elm Street
Wausau, WI 54401
tel: (715) 845-5664 or (888) 435-7131
fax: (715) 845-8076
E-mail: design@dwave.net
Web: www.designresumes.com

Jean F. West, CPRW, JCTC
Impact Resume & Career Services
(currently "Career Services")
207 10th Avenue
Indian Rocks Beach, FL 33785
tel: (888) 596-2534
fax: (727) 593-7386
Web: www.impactresumes.com

Pearl White, CEIP
A 1st Impression Resume Service
41 Tangerine
Irvine, CA 92618
tel: (949) 651-1068
fax: (949) 651-9415
Web: www.a1stimpression.com

Sharon Pierce-Williams, M.Ed., CPRW
The Résumé.Doc
609 Lincolnshire Lane
Findlay, OH 45840
tel: (419) 422-0228
fax: (419) 425-1185
Web: www.TheResumeDoc.com

Janice Worthington-Loranca CPRW, JCTC
Fortune 500 Communications
EVP National Resume Wriers Association
"Top 10 Industry Leaders" Professional
Association of Resume Writers
Resident Resume Expert,
careerInvestors.com
F500resume@aol.com

Linda Wunner, CPRW, CEIP, JCTC
Career & Resume Design / Linda's
Page Works
"Advanced career development
concepts that WORK!"
E-mail: Linda@successfulresumes.com
Web: www.successfulresumes.com

Online Resources

1st Impressions Resumes and Careers
www.1st-imp.com

A+ Online Resumes
www.ol-resume.com

Affordable Resume
www.aaow.com/john_schwartz

Bakos Group
www.bakos.com

Career & Resume Management
www.crm21.com

Career Marketing-Resume service
www.careermarketing.com

Career Transitions
www.bfservs.com:80/bfserv.html

Careerpro
www.career_pro.com

eResumes
www.resumelink.com

Keyword Resume & Fax Service
www.ourworld.compuserve.com/home
pages/deckerservices

North American Business Concepts
www.digimark.net/noam/

One-way Resume
www2.connectnet.com/users/blorincz

Protype
www.members.aol.com/criscito

Resume Publishing Company
www.csn.net

Resumes on the Web
www.resweb.com

Resumexpress
www.resumexpress.com

Superior Resumes
www.mindtrust.com

Resume Banks

Resume banks are the reverse of job banks. Instead of employers listing available jobs to be scanned by job hunters, resume banks are made up of resumes supplied by job applicants, intended to be scanned by prospective employers. In most resume banks, you either upload your resume in file or HTML form into the site, or fill out an online form, which will generate a resume-like document for employers to scan.

An employer requesting a search from a resume database will describe the available job with a number of keywords. The computer then searches for those words and phrases in all the resumes in the database. An employer can typically search for up to twenty keywords or phrases. It isn't necessary that you match them all —just one match is usually all it takes.

If you are going to post your resume online, you will most likely use one of the resume generators supplied by the job bank in question. If not, follow these guidelines.

- Use 14 point (size) Courier type, or a similar plain font.
- Avoid italics, script, underlining, and boldface, along with two-column or other nontraditional formatting.
- Use upper/lower case to differentiate headings.
- Use plenty of white space.
- Do not include large paragraphs of text.
- You can use bulleted lists, but use a dash as your bullet "point."

If you are an experienced professional with qualifications for more than one job, you may want to post additional resumes under appropriate job titles, including the appropriate keywords and phrases for that job. Some people are concerned about confidentiality. If you upload your resume into a resume bank, theoretically your employer may find your resume online. Practically speaking, most active resume banks have ways to protect your confidentiality. You can try to improve your odds by replacing the name of your current employer

with a generic name. For example, you could change "The First International Bank of Last Resort" to "A Major Bahamian Bank"; headhunters do this for their clients all the time.

Most resume banks are free (at present). The few who do charge typically offer special additional services, and the fees for these are usually quite reasonable. Note that most job banks have resume banks and vice versa.

A+ Online Resumes
www.ol-resume.com/
e-mail: webmaster@ol-resume.com
This is a professional resume service that will convert your resume to HTML and post it on the Web, where HR professionals and business owners can have access to it around the clock. Employers can find your resume either by job category or location. Resumes are registered with the most popular search engines. You are given your own home page with a URL. Postings cost $40 for three months, $60 for six months, $80 for nine months, and $100 for a full year. A+ aggressively promotes the site throughout the Internet on highly targeted hyperlinks to ensure that it maintains a high profile.

You can view the guest book, which contains a list of employers who use the site. These companies are listed by state. This site advises that you don't have to restrict a resume to one or two pages. While space considerations are different online, the reader's attention hasn't increased any, so stick to two pages.

America's Employers Resume Bank
www.americasemployers.com/resume.html
This subsidiary site of the America's Employers Career Center caters primarily to executives who have been prescreened by America's Employers career counselors. The resume database has grown by leaps and bounds since last year. When I searched this site, I found 17 resumes in accounting and finance, 11 in health care, and 26 in information systems. This year I found several hundred resumes in accounting alone.

Member companies are able to access contact information on the candidates directly. If nonmember company of America's Employers is in-terested in contacting you, the service will notify you.

America's Job Bank
www.ajb.dni.us

This is the big one, 1.4 million jobs, in all specialties, at all levels, and most importantly in your town. You can search for jobs by title or function, state, or zip code. How is such a large and detailed job bank possible? It's run by the Department of Labor.

You have three choices once you get into the Job Bank: menu search, keyword search, or code search (for those savvy individuals who know the D.O.T.—Dictionary of Occupational Titles—code for their profession). Menu search gives you a scroll list of 22 standard job categories. The 3,326 computer jobs on file for New York came up onto the screen in less than 30 seconds. I was impressed, having done so much waiting for so much less at other, more self-important sites. Each listing shows job title, location, salary, education required, experience required, and whether the job is full-time or part-time. I was even able to learn which industries the jobs were in. New listings are asterisked to save regular users' time. The really neat thing about this site is that once the jobs are on screen, you can re-sort the order they are listed in by state, city, job title, salary, or new jobs. America's Job Bank is friendly, flexible, fast—and it delivers.

America's Job Bank also has a resume builder, which will automatically load your profile in its resume database called America's Talent Bank. This database is also enormous and therefore frequently searched by employers and headhunters.

Bilingual Jobs
www.bilingual-jobs.com

If you are bi-lingual in English and one other language, this site can offer you an edge. The job bank offers jobs from all kinds of industries: Information Technology, Finance, Publishing, Construction, Manufacturing, and more. Many of the positions offer the opportunity of international exposure for the bi-lingual. In a global economy and with America's economic dominance in all fields, a job through this site could be the means to an important career boost. Obviously, you will post your resume in the resume bank too.

Brassring.com
www.brassring.com

A site with a strong IT slant, 50,000 jobs and 1,200 plus advertisers. Brassring.com was one of the first to offer an active database that automatically matches candidates and employers and notifies both (via e-mail) of any and all matches—sending the matching resumes to the employer, and the job description to the job seeker. Job seekers can "protect" their resume—so that their current employer doesn't accidentally pick up their resume as a match—and can specify which Usenet newsgroups they want to be listed on. The database automatically discards job listings/resumes you have already reviewed, so that you don't constantly have to go over the same material when you check in. If you're not happy with the results, you can adjust your profile with more or less information at any point. And you have the option of independently searching the database just like on the listings systems. It costs $20 to post your resume for six months. You can also do a keyword job search, which gives you an idea of what they have to offer.

Aside from the above, this site also offers goodies such as tips on resume writing and corporate profiles, and information on scholarships from educational institutions.

Careerbabe
www.careerbabe.com

A great site. Fran Quittel (the Careerbabe) cares and really knows her stuff. You won't find the standard job and resume banks here but you will get good and timely advice.

"The babe" is a columnist for a number of newspapers and magazines. She answers questions and has regular chats, as often as she can get worthwhile guests. The site also has a good library of articles with informative commentary on resumes, job hunting, and careers.

Careerbrain.com
www.careerbrain.com

Now this is something different, and right off the bat I have to tell you why: It's my site, and what is known in the business as a "heavy content" site. At Careerbrain you can take my free online job hunting course, which complements everything you are reading in this section and shows you how to use the Internet effectively in a job hunt. Also has free career choice tests, free resume evaluations, and free job hunting TV and radio shows starring yours truly. You'll also find resume blasters, reference checking tools, and other goodies. There's no site like it. You also get to ask me questions directly.

Careerbuilder
www.careerbuilder.com

Significant job and resume banks and e-mail alerts on suitable job openings make Careerbuilder worth a visit. Allied with ADP, Careerbuilder has marketing muscle and a presence in Canada, Europe, and Asia—which could be useful if you're seeking to gain a little international exposure.

A nice time-saving feature on the job bank page is that they tell you if there are advertised jobs in the bank for the geographic target of your search. The site also has some good job hunting advice on other career management issues.

Careerbuilder has developed a job scout that does more than e-mail alert you to suitable job openings in their job bank. This new tool searches all the job banks on the net and tells you who has openings in your area of expertise. This is a first and I predict will cause tremendous upheavals in the online recruitment advertising field.

CareerCity
www.careercity.com

Includes an impressive array of features for job seekers, including the following.

- A me   job search tool that allows you to instantly search 4 million job openings at all the leading career sites

- Descriptions and hot links to thousands of U.S. companies
- Job searches by state, country, job category, description, title, or company
- Free electronic resume posting directly to potential employers

CAREERMagazine
www.careermag.com/
e-mail: editor@careermag.com

CAREERMagazine has all the essentials of a thorough Career Site, a keyword-based job database, employer profiles, a resume bank, a career forum, job fairs, a recruiter directory, relocation resources. It also features articles on employment, employment book excerpts and reviews, a bookstore where you can order books, On Campus update, the 30 fastest growing occupations, and areas covering such subjects as diversity and self-employment.

Career Mosaic
www.careermosaic.com

The job bank is searchable by job title, geography (within a 50 mile radius of your specific location), or keyword. As of my last visit they did not have an e-mail alert for suitable job openings, so you won't automatically get a "heads up" on a desired employer.

This great site is marred only by the abysmal career center run by *Fortune* magazine. You will find some good *Fortune* inspired lists (The *Fortune 500*, etc.) but no real job hunting or career advice of any significance.

This is definitely one of the larger employment sites around, and another that claims to be the first, biggest, and best. Career Mosaic offers:

- A career resource center with advice for job seekers and links
- Free resume posting!
- The College Connection—for students or first-time job searchers
- Online job fairs
- Employer profiles
- A special area for health care jobs

- USENET jobs offered featuring 60,000 postings daily, rebuilt daily, cleared weekly
- J.O.B.S. database featuring "thousands of up-to-date job opportunities"

This site is all business, and has expanded rapidly. Their international gateway features Career Mosaic for Japan, Canada, the UK, Australia, Asia, France, Hong Kong, Korea, New Zealand, and Indonesia.

CareerPath
www.careerpath.com
e-mail: webmaster@careerpath.com
Careerpath is an ever-growing alliance of newspapers that put their recruitment advertising together to create a mammoth job bank. Starting with just seven newspapers, you can now check the help-wanted advertising of 80 plus newspapers; and this number will continue to grow. There are hundreds of thousands of job listings on the site, and you can search for jobs by newspaper, industry, or a keyword. Claims no job is older than two weeks.

The site also has a resume bank for employers and headhunters to search. It is worth taking a few minutes to use their resume creator, which will then automatically load your resume in the resume bank. The ads are updated daily by 6 A.M. Eastern Standard Time. They also post each day's number of ads.

You can search this site without registering to get a feel for what's available, but I guarantee that you will ultimately register. For one thing, registration is free. Registering involves filling in your name and e-mail address, and choosing a password and a screen name. Once you begin your search, the site is responsive, and easy to use. You simply select a job title and geography. You can also enter additional keywords that the database will use to narrow your search.

Career Roadblocks
www.careerroadblocks.com
If there is something blocking your career path, this site is there to help you. First the site identifies what the problem is, then offers solutions. Don't know what you want to do?

Can't pinpoint your career path? Is it your resume? Not enough interviews? Maybe it's your references?

Career Shop
www.careershop.com
e-mail: webmaster@tenkey.com
A substantial career site; the job bank also has an e-mail alert: a resume bank, job fair listings, relocation, a salary calculator, and links round out the standard fare. They do however have a few features that help them stand out.

They have a training area within the site that enlightens you about online, self-paced (CDROM), and on the ground-in-your-town training seminars.

They recently introduced careertv.com which, glamorous as it sounds, is basically the opportunity to see a couple of minor TV actors pitch the jobs of technology companies.

My favorite part of this whole site is their Career Doctor Dr. Randall Hansen answers questions and his input is relevant. Especially nice is that he'll give you an answer and then refer you to other resources and provide the links right there on the page. Good guy, sensible advice, kudos to careershop.com. This site has recently been bought by Personnel Group of America.

Career Tips
www.careertips.com
An interesting take on the global workplace. If you want to pursue work or education outside of the U.S. this is a good place to start. The site addresses career prospects, education and training facilities, employment opportunities and immigration rules in developed countries all around the world. This is an intelligently conceived site and well worth a visit if you are considering working overseas or completing part of your education in another country.

CareerWeb
www.careerweb.com
e-mail: info@cweb.com
A continually growing site with the requisite job and resume bank. Once you have filled out a

job profile, careerweb.com alerts you to suitable job openings via e-mail. This neat service is becoming increasingly common on the majority of career sites with job banks.

Careerweb also has a resume bank that is well worth the time to load a resume. However from the job hunters viewpoint, there is a problem with this resume bank—and every other resume bank! Your resume gets wiped out after 90 days. Fresh resumes are thought to be a selling point to employers and recruiters, but if you aren't settled in a new job in 90 days you'll have to re-register. Features include:

- Articles and essays (The Career Doctor)
- Books, publications, and news articles
- Career fairs
- Consulting and counseling services
- Directories
- Internships
- Professional training and career development
- Salary calculator
- Resume bank
- Job Bank

Check Your References
www.myreferences.com
(800) 750-3469

Getting interviews but no job offers? Have you ever wondered what your past employers and references are really saying about you? Maybe MyReferences.com could be the solution for your situation. For as little as $59, the people at MyReferences.com will do a professional reference check on your behalf and report to you on exactly what past employers say about you, including their tone of voice and how difficult they were to reach. An exemplary service that's been in business since the early eighties.

Community Career Center
www.nonprofitjobs.org

A job and resume bank site focused on community centered nonprofit jobs.

Company & Interview Research Assistant
Dianne Eisenhardt, Internet Research Expert

(800) 663-4056
dianne@alisontaylor.com

The Internet is full of great information. You can use it to identify companies you want to work for and to gather information on these companies to customize your resume and cover letters and then to prepare for the interview. However, when you are conducting a job search, time is of the essence and expert assistance can be invaluable. With 10+- years of research experience as the lead researcher for two Internet job-hunting books, Dianne Eisenhardt and her team can be a great asset to your job-hunting and interview preparation efforts. Available on an hourly basis, you can utilize this service to your best advantage.

Contract Employment Connection
www.ntes.com

A job bank addressing the needs of employers looking for contractors rather than full-time employees. Its strength is Information Technology people.

Contract Executives
www.imcor.com

Now owned by Norrel, a temporary help company, Imcor specializes in contract positions for executives; you won't find anything here for under $75K a year. All of the jobs in the job bank are contract positions; many of them come with a greater or lesser degree of opportunity for converting the contract position to permanent employment. If you are an executive in the 75K range the resume bank is worthwhile too.

Cool Works
www.coolworks.com

Jobs away from the madding crowd. A cool job bank with thousands of jobs in ski resorts, theme parks, national parks, sports, and the travel industry.

Diversity
www.eop.com

This site is the home of The Career Center for Workplace Diversity. It is owned by a publisher who specializes in special interest diversity magazines for equal opportunity, engineering, and the disabled. The site has a job bank, which leverages the recruitment advertising from the magazines, so if you belong to an identifiable minority, these advertisers would love to hear from you.

There are articles from the magazines re-purposed for the site, plus updates on career fairs around the country. If you are part of a minority or are challenged in some way, you know it can be tough finding good jobs and career advice, so spread the word.

DiversityLink
www.diversitylink.com

Another good diversity job bank with some very visible corporate advertisers. DiversityLink also has a resume bank you can be sure is accessed by the same major corporations and by recruiters whose clients are striving to achieve and maintain diversity in their workforce. If you belong to an identifiable minority you can gain an edge by posting your resume and responding to matching job openings.

Employment Spot
www.employmentspot.com

The site features lots of links to job and resume banks, as you would expect, plus career related news, diversity oriented employers, government organizations, internships, relocation resources, and maps to your next interviews. Well thought out and worth a visit.

Exec.U.Net
www.execunet.com
e-mail: Canada@execunet.com

This is a good database and networking connection for professionals in the $100K plus category. The site is also different in that while the job bank is free to employer and recruiters, there is a fee to the job hunter. The site requires membership at $135 for three months. For the Internet phobic, job leads can also be delivered through regular mail. Execunet also sponsors networking meetings around the country.

Exec.U.Net continues to add useful information, including more data on market trends, and resources for job search and career management. This is where you'll get the best chance to meet and be wooed by the headhunters.

Executive Jobs
www.jobreports.net

A special site that focuses on higher level jobs ($50–300K) in the sales and marketing disciplines. The site claims that none of these jobs are widely advertised and that many of them have never been advertised at all. This is a subscription site with monthly issues of a 50-page report that features 250–300 jobs per issue. Jobs are not repeated from issue to issue. If you register your resume, they will give you e-mail alerts when matching jobs are located from the newsletter. One monthly issue costs $29.95; the price drops the more issues you subscribe to.

Jobreports also offers a free resume evaluation service. There is also a for fee resume wiring and distribution service. This is a conscientiously run service, and for the Internet phobic it can all be done through hardcopy and the telephone. Reach them at (716) 485-3454.

FedWorld
www.fedworld.gov
e-mail: webmaster@Fedworld.gov

The FedWorld Information Network is a service designed to give the general public access to government information. FedWorld provides access to 100-plus dialup bulletin boards that are not otherwise available on the Internet. Search the job bank, register your profile and needs, and an e-mail alert will update you about appropriate openings.

FedWorld's Federal Job Announcement search capability allows you to search a database of about 2,000 U.S. government job announcements that are updated daily from Tuesday through Saturday at 9:30 A.M. Eastern Standard Time. From the initial home page, key in "Job Announcements," which brings you to a keyword search that allows you to enter one or two relevant job field words.

Flipdog.com
www.flipdog.com
Flipdog is something new. It will link you to the sites of upwards of 50,000 employers and their specific job openings. They are claiming over half a million job openings, which doesn't surprise me at all. The vast majority of the jobs are in the continental U.S.

Register with their job hunter tool (a variation on the standard e-mail alert), and it will alert you to when any company in their database has jobs posted on that company's own Web site that fit your needs.

How is this different? Flipdog isn't asking you to rely on companies who advertise with them, it goes directly to company Web sites and searches their Job Opportunity pages for you.

You can also subscribe to their monthly Job Opportunity Index, which gives you an overview of employment in 50 major Metropolitan areas and the number of jobs available in different major categories. This won't help you find a specific job, but if you are considering relocation it can give you a snapshot of types of employment opportunities in a given area, and the concentration of the core industries in that area.

Getting a Job
www.americanexpress.com/student/
A good-sized database of intern programs from corporate America and the non-profit world. Backed by Amex Financial Assistance services you can also learn a good deal about how far in debt you'll get for a good education!

Global careers
www.globalcareers.com
A job bank with international appeal. Jobs from around the world, mainly in finance, business, management, and transportation. There's also a resume bank, so if you want international exposure, or are bilingual this is the place to post your resume.

Gonyea Online Career Center
You must be a subscriber to America Online to access these services. To get to this site, search AOL by keyword and type in either "career" or "career center." You'll see the Gonyea Online Career Center as one of the search results. Formerly the America Online Career Center, the Gonyea Online Career Center was the power behind that throne, and still offers a good selection of career-related services, including:

- Help Wanted–USA
- Worldwide Resume Bank
- Career Guidance Services
- Government Jobs Central
- Career Resource Mall
- Occupational Profiles
- Employment Agencies
- Online Job Hunting

One service that will be of primary interest is Help Wanted—USA, where you can key in a preset job code and location for job categories and receive a list of matching job openings.

This site claims to have 10,000 new job listings per week, updated weekly. It recommends that the best time to check for new listings is Wednesday morning. The Gonyea Online Career Center also boasts over 1 million users a month. This makes it one of the most visited career sites available today.

Great Summer Jobs
www.gsj.petersons.com
Another niche site. This one offering a job bank with an endless supply of counselor jobs at summer camps around the country. Good content fills you in on what camp directors look for in the counselors they hire, what the jobs are, and how much they pay.

This is a seasonal site to the degree that you won't find jobs posted in the summer, because they have all been filled. The job listings start building in October and begin to fall off in the spring.

Headhunter.net
www.headhunter.net
The other awesome headhunter site. A major job bank with multiple postings from thousands of headhunting firms in most disciplines. This is a great job bank that gets you in front of the elusive

headhunter with hundreds of thousands of job openings, with an e-mail alert option. It also has an extensive resume bank you'll want to be in. This site has enormous respect in the professional community. If you are a mid-career professional (there's not a lot for entry level here) you must visit headhunter.net

Help Wanted USA
www.iccweb.com

Run by Jim Gonyea, an Internet careersite pioneer, you can also find this site on AOL as the Gonyea Career Center. It has a comprehensive job bank that feature jobs from cities throughout the nation, and an equally important resume bank. You'll also find a resume blaster, salary calculator, and other useful job hunting tools here. It is one of the most comprehensive sites around and reflects Jim's depth of knowledge.

Hoovers Online
www.hoovers.com

This is the online version of the Hoovers directories, a valuable research tool to job hunters. Use it to identify potential employers, or gather information for an upcoming interview. This is a subscription site costing about $12 a month, although many parts of the site are free.

Hot Jobs
www.hotjobs.com

A good and getting better, job bank with e-mail alerts. Great companies advertise with hotjobs.com in most fields. This growing job bank has lots of mid- to higher-level postings with plenty of information about the job, but not much about the employer, so you'll have to do that research yourself.

The site also has a pretty decent resume bank frequently scanned by employers and recruiters. A neat feature of the resume bank is that it can tell you how many times your resume has been accessed. This could give you useful feedback on the effectiveness of your resume; many hits but no calls for interview might suggest a review of your resume structure and content.

Industry Insite
www.industryinsite.com

A networking site for college graduates from an increasing number of colleges like Stanford, Harvard, Yale, Duke, Northeastern, Berkeley, University of Chicago, Cornell, Princeton, and MIT, to name a few. There is a job bank, but the real benefit is the opportunity to network with alumnae from your and other schools who have similar professional interest areas as you.

Industry Insite is a community-oriented site and a great way to leverage the contacts that can come from an expensive education. Expect this site to continue adding alumnae associations to its membership.

International Jobs
www.internationaljobs.org

Online version of a print newsletter. Job bank of openings outside the U.S., but you pay to see them, about $26 dollars for six weeks. You also get the hardcopy newsletter.

Internet Business Network
Interbiznet.com

Fresh news everyday that's relevant to online jobhunters. This site is geared mainly towards the professional recruitment community. However, you can glean lots of information about specific recruiters and trends in employment. They also have a career advice section that is way above average. You get the idea that the writers know something about job hunting, which is a refreshing change from most sites. Each day's fare features three to six short articles with links to other information sources.

Internet Job Search Report
Career Advancement Publications
(800) 663-5927
www.jobreports.net

This is one of the greatest timesaving reports. A good Internet job search strategy will include the large, popular sites as well as smaller industry and geographically specific sites. This company has compiled a massive database of thousands of career sites. For a nominal fee, you can purchase a list of career sites, job banks, resume banks and associations specific to your background. A great way to jump-start your job search!

Jaegers' Interactive
www.jaegerinc.com
A job bank run by a recruitment-advertising agency. The jobs come from their corporate advertisers. Jobs are across the board, most valuable if you are in the Ohio area.

JobDirect.com
www.jobdirect.com
Job and resume bank with a strong presence in the college educated entry level space. JobDirect has aggressively pursued colleges and graduating students across the U.S. and the resume bank shows it. Consequently employers scan the resume bank and post jobs in the job bank. If you are at the entry-level point of your career, this is a must go-to site.

JOBTRAK
www.jobtrak.com
e-mail: www@jobtrak.com
tel: (800) 999-8725
Established in 1987 as a service for college students, graduates, and alumni, this has developed into one of the most critically acclaimed sites on the Web. Also chosen as one of the University of Michigan's top four "Best of the Best" in job search sites, JOBTRAK was distinguished in 1992 as Entrepreneur of the Year by the state of California, semifinalist in the 1997 National Information & Infrastructure Awards, as well as earning 10 other online awards. This service is completely free. There is only one prerequisite. You must be a college student or an alum, since the only way you can get a password is through your campus or *alma mater*.

You can see why employers would register with and frequent this site! It is also user-friendly for employers: They can phone in their ads rather than have to master the Net in order to get access to this wonderful pool of talent.

In the past year Job Track has continued its regular launch of new features, including salary calculators, Career Fair calendars, more relocation information, and an expanded resource center.

Job Web
www.jobweb.org
e-mail: webmaster@jobweb.org
The first Internet site developed by a human resources organization, this one is owned and maintained by the National Association of Colleges and Employers (NACE), a nonprofit organization comprised of over 1,700 colleges and universities and over 1,400 business organizations. It caters to the college-educated work force.

Winner of the 1997 Gutenberg award for the Best HTML Career/Employment Publications, the features of Job Web are impressive, including:

- Jobs—a keyword search database, free for job seekers
- Employer profiles, hundreds of companies listed alphabetically
- Job search and industry information
- Career services professionals
- Catalogs for job seekers
- Relocation resources
- International resources

This site is especially worth visiting if you are in the human resources field or if you are a college graduate looking for your first job. This job site is likely to be a winner because of all the campus recruiters who belong to the sponsoring organization. Expect it to achieve greatness!

Kelly Services
www.kellyservices.com
The job bank features jobs from all over the Kelly Temporary Services network. The resume bank makes your resume available to the thousand plus Kelly offices and their recruiters. Lots of administrative positions and also an increasingly good source for technical and managerial temporary positions.

Local Opportunities
www.Abracat.com

Sick of the city and yearning for a meaningful career with small-town quality-of-life? Then visit this site, the job bank has help-wanted advertising from over 700 small town newspapers throughout North America. Register and identify your skills and geographic interests and you'll get e-mail alerts of matching jobs. Nifty site.

Manpower
www.manpower.com

A global employment services company (temporary and permanent) with a presence in 435 countries. You can search by title, keyword, state, or nation. There is a significant resume bank too, which makes your resume available to all the Manpower branch offices.

Med Search America
www.medsearch.com

There is no better site for health care professionals to find the perfect job. Thousands of job opportunities from all over the country are accessible to job seekers for *free!* It is powered by Monster Board and features a similar format. (When you see a Web site that says "powered by" it means the site has reached a commercial agreement to use products and services of another vendor under their own banner.)

Monster Board
www.monster.com

The aptly named Monster Board was one of the very first job search web sites. In fact their founder Jeff Taylor tells me their site was the 436th domain name registered.

The Monster job bank approaches the size of the one at Careerpath. It has hundreds of thousands of jobs for people at all levels and in all fields, it's a must visit job bank; and with over a million resumes, their resume bank may be the biggest there is. Combined, this tells you that employers and recruiters will all consider advertising in the job bank and searching the resume database.

The site has chats and resident "experts" to address your questions, although the response isn't always timely and sometimes lacks depth. This trend setting site also has a lot of other bells and whistles.

- Career insight & advice—including links and career advice columns by renowned employee advocate Joyce Lain Kennedy
- A resume builder
- A resume database
- Relocation services
- Personal job search agent

The jobs listed here seem to be primarily located on the East Coast and are mostly in technical fields. You can search the database by discipline (almost 300 very specific titles), location (over 200 towns/states), or keyword, and get a list of available positions.

Nationjob
www.nationjob.com

An excellent national site with strong job and resume banks and perhaps the premier site for jobs in the heartland. E-mail alerts on suitable jobs for registered users. Lots of additional content and a site owner who understands the world of work and cares about his customers make this site a consistent winner.

Newspage
www.newspage.com

No job or resume bank. What you do get is daily news coverage about corporate expansion and contraction activities. This is a subscription site with a nominal price of $5 a month; you can request news in a number of different areas. You can specify any region in the world. A useful research tool.

Penton Publishing
www.penton.com

Another job bank site owned by a publisher of professional niche magazines: sales, hospitality, travel, electronics, manufacturing, and management. The job bank reflects these specialties. It is not a big job bank, but because the magazines are also published overseas, there is an international component to some of the jobs.

Personal Internet Assistant
A service of Karrus Evergreen, Inc.
(800) 475-4146
terra@netsync.net

How you post your resume and complete online profiles will make a huge difference in your online job search effectiveness. It is not just a matter of completing the online questionnaire or pasting sections of your resume. This company and its staff of experts understand that these online profiles and registrations are screening tools—tools to screen you out. As such, they have found ways to trick these tools, ways to make you more successful online. With a comprehensive knowledge of the Internet, they will customize your online job hunt, completing your online presence to maximize your time and effectiveness.

Recruiters Online Network
www.ipa.com

This is one of the best places to get your resume in front of some 8,000 headhunters from around the world. You can now also view all those job openings the mysterious headhunters are working to fill. Once you have loaded your resume in the resume bank you'll get e-mail updates on suitable opportunities. At the same time, the member recruiters will be alerted to your presence when your skills match an open requisition. There are so many different specialist recruiters using this site, your profession and specialty are almost certainly represented.

Resume Express
www.resumexpress.com

Load your resume onto the Resume Express launcher and get it automatically distributed to over 4,000 targeted employers and recruiters. The cost is $99, and when you consider the time saving and comprehensive coverage, it is well worth the bucks. Started in 1994 by pioneer Wayne Gonyea, this site was the first of its kind. It is often said that you can't get $100K plus jobs on the Internet. I recommended a friend making way over the magic $100K mark to Resume Express, he got twenty calls, multiple interviews, and a great job well into six figures. It was also the only vehicle that got his resume any significant response.

Resumes on the Web
www.resweb.com
e-mail: sdas@ifu.net

Resume postings are now free and this site now has a jobbank (powered by jobsonline) with over 200,000 listings.

There is no fee for searching the site, making it attractive to recruiters and employers alike. You simply click onto the job category and the names of candidates appear. Click again and a complete resume with contact information appears—very straightforward. This is not a huge resume bank as yet, but the resumes I looked at had impressive credentials, making this site a place that employers and recruiters could well come to respect.

Retail Jobs
www.retailjobnet.com

A good niche site for the retail profession, if you are in the management or executive ranks, but not strong in sales floor positions. There is also a resume bank which in the last couple of years has been both for free and for fee, so who knows what it will be when you get there, as there are rumors that it may flip again.

Sales & Marketing Jobs Report
Faith, Winter & Grace, Inc.
www.jobreports.net
(800) 750-2621

This is a special site that focuses on high level jobs ($50–$300K) in the sales and marketing disciplines. It is a subscription based service with monthly issues of a 50+-page report that features 250 to 300 jobs. Jobs are not repeated from issue to issue. One introductory issue costs $33.90 (including shipping); the price drops the longer your subscribe. Jobreports.net also offers a free resume evaluation service. For a fee, they have a resume writing and distribution service.

Shawn's Internet Resume Center
www.inpursuit.com/sirc

For a one-time fee of $30 you can post your resume on this very heavily visited site, which caters to high-end management. Check out the guest book, and you'll be impressed by the employers and recruiters who are searching the site. Check out your competition by doing a resume search on others looking for work in your field—an idea of what kind of qualifications they have and how they're presenting themselves to employers could be time and money well spent.

Socrates Careers
www.socratescareers.com

No job or resume bank, as such. This is an association of career management professionals whose common bond is services to working professionals and executives. All the members are respected in their professional community, and all of them have extensive track records. The site will link you to individual members who provide a wide range of services: reference checking, career counselling, resume writing and distribution, headhunter lists, job lists by industry, testing and assessment tools, employment law, and discrimination attorneys, including the attorney who won the much publicized discrimination case against the Hooters restaurant chain. There's a lot of qualified help here.

Telecommuting Jobs
www.tjobs.com

A niche site which will develop growing importance in the changing world of work. You will find jobs here that don't require you in the office everyday: Mostly you'll find sales, programming, graphics, and writing jobs. There is a resume bank, but one that you pay to be in, albeit a token ten bucks a year. Also you'll find useful content on telecommuting trends and the issues that face telecommuters and their employers.

Wall Street Journal
www.wsj.com

On the homepage, click on careers. This is the Wall Street Journal's foray into online help-wanted advertising. The job bank features recruitment advertising from all the prestigious business-oriented advertisers who also use the newspaper's national and regional editions.

What makes the site stand out is some truly useful content. The site now includes a significant amount of job hunting and career management articles written by respected career and job hunting experts. These articles are now available online and comprise some of the most sensible advice available on the Internet.

Yahoo Resume Bank
www.yahoo.com

When you get into Yahoo, just type in "individual resumes" and you will be presented with 91 headings you can link to, covering all major industries.

This bank has a growing roster of thousands of professional resumes. When you check on a category (there are also subcategories within job categories) you are instantly presented with a list of names, each annotated with a quick quip designed to attract your attention.

Once you click on a name, you get a full resume with all the details: experience, education, activities, references, etc. For an employer, the Yahoo resume bank is accessible, easy to use, and fast; for you, it is free. Go on, post your resume!

Also see these other valuable resume sites:

Resumail Network
www.rsumail.com

Resumania Online
www.umn.edu/ohr/ecep/resume

Resume link
www.resume-link.com

Resources

HEALTH CARE

Publications
Hospital Phone Book
U.S. Directory Service, Miami, FL
Provides information on over 7,940
government and private hospitals in the U.S.

*National Association of County Health
Officials Sustaining Membership Directory*
National Association of County Health
Officials, Washington, DC
Lists national health officials for almost every
county in the U.S. Published annually. $10.
Call 202-783-5550 for more information.

National Jobs in Dietetics
Jobs in Dietetics, Santa Monica, CA
Lists jobs nationwide in the field of dietetics.
Published monthly; an annual subscription is
$84. Call 310-453-5375 for more information.

U.S. Medical Directory
U.S. Directory Service, Miami, FL
Over one thousand pages of information on
doctors, hospitals, nursing facilities, medical
laboratories, and medical libraries.

Associations

HEALTH CARE ADMINISTRATION

American Association of Medical Assistants
20 North Wacker Drive, Suite 1575
Chicago, IL 60606-2903; tel: 312-899-1500

American College of Healthcare Executives
1 North Franklin, Suite 1700
Chicago, IL 60606-3491; tel: 312-424-2800

American Health Care Association
1201 L Street NW
Washington, DC 20005; tel: 202-842-4444

American Health Information Management
Association
919 North Michigan Avenue
Chicago, IL 60611; tel: 312-787-2672

American Medical Technologists
710 Higgins Road
Park Ridge, IL 60068; tel: 708-823-5169

Healthcare Financial Management Association
Two Westbrook Corporate Center, Suite 700
Westchester, IL 60154; tel: 708-531-9600

National Association of Emergency Medical
Technicians
102 West Leake Street
Clinton, MS 39056; tel: 601-924-7747

Nuclear Medicine Technology Certification
Board
2970 Clairmont Road, Suite 610
Atlanta, GA 30329-1634; tel: 404-315-1739

NURSING

American Association of Nurse Anesthetists
222 South Prospect Avenue
Park Ridge, IL 60068-4001; tel: 708-692-7050

American Association of Occupational
Health Nurses
50 Lenox Pointe
Atlanta, GA 30324; tel: 404-262-1162
or 800-241-8014

American Hospital Association
1 North Franklin
Chicago, IL 60606; tel: 312-422-3000

American Nurses Association
600 Maryland Avenue SW, Suite 100 W
Washington, DC 20024-2571;
tel: 202-651-7000

Medical Economics Publishing
5 Paragon Drive
Montvale, NJ 07645-1742; tel: 201-358-7200

National Association for Home Care
519 C Street NE
Washington, DC 20002; tel: 202-547-7424
(send SASE for general information)

National Association for Practical Nurse
Education and Service
1400 Spring Street, Suite 310
Silver Spring, MD 20910; tel: 301-588-2491

National Association of Pediatric Nurse
Associates and Practitioners
1101 Kings Highway N, Suite 206
Cherry Hill, NJ 08034-1921;
tel: 609-667-1773

National Federation of Licensed
Practical Nurses
1418 Aversboro Road
Garner, NC 27529-4547; tel: 919-779-0046

National League for Nursing Communications
Department
350 Hudson Street
New York, NY 10014; tel: 212-989-9393

National Rehabilitation Association
633 South Washington Street
Alexandria, VA 22314; tel: 703-836-0850

PHYSICAL HEALTH

Accreditation Council for Graduate Medical
Education
515 North State Street, Suite 2000
Chicago, IL 60610; tel: 312-464-4920

American Association for
Respiratory Care
11030 Ables Lane
Dallas, TX 75229-4593; tel: 214-243-2272

American Association of Colleges of
Pediatric Medicine
1350 Piccard Drive, Suite 322
Rockville, MD 20850; tel: 301-990-7400

American Board of Preventive Medicine
9950 West Lawrence Avenue, Suite 106
Schiller Park, IL 60176; tel: 847-671-1750

American Medical Association
515 North State Street
Chicago, IL 60610; tel: 312-464-5000

American Occupational Therapy Association
4720 Montgomery Lane, P.O. Box 31220
Bethesda, MD 20824-1220; tel: 301-652-2682

American Physical Therapy Association
1111 North Fairfax Street
Alexandria, VA 22314;
tel: 703-684-2782 or 800-999-2782

American Podiatric Medical Association
9312 Old Georgetown Road
Bethesda, MD 20814-1621;
tel: 301-571-9200

American Society of Radiology Technologists
15000 Central Avenue SE
Albuquerque, NM 87123-4605;
tel: 505-298-4500

Society of Diagnostic Medical Sonographers
12770 Coit Road, Suite 508
Dallas, TX 75251; tel: 214-239-7367

DENTISTRY

American Association of Dental Assistants
203 North LaSalle Street, Suite 132
Chicago, IL 60601-1225;
tel: 312-541-1550

American Association of Dental Schools
1625 Massachusetts Avenue NW
Washington, DC 20036; tel: 202-667-9433

American Association of Orthodontists
401 North Lindbergh Blvd.
St. Louis, MO 63141-7816;
tel: 314-993-1700

American Dental Association
211 East Chicago Avenue
Chicago, IL 60611; tel: 312-440-2500
(for Commission on Dental Accreditation,
direct correspondence to Suite 3400; for
SELECT Program, direct correspondence to
Department of Career Guidance, Suite 1804)

American Dental Hygienists Association
Division of Professional Development
444 North Michigan Avenue, Suite 3400
Chicago, IL 60611; tel: 312-440-8900

National Association of Dental Laboratories
555 East Braddock Road
Alexandria, VA 22305; tel: 703-683-5263

National Board for Certification in
Dental Technology
555 East Braddock Road
Alexandria, VA 22305; tel: 703-683-5263

MENTAL HEALTH

American Association for Counseling
and Development
5999 Stevenson Avenue
Alexandria, VA 22304; tel: 703-823-9800

American Association for Marriage and
Family Therapy
11331 5th Street NW, Suite 300
Washington, DC 20005; tel: 202-452-0109

American Association of Mental Retardation
444 North Capitol Street, NW, Suite 846
Washington, DC 20001-1512;
tel: 202-387-1968 or 800-424-3688

American Psychiatric Association
1400 K Street NW
Washington, DC 20005; tel: 202-682-6000

American Psychological Association
750 First Street NE
Washington, DC 20002; tel: 202-336-5500

National Board for Certified Counselors
3 Terrace Way, Suite D
Greensboro, NC 27403-3660;
 tel: 910-547-0607

BIOTECHNOLOGY AND ENVIRONMENTAL TECHNOLOGY

Publications

Corporate Technology Directory
CorpTech, Woburn, MA
Lists over 35,000 businesses and 110,000
executives. Describes products and services in
such fields as automation, biotechnology,
chemicals, computers and software, defense,
energy, environment, manufacturing
equipment, advanced materials, medical,
pharmaceuticals, photonics, subassemblies and
components, testing and measurements,
telecommunications, and transportation and
holding companies. Published annually.

CorpTech Fast 5,000 Company Locator
CorpTech, Woburn, MA
Lists over five thousand of the fastest-growing
companies listed in the Corporate Technology
Directory, but includes addresses and phone
numbers, number of employees, sales, and
industries by state. Published annually.

Directory of Environmental Information
Government Institutes, Rockville, MD
Lists federal and state government resources,
trade organizations, and professional and
scientific newsletters, magazines, and
databases. Published every other year.

Environmental Telephone Directory
Governmental Institutes, Rockville, MD
Lists detailed information on governmental
agencies that deal with the environment. The
directory also identifies the environmental
aides of U.S. Senators and Representatives.
Published every other year.

Sales Guide to High-Tech Companies
CorpTech, Woburn, MA
Covers over three thousand company profiles
and twelve thousand executive contacts.
Includes specific details on each company's
products and services. Published quarterly; a
yearly subscription is $185. Call 617-932-3939
for more information.

Transportation Officials and Engineers Directory
American Road and Transportation Builders
Association, Washington, DC
Lists over four thousand state transportation
officials and engineers at local, state, and
federal levels. Published annually.

Associations

Air and Waste Management Association
1 Gateway Center, 3rd Floor
Pittsburgh, PA 15222; tel: 412-232-3444

American Chemical Society
1155 16th Street NW
Washington, DC 20036;
tel: 202-872-4600 or 800-227-5558

American Institute of Biological Sciences
1444 Eye Street NW, Suite 200
Washington, DC 20005; tel: 202-628-1500

American Institute of Chemists
501 Wythe Street
Alexandria, VA 22314-1917; tel: 703-836-2090

American Institute of Physics
1 Physics Ellipse
College Park, MD 20740-3843;
tel: 301-209-3100

American Society for Biochemistry and
Molecular Biology
9650 Rockville Pike
Bethesda, MD 20814-3996; tel: 301-530-7145

American Society for Microbiology
1325 Massachusetts Avenue NW
Washington, DC 20005; tel: 202-737-3600

American Society of Biological Chemists
9650 Rockville Pike
Bethesda, MD 20814-3996; tel: 301-530-7145

American Zoo and Aquarium Association (AZA)
Office of Membership Service
Oglebay Park, Route 88
Wheeling, WV 26003; tel: 304-242-2160

Association of American Geographers
1710 16th Street NW
Washington, DC 20009-3198; tel: 202-234-1450

Botanical Society of America
1735 Nell Avenue
Columbus, OH 43210; tel: 614-292-3519

Center for American Archeology
P.O. Box 366
Kampsville, IL 62053; tel: 618-653-4316

Department of Energy Headquarters
Operations Division
1000 Independence Avenue SW, Room 4E-090
Washington, DC 20585; tel: 202-586-4333
(hotline for job vacancies, updated every Friday)

Environmental Protection Agency
Recruitment Center
401 Main Street SW, Room 3634
Washington, DC 20460;
tel: 202-260-2090/3308

Federation of American Societies for
Experimental Biology
9650 Rockville Pike
Bethesda, MD 20814; tel: 301-530-7000

Genetics Society of America
9650 Rockville Pike
Bethesda, MD 20814-3998;
tel: 301-571-1825
Geological Society of America
3300 Penrose Place, P.O. Box 9140
Boulder, CO 80301; tel: 303-447-2020

National Accrediting Agency for Clinical
Laboratory Sciences
8410 West Bryn Mawr Avenue, Suite 670
Chicago, IL 60631; tel: 312-714-8880

National Solid Wastes Management Association
4301 Connecticut Avenue NW, Suite 300
Washington, DC 20008; tel: 202-244-4700

Natural Resource Conservation Service,
Personnel Division
P.O. Box 2980
Washington, DC 20013; tel: 202-720-4264

ENGINEERING

Associations
American Association of Engineering
Societies
1111 19th Street NW, Suite 608
Washington, DC 20034; tel: 202-296-2237

American Chemical Society
1155 16th Street NW
Washington, DC 20036;
tel: 202-872-4600 or 800-227-5558

American Institute of Chemical Engineers
345 East 47th Street
New York, NY 10017;
tel: 212-705-7338 or 800-242-4363

American Society for Engineering Education
1818 N Street NW, Suite 600
Washington, DC 20036; tel: 202-331-3500

American Society of Civil Engineers
1801 Alexander Bell Drive
Reston, VA 20191-4400; tel: 800-548-ASCE

American Society of Mechanical Engineers
(ASME)
345 East 47th Street
New York, NY 10017; tel: 212-705-7722

Institute of Electrical and Electronics
Engineers
345 East 47th Street
New York, NY 10017; tel: 212-705-7900

Institute of Industrial Engineers
25 Technology Park
Atlanta, GA 30092-0460; tel: 770-449-0460

Society of Manufacturing Engineers (SME)
1 SME Drive, P.O. Box 930
Dearborn, MI 48121; tel: 313-271-1500

INFORMATION TECHNOLOGY

Publications

Access
1900 West 47th Place, Suite 215
Shawnee Mission, KS 66205;
tel: 800-362-0681
(initial six-month nonmember listing, $15;
each additional three months, $15; initial six-
month listing for members of the Data
Processing Management Association, $10)

AIIM Job Bank Bulletin
Association for Information and Image
Management
1100 Wayne Avenue, Suite 1100
Silver Spring, MD 20910;
tel: 301-587-8202
(four-month subscription: nonmember, $100;
member, $25; issued semimonthly)

Associations

ASIS Jobline
American Society for Information Science
8720 Georgia Avenue, Suite 501
Silver Spring, MD 20910-3602;
tel: 301-495-0900
(free; monthly)

Association for Computing Machinery
1515 Broadway
New York, NY 10036; tel: 212-869-7440

Association for Systems Management
1433 West Bagley Road, P.O. Box 38370
Cleveland, OH 44138; tel: 216-243-6900

COMPUTERS

Publications

ComputerWorld
500 Old Connecticut Path
Framingham, MA 01701-9171; tel: 508-879-
0700 or 800-343-6474
(annual subscription: U.S., $39.95; Canada,
$110; issued weekly)

ComputerWorld, Campus Edition
500 Old Connecticut Path
Framingham, MA 01701-9171;
tel: 508-879-0700
(annual subscription, $5; free to students;
published each October)

High Technology Careers Magazine
4701 Patrick Henry Drive, Suite 1901
Santa Clara, CA 95054; tel: 408-970-8800
(six issues per year, $29)

Technical Employment News
P.O. Box 1285
Cedar Park, TX 78613;
tel: 512-250-9023 or 800-678-9724
(weekly subscription, $55; annual
subscription, $88, U.S. and Canada)

Associations

IEEE Computer Society
1730 Massachusetts Avenue NW
Washington, DC 20036; tel: 202-371-0101
(available to members only)

CU Career Connection
University of Colorado, Campus Box 133
Boulder, CO 80309-0133; tel: 303-492-4727
(two-month fee for passcode to the job hotline,
$30)

Data Processing Management Association
505 Busse Highway
Park Ridge, IL 60068; tel: 708-825-8124

Institute for Certification of Computing
Professionals
2200 East Devon Avenue, Suite 247
Des Plaines, IL 60018;
tel: 708-299-4227

Quality Assurance Institute
7575 Philips Boulevard, Suite 350
Orlando, Fl 32819; tel: 407-363-1111

Semiconductor Equipment and Materials
International
805 East Middlefield Road
Mountain View, CA 94043; tel: 415-964-5111

BUSINESS AND PROFESSIONAL

Publications

*The Almanac of American Employers
Corporate Jobs Outlook*
Boeme, TX
Lists five hundred of the country's most
successful, large companies; profiles salary
ranges, benefits, financial stability, and
advancement opportunities.

Corporate Jobs Outlook
Corporate Jobs Outlook, Inc., Dallas, TX
Each issue reviews fifteen to twenty major
(five thousand employees or more) firms.
The report rates the firms and provides
information on salaries and benefits, current
and projected development, where to apply
for jobs, potential layoffs, benefit plans, the
company's record for promoting women or
minorities to executive positions, and college
reimbursement packages. Also includes
personnel contact information for each firm.
Published bimonthly; a yearly subscription is
$159.99. Call 214-824-3030. Note: This
resource is also available online at
www.vinnelljobcorps.org.

Directory of Corporate Affiliations
Reed Reference Publishing Company, New
Providence, NJ
Lists key personnel in 4,700 parent companies
and forty thousand divisions, subsidiaries, and
affiliates. Includes addresses and phone numbers
of key executives and decision makers. Published
once a year, with quarterly updates. For more
information, call 800-323-6772.

Directory of Leading Private Companies
National Register Publishing Company,
Wilmette, IL
Profiles over seven thousand U.S. private
companies in the service, manufacturing,
distribution, retail, and construction fields.
Includes companies in such areas as health
care, high technology, entertainment, fast-food
franchises, leasing, publishing, and
communications. Published annually.

Encyclopedia of Associations
Gale Research, Inc., Detroit, MI
Published in three volumes. Volume 1 lists
national organizations in the U.S. and includes
over twenty-two thousand associations,
including hundreds for government
professions. Volume 2 provides geographic
and executive indexes. Volume 3 features full
entries on associations that are not listed in
Volume 1. Note: This resource is also
available online through Dialog Information
Services at www.dialog.com (or 800-334-
2564). Call for more information.

*International Directory of Corporate
Affiliations*
National Register Publishing Company,
Wilmette, IL
Lists over fourteen hundred major foreign
companies and their thirty thousand U.S. and
foreign holdings. Published annually.

The JobBank Series
Adams Media Corporation, Avon, MA
A top-notch series of paperback local
employment guides. The recent editions profile
virtually every local company in a given metro
area. Company listings are arranged by industry
for easy use. The series covers twenty-four
major metropolitan areas, including Atlanta,
Boston, the Carolinas, Chicago, Colorado,
Dallas/Ft. Worth, Detroit, Florida, Houston,
Los Angeles, Minneapolis/St. Paul, Missouri,
New York, Ohio, Philadelphia, Phoenix, San
Francisco, Tennessee, and Washington, DC.
Many listings feature contact names, common
positions hired for, benefits, fax numbers,
internship information, staff size, and more.
The series also includes *The JobBank Guide to
Computer & High-Tech Companies* as well as
The JobBank Guide to Health Care Companies.
Available at most bookstores.

*National Trade and Professional Associations
of the United States*
Columbia Books, Washington, DC
Lists information on over sixty-five hundred
trade and professional associations. Published
annually.

Resume Bank
American Corporate Counsel Association
1225 Connecticut Avenue NW, Suite 302
Washington, DC 20036; tel: 202-296-4522
(six-month registration: nonmembers, $65;
members, $25; complete job-matching
application, and five copies of resume free)

FINANCIAL SERVICES

Associations

BANKING

American Bankers Association
1120 Connecticut Avenue NW
Washington, DC 20036; tel: 202-663-5000
American Institute of Banking
1213 Bakers Way
Manhattan, KS 66502; tel: 913-537-4750

Association of Master of Business
Administration Executives
AMBA Center
South Summit Place
Branford, CT 06405; tel: 203-315-5221

Banking Federation of the European Economic
Community (BFEC)
Federation Bancaire de la Communaute
Europeenne (FBCE)
c/o Umberto Burani
10, rue Montoyer, B-1040
Brussels, Belgium; tel: 32-2-5083711;
fax: 32-2-5112328

Banking Law Institute (BLI)
22 West 21st Street
New York, NY 10010;
tel: 212-645-7880 or 800-332-1105;
fax: 212-675-4883

BANKPAC
(formerly: Bankers Political Action Committee;
Banking Profession Political Action Committee)
c/o Meg Bonitt
American Bankers Association
1120 Connecticut Avenue NW
Washington, DC 20036;
tel: 202-663-5115/5076
or 202-663-7544 (fax)

Electronic Banking Economics Society
(EBES)
P.O. Box 2331
New York, NY 10036; tel: 203-295-9788

Savings and Community Bankers of America
Educational Services
Center for Financial Studies
900 19th Street NW, Suite 400
Washington, DC 20006; tel: 202-857-3100

U.S. Council on International Banking
(USCIB)
1 World Trade Center, Suite 1963
New York, NY 10048;
tel: 212-466-3352; fax: 212-432-0544

Women in Banking and Finance
55 Bourne Vale
Bromley, Kent BR2 7NW, England;
tel: 44-181-4623276

Women's World Banking—USA
8 West 40th Street
New York, NY 10018;
tel: 212-768-8513; fax: 212-768-8519

SECURITIES

Association of Securities and Exchange
Commission Alumni
West Tower, Suite 812
1100 New York Avenue NW
Washington, DC 20005; tel: 202-408-7600;
fax: 202-408-7614

International Securities Market Association—
England
7 Limeharbour
London E14 9NQ, England;
tel: 44-171-538-5656; fax: 44-171-538-4902

National Association of Securities Dealers
(NASD)
1735 K Street NW
Washington, DC 20006-1506;
tel: 202-728-8000; fax: 202-293-6260

National Association of Securities
Professionals (NASP)
700 13th Street NW, Suite 950
Washington, DC 20005;
tel: 202-434-4535; fax: 202-434-8916

North American Securities Administrators
Association (NASAA)
1 Massachusetts Avenue NW, Suite 310
Washington, DC 20001;
tel: 202-737-0900; fax: 202-783-3571

Securities and Futures Authority
Cottons Centre, Cottons Lane
London SE I 2QB, England;
tel: 44-171-378-9000;
tel: 44-171-403-7569

Securities Industry Association (SIA)
120 Broadway
New York, NY 10271; tel: 212-608-1500;
fax: 212-608-1604

Securities Transfer Association (STA)
55 Exchange Place
New York, NY 10260-0001;
tel: 212-748-8000

Western Pennsylvania Securities
Industry Agency
1 Oxford Centre, 40th Floor
Pittsburgh, PA 15219; tel: 412-731-7185

ACCOUNTING

Academy of Accounting Historians (AAH)
University of Arkansas, Department of
Accounting
Fayetteville, AR 72701; tel: 501-575-6125;
fax: 501-575-7687

Accounting Aid Society of Detroit (AASD)
719 Griswold, Suite 2026
Detroit, MI 48226; tel: 313-961-1840;
fax: 313-961-6257
E-mail: itpass@igc.apc.org

Affiliation of Independent Accountants
9200 South Dadeland Boulevard, Suite 510
Miami, FL 33156; tel: 305-670-0580;
fax: 305-670-3818

American Accounting Association
5717 Bessie Drive
Sarasota, FL 34223; tel: 941-921-7747

American Institute of Certified Public
Accountants (AICPA)
1211 Avenue of the Americas
New York, NY 10036-8775;
tel: 212-596-6200 or 800-862-4272 or
212-596-6213 (fax)

American Society of Tax Professionals
P.O. Box 1024
Sioux Falls, SD 57101; tel: 605-335-1185

American Society of Women Accountants
1255 Lynnfield Road, Suite 257
Memphis, TN 38119;
tel: 901-680-0470

American Women's Society of Certified
Public Accountants
401 North Michigan Avenue, Suite 2200
Chicago, IL 60611; tel: 312-644-6610

Associated Accounting Firms International
(AAFI)
(formerly: Association of Regional CPA Firms)
1000 Connecticut Avenue, Suite 1006
Washington, DC 20036; tel: 202-463-7900;
fax: 202-296-0741

Associated Regional Accounting Firms
(ARAF)
3700 Crestwood Parkway, Suite 350
Duluth, GA 30136; tel: 770-279-4560;
fax: 770-279-4566 (fax)

Association for Accounting Administration
(AAA)
136 South Keowee Street
Dayton, OH 45402; tel: 513-222-0030;
fax: 513-2212-5794

Association of Accounting Technicians (AAT)
154 Clerkenwell Road
London EC I R 5AD, England;
tel: 44-171-837-8600/814-6999;
fax: 44-171-837-6970
E-mail: aatuk@pipex.com

Association of Government Accountants
2200 Mount Vernon Avenue
Alexandria, VA 22301; tel: 703-684-6931

EDP Auditors Association
3701 Algonquin Road, Suite 1010
Rolling Meadows, IL 60008;
tel: 708-253-1545

European Accounting Association (EAA)
European Institute for Advanced Studies in
Management
13 Rue d'Egmont, B-1050
Brussels, Belgium; tel: 32-2-511-9116;
fax: 32-2-512-1929
E-mail: vandyck@ciasm.be

Foundation for Accounting Education (FAE)
530 Fifth Avenue, 5th Floor
New York, NY 10036; tel: 212-719-8300 or
800-537-3635

Governmental Accounting Standards Board
(GASB)
401 Merrit 7, P.O. Box 5116
Norwalk, CT 06856-5116; tel: 203-847-0700;
fax: 203-849-9714

Information Systems Audit and Control
Association
3701 Algonquin Road, Suite 1010
Rolling Meadows, IL 60008;
tel: 708-253-1545

Institute of Certified Management Accountants
(ICMA)
10 Paragon Drive
Montvale, NJ 07645; tel: 201-573-9000 or
800-638-4427; fax: 201-573-8438

Institute of Internal Auditors
249 Maitland Avenue
Altamonte Springs, FL 32701-4201;
tel: 407-830-7600

Institute of Management Accountants
10 Paragon Drive
Montvale, NJ 07645; tel: 201-573-9000;
fax: 201-573-9000

InterAmerican Accounting Association (IAA)
(formerly: InterAmerican Accounting
Conference)
275 Fontainebleau Boulevard, Suite 245
Miami, Fl 33172; tel: 305-225-1991;
fax: 305-225-2011

National Association of State Boards of
Accountancy
545 Fifth Avenue
New York, NY 10168-0002;
tel: 212-490-3868

National Society for Public Accountants
1010 North Fairfax Street
Alexandria, VA 22314; tel: 703-549-6400

INSURANCE

Publications

Insurance Field Directories
Insurance Field Company
P.O. Box 948
Northbrook, IL 60065; tel: 708-498-4010
($55; published each September)

Insurance Phone Book and Directory
US Directory Service
121 Chanlon Road
New Providence, NJ 07074;
tel: 908-464-6800
($67.95, plus $4.75 shipping)

Associations

ACFE Job Bank
Association of Certified Fraud Examiners
716 West Avenue
Austin, TX 78701; tel: 512-478-9070 or
800-245-3321
(membership fee $75; send two copies of
resume and cover letter indicating salary
requirements and where you are willing to
relocate)

Actual Training Program Directory Society
of Actuaries
475 North Martingale Road, Suite 800
Schaumburg, IL 60173-2226;
tel: 708-706-3500
(free; published each January)

American Academy of Actuaries
1100 17th Street NW, 7th Floor
Washington, DC 20036;
tel: 202-223-8196

American Agents & Brokers
330 North 4th Street
St. Louis, MO 63012; tel: 314-421-5445

Best's Insurance Reports, Property/Casualty
Edition
A.M. Best Company
Ambest Road
Oldwick, NJ 08858-9988; tel: 908-439-2200
(annual fee $70)

Independent Insurance Agents of America
127 South Peyton
Alexandria, VA 22314;
tel: 703-683-4422 or 800-962-7950

Insurance Information Institute
110 William Street
New York, NY 10038; tel: 212-669-9200

Insurance Institute of America
720 Providence Road
Malvern, PA 19355; tel: 610-644-2100

Life Insurance Marketing and Research
Association
P.O. Box 208
Hartford, CT 16141-0208; tel: 203-777-7000

National Association of Life Underwriters
1922 F Street NW
Washington, DC 20006; tel: 202-332-6000

National Association of Professional Insurance
Agents
400 North Washington Street
Alexandria, VA 22314; tel: 703-836-9340

Professional Insurance Agents
400 North Washington Street
Alexandria, VA 22314; tel: 703-836-9340

Society of Actuaries
475 North Martingale Road, Suite 800
Schaumburg, IL 60173-2226;
tel: 708-706-3500

FINANCIAL MANAGEMENT

Associations

American Education Finance Association
(AEFA)
5249 Cape Leyte Drive
Sarasota, FL 34242; tel: 941-349-7580;
fax: 941-349-7580
E-mail: gbabigianc@aol.com

American Finance Association (AFA)
Stern, 44 West 4th Street, Suite 9-190
New York, NY 10012; tel: 212-998-0370

Association of Commercial Finance Attorneys
(ACFA)
1 Corporate Center, 18th Floor MSN 712
Hartford, CT 06103; tel: 203-520-7094; fax:
203-240-5077

Commercial Finance Association (CFA)
225 West 34th Street
New York, NY 10122; tel: 212-594-3490 or
212-564-6053

Financial Analysts Federation
P.O. Box 3726
Charlottesville, VA 22903; tel: 804-977-8977

Financial Management Association International
College of Business Administration
University of South Florida
Tampa, FL 33620-5500

Financial Management Service
Department of the Treasury
401 14th Street SW
Washington, DC 20227;
tel: 202-874-6750

Financial Managers Society
8 South Michigan Avenue, Suite 500
Chicago, IL 60603; tel: 312-578-1300

Government Finance Officers Association
of United States and Canada
ISO North Michigan Avenue, Suite 800
Chicago, IL 60601; tel: 312-977-9700;
fax: 312-977-4806

Institute of Certified Financial Planners
3801 East Florida Avenue, Suite 708
Denver, CO 80210; tel: 303-751-7600;
fax: 303-759-0749

Institute of Chartered Financial Analysts
P.O. Box 3668
Charlottesville, VA 22903; tel: 804-977-6600

Institute of International Finance (IIF)
2000 Pennsylvania Avenue NW, Suite 8500
Washington, DC 20006-1812;
tel: 202-857-3600; fax: 202-775-1430

International Association for Financial
Planning
2 Concourse Parkway, Suite 800
Atlanta, GA 30328; tel: 404-395-1605

National Association of County Treasurers and
Finance Officers
c/o National Association of Counties
440 First Street NW, 8th Floor
Washington, DC 20001;
tel: 202-393-6226

National Society for Real Estate Finance
(NSREF)
2300 M Street NW, Suite 800
Washington, DC 20037; tel: 202-973-2801

New York State Consumer Finance
Association (NYSCFA)
90 South Swan Street
Albany, NY 12210; tel: 518-449-7514;
fax: 518-426-0566

New York State Government Finance Officers
Association
119 Washington Avenue
Albany, NY 12210-2204;
tel: 518-465-1512; fax: 518-434-4640

North American Economics and Finance
Association (NAEFA)
Department of Finance
Syracuse University
Syracuse, NY 13244-2130;
tel: 315-443-2963; fax: 315-443-5389

Securities Industry Association
120 Broadway
New York, NY 10271; tel: 212-608-1500

HUMAN RESOURCES

Publications

HR Magazine
606 North Washington Street
Alexandria, VA 22314; tel: 703-548-3440

Associations

American Society for Training and
Development
1640 King Street, Box 1443
Alexandria, VA 22313; tel: 703-683-8100
Employment Management Association
4101 Lake Boone Trail, Suite 201
Raleigh, NC 27607; tel: 919-787-6010

Institute of Management Consultants
521 Fifth Avenue, 35th Floor
New York, NY 10175; tel: 212-697-8262

International Personnel Management
Association
1617 Duke Street
Alexandria, VA 22314; tel: 703-549-7100

National Training Laboratory
1240 North Pitt Street
Alexandria, VA 22314; tel: 703-548-1500

Society for Human Resource Management
606 North Washington Street
Alexandria, VA 22314; tel: 703-548-3440

LAW

Publications

ALA Management Connections
Association of Legal Administrators
175 E. Hawthorn Parkway, Suite 325
Vernon Hills, IL 60061-1428;
tel: 708-816-1212
(free; updated weekly)

Federal Careers for Attorneys
Federal Reports, Inc., Washington, DC
A guide to legal careers with over three
hundred U.S. government general counsel and
other legal offices in the U.S. Explains where
to apply, the types of legal work common to
each field, and information on special
recruitment programs.

Judicial Staff Directory
Staff Directories, Ltd., Mt. Vernon, VA
Lists over eleven thousand individuals
employed in the 207 federal courts, as well as

thirteen thousand cities and their courts.
The book also has information on court
administration, U.S. marshals, U.S. attorneys,
and the U.S. Department of Justice. Includes
eighteen hundred biographies.

NDAA Membership Directory
National District Attorneys Association,
Alexandria, VA
Lists all district attorneys' offices across
the U.S.
$15 for nonmembers, $10 for members.
Call 703-549-9222 for more information.

Paralegal's Guide to Government Jobs
Federal Reports, Inc., Washington, DC
Explains federal hiring procedures for both
entry-level and experienced paralegals. The
volume describes seventy law-related careers
for which paralegals qualify and lists over one
thousand federal agency personnel offices that
hire the most paralegal talent. Also profiles
special hiring programs.

Associations

American Association for Paralegal Education
P.O. Box 40244
Overland Park, KS 66204; tel: 913-381-4458

American Bar Association Information
Services
750 North Lake Shore Drive
Chicago, IL 60611; tel: 312-988-5000 or
800-621-6159

Internships for College Students Interested in
Law, Medicine, and Politics
Graduate Group
86 Norwood Road
West Hartford, CT 06117;
tel: 203-236-5570 or 203-232-3100
($27.50, published annually)

National Association for Law Placement
1666 Connecticut Avenue, Suite 328
Washington, DC 20009; tel: 202-667-1666

National Association of Legal Assistants
1516 South Boston Avenue, Suite 200
Tulsa, OK 74119; tel: 918-587-6828

National Federation of Paralegal Associations
P.O. Box 33108
Kansas City, MO 64114;
tel: 816-941-4000
National Paralegal Association
Box 406
Solebury, PA 18963; tel: 215-297-8333

NCRA Employment Referral Service
National Court Reporters Association
8224 Old Courthouse Road
Vienna, VA 22182; tel: 703-556-6272
(six-month registration: nonmembers, $20;
free to members)

Paralegal Placement Network Inc.
P.O. Box 406
Solebury, PA 18963; tel: 215-297-8333
(regular fee, $10; Nat. Paralegal Association
members, $15)

MEDIA/COMMUNICATION/
PUBLIC RELATIONS

Publications

P.R. Reporter
P.O. Box 6000
Exeter, NH 03833

Public Relations Consultants Directory
American Business Directories Inc.
5711 East 86th Circle
Omaha, NE 68127; tel: 402-331-7169

*SMPS Employment Referral Society for
Marketing Professional Services*
99 Canal Plaza, Suite 250
Alexandria, VA 22314;
tel: 703-549-6117 or 800-292-7677
(nonmembers, $100; members, $50; five
copies resume and SMPS application—on file
for three months)

Associations

American Society for Health Care Marketing
and Public Relations
American Hospital Association
1 North Franklin
Chicago, IL 60606; tel: 312-422-3737

American Society of Journalists and Authors
1501 Broadway, Suite 302
New York, NY 10036; tel: 212-997-0947

Council of Sales Promotion Agencies
750 Summer Street
Stamford, CT 06901; tel: 203-325-3911

Dow Jones Newspaper Fund
P.O. Box 300
Princeton, NJ 08543-0300; tel: 609-452-2820

Editorial Freelancers Association
71 West 23rd Street, Suite 1504
New York, NY 10010; tel: 212-929-5400

Institute for Public Relations Research and
Education (IPRRE)
University of Florida
P.O. Box 118400
Gainesville, FL 32611-8400;
tel: 904-392-0280

International Advertising Association
521 Fifth Avenue, Suite 1807
New York, NY 10175; tel: 212-557-1133

Investigative Reporters & Editors
University of Missouri
26A Walter Williams Hall
Columbia, MO 65211; tel: 314-882-2042

League of Advertising Agencies Directory
2 South End Avenue #4C
New York, NY 10280; tel: 212-945-4314

National School Public Relations Association
(NSPRA)
1501 Lee Highway, Suite 201
Arlington, VA 22209; tel: 703-528-5840

PR Newswire Job Bank
865 South Figueroa, Suite 2310
Los Angeles, CA 90017;
tel: 213-626-5500 or 800-321-8169
(send resume and cover letter)

Promotion Marketing Association of
America, Inc.
Executive Headquarters
257 Park Avenue South, 11th Floor
New York, NY 10001; tel: 212-420-1100

Public Relations Society of America
33 Irving Place, 3rd Floor
New York, NY 10003; tel: 212-995-2230

Public Relations Student Society of America
(PRSSA)
33 Irving Place, 3rd Floor
New York, NY 10003; tel: 212-460-1474

Society for Technical Communication
901 North Stuart Street, Suite 904
Arlington, VA 22203; tel: 703-522-4114

Writers Guild of America
555 West 57th Street
New York, NY 10019; tel: 212-767-7800

SALES AND MARKETING

Associations

TRAVEL

Adventure Travel Society
6551 South Revere Parkway, Suite 160
Englewood, CO 80111;
tel: 303-649-9016; fax: 303-649-9017

Air Transport Association of America
1301 Pennsylvania Avenue NW, Suite 1100
Washington, DC 20004-7017; tel: 202-626-4000

Airline Employees Association, Intl.
Job Opportunity Program
5600 South Central Avenue
Chicago, IL 60638-3797

American Society of Travel Agents (ASTA)
1101 King Street, Suite 200
Alexandria, VA 22314;
tel: 703-739-2782; fax: 703-684-8319

American Travel Inns (ATI)
(formerly: American Travel Association)
36 South State Street, Suite 1200
Salt Lake City, UT 84111-1416;
tel: 801-521-0732; fax: 801-521-0732

Association of Flight Attendants
1625 Massachusetts Avenue NW
Washington, DC 20036; tel: 202-328-5400

Association of Retail Travel Agents (ARTA)
845 Sir Thomas Court, Suite 3
Harrisburg, PA 17109; tel: 717-545-9548 or
800-969-6069; fax: 717-545-9613

Cruise Lines International Association
500 Fifth Avenue, Suite 1407
New York, NY 10110; tel: 212-921-0066

Freighter Travel Club of America
3524 Harts Lake Road
Roy, WA 98580; tel: 360-458-4178

Future Aviation Professionals of America
4959 Massachusetts Boulevard
Atlanta, GA 30337; tel: 404-997-8097 or
800-JET-JOBS

Greater Independent Association of National
Travel Services (GIANTS)
2 Park Avenue, Suite 2205
New York, NY 10016; tel: 212-545-7460 or
800-442-6871; fax: 212-545-7428

Independent Travel Agencies of America
Association (ITAA)
5353 North Federal Highway, Suite 300
Fort Lauderdale, Fl 33308; tel: 305-772-4660
or 800-950-5440; fax: 305-772-5797

Institute of Certified Travel Agents (ICTA)
148 Linden Street, P.O. Box 812059
Wellesley, MA 02181-0012; tel: 617-237-
0280 or 800-542-4282; fax: 617-237-3860

International Association for Air Travel Couriers
P.O. Box 1349
Lake Worth, FL 33460;
tel: 407-582-8320; fax: 407-582-1581

International Association of Travel Exhibitors
(IATE)
P.O. Box 2309
Gulf Shores, AL 36547;
tel: 205-948-6690; fax: 205-948-6690

International Association of Travel Journalists
(IATJ)
P.O. Box D
Hurleyville, NY 12747; tel: 914-434-1529

International Federation of Women's Travel
Organizations (IFWTO)
13901 North 73rd Street, #210B
Scottsdale, AZ 85260-3125;
tel: 602-596-6640; fax: 602-596-6638

Travel Industry Association of America
1100 New York Avenue NW, Suite 450
Washington, DC 20005-3934;
tel: 202-408-8422

U.S. Travel Data Center
(affiliate of the Travel Industry Association of
America)
2 Lafayette Center
1100 New York Avenue NW, Suite 450
Washington, DC 20005; tel: 202-408-1832

Yours in Travel Personnel Agency
12 West 37th Street
New York, NY 10018; tel: 212-697-7855

MARKETING/ADVERTISING

American Advertising Federation
Education Services Department
1101 Vermont Avenue NW, Suite 500
Washington, DC 20005; tel: 202-898-0089

American Marketing Association
250 South Wacker Drive, Suite 200
Chicago, IL 60606-5819; tel: 312-648-0536

The Convention Liaison Council
1575 Eye Street NW, Suite 1190
Washington, DC 20005; tel: 202-626-2764

Direct Marketing Association
1120 Avenue of the Americas
New York, NY 10036-6700; tel: 212-768-7277

Meeting Planners International
Informant Building, Suite 5018
1950 Stemmons Freeway
Dallas, TX 75207; tel: 214-712-7700

Retail Advertising and Marketing Association
500 North Michigan Avenue, Suite 600
Chicago, IL 60611; tel: 312-251-7262

Sales and Marketing Executives International
977 Statler Office Tower
Cleveland, OH 44115; tel: 216-771-6650

Sales and Marketing Management
355 Park Avenue South
New York, NY 10010; tel: 212-592-6300

FOOD SERVICES

Associations

Alaska Culinary Association
P.O. Box 140396
Anchorage, AK 99514; tel: 907-265-7116

American Culinary Federation
10 San Bartola Road, P.O. Box 3466
St. Augustine, FL 32085-3466;
tel: 904-824-4468

Berks Lehigh Chef's Association
2012 Redwood Avenue
Wyomissing, PA 19610; tel: 610-678-1217

National Food Broker Association
2100 Reston Parkway, Suite 400
Reston, VA 22091; tel: 703-758-7790

National Restaurant Association
1200 17th Street NW
Washington, DC 20036; el: 202-331-5900

SUPPORT SERVICES

Associations

American Society of Corporate Secretaries
521 Fifth Avenue
New York, NY 10175-0003;
tel: 212-681-2000

California Federation of Legal Secretaries
2250 East 73rd Street, Suite 550
Tulsa, OK 74136; tel: 918-493-3540

National Association of Executive Secretaries
900 S. Washington Street, No. G-13
Falls Church, VA 22046; tel: 703-237-8616

PUBLIC SERVICES/SOCIAL SERVICES

Publications

*Directory of Legal Aid and Defender Offices
in the U.S. and Territories*
National Legal Aid and Defender Association,
Washington, DC
Lists legal aid and public defender offices across
the U.S. Published annually.

Associations

ACTION International
120 Beacon Street
Somerville, MA 02143;
tel: 617-492-4930

American Counseling Association
5999 Stevenson Avenue
Alexandria, VA 22304;
tel: 703-823-9800 or 800-347-6647

American Friends Service Committee
1501 Cherry Street
Philadelphia, PA 19102; tel: 215-241-7000

American School Counselor Association
801 North Fairfax Street, Suite 301
Alexandria, VA 22314; tel: 703-683-2722

American Vocational Association
1410 King Street
Alexandria, VA 22314;
tel: 703-683-3111 or 800-892-2274

Child Welfare League of America
440 First Street NW, Suite 310
Washington, DC 20001; tel: 201-638-2952

Council for Standards in Human Service
Education
Northern Essex Community College
Haverhill, MA 01830; tel: 508-374-5889

Council on Social Work Education
1600 Duke Street, Suite 300
Alexandria, VA 22314-3421;
tel: 703-683-8080
(send $10 for Directory of Accredited BSW
and MSW Programs)

Educators for Social Responsibility
23 Garden Street
Cambridge, MA 02138; tel: 617-492-1764

Human Service Council
3191 Maguire Boulevard, Suite 1150
Orlando, FL 32803; tel: 407-897-6465

National Association of Social Workers
750 First Street NE, Suite 700
Washington, DC 20002-4241;
tel: 202-408-8600

National Center for Charitable Statistics
1828 L Street NW, Suite 1200B
Washington, DC 20036; tel: 202-223-8100

National Civic League
1445 Market Street, Suite 300
Denver, CO 80202-1728; tel: 303-571-4343

National Exchange Club Foundation for the
Prevention of Child Abuse
3050 Central Avenue
Toledo, OH 43606; tel: 419-535-3232
or 800-760-3413

National Network for Social Work Managers
1316 New Hampshire Avenue NW, Suite 602
Washington, DC 20036; tel: 202-785-2814

National Organization for Human Service
Education
Fitchburg State College, Box 6257
160 Pearl Street
Fitchburg, MA 01420; tel: 508-345-2151

Save the Children Federation
54 Wilton Road
Westport, CT 06880; tel: 203-221-4000

Social Service Association
6 Station Plaza
Ridgewood, NJ 07450; tel: 201-444-2980

EDUCATION

Publications

*Who's Who in Special Libraries and
Information Centers*
Gale Research Inc., Detroit, MI
Lists special libraries alphabetically and
geographically. Published annually.

Associations

Academy for Educational Development (AED)
1875 Connecticut Avenue NW
Washington, DC 20009;
tel: 202-884-8000; fax: 202-884-8400
admind@aed-org (E-mail)

American Association of School
Administrators
1801 N Moore Street
Arlington, VA 22209-9988;
tel: 703-528-0700

American Association of School Librarians
50 E. Huron Street
Chicago, IL 60611; tel: 312-944-6780

American Association of University
Administrators
1012 14th Street NW, Suite 500
Washington, DC 20005; tel: 202-737-5900

American Association of University Professors
1012 14th Street NW, Suite 500
Washington, DC 20005; tel: 202-737-5900

American Educational Studies Association
(AESA)
University of Cincinnati
Graduate Studies and Research
Cincinnati, OH 45221; tel: 513-556-2256

American Federation of Teachers
555 New Jersey Avenue NW
Washington, DC 20001; tel: 202-879-4400

American Library Association
50 East Huron Street
Chicago, IL 60611; tel: 312-944-6780

Association for Community Based Education
(ACBE)
1805 Florida Avenue NW
Washington, DC 20009;
tel: 202-462-6333 or 202-232-8044

Association for Educational Communications
and Technology (AECT)
1025 Vermont Avenue NW, Suite 820
Washington, DC 20005;
tel: 202-347-7834; fax: 202-347-7839

Center for Adult Learning and Educational
Credentials (CALEC)
1 Dupont Circle NW
Washington, DC 20036;
tel: 202-939-9475; fax: 202-775-8574

College and University Personnel Association
1233 20th Street NW, Suite 301
Washington, DC 20036-1250;
tel: 202-429-0311

Council on International Educational
Exchange (CIEE)
205 East 42nd Street
New York, NY 10017;
tel: 212-661-1414; fax: 212-972-3231

Earthwatch
(formerly: Educational Expeditions
International)
680 Mount Auburn Street, Box 403
Watertown, MA 02272;
tel: 617-926-8200 or 800-776-0188;
fax: 617-926-8532
E-mail: info@earthwatch.org

Educational Research Service (ERS)
2000 Clarendon Blvd.
Arlington, VA 22201;
tel: 703-243-2100; fax: 703-243-1985

Federal Librarians Round Table
American Library Association,
Washington Office
1301 Pennsylvania Avenue NW, No. 403
Washington, DC 20004;
tel: 202-608-8410

High/Scope Educational Research Foundation
600 North River Street
Ypsilanti, MI 48198-2898;
tel: 313-485-2000 or 800-40-PRESS;
fax: 313-485-0704

Independent Educational Services (IES)
(formerly: Cooperative Bureau for Teachers)
353 Nassau Street
Princeton, NJ 08540; tel: 609-921-6195 or
800-257-5102; fax: 609-921-0155

Institute for Educational Leadership (IEL)
1001 Connecticut Avenue NW, Suite 310
Washington, DC 20036;
tel: 202-822-8405; fax: 202-872-4050

Intercultural Development Research
Association (IDRA)
5835 Callaghan Road, Suite 350
San Antonio, TX 78228;
tel: 210-684-8180; fax: 210-684-5389

International Association for Educational Assessment (IAEA)
P.O. Box 6665
Princeton, NJ 08541; tel: 609-921-9000;
fax: 609-520-1093

Madison Center for Educational Affairs (MCEA)
455 15th Street NW, Suite 712
Washington, DC 20005;
tel: 202-833-1801; fax: 202-467-0006

National Association of Educational Office Professionals (NAEOP)
P.O. Box 12619
Wichita, KS 67277; tel: 316-942-4822;
fax: 316-942-7100

National Association of Secondary School Principals
1904 Association Drive
Reston, VA 22091; tel: 703-860-0200

National Association of Student Personnel Administrators
1875 Connecticut Avenue NW, Suite 418
Washington, DC 20009; tel: 202-265-7500

National Council for Accreditation of Teacher Education
2010 Massachusetts Avenue NW, Suite 500
Washington, DC 20036; tel: 202-466-7496

National Council of Educational Opportunity Associations (NCEOA)
1025 Vermont Avenue NW, Suite 1201
Washington, DC 20005; tel: 202-347-7430

National Council on the Evaluation of Foreign Educational Credentials
c/o AACRAO
1 Dupont Circle NW, Suite 330
Washington, DC 20036;
tel: 202-293-9161 or 202-872-8857
E-mail: aacrao@umdd

National Education Association
1201 16th Street NW
Washington, DC 20036; tel: 202-833-4000

National Rural Education Association (NREA)
Colorado State University
230 Education Building
Fort Collins, CO 80523-1588;
tel: 970-491-7022; fax: 970-491-1317

Special Libraries Association
1700 18th Street NW
Washington, DC 20009-2508;
tel: 202-234-4700; fax: 202-265-9317

University Council for Educational Administration (UCEA)
Pennsylvania State University
212 Rackley Bldg.
University Park, PA 16802-3200;
tel: 814-863-7916/7917 or
fax: 814-863-7918

GOVERNMENT

Publications

The Capitol Source
National Journal, Inc., Washington, DC
Includes names, addresses, and phone numbers for key figures in the District of Columbia; also features information about corporations, interest groups, think tanks, labor unions, real estate organizations, financial institutions, trade and professional groups, law firms, political consultants, advertising and public relations firms, private clubs, and the media. Published twice a year.

Congressional Yellow Book
Monitor Publishing Co., New York, NY
Gives detailed information on congressional staff positions, committees and subcommittees, and top staff in congressional support agencies. Published annually.

COSLA Directory
The Council of State Governments, Lexington, KY
Provides information on state library agencies, consultant and administrative staff, plus ALANER numbers, electronic mail letters, and fax numbers. Published annually.

Directory of Federal Libraries
Includes library's administrator and selected staff for three thousand special and general, presidential and national libraries, as well as library facilities in technical centers, hospitals, and penal institutions.

Federal Executive Directory
Carroll Publishing Co., Washington, DC
Profiles a broad range of agencies, both executive and legislative, including cabinet departments, federal administrative agencies, and congressional committee members and staff. The directory also outlines areas of responsibility for legal and administrative assistants. Published six times a year; an annual subscription is $178. Call 202-333-8620 for more information.

Federal Organization Service: Military
Carroll Publishing Co., Washington, DC
Lists direct-dial phone numbers for 11,500 key individuals in fifteen hundred military departments and offices. Updated every six weeks; an annual subscription is $625. Call 202-333-8620 for more information.

Washington Information Directory
Congressional Quarterly Inc., Washington, DC
Provides important information on the federal government as a whole, and on each federal department and agency. The volume also provides details on regional federal information sources, nongovernmental organizations in the Washington area, and congressional committees and subcommittees. Published annually.

Washington 2000
Columbia Books, New York, NY
Contains addresses, phone numbers, and profiles of key institutions in the city. Includes chapters on the federal government, the media, business, national associations, labor unions, law firms, medicine and health, foundations and philanthropic organizations, science and policy research groups, and educational, religious, and cultural institutions. Published annually.

Associations

American Federation of State, County, and Municipal Employees
1625 L Street NW
Washington, DC 20036; tel: 202-429-1000

American Planning Association
122 South Michigan Avenue, Suite 1600
Chicago, IL 60603; tel: 312-431-9100

Civil Service Employees Association
P.O. Box 7125
Capitol State
Albany, NY 12210;
tel: 518-434-0191 or 800-342-4146

Council of State Governments
P.O. Box 11910
3560 Iron Works Pike
Lexington, KY 40578; tel: 606-244-8000

International Association of Fire Fighters
1750 New York Avenue NW
Washington, DC 21006; tel: 202-737-8484

International City/County Management
Association
777 North Capitol Street NE, Suite 500
Washington, DC 20002; tel: 202-289-4262

National Association of Counties (NACO)
440 First Street NW, 8th Floor
Washington, DC 20001; tel: 202-393-6226

National Association of Government
Communicators
669 South Washington Street
Alexandria, VA 22314; tel: 703-519-3902

National Planning Association
1424 16th Street NW, Suite 700
Washington, DC 20036; tel: 202-265-7685

New York State Professional Firefighters
Association
111 Washington Avenue, Suite 207
Albany, NY 12210; tel: 518-436-8827

State Services Organization (SSO)
444 North Capitol Street NW
Washington, DC 20001; tel: 202-624-5470

DISABILITIES

ADA Regional Disabled and Business Assistance Centers

Connecticut, Maine, Massachusetts, Rhode Island, and Vermont:
New England Disability and Business
Technical Assistance Center
145 Newbury Street
Portland, ME 04101;
tel: 207-874-6535 (voice/TDD)

New Jersey, New York, Puerto Rico, and Virgin Islands:
Northeast Disability and Business Technical
Assistance Center
354 South Broad Street
Trenton, NJ 08608; tel: 609-392-4004 (voice),
609-392-7044 (TDD)

Delaware, District of Columbia, Maryland, Pennsylvania, Virginia, and West Virginia:
Mid-Atlantic Disability and Business
Technical Assistance Center
2111 Wilson Boulevard, Suite 400
Arlington, VA 22201;
tel: 703-525-3268 (voice/TDD)

Alabama, Florida, Georgia, Kentucky, Mississippi, North Carolina, South Carolina, and Tennessee:
Southeast Disability and Business Technical
Assistance Center
1776 Peachtree Street, Suite 310 North
Atlanta, GA 30309;
tel: 404-888-0022 (voice/TDD)

Illinois, Indiana, Michigan, Minnesota, Ohio, and Wisconsin:
Great Lakes Disability and Business Technical
Assistance Center
1640 West Roosevelt Road (M/C 627)
Chicago, IL 60608;
tel: 312-413-1407 (voice/TDD)

Arkansas, Louisiana, New Mexico, Oklahoma, and Texas:
Southwest Disability and Business Technical
Assistance Center
2323 South Shepherd Boulevard, Suite 1000
Houston, TX 77019; tel: 713-520-0232
(voice), 713-520-5136 (TDD)

Iowa, Kansas, Nebraska, and Missouri:
Great Plains Disability and Business Technical
Assistance Center
4816 Santana Drive
Columbia, MO 65203;
tel: 314-882-3600 (voice/TDD)

Colorado, Montana, North Dakota, South Dakota, Utah, and Wyoming:
Rocky Mountain Disability and Business
Technical Assistance Center
3630 Sinton Road, Suite 103
Colorado Springs, CO 80907-5072;
tel: 719-444-0252 (voice/TDD)

Arizona, California, Hawaii, and Nevada:
Pacific Coast Disability and Business
Technical Assistance Center
440 Grand Avenue, Suite 500
Oakland, CA 94610; tel: 510-465-7884
(voice), 510-465-3167 (TDD)

Job Accommodation Network
P.O. Box 6123
809 Allen Hall
Morgantown, WV 26505-6123;
tel: 800-526-7234 (voice/TDD)

The President's Committee on Employment of
People with Disabilities
1331 F Street NW
Washington, DC 20004;
tel: 202-376-6200 (voice),
202-376-6205 (TDD)

U.S. Department of Justice, Civil Rights
Division
Office of the Americans with Disabilities Act
P.O. Box 66118
Washington, DC 20035-6118; tel: 800-514-
0301 (voice), 800-514-0383 (TDD)

Keyword Appendix

This keyword appendix has been compiled to help you "punch up" your resumes and cover letters. It contains some of the words frequently chosen by recruiters and human resources professionals when they are creating keyword lists for their resume database software. Depending upon the position to be filled and the profession involved, the recruiter chooses a selection of keywords he or she feels will best describe the capabilities and experiences desired of the job candidate. The software then searches the resume database for documents (resumes) containing any of these selected keywords. Each document found tabulates the number of times these selected keywords appear. The resumes with the most "hits" from the keyword selection list are then ranked in priority by the software.

You should use this keyword appendix in the editing process of your electronic resumes, cover letters, and Web site questionnaires. Once you have a draft that powerfully packages your credentials and capabilities, check it against both sections of keywords; this allows you to substitute common keywords for less effective synonyms you may have chosen.

You should also build your own keyword database from job postings you see. Whenever you encounter a skill set you possess used in want ad or job posting, add it to your own keyword list.

Key Verbs and Key Nouns

These keyword verbs describe your working actions while the keyword nouns showcase those actions in desirable work settings. Inclusion of these words will definitely have a favorable impact on the reception of your electronic job search correspondence. Read the profession-specific nouns for your field, and ask yourself: Have I done work in this area? If the answer is yes, ask yourself: Is it detailed in my resume?

If you possess experience in an area not captured on your resume, describe that experience. The goal isn't creating a resume including lots of keywords at the expense of an accurate description of your background, but making sure that your resume is the most powerful it can be. Once online, the important thing is to have the screening software work for you, pulling *your* resume back from cyberspace into the hands of employment managers—where it actually matters. Remember, you can always add keywords to the keyword/skill set area of your resume, and it takes only a little effort with no need to reformat.

Key Verbs

accepted	automated	controlled	educated
accomplished	balanced	coordinated	eliminated
achieved	budgeted	corresponded	emended
acted	built	counseled	enabled
adapted	calculated	created	encouraged
addressed	catalogued	critiqued	engineered
administered	chaired	cut	enlisted
advanced	clarified	decreased	established
advised	classified	defined	evaluated
allocated	coached	delegated	examined
analyzed	collected	demonstrated	executed
appraised	compiled	designed	expanded
approved	completed	developed	expedited
arranged	composed	devised	explained
assembled	computed	diagnosed	extracted
assigned	conceptualized	directed	fabricated
attained	conducted	dispatched	facilitated
audited	consolidated	distinguished	familiarized
authored	contained	diversified	fashioned
	contracted	drafted	focused
	contributed	edited	forecast

formulated	lectured	promoted	scheduled
founded	led	proposed	schooled
generated	maintained	provided	screened
guided	managed	publicized	set
headed up	marketed	published	shaped
identified	mediated	purchased	solidified
illustrated	moderated	recommended	solved
implemented	monitored	reconciled	specified
improved	motivated	recorded	stimulated
increased	negotiated	recruited	streamlined
indoctrinated	operated	reduced	strengthened
influenced	organized	referred	summarized
informed	originated	regulated	supervised
initiated	overhauled	rehabilitated	surveyed
innovated	oversaw	remodeled	systemized
inspected	performed	repaired	tabulated
installed	persuaded	represented	taught
instigated	planned	researched	trained
instructed	prepared	resolved	translated
integrated	presented	restored	traveled
interpreted	prioritized	restructured	trimmed
interviewed	processed	retrieved	upgraded
introduced	produced	revamped	validated
invented	programmed	revitalized	worked
launched	projected	saved	wrote

Key Nouns

Administration
administration
administrative infrastructure
administrative processes
administrative support
back office
budget administration
client communications.
confidential correspondence
contract administration
corporate record keeping
corporate secretary
customer liaison
document management
efficiency improvement.
executive liaison
executive officer support facilities
   management
front office operations
government affairs
liaison affairs
mail and messenger services
meeting planning
office management
office services
policy and procedure
product support
productivity improvement
project management
records management
regulatory reporting
resource management
technical support
time management
workflow planning/prioritization

Association and Not-for-Profit Management
advocacy
affiliate members
board relations
budget allocation
budget oversight.
community outreach
corporate development
corporate giving
corporate sponsorship
education foundation.
educational programming
endowment funds
foundation management
fundraising
grassroots campaign
industry association
industry relations
leadership training
marketing communications.
media relations
member communications
member development
member-driven organization
member retention
member services
mission planning
not-for-profit
organization (al) leadership

organization (al) mission
organization (al) vision
policy development
political affairs
press relations
public policy development
public relations.
public/private partnerships
regulatory affairs
research foundation
speakers bureau
special events management
volunteer recruitment
volunteer training

Banking
asset management
asset-based lending
audit examination
branch operations
cash management
commercial banking
commercial credit
consumer banking
consumer credit
correspondent banking
credit administration
credit analysis
debt financing
deposit base
depository services
equity financing
fee income
foreign exchange (FX)

global banking
investment management
investor relations
lease administration.
letters of credit
liability exposure
loan administration
loan processing
loan quality
loan recovery
loan underwriting
lockbox processing
merchant banking
nonperforming assets
portfolio management
receivership
regulatory affairs
relationship management
retail banking
retail lending
return-on-assets
return-on-equity
return-on-investment
risk management
secondary markets
secured lending
securities management
transaction banking
trust services
unsecured lending
wholesale banking
workout

Customer Service

account relationship management
customer communications
customer development
customer focus groups
customer loyalty
customer management
customer needs assessment
customer retention
customer satisfaction
customer service
customer surveys
field service operation
inbound service operation
key account management
order fulfillment
order processing
outbound service operation
process simplification
records management
relationship management
sales administration
service benchmarks
service delivery
service measures
service quality
telemarketing operations
telesales operations

Engineering
benchmark
capital project
chemical engineering
commissioning
computer-aided design (CAD)
computer-aided engineering (CAE)
computer-aided manufacturing
   (CAM)
cross-functional team
customer management
development engineering
efficiency
electrical engineering
electronics engineering
engineering change order (ECO)
engineering documentation
environmental engineering
ergonomic techniques
experimental design
experimental methods
facilities engineering
fault analysis
field performance
final customer acceptance
hardware engineering
industrial engineering
industrial hygiene
maintenance engineering
manufacturing engineering
manufacturing integration
methods design
mechanical engineering
nuclear engineering

occupational safety
operating and maintenance (O&M)
optics engineering
plant engineering
process development
process engineering
process standardization
product design
product development cycle
product functionality
product innovation
product lifecycle management
product manufacturability
product reliability
productivity improvement
project costing
project planning
project management
prototype
quality assurance
quality engineering
regulatory compliance
research and development (R&D)
resource management
root cause
scale-up
software engineering
specifications
statistical analysis
systems engineering
systems integration
technical briefings
technical liaison affairs
technology development
test engineering
turnkey
work methods analysis

**Finance, Accounting, and
   Auditing**
accounts payable
accounts receivable
asset disposition
asset management
asset purchase
audit controls
audit management
cash management
commercial paper
corporate development
corporate tax
cost accounting
cost avoidance
cost reduction
cost/benefit analysis
credit and collections
debt financing
divestiture
due diligence
employee stock ownership plan
   (ESOP)
equity financing

feasibility analysis
financial analysis
financial audits
financial controls
financial models
financial planning
financial reporting
foreign exchange (FX)
initial public offering (IPO)
internal controls
international finance
investment management
investor accounting
investor relations
job costing
letters of credit
leveraged buyout (LBO)
liability management
make/buy analysis
margin improvement
merger
operating budgets
operational audits
partnership accounting
profit/loss (P&L) analysis
profit gains
project accounting
project financing
regulatory compliance auditing
return on assets (ROA)
return on investment (ROI)
revenue gain
risk management
shareholder relations
stock purchase
strategic planning
treasury
trust accounting
work papers

**General Management, Senior
   Management, and Consulting**
accelerated growth
acting executive
advanced technology
benchmarking
business development
business reengineering
capital projects
competitive market position
consensus building
continuous process improvement
corporate administration
corporate communications
corporate culture change
corporate development
corporate image
corporate legal affairs
corporate mission
corporate vision
cost avoidance
cost reduction

crisis communications
cross-cultural communications
customer retention
customer-driven management
efficiency improvement
emerging business venture
entrepreneurial leadership
European economic community
   (EEC)
executive management
executive presentations
financial management
financial restructuring
global market expansion
high-growth organization
interim executive
leadership development
long-range planning
management development
margin improvement
market development
market-driven management
marketing management
matrix management
multi-function experience
multi-industry experience
multi-site operations management
new business development
operating infrastructure
operating leadership
organization (al) culture
organization (al) development
participative management
policy development
performance improvement
process ownership
process reengineering
productivity improvement
profit & loss (P&L) management
profit growth
project management
quality improvement
relationship management
reengineering
reorganization
return-on-assets (ROA)
return-on-equity (ROE)
return-on-investment (ROI)
revenue growth
sales management
service design/delivery
signatory authority
start-up venture
strategic development
strategic partnership
tactical planning/leadership
team building
team leadership
total quality management (tqm)
transition management
turnaround management
world class organization

Health Care

acute care facility
ambulatory care
assisted living
capital giving campaign
case management
certificate of need (CON)
chronic care facility
clinical services
community hospital
community outreach
continuity of care
cost center
electronic claims processing
employee assistance program (EAP)
emergency medical systems (EMS)
fee billing
full time equivalent (FTE)
grant administration
healthcare administrator
healthcare delivery systems
health maintenance organization (HMO)
home healthcare
hospital foundation
industrial medicine
inpatient care
long-term care
managed care
management service organization (MSO)
multi-hospital network
occupational health
outpatient care
patient accounting
patient relations
peer review
physician credentialing
physician relations
practice management
preferred provider organization (PPO)
preventive medicine
primary care
provider relations
public health administration
quality of care
regulatory standards (JCAHO)
rehabilitation services
reimbursement program
risk management
service delivery
skilled nursing facility
third party administrator
utilization review
wellness programs

Hospitality

amenities
back-of-the-house operations
banquet operations
budget administration
catering operations
club management
conference management
contract F&B operations
corporate dining room
customer service
customer retention
food and beverage operations (F&B)
food cost controls
front-of-the-house operations
guest retention
guest satisfaction
hospitality management
inventory planning/control
labor cost controls
meeting planning
member development/retention
menu planning
menu pricing
multi-unit operations
occupancy
portion control
property development
purchasing
resort management
service management
signature property
vendor sourcing
vip relations

Human Resources

american disabilities act (ADA)
benefits administration
career pathing
change management
chief talent officer (CTO)
claims administration
college recruitment
compensation
competency-based performance
corporate culture change
cross-cultural communications
diversity management
equal employment opportunity (EEO)
employee communications
employee empowerment
employee involvement teams
employee relations
employee retention
employee surveys
expatriate employment
grievance proceedings
human resources (HR)
human resources generalist affairs
human resources partnerships
incentive planning
international employment
job task analysis
labor arbitration
labor contract negotiations
labor relations
leadership assessment

leadership development
management training and development
manpower planning
merit promotion
multimedia training
multinational workforce
organization (al) design
organization (al) development (OD)
organization (al) needs assessment
participative management
performance appraisal
performance incentives
performance reengineering
position classification
professional recruitment
regulatory affairs
retention
safety training
self-directed work teams
staffing
succession planning
train-the-trainer
training & development
union negotiations
union relations
wage & salary administration
workforce reengineering

Human Services

adult services
advocacy
behavior management
behavior modification
casework
client advocacy
client placement
community-based intervention
community outreach
counseling
crisis intervention
diagnostic evaluation
discharge planning
dually diagnosed
group counseling
human services
independent life skills training
inpatient
integrated service delivery
mainstreaming
outpatient
program development
protective services
psychoanalysis
psychological counseling
psychotropic medication
school counseling
social services
social welfare
substance abuse
testing
treatment planning

vocational rehabilitation
vocational placement
vocational testing
youth training program

International Business Development

acquisition
barter transactions
channel development
competitive intelligence
corporate development
cross-border transactions
cross-cultural communications
diplomatic protocol
emerging markets
expatriate
export
feasibility analysis
foreign government affairs
foreign investment
global expansion
global market position
global marketing
global sales
import
intellectual property
international business development
international business protocol
international financing
international liaison
international licensee
international marketing
international subsidiary
international trade
joint venture
licensing agreements
local national
market entry
marketing
merger
multichannel distribution network
offshore operations
public/private partnership
technology licensing
start-up venture
strategic alliance
strategic planning
technology transfer

Law and Corporate Legal Affairs

acquisition
adjudicate
administrative law
antitrust
briefs
case law
client management
contracts law
copyright law

corporate by-laws
corporate law
corporate record keeping
criminal law
cross-border transactions
depositions
discovery
due diligence
employment law
environmental law
ethics
family law
fraud
general partnership
intellectual property
interrogatory
joint venture
judicial affairs
juris doctor (JD)
labor law
landmark decision
legal advocacy
legal research
legislative review/analysis
licensing
limited liability corporation (LLC)
limited partnership
litigation
mediation
memoranda
mergers
motions
negotiations
patent law
personal injury
probate law
risk management
sec affairs
shareholder relations
signatory authority
strategic alliance
tax law
technology transfer
trade secrets
trademark
transactions law
trial law
unfair competition
workers' compensation litigation

Manufacturing
asset management
automated manufacturing
capacity planning
capital budget
capital project
cell manufacturing
computer integrated
    manufacturing (CIM)
concurrent engineering
continuous improvement
cost avoidance

cost reductions
cross-functional teams
cycle time reduction
distribution management
efficiency improvement
environmental health and safety
    (EHS)
equipment management
ergonomically efficient
facilities consolidation.
inventory control
inventory planning
just-in-time (JIT)
kaizen
labor efficiency
labor relations
lean manufacturing
logistics management
manufacturing engineering
manufacturing integration
manufacturing technology
master schedule
materials planning
materials replenishment system
    (MRP)
multi-site operations
occupational health & safety
    (OH&S)
on-time delivery
operating budget.
operations management
operations reengineering
operations start-up
optimization
order fulfillment
order processing
outsourcing
participative management
performance improvement
physical inventory
pilot manufacturing
plant operations
process automation
process redesign/reengineering
procurement
product development and
    engineering
product rationalization.
production forecasting
production lead time
production management
production plans/schedules
production output
productivity improvement
profit & loss (P&L) management
project budget
purchasing management
quality assurance/quality control
quality circles
safety management
safety training
shipping and receiving operation

spares and repairs management
statistical process control (SPC)
technology integration.
time and motion studies
total quality management (TWM)
traffic management
turnaround management
union negotiations
value-added processes
vendor management
warehousing operations
work in progress (WIP)
workflow optimization
workforce management
world class manufacturing (WCM)
yield improvement

**Public Relations and Corporate
    Communications**
advertising communications
agency relations - directed
brand management
brand strategy
broadcast media
campaign management
community affairs
competitive market lead
community outreach
conference planning
cooperative advertising
corporate communications
corporate identity
corporate sponsorship
corporate vision
creative services
crisis communications
customer communications
direct mail campaign
electronic advertising
electronic media
employee communications
event management
fundraising
government relations
grassroots campaign
investor communications
issues management
legislative affairs
logistics
management communications
market research
marketing communications
media buys
media placement
media relations
media scheduling
merchandising
multimedia advertising
political action committee (pac)
premiums
press releases
print media

promotions
public affairs
public relations
public speaking
publications
publicity
sales incentives
shareholder communications
special events
strategic communications plan
strategic planning
strategic positioning
tactical campaign
trade shows
vip relations

Purchasing and Logistics
acquisition management
barter trade
bid review
buy vs. lease analysis
capital equipment acquisition
commodities purchasing
competitive bidding
contract administration
contract change order
contract negotiations
contract terms and conditions
cradle-to-grave procurement
distribution management
economic ordering quantity
    methodology
fixed price contracts
indefinite price/indefinite quantity
international sourcing
inventory planning/control
just-in-time (JIT) purchasing
logistics management
materials replenishment ordering
    (MRO) purchasing
multisite operations
negotiation
offshore purchasing
outsourced
price negotiations
procurement
proposal review
purchasing
regulatory compliance
request for proposal (RFP)
request for quotation (RFQ)
sourcing
specifications compliance
subcontractor negotiations
supplier management
supplier quality
vendor partnerships
vendor quality certification
warehousing

Real Estate, Construction, and Property Management
acquisition
American disabilities act (ADA)
asset management
asset valuation
asset workout/recovery
building code compliance
building trades
capital improvement
claims administration
commercial development
community development
competitive bidding
construction management
construction trades
contract administration
contract award
critical path method (CPM) scheduling
design and engineering
divestiture
engineering change orders (ECOS)
estimating
environmental compliance
facilities management
fair market value pricing
grounds maintenance
historic property renovation
industrial development
infrastructure development
leasing management
master community association
master scheduling.
mixed use property
occupancy
planned use development (PUD)
portfolio
preventive maintenance
project concept - drove
project development
project management
project scheduling
property management
property valuation
real estate appraisal
real estate brokerage
real estate development
real estate investment trust (REIT)
real estate law
real estate partnership
regulatory compliance
renovation
return on assets (ROA)
return on equity (ROE)
return on investment (ROI)
site development
site remediation
specifications
syndications
tenant relations
tenant retention

turnkey construction

Sales/Marketing/Business Development
account development
account management
account retention
brand management.
business development
campaign management
competitive analysis
competitive contract award
competitive market intelligence
competitive product positioning
consultative sales
customer loyalty
customer needs assessment
customer retention
customer satisfaction
customer service
direct mail marketing
direct response marketing
direct sales
distributor management
emerging markets
field sales management
fulfillment
global markets
global sales
headquarters account management
high-impact presentations
incentive planning
indirect sales
international sales
international trade
key account management
line extension
margin improvement
market launch
market positioning
market research
market share ratings
market surveys
marketing strategy
mass merchants
multichannel distribution
multichannel sales
multimedia advertising
multimedia marketing communications
national account management
negotiations
new market development
new product introduction
product development
product launch
product lifecycle management
product line rationalization
product positioning
profit & loss (P&L) management
promotions
profit growth

public relations
public speaking
revenue growth
revenue stream
sales closing
sales cycle management
sales forecasting
sales training
sales presentations
solutions selling
strategic market planning
tactical market plans
team building/leadership
trend analysis

Law Enforcement and Security
asset protection
corporate fraud
corporate security
crisis communications
crisis response
electronic surveillance
emergency planning & response
emergency preparedness
industrial espionage
industrial security
interrogation
investigations management
law enforcement
media relations
personal protection
public relations
safety training
security operations
surveillance
tactical field operations
vip protection
white collar crime

Teaching and Education Administration
academic advisement
accreditation
admissions management
alumni relations
campus life
capital giving campaign
career counseling
career development
classroom management
course design
conference management
curriculum development
education administration
enrollment
extension program
field instruction
grant administration
higher education
holistic learning
instructional media
instructional programming

intercollegiate athletics
leadership training
lifelong learning
management development
peer counseling
program development
public/private partnerships
public speaking
recruitment
residential life
scholastic standards
seminar management
student retention
student services
student-faculty relations
textbook review
training and development

Transportation
agency operations
asset management
cargo handling
carrier management
common carrier
container transportation
contract transportation services
customer delivery operations
dedicated logistics operations
dispatch operations
distribution management
driver leasing
equipment control
export operations
facilities management
fleet management
freight consolidation
freight forwarding
import operations
inbound transportation
intermodal transportation network
line management
load analysis
logistics management
maritime operations
outbound transportation
over-the-road transportation
port operations
regulatory compliance
route planning/analysis
route management
safety management
safety training
terminal operations
traffic planning
traffic management
transportation planning
transportation management
warehouse management
workflow optimization

Index